HiSET®
POWER PRACTICE

LEARNINGEXPRESS®

NEW YORK

Cataloging-in-Publication Data is on file with the Library of Congress.

ISBN 978-1-61103-066-2

Printed in the United States of America

9 8 7 6 5 4 3 2 1

For more information on LearningExpress, other LearningExpress products, or bulk sales, please write to us at:
  LearningExpress/An EBSCO Company
  224 West 29th Street
  3rd Floor
  New York, NY 10001

CONTENTS ▶

CONTENTS

HOW TO USE THIS BOOK ▶

Welcome to *HiSET® Power Practice*! Congratulations on taking a big step toward preparing for your HiSET® exam and earning a diploma. One of your main goals on test day is to be confident that you know the exam inside and out—that's where this book comes in.

Practice Makes Perfect

As you might know, the HiSET® is a five-section test given both on the computer and via pencil and paper. You'll learn all about the HiSET® and its question types in Chapter 1. You'll also find three full-length practice exams in this book, which closely resemble the actual HiSET® test. You will also have a chance to work with a computerized HiSET® exam on the free online test you have access to via this book. Visit page 375 to find out how to take this computerized exam.

Taking Your Tests

Try to take the tests in this book under the same conditions you would have to on the actual test day. The beginning of each test tells you how long you have. Sit down in a quiet spot, set your timer, and try to take each test without any interruptions. After you finish each exam, you will find detailed answer explanations for every question along with scoring information and sample essays for the essay section.

Scoring Your Best

Practicing with test-like questions is the best way to prepare for the HiSET® exam. This book is filled with questions that mirror the ones you will see on test day. Taking these practice tests, especially under the same timing conditions as the real HiSET® exam, will help you get used to pacing yourself. You also see which subjects you excel in, and which you need a bit more study in. Use this book as a part of your study toolkit, and you'll be well on your way to exam success and a diploma!

1 ▶ INTRODUCTION TO THE HiSET®

Everyone takes a different path in life, so why should continuing education be one size fits all? Until 2014, the only nationwide option for a high school equivalency test was the GED® exam. Since then, 22 U.S. states and territories have adopted an alternative test: the **High School Equivalency Test (HiSET®)**.

Higher education programs—and more employers than ever—require that applicants have a high school credential, so exams like the HiSET® are often an essential first step toward continuing your education or going after a rewarding career. Congrats on taking the first step on your path to the future!

What Is the HiSET®?

The HiSET® was developed and is offered by the Educational Testing Service (ETS), and offers high school equivalency certification to students who have not earned a standard high school diploma, and are not currently enrolled in high school.

The HiSET® exam is available in both computer- and paper-based formats, and is offered in both English and Spanish. It's geared toward test takers who are 18 years old or older, although 16- and 17-year-olds may be able to apply for "special circumstances" exemptions, depending on their states' rules. (Check with your state's HiSET® guidelines if you're between 16 and 18 years old and want to register to take the test.) Individuals who are younger than 16 years old are typically not allowed to register for the test, but double-check your state's requirements to confirm.

Individual state requirements can be found at http://hiset.ets.org/requirements.

What's on the HiSET® Exam?

The exam tests general, high school–level knowledge in five key areas:

- Language Arts—Reading
- Language Arts—Writing
- Mathematics
- Science
- Social Studies

Each of these five areas is a subtest on the HiSET®. They can be taken one at a time (on different days if you prefer), or all in one sitting, which is known as "the battery." The overall exam is aligned to the Office of Vocational and Adult Education's (OVAE) College and Career Readiness (CCR) Standards for Adult Education. With its alignment to the educational standards, the test is considered a reliable indicator of college and career readiness.

Language Arts—Reading

Test Name	Language Arts—Reading
Time	65 minutes
Number of Questions	40
Format	Multiple-choice questions

The Language Arts—Reading subtest evaluates your ability to understand, interpret, and analyze different types of reading material. In this section, you're given passages to read from literary and informational texts, and 40 multiple-choice questions to answer based on those passages. The texts (60% literary, 40% informational) are from different genres and a range of subjects that vary in style and subject matter. Each text is 400 to 600 words long, and can be taken from a variety of formats, including essays, biographies, narratives, personal memoirs, and poetry.

The questions test the ability to:

- Comprehend the text
- Make inferences and interpretations
- Draw conclusions
- Apply information
- Recognize figurative language
- Analyze the style, tone, main idea, topic, structure, or theme
- Identify the purpose and/or viewpoint
- Recognize an author's style, structure, mood, or tone
- Identify literary techniques and argument styles
- Apply, compare, and contrast information
- Make predictions
- Make connections between multiple sources

Language Arts—Writing

Test Name	Language Arts—Writing
Time	120 minutes
Number of Questions	51
Format	50 multiple-choice questions (Part 1) 1 essay question (Part 2)

The Language Arts—Writing subtest focuses on a candidate's ability to read and write standard American English. The test breaks down into two parts.

Part 1 presents "draft" versions of different kinds of texts (e.g., articles, personal narratives, letters, essays, and reports), and asks you to make choices about how to revise and fix the text. The test questions are embedded as underlined or highlighted parts of the text, and the multiple-choice questions ask readers how to revise the underlined or highlighted text for organization, grammar, or clarity. In this subtest, you may be asked to evaluate style, structure, organization, conciseness, clarity, relevance, language usage, or mechanics.

The content is broken down into three general categories:

- Language Facility: 43%
- Writing Conventions: 35%
- Organization of Ideas: 22%

Part 2 requires you to write an essay and demonstrate writing and organization skills. Each essay question presents one or more pieces of evidence-based writing, and asks the test taker to write an argument based on evidence and reasoning drawn from those pieces. Test takers are expected to demonstrate writing skills in these general areas:

- Development of ideas
- Organization of ideas
- Language facilities

Mathematics

Test Name	Mathematics
Time	90 minutes
Number of Questions	50
Format	Multiple-choice questions

The Mathematics subtest assesses math knowledge and problem-solving skills. The multiple-choice questions present realistic, practical problems that test the following subject areas:

- Numbers and operations
- Measurement
- Geometry
- Data analysis
- Probability
- Statistics
- Algebra

In addition to the basic content knowledge, the Mathematics section also tests:

- Mathematical concepts and procedures
- Analyzing and interpreting information
- Synthesizing data
- Solving problems

A calculator is not required (the Mathematics subtest is considered "calculator neutral"), and you are not allowed to bring outside calculators into the test center. However, you *can* request a calculator after arriving at the test center. If you request one, the test center is obligated to provide a four-function or scientific calculator for the test. Calculator options can vary depending on state standards, so be sure to check your own state's HiSET® policies before taking the exam.

Science

Test Name	Science
Time	80 minutes
Number of Questions	50
Format	Multiple-choice questions

The Science subtest tests your general science knowledge, and your ability to apply scientific principles, interpret scientific information, and evaluate scientific information. The questions present information in the form of reports, graphs, tables, and charts, and ask you to draw conclusions about the results.

The content areas on the Science subtest include:

- Life Sciences—49%
  - Botany
  - Biology
  - Health
  - Zoology
- Physical Sciences—28%
  - Chemistry
  - Physics
- Earth Sciences—23%
  - Astronomy
  - Geology

The multiple-choice questions may ask you to do any of the following:

- Interpret data
- Apply scientific principles
- Identify the research questions to be considered
- Identify the best procedure for answering questions
- Draw conclusions from given results
- Recognize the differences between hypotheses, assumptions, and observations
- Judge the reliability of information sources

Social Studies

Test Name	Social Studies
Time	70 minutes
Number of Questions	50
Format	Multiple-choice questions

The Social Studies subtest measures your ability to analyze and interpret information given in different written formats. The subtest presents information in reading passages, documents, posters, political cartoons, timelines, maps, graphs, tables, and charts. Depending on the topic, the multiple-choice questions may ask you to:

- Judge the reliability of the text sources
- Distinguish fact from opinion
- Judge the validity of inferences and conclusions from the text
- Determine whether there's enough information presented to draw conclusions

Where Can I Take the HiSET®?

The HiSET® is offered in 25 U.S. states and territories. Each state may have different policies for the exam, including:

- State/national residency requirements
- Minimum age requirements (and waiver availability for test takers under 18)
- ID requirements at the test centers
- Mandatory HiSET® practice tests or classes before taking the exam

Before you register for the test, be sure to check http://hiset.ets.org/requirements for the most up-to-date information for your state.

HiSET® State Availability

The HiSET® is available in the following U.S. states and territories:

- American Samoa
- California
- Colorado
- Guam
- Hawaii
- Illinois
- Iowa
- Louisiana
- Maine
- Marshall Islands
- Massachusetts
- Mississippi
- Missouri

- Montana
- Nevada
- New Hampshire
- New Jersey
- New Mexico
- North Carolina
- Northern Mariana Islands
- Oklahoma
- Palau
- Pennsylvania
- Tennessee
- Wyoming

When Can I Take the HiSET®?

The HiSET® is offered year-round, whenever test centers are open. The ETS website has a test center locator tool, which can help you find test centers in your area that offer the HiSET®, along with the available dates and times.

How Do I Register for the HiSET®?

If the HiSET® is offered in your state and you are eligible to take the test, you can create a "My HiSET®" account on the ETS website (http://hiset.ets.org/take/hiset_account/). Once you've registered, you can search for test locations, find out state-specific test information, schedule and reschedule a test, pay for a test, and view your scores. You can access all of your personal HiSET® information through this portal.

What Test Accommodations Are Available?

If you need additional accommodations due to disabilities or health-related needs, you can request them before test day. Accommodations that need to be requested and approved by your test center ahead of time include:

- Extended test time (paper test and computer-based test)
- Separate test space (paper test and computer-based test)
- Audio test (paper test)
- Large print test (paper test)
- Screen magnification (computer-based test)
- Calculator/talking calculator (paper test and computer-based test)
- Scribe or keyboard entry aide (paper test and computer-based test)
- Supervised break time (paper test and computer-based test)
- Sign language instructions (paper test and computer-based test)

Some accommodations do not need to be approved ahead of time, which means they'll be available at the test center on test day, by request:

- Large print test book and answer sheet
- Scratch paper (which cannot be removed from the test center)
- Wheelchair access

What Can't I Bring on Test Day?

The following items are not allowed in the test center on test day:

- Outside calculators
- Tablets and cell phones
- Cameras or recording devices
- Books or papers
- Highlighters
- Food or drinks
- Any test aids that have not been approved by ETS or the test center

If you have any concerns about whether an item will be allowed in with you, check with the test center and/or the ETS website before test day.

How Is the HiSET® Scored?

Multiple-choice questions are scored by machine, which assigns 1 raw point for each correct answer. The total raw score for each subtest is then scaled by the test makers depending on the difficulty of the questions. Essay questions are scored by human reviewers (two or more per essay), who use a strict scoring grid to assign a score from 1 to 6 points.

The most important takeaway is that *you should answer every question you can on the HiSET®*! You are NOT penalized for incorrect answers—you are only awarded points for correct answers. So try not to leave any blanks on the test!

Each subtest receives a scaled score ranging from 1 to 20 (except the essay, which is scored on a scale of 1 to 6). The minimum passing score is 8 for an individual subtest, 2 for the essay, and 45 for the complete HiSET® exam.

TEST	PASSING SCORE	TOTAL SCALED SCORE
Language Arts—Reading	8	20
Language Arts—Writing	8	20
Battery (all subtests combined)	45	100
Mathematics	8	20
Science	8	20
Social Studies	8	20
Essay	2	6

After you take a subtest or the battery, you'll have access to a comprehensive score report that includes general and detailed summaries of how you did on each subtest and overall. These score reports are available through your ETS HiSET® account, and will not be sent to you via traditional mail.

If you take a paper-based HiSET® test, your multiple-choice subtest scores should be available online 3 to 5 business days after ETS receives your answer sheet, and your essay score should be available 6 to 10 days after ETS receives your answer sheet. If you take the computer-based HiSET®, you'll see an unofficial score on screen at the end of your test. Official scores will be available online after 3 business days for multiple-choice subsets, and after 6 business days for the essay test.

Let's Get Started!

Now that you know what to expect with the HiSET®, it's time to dig in and start your powerful practice! The exams in this book are designed to be as close as possible to the actual tests you will see on your exam day. Each question in the exams that come in this book is accompanied by a very detailed answer explanation—you will be able to see not only why the correct answer is right, but also why each of the other answer choices is incorrect. You will also see sample essays at all levels for Part 2 of the Language Arts—Writing section.

Best of luck on your HiSET® test study journey and on your test-taking experience!

2 ▶ HiSET®
PRACTICE TEST 1

This practice test is modeled on the format, content, and timing of the official HiSET® test.

You can choose either to take each test separately, or to take all five tests together. However you decide to use this practice test, try to take each part under the most test-like conditions you can.

Try to take your test in a quiet spot, as free from distraction as possible. At the beginning of each test section, you will find test information, including the actual time limits you will be given on your exam day. If you want to work under testing conditions, set a timer and aim to complete each test section within the given time limit.

You should work carefully, but not spend too much time on any one question. And remember—be sure you answer every question! You *are not* penalized for incorrect answers; you are only rewarded for correct ones!

When you complete this entire practice exam, you will find complete answer explanations for every question that explain not only why correct answers are right, but also why incorrect answers are wrong. You will also find sample essays at every level, and information on scoring your exam.

Good luck!

Language Arts—Reading

65 Minutes
40 Questions

This practice test is modeled on the content and timing of the official HiSET® Language Arts—Reading test and, like the official test, presents a series of questions that assess your ability to understand, interpret, and analyze a broad range of literary and informational texts. Refer to the passages as often as necessary when answering the questions.

Use the following information to answer questions 1–6.

A man is on a time-traveling mission. This excerpt from *Of All Possible Worlds* by William Tenn explains how the man became a time traveler.

(1)

It was a good job and Max Alben knew whom he had to thank for it—his great-grandfather.

(2)

"Good old Giovanni Albeni," he muttered as he hurried into the laboratory slightly ahead of the escorting technicians, all of them, despite the excitement of the moment, remembering to bob their heads deferentially at the half-dozen full-fleshed and hard-faced men lolling on the couches that had been set up around the time machine.

(3)

He shrugged rapidly out of his rags, as he had been instructed in the anteroom, and stepped into the housing of the enormous mechanism. This was the first time he had seen it, since he had been taught how to operate it on a dummy model, and now he stared at the great transparent coils and the susurrating energy bubble with much respect.

(4)

This machine, the pride and the hope of 2089, was something almost outside his powers of comprehension. But Max Alben knew how to run it, and he knew, roughly, what it was supposed to accomplish. He knew also that this was the first backward journey of any great duration and, being scientifically unpredictable, might well be the death of him.

(5)

"Good old Giovanni Albeni," he muttered again affectionately.

(6)

If his great-grandfather had not volunteered for the earliest time-travel experiments way back in the nineteen-seventies, back even before the Blight, it would never have been discovered that he and his seed possessed a great deal of immunity to extra-temporal blackout.

(7)

And if that had not been discovered, the ruling powers of Earth, more than a century later, would never have plucked Max Alben out of an obscure civil-service job as a relief guard at the North American Chicken Reservation to his present heroic and remunerative eminence. He would still be patrolling the barbed wire that surrounded the three white leghorn hens and two roosters—about one-sixth of the known livestock wealth of the Western Hemisphere—thoroughly content with the half-pail of dried apricots he received each and every payday.

(8)

No, if his great-grandfather had not demonstrated long ago his unique capacity for remaining conscious during time travel, Max Alben would not now be shifting from foot to foot in a physics laboratory, facing the black market kings of the world and awaiting their final instructions with an uncertain and sub-missive grin.

(9)

Men like O'Hara, who controlled mush-rooms, Levney, the blackberry tycoon, Sorgasso, the packaged-worm monopolist—would black marketeers of their tremendous stature so much as waste a glance on someone like Alben ordinarily, let alone confer a lifetime pension on his wife and five children of a full spoonful each of non-synthetic sugar a day?

(10)

Even if he didn't come back, his family was provided for like almost no other family on Earth. This was a . . . good job and he was lucky.

(11)

Alben noticed that Abd Sadha had risen from the straight chair at the far side of the room and was approaching him with a sealed metal cylinder in one hand.

(12)

"We've decided to add a further precaution at the last moment," the old man said. "That is, the scientists have suggested it and I have—er—I have given my approval."

1. After receiving his instructions from Abd Sadha, Max Alben will most likely
   a. travel to the 1970s.
   b. travel into the future.
   c. enter the time machine.
   d. meet his great-grandfather.

2. Which of the following meanings associated with the word "powers" seems most intended in paragraph 7?
   a. authorities
   b. strengths
   c. abilities
   d. resources

3. The narrator mentions the fact that Max Abden's trip through time is scientifically unpredictable and "might well be the death of him" (paragraph 4) in order to create a tone of
   a. sadness.
   b. horror.
   c. tension.
   d. humor.

4. Max Alben most likely considers his great-grandfather to be a
   a. gentle person.
   b. role model.
   c. great genius.
   d. foolish man.

5. Which of the following lines from paragraphs 8 to 11 refines information from paragraph 6?
   a. "No, if his great-grandfather had not demonstrated long ago his unique capacity for remaining conscious during time travel"
   b. "Max Alben would not now be shifting from foot to foot in a physics laboratory, facing the black market kings of the world"
   c. "would black marketeers of their tremendous stature so much as waste a glance on someone like Alben ordinarily"
   d. "Alben noticed that Abd Sadha had risen from the straight chair at the far side of the room and was approaching him with a sealed metal cylinder in one hand."

6. Abd Sadha most likely pauses to say as "er" in paragraph 12 because he
   a. forgot that he did not suggest the precaution.
   b. believes the scientists do not know what they are doing.
   c. is concerned about Max Abden's safety.
   d. is unsure of exactly what he is saying.

Use the following information to answer questions 7–11.

On September 25, 1789, the Second Continental Congress created ten amendments to the United States Constitution. These amendments, written by James Madison, are known as the Bill of Rights.

(1) The Conventions of a number of the States, having at the time of their adopting the Constitution, expressed a desire, in order to prevent misconstruction or abuse of its powers, that further declaratory and restrictive clauses should be added: And as extending the ground of public confidence in the Government, will best ensure the beneficent ends of its institution.

(2) Resolved by the Senate and House of Representatives of the United States of America, in Congress assembled, two thirds of both Houses concurring, that the following Articles be proposed to the Legislatures of the several States, as amendments to the Constitution of the United States, all, or any of which Articles, when ratified by three fourths of the said Legislatures, to be valid to all intents and purposes, as part of the said Constitution; viz.

(3) Articles in addition to, and Amendment of the Constitution of the United States of America, proposed by Congress, and ratified by the Legislatures of the several States, pursuant to the fifth Article of the original Constitution.

(4) **Amendment I**

Congress shall make no law respecting an establishment of religion, or prohibiting the free exercise thereof; or abridging the freedom of speech, or of the press; or the right of the people peaceably to assemble, and to petition the Government for a redress of grievances.

(5) **Amendment II**

A well regulated Militia, being necessary to the security of a free State, the right of the people to keep and bear Arms, shall not be infringed.

(6) **Amendment III**

No Soldier shall, in time of peace be quartered in any house, without the consent of the Owner, nor in time of war, but in a manner to be prescribed by law.

(7) **Amendment IV**

The right of the people to be secure in their persons, houses, papers, and effects, against unreasonable searches and seizures, shall not be violated, and no Warrants shall issue, but upon probable cause, supported by Oath or affirmation, and particularly describing the place to be searched, and the persons or things to be seized.

(8) **Amendment V**

No person shall be held to answer for a capital, or otherwise infamous crime, unless on a presentment or indictment of a Grand Jury, except in cases arising in the land or naval forces, or in the Militia, when in actual service in time of War or public danger; nor shall any person be subject for the same offence to be twice put in jeopardy of life or limb; nor shall be compelled in any criminal case to be a witness against himself, nor be deprived of life, liberty, or property, without due process of law; nor shall private property be taken for public use, without just compensation.

(9) **Amendment VI**

In all criminal prosecutions, the accused shall enjoy the right to a speedy and public trial, by an impartial jury of the State and district wherein the crime shall have been committed, which district shall have been previously ascertained by law, and to be informed of the nature and cause of the accusation; to be confronted with the witnesses against him; to have compulsory process for obtaining witnesses in his favor, and to have the Assistance of Counsel for his defence.

(10) **Amendment VII**

In Suits at common law, where the value in controversy shall exceed twenty dollars, the right of trial by jury shall be preserved, and no fact tried by a jury, shall be otherwise re-examined in any Court of the United States, than according to the rules of the common law.

(11) **Amendment VIII**

Excessive bail shall not be required, nor excessive fines imposed, nor cruel and unusual punishments inflicted.

(12) **Amendment IX**

The enumeration in the Constitution, of certain rights, shall not be construed to deny or disparage others retained by the people.

(13) **Amendment X**

The powers not delegated to the United States by the Constitution, nor prohibited by it to the States, are reserved to the States respectively, or to the people.

7. Which of the following states the primary purpose of this passage?
   a. to explain why Americans have rights other people do not
   b. to prove that Americans enjoy a number of exclusive rights
   c. to show how a country is supposed to treat its citizens
   d. to establish the basic rights and freedoms of Americans

8. Information in this passage would be most useful for
   a. ensuring a criminal trial is fair.
   b. figuring out the cost of bail.
   c. understanding a soldier's rights.
   d. establishing a new religion.

9. The author of the Bill of Rights most likely
   a. thought soldiers deserved special rights.
   b. valued the freedom to express oneself.
   c. believed people rarely committed crimes.
   d. did not support the American legal system.

10. According to the passage, both state governments and citizens
    a. should enforce the Bill of Rights.
    b. deserve to be delegated powers.
    c. have the right to a trial by jury.
    d. must form militias to ensure security.

11. The Bill of Rights was created on the assumption that the United States Constitution
    a. applied to all states.
    b. was seriously flawed.
    c. required clarification.
    d. was widely misunderstood.

Use the following information to answer questions 12–17.

A little girl is sent to live with her wealthy relatives. This excerpt from *Mansfield Park* by Jane Austen describes the family's first impressions of the girl.

(1)

Fanny Price was at this time just ten years old, and though there might not be much in her first appearance to captivate, there was, at least, nothing to disgust her relations. She was small of her age, with no glow of complexion, nor any other striking beauty; exceedingly timid and shy, and shrinking from notice; but her air, though awkward, was not vulgar, her voice was sweet, and when she spoke her countenance was pretty. Sir Thomas and Lady Bertram received her very kindly; and Sir Thomas, seeing how much she needed encouragement, tried to be all that was conciliating: but he had to work against a most untoward gravity of deportment; and Lady Bertram, without taking half so much trouble, or speaking one word where he spoke ten, by the mere aid of a good-humored smile, became immediately the less awful character of the two. . . .

(2)

They were a remarkably fine family, the sons very well-looking, the daughters decidedly handsome, and all of them well-grown and forward of their age, which produced as striking a difference between the cousins in person, as education had given to their address; and no one would have supposed the girls so nearly of an age as they really were. There were in fact but two years between the youngest and Fanny. Julia Bertram was only twelve, and Maria but a year older. The little visitor meanwhile was as unhappy as possible. Afraid of everybody, ashamed of herself, and longing for the home she had left, she knew not how to look up, and could scarcely speak to be heard, or without crying. Mrs. Norris had been talking to her the whole way from Northampton of her wonderful good fortune, and the extraordinary degree of gratitude and good behaviour which it ought to produce, and her consciousness of misery was therefore increased by the idea of its being a wicked thing for her not to be happy. The fatigue, too, of so long a journey, became soon no trifling evil. In vain were the well-meant condescensions of Sir Thomas, and all the officious prognostications of Mrs. Norris that she would be a good girl; in vain did Lady Bertram smile and make her sit on the sofa with herself and pug, and vain was even the sight of a gooseberry tart towards giving her comfort; she could scarcely swallow two mouthfuls before tears interrupted her, and sleep seeming to be her likeliest friend, she was taken to finish her sorrows in bed.

(3)

"This is not a very promising beginning," said Mrs. Norris, when Fanny had left the room. "After all that I said to her as we came along, I thought she would have behaved better; I told her how much might depend upon her acquitting herself well at first. I wish there may not be a little sulkiness of temper—her poor mother had a good deal; but we must make allowances for such a child—and I do not know that her being sorry to leave her home is really against her, for, with all its faults, it was her home, and she cannot as yet understand how much she has changed for the better; but then there is moderation in all things."

(4)

It required a longer time, however, than Mrs. Norris was inclined to allow, to reconcile Fanny to the novelty of Mansfield Park, and the separation from everybody she had been used to. Her feelings were very acute, and too little understood to be properly attended to. Nobody meant to be unkind, but nobody put themselves out of their way to secure her comfort.

12. When Fanny saw how good-looking her cousins were, it most likely caused her to feel
    a. self-conscious.
    b. rejected.
    c. irritated.
    d. proud.

13. One of this passage's themes is the difficulty of
    a. meeting new people.
    b. being a young person.
    c. relating to older people.
    d. adjusting to new situations.

14. What does "conciliating" (paragraph 1) mean?
    a. terrifying
    b. soothing
    c. horrible
    d. wonderful

15. Which of the following lines from paragraphs 3 and 4 sums up information from earlier in the passage?

   a. "After all that I said to her as we came along, I thought she would have behaved better"

   b. "I told her how much might depend upon her acquitting herself well at first"

   c. "It required a longer time, however, than Mrs. Norris was inclined to allow, to reconcile Fanny to the novelty of Mansfield Park"

   d. "Her feelings were very acute, and too little understood to be properly attended to."

16. Mrs. Norris seems to have

   a. little faith that Fanny will get used to Mansfield Park.

   b. conflicting feelings about Fanny's behavior.

   c. a lack of patience for Fanny's rudeness.

   d. complete sympathy for Fanny's sadness.

17. What is the most likely reason that the first two paragraphs mostly describe Fanny's impressions of her new family?

   a. Fanny is the central character of the story.

   b. The story is told from the first-person point of view.

   c. The author is establishing Fanny as a judgmental character.

   d. Fanny's new family members are the most important characters in the story.

Use the following information to answer questions 18–22.

Tea holds a very special place in Chinese culture. This excerpt from *The Book of Tea* by Kakuzo Okakura, a nonfictional work, discusses tea in ancient China.

(1)

Like Art, Tea has its periods and its schools. Its evolution may be roughly divided into three main stages: the Boiled Tea, the Whipped Tea, and the Steeped Tea. We moderns belong to the last school. These several methods of appreciating the beverage are indicative of the spirit of the age in which they prevailed. For life is an expression, our unconscious actions the constant betrayal of our innermost thought. Confucius said that "man hideth not." Perhaps we reveal ourselves too much in small things because we have so little of the great to conceal. . . . The Cake-tea which was boiled, the Powdered-tea which was whipped, the Leaf-tea which was steeped, mark the distinct emotional impulses of the Tang, the Sung, and the Ming dynasties of China. If we were inclined to borrow the much-abused terminology of art-classification, we might designate them respectively, the Classic, the Romantic, and the Naturalistic schools of Tea.

(2)

The tea-plant, a native of southern China, was known from very early times to Chinese botany and medicine. It is alluded to in the classics under the various names of Tou, Tseh, Chung, Kha, and Ming, and was highly prized for possessing the virtues of relieving fatigue, delighting the soul, strengthening the will, and repairing the eyesight. It was not only administered as an internal dose, but often applied externally in form of paste to alleviate rheumatic pains. The Taoists claimed it as an important ingredient of the elixir of immortality. The Buddhists used it extensively to prevent drowsiness during their long hours of meditation.

(3)

By the fourth and fifth centuries Tea became a favourite beverage among the inhabitants of the Yangtse-Kiang valley. It was about this time that modern ideograph Cha was coined, evidently a corruption of the classic Tou. The poets of the southern dynasties have left some fragments of their fervent adoration of the "froth of the liquid jade." Then emperors used to bestow some rare preparation of the leaves on their high ministers as a reward for eminent services. Yet the method of drinking tea at this stage was primitive in the extreme. The leaves were steamed, crushed in a mortar, made into a cake, and boiled together with rice, ginger, salt, orange peel, spices, milk, and sometimes with onions! The custom obtains at the present day among the Tibetans and various Mongolian tribes, who make a curious syrup of these ingredients. The use of lemon slices by the Russians, who learned to take tea from the Chinese caravansaries, points to the survival of the ancient method.

18. Which of the following states the primary purpose of the passage?
   a. to explain the different kinds of tea that people drank in ancient China
   b. to compare tea's role in Chinese culture to its roles in other cultures
   c. to show that tea is extremely important in Chinese religious ceremonies
   d. to provide an overview of tea's evolution and role in ancient Chinese culture

19. Which of the following meanings associated with the word "school" seems most intended in paragraph 1?
   a. academy of learning
   b. specific approach
   c. to educate
   d. circle of associates

20. The author expresses the opinion that
   a. there are several periods in the evolution of tea.
   b. the terminology of art classification is often abused.
   c. tea was described by different names in classic literature.
   d. tea was once the favorite beverage of people in the Yangtse-Kiang valley.

21. Read the following paragraph:

   The tea ceremony is one of the key traditions in Chinese weddings. It is an expression of respect between the families united through matrimony. Although it has a long history, the tea ceremony is still often practiced to honor twenty-first century marriages in China.

   The author of this paragraph and Kakuzo Okakura agree that tea

   a. is an essential component of Taoist and Buddhist traditions.
   b. represents respect between different groups of people.
   c. has deep and long-lasting bonds to Chinese culture.
   d. still holds an important place in the twenty-first century.

22. According to information in the second paragraph, Buddhists
   a. had more realistic expectations of tea than Taoists did.
   b. were inspired by Taoists to use tea in their religious traditions.
   c. were particularly sensitive to the properties of tea.
   d. valued tea drinking as their most important tradition.

Use the following information to answer questions 23–28.

A garden is the setting in the poem "A Child's Voice" by E.C. Dickinson.

   (1) 'Twas in a far back swallow-time
       When the air was filled with chime
       Of Sunday bells that danced in tune
       With Eastern phantasies,
       A child within a garden's boon
       Oft sighed with saddened eyes.

(2) A swallow screamed and wheeled at him
    Beside the greenhouse door;
    It knew that there he strove to limn
    The need in his soul's core:
    And he is lonely and sad who tells
    His need to Sunday bells.

(3) Of playfellows there was not one
    To whom at wake of sun
    The child might turn to speak a dream
    Of lazy summer seas
    O'er which a ship rode fair of beam
    Bringing his soul's keys;

(4) And how a wondrous alien boy
    Trod proud that ship of Fate.
    There mid the bells of Sunday joy
    He whispered, "Come not late
    Within my longing, for my play
    Won't keep for any day."

(5) "The greenhouse tank is stagnant now
    Under the cherry bough;
    And there a ship is by the quay,
    The joy of my Baghdad.
    Oh come, oh come and play with me
    That I should not be sad."

(6) The jewelled shade of evening's hood
    Held many Eastern tales;
    And cinnamon and sandalwood
    Lurked in his camels' bales.
    But then a swallow harshly screamed
    And tumbled what he dreamed.

(7) And that was back in swallow-time
    With life a child's rhyme.
    And some came true of what he dreamed,
    And some has been forgot.
    But life with sadness still is seamed,
    And thorns take long to rot.

23. The poet describes a particular time and particular sounds in the first stanza to
    a. show they will be important in the poem.
    b. establish the poem's setting.
    c. reveal a character's memories.
    d. set the poem's mood.

24. This poem is mainly about a boy who
    a. enjoys the sounds of bells.
    b. works in a greenhouse.
    c. travels by ship.
    d. hears a swallow singing.

25. The boy in the poem most likely
    a. has a terrible fear of birds.
    b. traveled to a new country aboard a ship.
    c. kept a garden when he lived in Baghdad.
    d. is too shy to make friends in his new home.

26. The boy most likely refers to the fact that "the greenhouse tank is stagnant now" (stanza 5) in order to
    a. explain that he has to replace the water in the tank.
    b. prove that life in his new country is miserable.
    c. express his feelings of sadness about his new country.
    d. describe one of the things he dislikes about his new country.

27. In the sixth stanza, the phrase "tumbled what he dreamed" means that the swallow
    a. ruined the boy's life.
    b. made the boy wake from sleep.
    c. broke the boy's concentration.
    d. caused the boy to have strange dreams.

28. This poem would have the greatest meaning to people who are

    a. doing jobs they dislike.

    b. relaxing on a Sunday.

    c. shooing birds from gardens.

    d. separated from loved ones.

Use the following information to answer questions 29–34.

Before becoming the sixteenth president of the United States, Abraham Lincoln ran for a seat in the state legislature. This excerpt from *The Every-Day Life of Abraham Lincoln* by Francis Fisher Browne describes the election.

(1)

Lincoln's popularity among his comrades in the field was so great that at the close of his military service, which had lasted three months, he was nominated as a candidate for the State Legislature. "His first appearance on the stump in the course of the canvass was at Pappsville, about eleven miles west of Springfield, upon the occasion of a public sale. The sale over, speech-making was about to begin, when Lincoln observed some strong symptoms of inattention in his audience which had taken that particular moment to engage in a general fight. Lincoln saw that one of his friends was suffering more than he liked, and stepping into the crowd he shouldered them sternly away from his man until he met a fellow who refused to fall back. Him he seized by the nape of the neck and the seat of his breeches, and tossed him 'ten or twelve feet easily.' After this episode—as characteristic of him as of the times—he mounted the platform and delivered with awkward modesty the following speech: 'Gentlemen and Fellow-Citizens, I presume you all know who I am. I am humble Abraham Lincoln. I have been solicited by my friends to become a candidate for the Legislature. My politics are short and sweet, like the old woman's dance. I

am in favor of a national bank. I am in favor of the internal-improvement system and a high protective tariff. These are my sentiments and political principles. If elected I shall be thankful. If not, it will be all the same.'"

(2)

Lincoln's friend, Mr. A.Y. Ellis, who was with him during a part of this campaign, says: "He wore a mixed-jeans coat, claw-hammer style, short in the sleeves and bobtail,—in fact, it was so short in the tail that he could not sit down on it,—flax and tow linen pantaloons, and a straw hat. I think he wore a vest, but I do not remember how it looked. He wore pot-metal boots. I went with him on one of his electioneering trips to Island Grove, and he made a speech which pleased his party friends very well, although some of the Jackson men tried to make sport of it. He told several good anecdotes in the speech, and applied them very well, I thought."

(3)

The election took place in August, and although Lincoln was defeated he received two hundred and seventy-seven out of the two hundred and eighty-four votes cast in his precincts. He was so little known outside of New Salem that the chances of election were hopelessly against him, yet the extraordinary evidence of favor shown by the vote of his fellow-townsmen was a flattering success in the midst of defeat. His failure to be elected, however, left him once more without occupation. He was without means, and felt the necessity of undertaking some business that would provide him an income, however small. It seems that at this time he considered seriously learning the blacksmith's trade, but while entertaining the idea an event occurred which opened the way in another direction. The particulars of this event are given by Mr. W.G. Greene. "A man named Reuben Radford," says Mr. Greene, "was the keeper of a small store in the village of New Salem. A friend told him to look out for the 'Clary Grove boys' or they would smash him up. He said he was not afraid."

29. Based on information in the first paragraph, Lincoln was
  a. not as humble as he claimed to be.
  b. unclear about his own political policies.
  c. at his strongest when making speeches.
  d. someone who valued friendship as well as success.

30. Read the following paragraph from Harry A. Lewis's *Hidden Treasures; or Why Some Succeed While Others Fail*:

About this time he became a clerk in a country store, where his honesty and square dealing made him a universal favorite, and earned for him the sobriquet of "Honest Abe." He next entered the Black Hawk war, and was chosen captain of his company. Jefferson Davis also served as an officer in this war. In the fall of 1832 he was a candidate for the legislature, but was defeated. He then opened a store with a partner named Berry.

How does this paragraph differ from Browne's passage?

  a. Only Lewis's paragraph illustrates Lincoln's honesty.
  b. Only Browne's passage explains Lincoln's failure to be elected to the legislature.
  c. Only Lewis's paragraph refers to one of Lincoln's failures.
  d. Only Browne's passage describes how Lincoln opened a store with a partner.

31. Which of the following meanings associated with the word "means" seems most intended in paragraph 3?
  a. purposes
  b. resources
  c. indicates
  d. certainties

32. Why does the author devote the entire second paragraph to an extended quote from one of Lincoln's friends?
  a. to add a humorous tone to a passage that is serious overall
  b. to make his writing more interesting by varying its style
  c. to give the reader information that could not be given in any other way
  d. to support his secondhand observances with a first-person anecdote

33. How was Lincoln most likely different after he ran for state legislature?
  a. He became focused on his political career only.
  b. He decided he needed to become more aggressive.
  c. He gained a higher profile throughout his state.
  d. He gave up politics after he lost the election.

34. In paragraph 1, the phrase "short and sweet" means
  a. delightful.
  b. inadequate.
  c. common.
  d. simple.

Use the following information to answer questions 35–40.

Sherlock Holmes is the most famous private detective in the history of literature. This excerpt from "The Adventure of the Cardboard Box" by Arthur Conan Doyle describes one of Holmes's discussions with his faithful assistant, Dr. Watson.

(1)

It was a blazing hot day in August. Baker Street was like an oven, and the glare of the sunlight upon the yellow brickwork of the house across the road was painful to the eye. . . . A depleted bank account had caused me to postpone my holiday, and as to my companion, neither the country nor the sea presented the slightest attraction to him. He loved to lie in the very center of five millions of people, with his filaments stretching out and running through them, responsive to every little rumor or suspicion of unsolved crime. Appreciation of nature found no place among his many gifts, and his only change was when he turned his mind from the evil-doer of the town to track down his brother of the country.

(2)

Finding that Holmes was too absorbed for conversation I had tossed aside the barren paper, and leaning back in my chair I fell into a brown study. Suddenly my companion's voice broke in upon my thoughts:

(3)

"You are right, Watson," said he. "It does seem a most preposterous way of settling a dispute."

(4)

"Most preposterous!" I exclaimed, and then suddenly realizing how he had echoed the inmost thought of my soul, I sat up in my chair and stared at him in blank amazement.

(5)

"What is this, Holmes?" I cried. "This is beyond anything which I could have imagined."

(6)

He laughed heartily at my perplexity.

(7)

"You remember," said he, "that some little time ago when I read you the passage in one of Poe's sketches in which a close reasoner follows the unspoken thoughts of his companion, you were inclined to treat the matter as a mere tour-de-force of the author. On my remarking that I

was constantly in the habit of doing the same thing you expressed incredulity."

(8)

"Oh, no!"

(9)

"Perhaps not with your tongue, my dear Watson, but certainly with your eyebrows. So when I saw you throw down your paper and enter upon a train of thought, I was very happy to have the opportunity of reading it off, and eventually of breaking into it, as a proof that I had been in rapport with you."

(10)

But I was still far from satisfied. "In the example which you read to me," said I, "the reasoner drew his conclusions from the actions of the man whom he observed. If I remember right, he stumbled over a heap of stones, looked up at the stars, and so on. But I have been seated quietly in my chair, and what clues can I have given you?"

(11)

"You do yourself an injustice. The features are given to man as the means by which he shall express his emotions, and yours are faithful servants."

(12)

"Do you mean to say that you read my train of thoughts from my features?"

(13)

"Your features and especially your eyes. Perhaps you cannot yourself recall how your reverie commenced?"

(14)

"No, I cannot."

(15)

"Then I will tell you. After throwing down your paper, which was the action which drew my attention to you, you sat for half a minute with a vacant expression. Then your eyes fixed themselves upon your newly framed picture of General Gordon, and I saw by the alteration in your face that a train of thought had been started. But it did not lead very far. Your eyes flashed across to the unframed portrait of Henry Ward Beecher which stands upon the top of your books. Then you glanced up at the wall, and of course your meaning was obvious. You were thinking that if the portrait were framed it would just cover that bare space and correspond with Gordon's picture there."

(16)

"You have followed me wonderfully!" I exclaimed.

35. In paragraph 1, the author has used the discussion of a holiday as an opportunity to do which of the following?
   a. Establish the setting of the story.
   b. Reveal details about Dr. Watson's personal life.
   c. Establish Sherlock Holmes's interest in travel.
   d. Reveal details about Sherlock Holmes's personality.

36. Which line from paragraphs 9 to 11 clarifies information from earlier in the passage?
   a. "I saw you throw down your paper and enter upon a train of thought"
   b. "I was very happy to have the opportunity of reading it off"
   c. "the reasoner drew his conclusions from the actions of the man whom he observed"
   d. "The features are given to man as the means by which he shall express his emotions"

37. Based on the way Watson reacts to how Holmes reads Watson's body language, Watson is most likely
   a. irritated by Holmes.
   b. bored by Holmes.
   c. confused by Holmes.
   d. delighted by Holmes.

38. Both Watson and Holmes share a fascination with
   a. studying body language.
   b. taking holidays.
   c. human behavior.
   d. Henry Ward Beecher.

39. Watson most likely says "Oh, no!" (paragraph 8) because he
   a. did not think he made his incredulity clear.
   b. was not really incredulous.
   c. did not want Holmes to be offended.
   d. was incapable of feeling incredulous.

40. What will likely happen after the conversation in this passage?
   a. Holmes and Watson will discuss Edgar Allan Poe.
   b. Holmes will turn his attention to solving a crime.
   c. Watson will deny that he'd expressed incredulity.
   d. Watson will go on his holiday.

Language Arts—Writing

Part 1: Multiple Choice
50 Questions
75 Minutes

This practice test is modeled on the content and timing of the official HiSET® Language Arts—Writing test and, like the official test, presents a series of questions that assess your ability to recognize and produce effective standard American written English. Like the official test, this practice is broken up into two parts: Part 1 consists of multiple-choice questions; Part 2 consists of an essay.

Part 1 is a test of skills involved in revising written materials that contain grammatical and stylistic errors. In this section, you will find the types of passages you come across in everyday life—letters, memos, articles, and so on.

You will find each passage presented twice: first in a box without any marks so you can read it uninterrupted, and then in a spread-out format with certain parts underlined and numbered.

For each numbered portion of the passage, you will be asked to choose the alternative that fixes the writing to make it correct, clear, organized, and free of grammatical errors. If you think the original underlined version is best, choose "No change."

Read through the draft press release. Then proceed to the suggestions for revision that follow.

On April 1, the Evergreen Hills community will be kicking off a town-wide composting program. This program is the first of it's kind in the county and is part of the town council's "Put the Green Back in Evergreen" environmental sustainability campaign.

Composting takes natural waste that would otherwise go into the food scraps and plant matter, garbage, and converts it into nutrient-rich soil that can then be used for planting. The main Evergreen Hills compost site will be hosted and maintained at the Blueberry Fields Community Garden. Any soil not used by the garden's staff will be available to town residents on a first-come, first-served basics.

To take part, residents can drop off compostable materials in the orange bins that will be located at 35 locations around town. Many items can be composted. These include fruit and vegetable scraps, eggshells, shredded newspaper, leaves, pine needles, sawdust, grass clippings, coffee grounds, and other natural materials. Items that should not be dropped off for composting include colored paper, plastics, meat, bones of any kind, and dairy products.

"This initiative is so exciting," said Town Councilor Marguerite Cobb. We waste so much material that could be benefiting our town and our environment instead of overflowing our landfill."

Other residents are more skeptical about how the composting program will actually work. "Will people actually take the time to separate out their garbage? I think that remains to be seen," commented Benny Matthews, a local restaurant owner. Benny Matthews is also a registered Independent voter. Like many others in the community, Benny is waiting to see if composting is a positive use of town resources.

(1)

On April 1, the Evergreen Hills community will be kicking off a town-wide composting program. This program is the first of it's [1] kind in the county and is part of the town council's "Put the Green Back in Evergreen" environmental sustainability campaign.

(2)

Composting takes natural waste that would otherwise go into the food scraps and plant matter, garbage, [2] and converts it into nutrient-rich soil that can then be used for planting. The main Evergreen Hills compost site will be hosted and maintained at the Blueberry Fields Community Garden. Any soil not used by the garden's staff will be available to town residents on a first-come, first-served basics. [3]

(3)

To take part, residents can drop off compostable materials in the orange bins that will be located at 35 locations around town. Many items can be composted. These include fruit and vegetable scraps, eggshells, shredded newspaper, leaves, pine needles, sawdust, grass clippings, coffee grounds, and other natural materials. [4] Items that should not be dropped off for composting include colored paper, plastics, meat, bones of any kind, and dairy products. [5]

(4)

"This initiative is so exciting," said Town Councilor Marguerite Cobb. We waste so much material that could be benefiting our town and our environment instead of overflowing our landfill." [6]

(5)

Other residents are more skeptical about how the composting program will actually work. "Will people actually take the time to separate out their garbage? I think that remains to be seen," commented Benny Matthews, a local restaurant owner.

Benny Matthews is also a registered Independent voter. [7] Like many others in the community, Benny is waiting to see if composting is a positive use of town resources.

1. **a.** *(No change)*
   b. it is
   c. its
   d. its'

2. **a.** *(No change)*
   b. garbage, such as food scraps and plant matter,
   c. garbage, food scraps, and plant matter
   d. food scraps and plant matter

3. **a.** *(No change)*
   b. first-come, first-serve base
   c. first-come, first-served basis
   d. first-come, first-serve basis

4. Which of the following would be the best way to combine the indicated sentences?
   a. Many items include fruit and vegetable scraps, eggshells, shredded newspaper, leaves, pine needles, sawdust, grass clippings, coffee grounds, and other natural materials.
   b. Many items can be composted, fruit and vegetable scraps, eggshells, shredded newspaper, leaves, pine needles, sawdust, grass clippings, coffee grounds, and other natural materials.
   c. Many items, fruit and vegetable scraps, eggshells, shredded newspaper, leaves, pine needles, sawdust, grass clippings, coffee grounds, and other natural materials, can be composted.
   d. Many items can be composted: fruit and vegetable scraps, eggshells, shredded newspaper, leaves, pine needles, sawdust, grass clippings, coffee grounds, and other natural materials.

5. Which of the following sentences, added at the end of paragraph 3, would provide the best concluding sentence for the paragraph?

   a. If you have questions about which materials are compostable, please e-mail compost@evergreenhills.gov.

   b. The city landfill's hours are 8:00 A.M. to 7:00 P.M., Monday through Saturday.

   c. Compost programs in other cities have had mixed results.

   d. Remember, 35 orange bins will be available around town.

6. **a.** *(No change)*

   b. We waste so much material that could be benefiting our town and our environment instead of overflowing our landfill.

   c. . . . We waste so much material that could be benefiting our town and our environment instead of overflowing our landfill."

   d. "We waste so much material that could be benefiting our town and our environment instead of overflowing our landfill."

7. The writer is considering deleting the indicated information. Should the writer delete this material?

   a. No, because Matthews' political beliefs help the reader understand his positions on all issues.

   b. No, because by specifying Matthews' politics, the author makes the composting program a political issue.

   c. Yes, because Matthews' politics are irrelevant to his position on the composting program.

   d. Yes, because readers might disagree with Matthews' position on the composting program if they dislike his politics.

Read through the draft article. Then go on to the suggestions for revision that follow.

How do you steal 13 paintings from a museum, and get away without leaving a bit? It may sound like the plot to an Ocean's Eleven–type movie, but it is also a very real question that has stumped police for more than 25 years.

In the wee hours of March 20, 1990, two men disguised as Boston police officers tricked security guards at the Isabella Stewart Gardner Museum into letting them in through a back door. The two "officers" proceeded to tie up the guards. By the time the thieves finished ransacking the museum, he had stolen 13 paintings worth more than $500 million. They escaped into the night, and according to sources, the heist was not discovered until museum employees came in the next morning.

The thieves had access to the entire museum, yet they only chose 13 pieces of art to steal. Some other pieces that were even more valuable were left untouched. Without knowing who did this and what their motives could have been, it's impossible to understand why they chose those specific paintings.

At the time, both the police and the FBI investigated the theft but discovered no concrete leads. They believe the artwork was offered for sale in Philadelphia in the 2000s, police were never able to trace it directly, all 13 pieces have since gone back underground. The FBI eventually identified a number of suspects, but there was never enough evidence to arrest them, and at least two suspects died before investigators could find proof tying them to the stealing.

Now the trail has gone cold, and experts wonder if any of these famous works of art will ever be found. If you visit the Gardner Museum today, you'll see that the empty frames from the stolen paintings are still on the walls as a memorial to the lost art. I think that if the paintings ever turn up, the story will make one heck of a movie!

(1)

How do you steal 13 paintings from a museum, and get away without leaving a bit [8]? It may sound like the plot to an *Ocean's Eleven*–type movie, but it is also a very real question that has stumped police for more than 25 years.

(2)

In the wee hours of March 20, 1990, two men disguised as Boston police officers tricked security guards at the Isabella Stewart Gardner Museum into letting them in through a back door. The two "officers" proceeded to tie up the guards. By the time the thieves finished ransacking the museum, he had [9] stolen 13 paintings worth more than $500 million. They escaped into the night, and according to sources, [10] the heist was not discovered until museum employees came in the next morning.

(3)

[11] The thieves had access to the entire museum, yet they only chose 13 pieces of art to steal. Some other pieces that were even more valuable were left untouched. Without knowing who did this and what their motives could have been, it's impossible to understand why they chose those specific paintings.

(4)

At the time, both the police and the FBI investigated the theft but discovered no concrete leads. They believe the artwork was offered for sale in Philadelphia in the 2000s, police were never able to trace it directly, all 13 pieces have since gone back underground. [12] The FBI eventually identified a number of suspects, but there was never enough evidence to arrest them, and at least two suspects died before investigators could find proof tying them to the stealing. [13]

(5)

Now the trail has gone cold, and experts wonder if any of these famous works of art will ever be found. If you visit the Gardner Museum today, you'll see that the empty frames from the stolen paintings are still on the walls as a memorial to the lost art. I think that if the paintings ever turn up, the story will make one heck of a movie! [14]

8. a. (*No change*)
   b. a sample
   c. a trace
   d. an evidence

9. a. (*No change*)
   b. they had
   c. he'd
   d. it had

10. Which of these would be an appropriate source for the writer to quote here?
   a. the writer's cousin, who recently started volunteering at the museum
   b. a police officer who has worked on the case
   c. another newspaper article on the same topic
   d. an Internet message board where people post theories about what happened

11. Which of the following sentences, added at the beginning of paragraph 3, would provide the best opening sentence for the paragraph?
   a. In addition to the "whodunit," the "why" has long plagued investigators.
   b. Anyway, nobody really knows anything.
   c. Why?
   d. Investigators ask themselves, "Why?"

12. a. (*No change*)
   b. They believe the artwork was offered for sale in Philadelphia in the 2000s police were never able to trace it directly. All 13 pieces have since gone back underground.
   c. Because they believe the artwork was offered for sale in Philadelphia in the 2000s, police were never able to trace it directly, and all 13 pieces have since gone back underground.
   d. Although they believe the artwork was offered for sale in Philadelphia in the 2000s, police were never able to trace it directly, and since then all 13 pieces have gone back underground.

13. a. (*No change*)
   b. stolen
   c. heist
   d. loss

14. a. (*No change*)
   b. Personally, I don't believe any of the paintings will ever turn up.
   c. Who knows whether the lost paintings will ever be recovered, and who cares?
   d. With all the twists and turns in this case, it's possible that the paintings will be found someday and there will be a Hollywood ending.

Read through the draft cover letter. Then go on to the suggestions for revision that follow.

Dear Sir or Madam,

I am interested in your job opening for a rodeo clown. I am a performer of more than 16 years, traveling all over the country. I am confident that these qualities make me well suited to join your company.

Clowning has been a cornerstone of my family for many years; it is kind of like a family business. My grandfather graduated from Central University's famous clowning program, and although the performing bug skipped a generation (my parents are accountants), I caught it early in life. Some of my earlier memories involve creating balloon animals and performing magic shows for my sisters and friends.

I'm also prepared for the challenges of performing with a traveling rodeo. I have worked with large animals before and spent a long time training safely with them. I am quick on my feet—both literally and figuratively! I spend the past five years homing my skills in improv comedy classes at the Joke Cellar.

I served as the head clown in the Arturo Brothers Circus. During my time there, I received rave reviews, and the show enjoyed healthy attendance numbers. However, the Arturo's have decided to close the circus, and it's time for me to seek a new, more challenging opportunity.

At this stage in my career. I'm ready to pack my suitcase and take my show on the road. Therefore, with your rodeo, I would love to learn more about the job.

Regards,
Charles "Chuckles" Brown

---

(1)

Dear Sir or Madam,
I am interested in your job opening for a rodeo clown. <u>I am a performer of more than 16 years, traveling all over the country.</u> [15] I am confident that these qualities make me well suited to join your company.

(2)

Clowning has been a cornerstone of my family for many years; it is kind of like a family business. My grandfather graduated from Central University's famous clowning program, and although the performing bug skipped a generation (my parents are accountants), I caught it early in life. Some of my <u>earlier</u> [16] memories involve creating balloon animals and performing magic shows for my sisters and friends.

(3)

I'm also prepared for the challenges of performing with a traveling rodeo. I have worked with large animals before and spent a long time training safely with them. I am quick on my feet—both literally and figuratively! <u>I spend the past five years</u> [17] <u>homing</u> [18] my skills in improv comedy classes at the Joke Cellar.

(4)

I served as the head clown in the Arturo Brothers
Circus. [19] During my time there, I received rave
reviews, and the show enjoyed healthy attendance
numbers. However, the Arturo's [20] have decided to
close the circus, and it's time for me to seek a new,
more challenging opportunity.

(5)

At this stage in my career. [21] I'm ready to
pack my suitcase and take my show on the road.
Therefore, with your rodeo, I would love to learn
more about the job. [22]

Regards,
Charles "Chuckles" Brown

15. **a.** *(No change)*
   b. I am a performer and have been for more
       than 16 years.
   c. Performing for more than 16 years, I have
       traveled all over the country.
   d. Delete the sentence.

16. **a.** *(No change)*
   b. earliest
   c. most early
   d. least early

17. **a.** *(No change)*
   b. I am spending the last five years
   c. I will have spent the last five years
   d. I spent the past five years

18. **a.** *(No change)*
   b. making
   c. honing
   d. finding

19. Which of the following, added at the beginning
   of the first sentence of paragraph 4, would provide the best opening to the sentence?
   a. In addition to my training,
   b. I was in the Arturo Bros. circus and
   c. But enough about my training,
   d. Thankfully,

20. **a.** *(No change)*
   b. Arturos'
   c. Arturo
   d. Arturos

21. **a.** *(No change)*
   b. At this stage in my career,
   c. This is the stage of my career.
   d. If you look at the stages of my career.

22. **a.** *(No change)*
   b. Your rodeo, I would love to learn more
       about it and the job opening.
   c. Therefore, I would love to learn more about
       the job opening with your rodeo.
   d. I would love to learn more about the job
       opening with your rodeo, therefore.

Read through the draft report. Then go on to the suggestions for revision that follow.

How young is too young to be posting on social media? Some people think that giving children access to sites such as Facebook and Instagram is a harmless way to allow them to communicate, but many others believe that the potential risks prevail the social benefits.

On one side of the issue, you have people who think children should have their own social media accounts. That is, with parental permission. They also think kids should have supervision. The kids can use these social networks to post pictures they've taken and to build communication skills by reading and writing posts. These advocates who include parents stress that because they are watching their kids' activities online, there is a benefit to letting children have these types of interactions early. Helps the children make healthier choices about what they do and post online.

On the other side of the issue, you have people who believe that young children should have limited exposure to the Internet. They say that cases of online bullying among students show the potential for kids' online social presence to spin out of control, even when they have permission to go online. There is also the "stranger danger" element, which means kids can be monitored and tricked into interacting with adults pretending to be other kids.

So where do the social media websites themselves fall on the issue? Both Facebook and Instagram requires users to be at least 13 years old. They also recommend that any users under the age of 16 have parental permission, and some youth advocates believe that these guidelines don't go far enough to protect kids' privacy.

(1)

How young is too young to be posting on social media? Some people think that giving children access to sites such as Facebook and Instagram is a harmless way to allow them to communicate, but many others believe that the potential risks prevail [23] the social benefits.

(2)

On one side of the issue, you have people who think children should have their own social media accounts. That is, with parental permission. They also think kids should have supervision. [24] The kids can use these social networks to post pictures they've taken and to build communication skills by reading and writing posts. These advocates who include parents [25] stress that because they are watching their kids' activities online, there is a benefit to letting children have these types of interactions early. Helps the children make healthier choices about what they do and post online. [26]

(3)

On the other side of the issue, you have people who believe that young children should have limited exposure to the Internet. They say [27] that cases of online bullying among students show the potential for kids' online social presence to spin out of control, even when they have permission to go online. There is also the "stranger danger" element, which means kids can be monitored and tricked into interacting with adults pretending to be other kids.

(4)

So where do the social media websites themselves fall on the issue? Both Facebook and

Instagram <u>requires users to be at least 13 years old</u>.
[28] They also recommend that any users under the
age of 16 have parental <u>permission, and some</u> [29]
youth advocates believe that these guidelines don't go
far enough to protect kids' privacy.

23. **a.** *(No change)*
  b. sway
  c. outweigh
  d. outplay

24. Which of the following is the best way to combine the indicated sentences?
  a. That is, with parental permission and they
     also think kids should have supervision.
  b. This usually means that kids have parental
     permission and supervision.
  c. With parental permission and also parental
     supervision.
  d. Likewise, this includes parental permission.

25. **a.** *(No change)*
  b. These advocates include parents
  c. These advocates may or may not be parents
  d. These advocates, who include parents,

26. **a.** *(No change)*
  b. Helping the children make healthier choices
     about what they do and post online.
  c. They believe it helps children make healthier
     choices about what they do and post online.
  d. Helps the children make healthier choices
     about what they do and post online.

27. **a.** *(No change)*
  b. admit
  c. pretend
  d. argue

28. **a.** *(No change)*
  b. required that users be at least 13 years old
  c. requiring that users be at least 13 years old
  d. require that users be at least 13 years old

29. **a.** *(No change)*
  b. permission, but some
  c. permission, some
  d. permission however some

Read through the draft memo. Then go on to the suggestions for revision that follow.

TO: Tenants of 15 Water Street
FROM: Building Management
RE: Updated Building Policies

Greetings tenants,

We'd like to take this opportunity to remind everyone that the below policies are in affect for everyone who currently lived in the building, as well as any visitors.

PETS: Large animals include dogs over 35 pounds. These are not allowed to live in the building. All pet owners must clean up after their animals and pay for any damage caused by their pets. Dog and cat owners are expected to notify the management company and pay a $200 "pet deposit," which is refundable upon moving out (provided there is no pet-related damage to the apartment). If they do not pay the deposit by October 31, you may be subject to an initial nonrefundable $300 fee. The fee will increase by $25 per month for every additional month you have failed to pay the initial fee.

All tenants are expected to put their trash in the bins near the basement entrance. Recyclable materials go in the bins near the basement entrance. In common areas, such as the lobby and laundry room, tenants are expected to clean up after themselves.

Peace, and see you at the block party.

(1)

TO: Tenants of 15 Water Street
FROM: Building Management
RE: Updated Building Policies

Greetings tenants,

We'd like to take this opportunity to remind everyone that the below policies [30] are in affect [31] for everyone who currently lived [32] in the building, as well as any visitors.

(2)

PETS: Large animals include dogs over 35 pounds. These are not allowed to live in the building. [33] All pet owners must clean up after their animals and pay for any damage caused by their pets. Dog and cat owners are expected to notify the management

company and pay a $200 "pet deposit," which is refundable upon moving out (provided there is no pet-related damage to the apartment). If they [34] do not pay the deposit by October 31, you may be subject to an initial nonrefundable $300 fee. The fee will increase by $25 per month for every additional month you have failed to pay the initial fee. [35]

(3)

[1] All tenants are expected to put their trash in the bins near the basement entrance. [2] Recyclable materials go in the bins near the basement entrance. [3] In common areas, such as the lobby and laundry room, tenants are expected to clean up after themselves. [36]

(4)

Peace, and see you at the block party. [37]

30. **a.** *(No change)*
   b. below
   c. policies below
   d. policies

31. **a.** *(No change)*
   b. in the effective
   c. affecting
   d. in effect

32. **a.** *(No change)*
   b. previously lived
   c. currently lives
   d. currently will live

33. Which of the following would be the best way to combine the indicated sentences?
   a. Large animals include dogs over 35 pounds; these are not allowed to live in the building.
   b. Large animals are not allowed to live in the building.
   c. Including animals over 35 pounds, large animals are not allowed to live in the building.
   d. Large animals, including dogs over 35 pounds, are not allowed to live in the building.

34. **a.** *(No change)*
   b. we
   c. you
   d. it

35. The writer is considering deleting the indicated information. Should the writer delete this material?
   a. No, because it is relevant information that further clarifies the consequences of not paying the pet deposit.
   b. No, because it will effectively frighten tenants into paying the required pet deposit.
   c. Yes, because it is an unnecessary extra penalty for people who fail to pay the initial pet deposit.
   d. Yes, because it is a minor piece of information that adds unnecessary details to an otherwise concise memo.

36. The writer would like to add the following information to paragraph 3:

> Failure to place refuse in the correct bins can result in a $10 fine for each infraction.

For the most logical organization of ideas, where should this sentence be placed?
   a. before sentence 1
   b. after sentence 1
   c. after sentence 2
   d. after sentence 3

37. **a.** *(No change)*
   b. That's all for now. (P.S.: Hope to see you at the block party.)
   c. You'd better be careful what you do in this building or there will be serious consequences.
   d. Thank you. We look forward to seeing you at the upcoming block party!

Read through the restaurant review. Then go on to the suggestions for revision that follow.

> If you're planning to go to the restaurant Billy Buddy's old town grill, do yourself a favor and save your money. Go to McDonald's instead. Go to Pizza Town. Eat leftovers on your couch.
>
> My experience at this restaurant was terrible from start to finish. I was looking forward to trying it out, and celebrating my birthday was a good reason to go. The problems started when we walked through the door. My husband had made a reservation for six people for 7:00. I had gone to the gym and run some errands before dinner. When we got there, not only had they lost the reservation, but they made us wait for more than 45 minutes when they said it would just be a 10-minute wait! They didn't even offer to let us sit at the coffee bar while we waited.
>
> By the time we sat down, we were ready to order right away. This was after we had been waiting hungrily in the lobby. Our waitress had other plans. I saw her over in the corner texting. She stopped only when my husband waved to get her attention. She helped make it up to us by bringing a basket of bread. But boy was the bread moldy? It sure was. We should have walked right out at that point.
>
> When we got our food, everyone at my table was willing to forgive and forget the bad service. Then we started eating. Each person at the table had something wrong with his or her dinner. My steak was barely cooked, and my sister's grilled chicken was more like a yoga mat with BBQ sauce than food. The last straw came at desert when the waitress brought out a special birthday cake my husband had preordered a week prior. The staff sang "Happy Birthday" to me but used the wrong name. I'm not sure who "Margaret" is, but I hope she had a better birthday dinner than I did!

(1)

If you're planning to go to the <u>restaurant Billy Buddy's old town grill</u> [38], do yourself a favor and save your money. Go to McDonald's instead. Go to Pizza Town. Eat leftovers on your couch. [39]

(2)

My experience at this restaurant was terrible from start to finish. [40] I was looking forward to trying it out, and celebrating my birthday was a good reason to go. The problems started when we walked through the door. My husband had made a reservation for six people for 7:00. <u>I had gone to the gym and run some errands before dinner.</u> [41] When we got there, not only had they lost the reservation, but they made us wait for more than 45 minutes when they said it would just be a 10-minute wait! They didn't even offer to let us sit at the coffee bar while we waited.

(3)

<u>By the time we sat down, we were ready to order right away. This was after we had been waiting hungrily in the lobby.</u> [42] Our waitress had other plans. I saw her over in the corner texting. She stopped only when my husband waved to get her attention. <u>She helped make it up to us by bringing a basket of bread. But boy was the bread moldy? It sure was.</u> [43] We should have walked right out at that point.

(4)

When we got our food, everyone at my table was willing to forgive and forget the bad service. Then we started eating. Each person at the table had something wrong with <u>his or her</u> [44] dinner. My steak was barely cooked, and my sister's grilled chicken was more like a yoga mat with BBQ sauce than food. The last straw came at desert [45] when the waitress brought out a special birthday cake my husband had preordered [45] a week prior [45]. The staff sang "Happy Birthday" to me but used the wrong name. I'm not sure who "Margaret" is, but I hope she had a better birthday dinner than I did!

38. a. *(No change)*
  b. the restaurant Billy Buddy's Old Town grill
  c. the Restaurant Billy Buddy's Old Town Grill
  d. the restaurant Billy Buddy's Old Town Grill

39. Which of the following sentences, added at the end of paragraph 1, would provide the best concluding sentence for the paragraph?
  a. My favorite restaurant is China Bistro on Central Avenue in the middle of town.
  b. There were some good things about my visit that I would also like to mention.
  c. Any of these choices would provide a much better dining experience.
  d. Just so you know, Billy Buddy's Old Town Grill is open Tuesday through Sunday.

40. Which of the following would be an effective transition to begin the second sentence of paragraph 2?
  a. After finishing my meal
  b. Without a second left to spare,
  c. As I was deciding how I felt about it,
  d. Before reaching my unfortunate conclusion,

41. The writer is considering deleting the indicated information. Should the writer delete this material?
  a. No, because the information helps establish the setting of the passage.
  b. No, because the information shows how the author became so hungry.
  c. Yes, because the information isn't related to the writer's restaurant experience.
  d. Yes, because the information was only included to make the reader feel sorry for the writer.

42. Which of the following would be the best way to combine the indicated sentences?
  a. By the time we sat down, we were ready to order right away; this was after we had been waiting hungrily in the lobby.
  b. By the time we were finally seated, we were hungry and ready to order.
  c. Hungrily waiting, we were seated and ready to order.
  d. We waited hungrily in the lobby, then we were seated, and then we were ready to order.

43. Which of the following would be the best way to combine the indicated sentences?
  a. She helped make it up to us by bringing a basket of bread, but boy was the bread moldy (it sure was).
  b. Our waitress helped by bringing us a basket of bread, but boy, was it moldy!
  c. She helps make it up to us by bringing a basket of bread—but the bread was moldy!
  d. She helped make it up to us by bringing a basket of bread—but the bread was moldy!

44. a. *(No change)*
    b. their
    c. our
    d. his

45. Which of the following words, if any, is misspelled?
    a. *(None)*
    b. desert
    c. preordered
    d. prior

Read through the speech. Then go on to the suggestions for revision that follow.

This town needs strong and positive leadership more than ever before, and if you support my bid to become the Mayor, I will be that leader. After 15 years on the town council and 30 years living in our fine city, I know the community we share inside and out. I know the nature of our struggles, and I know what we can do to meet these challenges with optimism and hard work.

One challenge is financial. I neither need nor want to rehash the chain of events that led to our former mayor being convicted of embezzlement. I simply believe in a fresh start for the community. Although you should know that I will request annual audits of our budget and spending and will take personal responsibility for any issues that arise during my administration. My word is as good as money.

We have some of the best beaches and most beautiful scenery in the state, but tourist revenues have decreased over the past 10 years. I am currently working to assemble a special marketing department to rebrand our image to reestablish our city as a timeless, not fleetingly trendy, vacation spot.

Despite these challenges, our best days lie ahead of us. So please support me on election day. I promise to devote my mayoral term to getting this city up to snuff for all of you.

(1)

This town needs strong and positive leadership more than ever before, and if you support my bid to become the Mayor [46], I will be that leader. After 15 years on the town council and 30 years living in our fine city, I know the community we share inside and out. I know the nature of our struggles, and I know what we can do to meet these challenges with optimism and hard work.

(2)

One challenge is financial. I neither need nor want to rehash the chain of events that led to our former mayor being convicted of embezzlement. I simply believe in a fresh start for the community. Although [47] you should know that I will request annual audits of our budget and spending and will take personal responsibility for any issues that arise during my administration. My word is as good as money. [48]

(3)

We have some of the best beaches and most beautiful scenery in the state, but tourist revenues have decreased over the past 10 years. [49] I am currently working to assemble a special marketing department to rebrand our image to reestablish our city as a timeless, not fleetingly trendy, vacation spot.

(4)

Despite these challenges, our best days lie ahead of us. So please support me on election day. I promise to devote my mayoral term to <u>getting this city up to snuff for all of you.</u> [50]

46. a. *(No change)*
   b. The Mayor
   c. The mayor
   d. the mayor

47. a. *(No change)*
   b. However,
   c. Even though
   d. Never

48. a. *(No change)*
   b. as solid as silver
   c. completely ironclad
   d. as good as gold

49. Which of the following sentences, added after the first sentence in paragraph 3, would provide the best transition into the next sentence?
   a. I am running for mayor and would appreciate your vote.
   b. Another major challenge for this town is tourism.
   c. However, I have a clear plan for repairing our standing among tourists.
   d. Perhaps it is because our beaches are in such a sorry state.

50. a. *(No change)*
   b. undoing everything our last mayor did to you and this city of ours
   c. improving our great city's image and the lives of every citizen who resides here
   d. making our city good and making all of your lives good, too

Part 2: Essay Question
45 Minutes

This part of the practice test will assess your writing skills. On the official exam, you will have a 45-minute limit to plan and write your essay. Your essay will be scored on how well you

- develop a main idea and support it with strong reasons, examples, and details
- clearly organize your ideas, including the use of an introduction and conclusion, logical paragraphs, and effective transitions
- use language, including varied word choice and sentence constructions and appropriate voice
- clearly and correctly use writing conventions

Each passage offers a different perspective on the same important issue. Read both passages carefully, taking note of the strengths and weaknesses of each author's discussion. Then write an essay that explains your own opinion on the important issue discussed in both passages.

The following article includes an excerpt from a U.S. Department of Transportation report called "How Bike Paths and Lanes Make a Difference."

Our state government is currently considering installing a new bike lane along twenty miles of road stretching across town. Early reaction to the proposal has been overwhelmingly positive. A bike lane will surely encourage commuters to "go green" by facilitating an alternative mode of travel to driving in gas-guzzling, pollution-spewing automobiles. Bicycling is also a path to personal health as it is a marvelous form of exercise that can help combat the current obesity epidemic. However, the proposed bicycle lane might prove most beneficial in terms of traffic safety. A report from the U.S. Department of Transportation explains how dedicated bicycle lanes provide riders with a greater sense of safety. The following is an excerpt from that report:

Those Who Have Access to a Bicycle Are Likely to Ride It

Nearly half (46%) of the adult population have access to a bicycle, and more than half with access (about 52 million) rode their bikes in the 30 days prior to answering the survey. Another 5 million people rode a bike during that time period, even though they didn't have direct access to one (presumably they rented or borrowed a bike) for a total of 57 million bicyclists each summer month. Of these, 58% (33 million) were infrequent bicyclists, riding one to five times per month, while 42% (24 million) were frequent bicyclists, riding more than five times per month. Thus, 12% of the adult population, or one in eight adults, rides a bicycle more than five days per month during the summer period.

Availability of Bike Paths and Lanes

Bike paths and lanes are the chief infrastructure features that might be expected to affect bicycling. About a quarter of the population has both bike paths and lanes available in the areas where it lives or rides, and approximately 3 out of 10 adult Americans have access to one or the other. Forty-three percent of adult Americans live in communities that don't have bike paths or bike lanes. As a rule, bike paths are specially created pathways away from the main roads, typically in recreational areas. Bike lanes provide the bicyclist his or her own lane on a road shared with motorists and typically provide direct routes for travelers wanting to get to work or school. The presence of bike paths and lanes does not appear to have a significant effect on whether people ride bicycles or on how frequently they ride. Instead, the significance of biking facilities—paths and lanes—lies in the increased sense of personal safety.

Presence of Bike Paths and Lanes and the Perception of Biking Safety

Nearly one out of eight (13%) people surveyed who rode one or more times during the previous month said they felt threatened for their personal safety at least once. In areas where both bike paths and lanes were available, the percent of bicyclists feeling threatened for their personal safety dropped to 10%. When neither bike paths nor lanes were available, the percentage increased to 17%. When only one was available, either bike paths or bike lanes, the percentage fearful was in between, at about 12%. Not surprisingly, the most frequently mentioned source of unease was from motorists. Of the bicyclists who felt endangered, 87% referred to feeling threatened by motorists. Thus, where lanes and paths are absent, bicyclists become more concerned for their personal safety.

The following article is a newspaper editorial about the proposed bike lane.

The proposal to create a new bike lane in our community has caused a surprising stir as of late. Public opinion seems overwhelmingly in favor of this proposal, and this is of little surprise considering the way it is being spun by its proponents. The image of cheery children and environmentally conscious adults zipping off to school or work on their own private bicycle lane without the dangers of sharing pavement with cars appeals to both our sentimentality and our fears. However, this is not as cut-and-dried an issue as the pro-bike-lane contingent would have you believe.

First we must consider the bill. The proposed lane is a 20-mile one, which will allegedly be a boon to commuters. Taxpayers, however, might not be as enthusiastic when they consider that the cost will be about $130,000 per mile, for a grand total of $2,600,000.

The safety issue is also questionable. While the U.S. Department of Transportation recently released a report with statistics relaying how safe bikers feel when sharing roads with cars versus riding on bike lanes, there is precious little data about the actual safety of bike lanes. The bottom line is that the proposed bike lane will still lie parallel to a car-populated road. Those cars are as likely to veer into a bike lane as they are to veer into bikers sharing a road with them.

Perhaps instead of wasting valuable public funds on a proposal that is very popular but may not actually be safer, we should encourage bikers and drivers to exercise greater safety precautions on the road. Considering that our roads are in terrible disrepair, those tax dollars would be put to better use repairing the roads cars and bikes both share than creating new lanes for bicycles alone. Regardless of where those dollars are ultimately put to use, we need to exercise more consideration for the con side of this issue before we heedlessly leap to vote pro.

Write an essay in which you explain your own position on the issue of whether your local government should use public funds to create a new bike lane.

Be sure to use evidence from the text passages provided, as well as specific reasons and examples from your own experience and knowledge to support your position. Remember that every position exists within the context of a larger discussion of the issue, so your essay should, at minimum, acknowledge alternate and/or opposing ideas. When you have finished your essay, review your writing to check for correct spelling, punctuation, and grammar.

_____

_____

_____

_____

_____

Mathematics

90 Minutes
50 Questions

This practice test is modeled on the content and timing of the official HiSET® Mathematics test and, like the official test, presents a series of questions that assess your ability to solve quantitative problems using fundamental concepts and reasoning skills.

1. If $3\frac{3}{4}$ cups of flour are needed to bake a batch of 36 cookies, how much flour is needed to make 90 cookies?
   a. $5\frac{5}{8}$ cups
   b. $9\frac{3}{8}$ cups
   c. $8\frac{1}{2}$ cups
   d. $7\frac{1}{2}$ cups
   e. $11\frac{1}{4}$ cups

2. The diameter of a circle is 16 cm. What is the area (in square centimeters) of a circle whose radius is triple the radius of such a circle?
   a. 24π
   b. 48π
   c. 96π
   d. $2,304\pi$
   e. 576π

3. Consider the following scenario:
   - Rabbits eat a certain type of plant in a neighborhood.
   - Initially, these plants are plentiful in the neighborhood and neighbors have many rabbit sightings.
   - As time goes on, the plants diminish in number and neighbors see fewer rabbits hopping about.
   - As the plants begin to flourish once again, the number of rabbit sightings increases.

Which of the following graphs accurately depicts this scenario?

a.

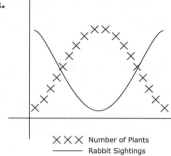

ⅩⅩⅩ Number of Plants
——— Rabbit Sightings

b.

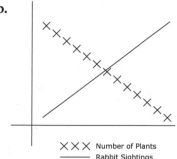

ⅩⅩⅩ Number of Plants
——— Rabbit Sightings

c.

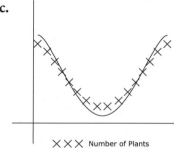

ⅩⅩⅩ Number of Plants
——— Rabbit Sightings

d.

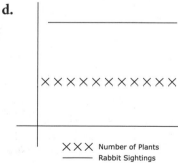

ⅩⅩⅩ Number of Plants
——— Rabbit Sightings

e.

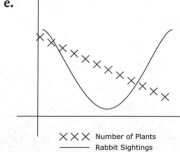

ⅩⅩⅩ Number of Plants
——— Rabbit Sightings

4. The number of bacteria observed in a biological experiment is described by the formula $P(t) = 68(\frac{1}{2})^{-t}$, where $t \geq 0$ is measured in minutes. Which of the following is a true statement?

    a. Every minute, the population increases by 68 bacteria.

    b. The population levels off after one hour.

    c. The population doubles every minute.

    d. The maximum number of bacteria is 68.

    e. The population diminishes by a factor of 2 each minute.

5. For which of the following values of a does the following system have no solution?

$$\begin{cases} y = ax - 3 \\ ay = x + 1 \end{cases}$$

    a. $a = \frac{1}{2}$

    b. $a = -1$

    c. $a = -2$

    d. $a = 4$

    e. $a = -4$

6. Which of the following number lines correctly illustrates the domain of the function $f(x) = \frac{x}{x - 2} + \sqrt{x + 1}$?

    a.

    b.

    c.

    d.

    e.

7. The following table gives the ages of the attendees of an awards banquet:

AGE	FREQUENCY
10 to 15	8
16 to 21	31
22 to 30	11
31 to 40	48
41 to 50	32
51 and up	20

What is the probability that the age of a randomly selected guest is greater than 40?

    a. $\frac{13}{25}$

    b. $\frac{2}{15}$

    c. $\frac{49}{75}$

    d. $\frac{16}{75}$

    e. $\frac{26}{75}$

8. The frame of the roof of the side of a shed is in the shape of the following right triangle:

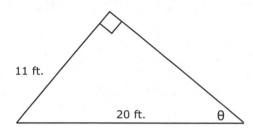

11 ft.

20 ft.

θ

Which of the following equations can be used to determine the value of the angle θ?

a. $\cos \theta = \frac{20}{11}$

b. $\tan \theta = \frac{11}{20}$

c. $\sin \theta = \frac{11}{20}$

d. $\cos \theta = \frac{11}{20}$

e. $\sin \theta = \frac{20}{11}$

9. Which of the following is a rational number?

a. $\frac{\pi}{\sqrt{2}}$

b. $\frac{\frac{1}{6}}{\left(\frac{2}{3}\right)^{-4}}$

c. $\sqrt[3]{2} \cdot \sqrt{2}$

d. $(3\pi)^2$

e. $3\sqrt{3} + 2\sqrt{2}$

10. Consider the following diagram:

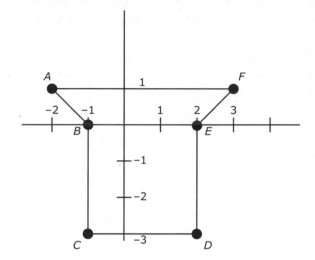

If the image of $\overline{ED}$ under a translation is the line segment $\overline{E'D'}$, where E' is the point (6,5) and D' is the point (6,2), what are the coordinates of the endpoints of the image $\overline{A'F'}$ of the line segment $\overline{AF}$?

a. $A'(3,5)$ and $F'(8,5)$

b. $A'(2,1)$ and $F'(8,1)$

c. $A'(-2,1)$ and $F'(3,6)$

d. $A'(-6,-4)$ and $F'(-1,-4)$

e. $A'(2,6)$ and $F'(7,6)$

11. Eight subway passengers are asked to tell a surveyor the number of sneezes they had heard on their trip that day, and then to rate their perception of their exposure to disease on a scale of 1 to 10, where 1 is very low exposure and 10 is very high. The data and the best fit line are shown:

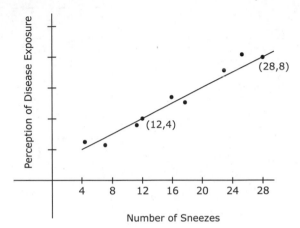

Based on this information, how many sneezes would you expect a passenger to have heard to rate his or her exposure to disease as 10?

a. 40
b. 30
c. 32
d. 34
e. 36

12. A cylinder has height 30 inches and base diameter D inches. What is the volume of a cylinder (measured in cubic inches) obtained by doubling the height and taking one-third of the diameter?

a. $\frac{5}{9}\pi D^2$
b. $\frac{4}{3}\pi(\frac{D}{6})^3$
c. $\frac{5}{3}\pi D^2$
d. $10\pi D$
e. $\frac{5}{6}\pi D^2$

13. Which of the following expressions is equivalent to $\frac{2}{x-1} - \frac{3}{x^2-1} - \frac{2}{x+1}$?

a. $-\frac{3}{x^2+2x}$
b. $\frac{4x+7}{x^2-1}$
c. $\frac{1}{x^2-1}$
d. $\frac{3}{x^2-1}$
e. $\frac{1}{1-x^2}$

14. Will invests a portion of $6,500 in a money market CD that earns 3% interest annually and deposits the remainder in a savings account that earns 1.4% interest annually. He earns $100.50 in interest in the first year. Let x represent the amount Will invests in the 3% CD. Which of the following equations could be used to determine the amount he invested in the CD and the amount he deposited in the savings account?

a. $0.03x + 0.014(6,500 - x) = 100.50$
b. $0.03x + 0.014(6,500 - x) = 6,500(0.044)$
c. $3x + 1.4(6,500 - x) = 100.50$
d. $1.4x + 3(x - 6,500) = 10,050$
e. $0.044[x + (x - 6,500)] = 100.50$

15. Which of the following quadratic equations has two distinct negative real solutions?

a. $9x^2 = 18x$
b. $25x^2 + 10x + 1 = 0$
c. $9x^2 + 9x + 2 = 0$
d. $x^2 + x + 3 = 0$
e. $8x^2 - 6x + 1 = 0$

16. Several singles tennis games are played in a given day at a weekend tournament. The following are the number of ace serves scored by various players in their matches that day:

NUMBER OF ACE SERVES	FREQUENCY
0	5
2	4
4	2
6	1
8	2
10	4
12	6

What is the median number of ace serves scored?

a. 7
b. 6
c. 8
d. 12
e. 6.25

17. Fill in the box with the correct exponent:

$$\frac{\sqrt{x^3}}{\sqrt[4]{x}} = x^{\square}$$

a. 6
b. $\frac{14}{3}$
c. $-\frac{10}{3}$
d. $\frac{7}{4}$
e. $\frac{5}{4}$

18. An audience member at a water fountain display wants to determine how high the highest geyser shoots. She measures its shadow as 13 feet, and she knows that a small geyser of x feet casts a shadow of y feet onto the ground. What is the height (in feet) of the highest geyser?

a. $\frac{x}{13y}$
b. $\frac{13 + x}{y}$
c. $13xy$
d. $\frac{13y}{x}$
e. $\frac{13x}{y}$

19. Sofia has a collection of nickels, dimes, and quarters. She has two fewer nickels than quarters, and the number of dimes is one more than twice the number of quarters. If her total amount of money is \$3.50, how many nickels are in her collection?

a. 5
b. 7
c. 14
d. 15
e. 25

20. Which of the following expressions is equivalent to $[(1 - 3x^2)(1 + 3x^2)]^2$?

a. $81x^8 - 18x^4 + 1$
b. $1 - 81x^8$
c. $81x^6 - 18x^4 + 1$
d. $1 + 36x^8$
e. $1 - 12x^4 + 36x^8$

21. Suppose you shuffle two standard 52-card decks of playing cards together and select one card at random. What is the probability of randomly selecting either a heart or an ace?

   a. $\frac{35}{52}$

   b. $\frac{4}{13}$

   c. $\frac{17}{52}$

   d. $\frac{1}{4}$

   e. $\frac{1}{13}$

22. The set $\{-2, -1, 1, 3\}$ is the complete set of zeros for which polynomial?

   a. $p(x) = (x-2)(x-1)(x+1)(x+3)$

   b. $p(x) = (x+2)^2(x^2-1)(x-3)$

   c. $p(x) = (x^2-4)(x^2-1)(x-3)$

   d. $x(x+1)(x-1)^3(x+2)(x-3)$

   e. $p(x) = (x^2-9)(x^2-1)(x^2-4)$

23. What is the solution set of the equation $2\sqrt{1-x} - 10 = 0$?

   a. $\{x \mid x = -26\}$

   b. $\{x \mid x = 16\}$

   c. $\{x \mid x = -24\}$

   d. $\{x \mid x = -4\}$

   e. empty set

24. Consider the following line segment, where $a > 0$ and $b > 1$:

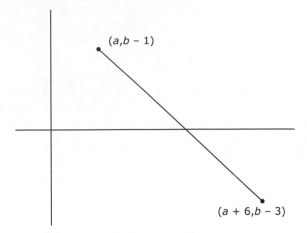

What is the midpoint of this segment?

   a. $(a+3, 0)$

   b. $(3, 2)$

   c. $(a+3, b-2)$

   d. $(a+6, b-4)$

   e. $(2a+6, 2b-4)$

25. A local arboretum wants to build a bridge across a pond. At the moment, the walkway around the pond has the measurements shown in the following figure:

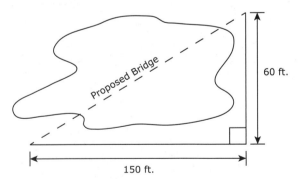

Which expression gives the length of the bridge?

   a. $\sqrt{150^2 - 60^2}$

   b. $150^2 + 60^2$

   c. $60 + 150$

   d. $\sqrt{150^2 + 60^2}$

   e. $150 - 60$

26. If a is an irrational number and b is a nonzero rational number, which of the following *could* be a rational number?

  a. $b + a$

  b. $a \cdot b$

  c. $2b - a$

  d. $\frac{a}{b}$

  e. a^2

27. Which of the following expressions is equivalent to $3x(1 - 2x) + 4x^2(x - 3) - 2x^3$?

  a. $2x^3 + x - 3$

  b. $2x^3 - 18x^2 + 3x$

  c. $2x^3 + x - 3$

  d. $2x + 18x^2 + 2x^3$

  e. $-2x^3 - 18x^2 - 3x$

28. A salad bar owner charges a base price of $5.75 for a basic salad with three toppings and $0.80 for each additional topping. A 6% tax is then applied to that price to get the total cost. Which of the following functions could be used to compute the cost of a salad based on the number of additional toppings x?

  a. $f(x) = (5.75 + 0.80x) + 6(5.75 + 0.80x)$

  b. $f(x) = 5.75 + 0.80x$

  c. $f(x) = 5.75 + 0.80x + 0.06$

  d. $f(x) = (5.75 + 0.80x) + 0.06(5.75 + 0.80x)$

  e. $f(x) = 0.80(5.75 + x) + 0.0048(5.75 + x)$

29. What is the solution set for the inequality $-x - 3[4(1 - 2x) + 5] > x$?

  a. $\{x \mid x > \frac{8}{9}\}$

  b. $\{x \mid x > \frac{27}{22}\}$

  c. $\{x \mid x > -\frac{7}{10}\}$

  d. $\{x \mid x > \frac{22}{27}\}$

  e. $\{x \mid x > \frac{9}{8}\}$

30. Solve for y: $\frac{7}{x} - \frac{3}{y} = \frac{4}{2x}$

  a. $y = \frac{3}{5}x$

  b. $y = -\frac{15}{14}x$

  c. $y = \frac{5}{3}x$

  d. $y = -x$

  e. $y = -\frac{14}{15}x$

31. The half-life of a radioactive isotope X is 2.3×10^4 years, and the half-life of a different radioactive isotope Y is 3.1×10^5 years. How many years greater is the half-life of Y than the half-life of X?

  a. 3.33×10^9 years

  b. 0.8×10^1 years

  c. 3.33×10^5 years

  d. 2.87×10^5 years

  e. 8×10^4 years

32. Which of the following is the graph of the equation $(x-3)^2 + (y+1)^2 = 4$?

a.

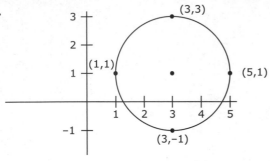

(Not to Scale)

b.

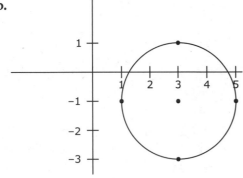

(Not to Scale)

c.

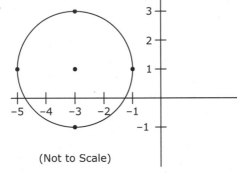

(Not to Scale)

d.

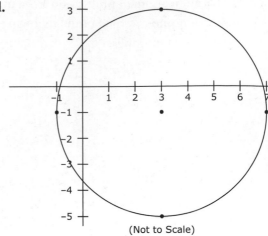

(Not to Scale)

e.

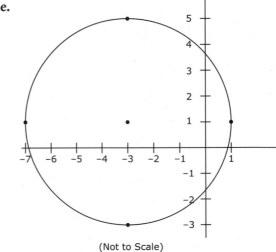

(Not to Scale)

33. A starting basketball player scores the following numbers of points in a series of playoff games:

$$48, 38, 38, 34, 44, 44$$

How many points must he score in a seventh game to ensure that the mean number of points scored for all seven games is 40?

a. 41

b. 34

c. 44

d. 38

e. 40

34. At a recent annual alumni event, the event coordinator asked every twentieth guest who came through the entrance, "How do you prefer to be informed of such events?" She recorded the results in this table:

METHOD OF CONTACT	FREQUENCY
Phone	3
Text message	11
E-mail	19
Newsletter	7

Based on this information, if there are 8,000 alumni total, how many would you expect would prefer being contacted by text message?

a. 3,800
b. 1,400
c. 5,800
d. 600
e. 2,200

35. John buys turkey sandwiches and roast beef sandwiches at a local sandwich shop. A turkey sandwich costs $5.50, and a roast beef sandwich costs $6.75. If he buys 12 sandwiches all told and spends $72.25, which system of equations could be used to determine the number of each type of sandwich he purchased?

a. $\begin{cases} x + y = 72.25 \\ 5.50x + 6.75y = 12 \end{cases}$

b. $\begin{cases} 12.25(xy) = 72.25 \\ x + y = 12 \end{cases}$

c. $\begin{cases} x + y = 12 \\ 5.50x + 6.75y = 72.25 \end{cases}$

d. $\begin{cases} 550x + 675y = 72.25 \\ x + y = 12 \end{cases}$

e. $\begin{cases} y = 12 + x \\ 6.75y = 72.25 - 5.50x \end{cases}$

36. Consider the following graph of a polynomial function $p(x)$:

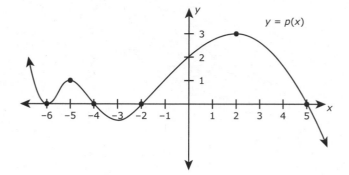

Which of the following is a complete collection of zeros for $p(x)$?

a. $\{-6, -5, -4, -3, -2, 2, 5\}$
b. $\{-4, -2, 5\}$
c. $\{-5, -3, 2\}$
d. $\{-6, -4, -2, 5\}$
e. $\{3\}$

37. What is the range of the function $y(x) = 2x^2 - 20x + 47$?
a. $\{y \mid y \leq 47\}$
b. all real numbers
c. $\{y \mid y \geq -3\}$
d. $\{y \mid y \geq 47\}$
e. $\{y \mid y \leq -3\}$

38. Which of the following expressions is equivalent to $2^4 \times 25^2$?
a. $(2 \times 25)^{4 \times 2}$
b. $(2 \times 5)^4$
c. $(2 \times 25)^{2 + 4}$
d. $(2 \times 5)^{4 + 4}$
e. $(2 \times 5)^{4 \times 4}$

39. What is the length (in centimeters) of the arc corresponding to the shaded sector?

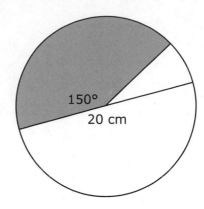

150°
20 cm

a. 20π
b. $\frac{50}{3}\pi$
c. 3,000
d. $\frac{25}{3}\pi$
e. 1,500

40. Suppose the probability of a spinner with red and green spaces landing on green is $\frac{2}{5}$. If you spin the spinner once, and then a second time, what is the probability of it landing on green on the second spin?

a. $\frac{3}{5}$
b. $\frac{1}{2}$
c. $\frac{4}{25}$
d. 0
e. $\frac{2}{5}$

41. Consider the following paired data:

x	−10	−5	−1	3	4
y	0	1	2	4	6

Which of the following is true about the best fit line?

a. The best fit line does not exist in this case.
b. The best fit line has a positive slope.
c. The best fit line is horizontal.
d. The best fit line has a negative slope.
e. The best fit line is vertical.

42. A couple traveled 2,871.46 miles cross-country and averaged 31.2 miles per gallon. How many gallons of gas did they use, rounded to three significant digits?

a. 92.0
b. 93.0
c. 92.03
d. 92.04
e. 92.0340

43. Five experimenters derive different expressions for the concentration, C, of a certain toxic chemical in well water in a neighborhood over time t. Which of the following expressions is NOT equivalent to all of the others?

a. $C = 57(\frac{2}{3})^{t+1}$
b. $C = \frac{171}{2}(\frac{2}{3})^{t}$
c. $C = 38(\frac{2}{3})^{t}$
d. $C = 38(\frac{3}{2})^{-t}$
e. $C = \frac{76}{3}(\frac{3}{2})^{1-t}$

44. What is the solution set of the equation $\frac{2}{x-3} - \frac{3}{2x-1} = 0$?

a. {1}
b. {−7}
c. {$\frac{1}{2}$,3}
d. {4}
e. empty set

45. Consider the following rectangle:

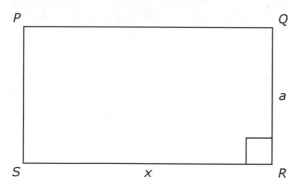

Which expression describes the sum of the lengths of the diagonals $\overline{SQ}$ and $\overline{PR}$ as a function of x?

a. $f(x) = \sqrt{a^2 + x^2} + \sqrt{a^2 - x^2}$
b. $f(x) = 2a^2 + 2x^2$
c. $f(x) = 2a + 2x$
d. $f(x) = 2\sqrt{a^2 + x^2}$
e. $f(x) = 2\sqrt{x^2 - a^2}$

46. An electronics retailer reduced the price of last year's laptops by p%. If the sale price, before tax, is x dollars, what was the original price (in dollars) of the laptop?

a. $\frac{100}{100 + p}x$
b. $\frac{100 - p}{100}$
c. $\frac{x}{p}$
d. $\frac{100x}{100 - p}$
e. $\frac{(100 - p)x}{100}$

47. What is the solution of the system
$$\begin{cases} 2x - 1 = y \\ -2y + 1 = x \end{cases}?$$
a. $x = 1, y = 0$
b. $x = \frac{3}{5}, y = \frac{1}{5}$
c. $x = \frac{2}{5}, y = -\frac{1}{5}$
d. $x = 1, y = 1$
e. any point on the line $y = -x$

48. Consider the graph of the function $f(x)$:

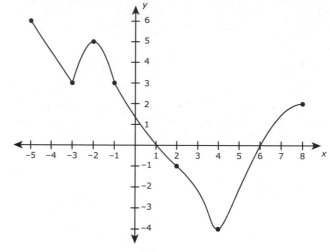

Which of the following statements is false?

a. All x values in $[-5,8]$ belong to the domain of $f(x)$.
b. The function has an inverse on its domain.
c. The function's minimum value occurs when $x = 4$.
d. The range of the function is $[-4,6]$.
e. The function is increasing on $[4,8]$.

49. Consider the graph of the function :

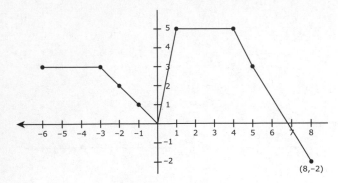

(8,−2)

Over which of the following intervals is the average value of $f(x)$ the largest?

a. (2,5)

b. (−1,1)

c. (−2,1)

d. (−6,5)

e. (4,8)

50. The formula $s = \frac{1}{2}gt^2 + v_0t + s_0$ describes the height of an object dropped from a height s_0 feet above ground with an initial vertical speed of v_0 feet per second. The constant g is the acceleration due to gravity, measured in feet per second squared. If the height of the object at $t = 3$ seconds is 140 feet and the initial height from which the object was dropped is 205 feet, which of the following expressions gives the initial speed v_0?

a. $-\frac{1}{3}(65 + 3g)$

b. $-(\frac{9}{2}g + 475)$

c. $-\frac{1}{6}(130 + 9g)$

d. $(\frac{9}{2}g + 625)$

e. $(3g + 625)$

Science

80 Minutes
50 Questions

This practice test is modeled on the content and timing of the official HiSET® Science test and, like the official test, presents a series of questions that assess your ability to use science content knowledge, apply principles of scientific inquiry, and interpret and evaluate scientific information.

Questions 1–5 are based on the following information.

Julian wanted to test whether or not light is required for photosynthesis, the chemical process that converts carbon dioxide to glucose in plants. He took a potted plant and placed it in the dark for 3 days to deplete its starch (glucose) stock. Next, he covered half of one leaf with black paper on both sides. He then placed the plant in sunlight for 3 hours. After the 3-hour incubation, he placed the leaf in boiling water for 10 minutes and then in boiling alcohol for 10 minutes to remove the chlorophyll. Finally, he rinsed the leaf under running water and added a few drops of iodine solution to the leaf. Iodine turns bluish black in the presence of starch. The part of the leaf that was covered in black paper did not change color, while the rest of the leaf turned bluish black.

1. What is the independent variable in this experiment?
   a. the type of potted plant
   b. the presence or absence of light
   c. the color change on the leaf
   d. the removal of chlorophyll from the leaf

2. Given the result obtained in this experiment, which of the following conclusions can be drawn?
   a. Light is essential for photosynthesis.
   b. Light is not essential for photosynthesis.
   c. Starch is essential for photosynthesis.
   d. Starch is not essential for photosynthesis.

3. What result would be obtained upon addition of iodine to the leaf if the plant were not incubated in the dark at the beginning of the experiment?
   a. There would be no color change throughout the entire leaf, regardless of black paper coverage.
   b. The entire leaf would turn bluish black, regardless of black paper coverage.
   c. The covered part of the leaf would turn bluish black, while the rest of the leaf would not change color.
   d. The same result would be obtained; the covered part of the leaf would not change color, while the rest of the leaf would turn bluish black.

4. The chlorophyll was removed after the incubation in light in order to
   a. remove any produced starch from the leaf.
   b. induce the color change that indicates starch presence.
   c. increase the absorption of light by the leaf cells.
   d. halt further photosynthetic production.

5. How could this experimental detection setup be used to determine the effect of dry conditions on photosynthesis in plant leaves?

   a. Place a potted plant in the dark to destarch; in the light, wrap part of a leaf tightly in water-tight plastic wrap, exposing the rest of the leaf to water at regular intervals for 3 hours; and use the iodine solution to detect photosynthetic production on the leaf.

   b. Place a potted plant in the dark to destarch; in the light, submerge the plant leaf in water for 3 hours; and use the iodine solution to detect photosynthetic production on the leaf.

   c. Place a potted plant in the dark to destarch; wrap part of a leaf tightly in black paper, exposing the rest of the leaf to light for 3 hours; and use the iodine solution to detect photosynthetic production on the leaf.

   d. Place a potted plant in the dark to destarch; in the light, place one leaf in a room at 35°C for 3 hours and place another leaf at 70°C for 3 hours; and use the iodine solution to detect photosynthetic production on the leaves.

Questions 6–10 are based on the following information.

The chemical 2-hydroxyphenazine (2-OH-PHZ) plays a key role in the biological control of plant diseases. The enzyme PhzO converts phenazine-1-carboxylic acid (PCA) to 2-OH-PHZ. The enzyme was found in past studies to be dependent on NADPH and Fe^{3+}, and the enzymatic reaction occurred optimally at 28°C.

A group of scientists decided to test the reaction without any enzyme whatsoever, and they found that the chemical reaction follows first-order kinetics. The scientists calculated the rate constant for each reaction based on the initial rate over the first hour, with higher rate constants indicating more rapid rates. The rate constants were determined by creating a best-fit straight-line graph, and the R^2 value indicates how close the best-fit line was to the points of interest; the closer an R^2 value is to 1, the better the fit is. Finally, the scientists determined the half-life for each reaction, which is the time it takes for the initial concentration to decrease to half of its value.

TEMPERATURE °C	REACTION ORDER	RATE CONSTANT (h^{-1})	R^2	HALF-LIFE (h)
28	1	0.0206	0.9979	33.64
37	1	0.0378	0.9898	18.33
55	1	0.1197	0.9993	5.79
70	1	0.1936	0.9818	3.58

Source: http://journals.plos.org/plosone/article?id=10.1371/journal.pone.0098537

6. Which of the following hypotheses reasonably predicts a possible outcome of this experiment?

 a. If pressure forces molecules to interact more regularly, then increasing pressure will increase the reaction rate.

 b. If temperature increases the frequency of interactions among molecules, then increasing temperature will increase the reaction rate.

 c. If pressure forces molecules to interact more regularly, then increasing pressure will decrease the reaction rate.

 d. If temperature increases the frequency of interactions among molecules, then increasing temperature will decrease the reaction rate.

7. Based on the data collected, the best-fit line that deviated the most from the data points of interest occurred at which temperature?

 a. 28°C

 b. 37°C

 c. 55°C

 d. 70°C

8. Which conclusion can be drawn, based on the data, about the relationship between reaction rate and half-life?

 a. There is no relationship between reaction rate and half-life.

 b. As reaction rate increases, half-life increases.

 c. As reaction rate increases, half-life decreases.

 d. As reaction rate increases, half-life remains constant.

9. How does the evidence gathered in this experiment relate to the following statement?

 Increasing the temperature speeds up the rate at which PCA is converted to 2-OH-PHZ when no enzyme is present.

 a. The evidence disproves the statement.

 b. The evidence proves the statement to be true.

 c. The evidence conflicts with the statement but does not disprove it.

 d. The evidence supports the statement but does not prove it to be true.

10. A student wants to test the reaction rate in the presence of PhzO at a wide range of temperatures, using the same general setup as the original experiment. Which of the following limitations would the student encounter during this experiment?

 a. PhzO might lose its structural and functional integrity at high temperatures.

 b. The dependent variable has changed in this experiment compared to the original one.

 c. The R^2 value tends to get worse at lower temperatures, decreasing reliability in this temperature range.

 d. Based on the half-life times, it could take days to collect the initial rate data.

Questions 11–15 are based on the following information.

A group of scientists wanted to test whether predators are attracted to the olfactory (smell) signals of prey. Since mice communicate through olfaction and are a common prey source in the field and forest ecosystems, the scientists collected a scent from a group of two adult male mice and a scent from a group of six adult male mice; the latter scent was stronger because it was derived from a greater number of mice. The scientists applied the scents to two distinct locations and recorded the number of free-roaming predators who visited each location over the course of six days. The scientists also tracked the number of free-roaming predators who visited an unscented control location over the same time period. Their results are shown in the following figure:

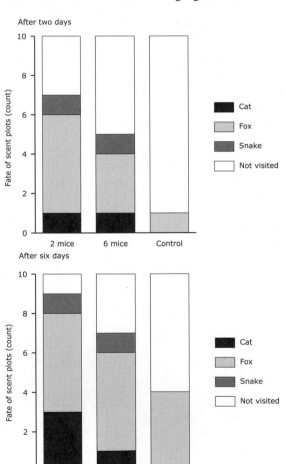

Source: http://journals.plos.org/plosone/article?id=10.1371/journal.pone.0013114

11. Which of the following pieces of evidence is NOT provided by the data collected in this experiment?
   a. the total number of predators attracted to each location
   b. the diversity of predators attracted to each location
   c. the average number of predators who visited the plots prior to scent addition
   d. the proportion of predators who visited locations with stronger versus weaker scents

12. Based on the evidence, the predators that visited only scented locations were
   a. cats and foxes.
   b. foxes and snakes.
   c. snakes and cats.
   d. cats, foxes, and snakes.

13. The purpose of the control location in the experiment is to
   a. compare the predators attracted to scents of different prey types.
   b. sample the kinds of predators typically attracted to areas with no prey scent for comparison with the scented locations.
   c. confirm that the prey scent will last for the duration of the six days over which this experiment was run.
   d. demonstrate the full diversity of predators in the region by attracting them to the control location.

14. How does the evidence gathered in this experiment relate to the following statement?

Stronger prey scents increase the total number of predators attracted to a given location relative to weaker prey scents.

  a. The evidence disproves the statement.
  b. The evidence proves the statement to be true.
  c. The evidence conflicts with the statement but does not disprove it.
  d. The evidence supports the statement but does not prove it to be true.

15. Based on the evidence, the total number of visiting predators was
  a. highest during the first two days for the scented locations and highest during the latter four days for the unscented locations.
  b. highest during the latter four days for the scented locations and highest during the first two days for the unscented locations.
  c. highest during the first two days for both the scented and unscented locations.
  d. highest during the latter four days for both the scented and unscented locations.

Questions 16–20 are based on the following information.

After reading about the nervous system, Jenna decided to test the reflex times of her fellow students after a sleepless night and after a full night of sleep. Jenna chose four subjects who had slept at least nine hours the previous night to test reflex times in the morning. To test reflex times, she had each of her subjects hold out his or her dominant hand with the palm facing sideways. Jenna then held a ruler with the 0-inch mark level with the subject's hand and the 12-inch mark at the top and, without warning, dropped the ruler. Each subject would then react as quickly as possible to catch the ruler. Jenna marked the position on the ruler at which the subject caught it.

Jenna then asked the four test subjects to pull all-nighters, with none of the four sleeping at all. The next day, at the same time as her previous test, she repeated the test to see how, if at all, their reflex times had changed. Jenna's data are shown in the table.

SUBJECT #	POSITION CAUGHT AFTER 9+ HOURS OF SLEEP (INCH)	POSITION CAUGHT AFTER 0 HOURS OF SLEEP (INCH)
1	1.5	3.5
2	2.2	5.0
3	1.9	3.2
4	2.0	2.1

16. Which of the following choices provides the scientific question Jenna investigated in this study?
  a. How does reflex time differ between male and female students?
  b. How does sleep location affect students' reflex times?
  c. What is the effect of students' reflex times on hours slept?
  d. What is the effect of hours slept on students' reflex times?

17. Which subject was least affected by the situational change between the trials?
  a. Subject #1
  b. Subject #2
  c. Subject #3
  d. Subject #4

18. What general conclusion can be drawn based on the collected evidence?
  a. One's reflexes are slower on less sleep.
  b. One's reflexes are quicker on less sleep.
  c. Slower reflexes increase one's ability to sleep through the night.
  d. Quicker reflexes increase one's ability to sleep through the night.

19. Which of the following changes would improve the reliability of the experiment?
   a. Use only male test subjects.
   b. Perform additional trials per test subject.
   c. Use a yardstick and measure in feet.
   d. Use fewer test subjects.

20. A constant among all experimental trials is
   a. reflex time.
   b. the ruler's starting point relative to the hand.
   c. the identity of the test subject.
   d. the number of hours slept.

Questions 21–25 are based on the following information.

A group of students wanted to test which color absorbs the most heat. The students decided to test white, yellow, blue, and black. The students obtained white, yellow, blue, and black construction paper. For each type of paper, the students folded it around a mercury thermometer, completely covering the end that detects temperature. Then the students placed the setups outside in the sunlight and recorded the temperature of each paper color every 20 minutes for one hour. Their results are shown in the graph.

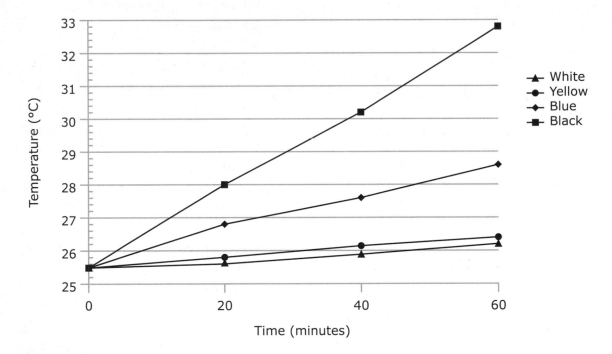

21. Based on the scientific question and experimental design, the students are detecting heat absorption by measuring the
   a. time spent in sunlight.
   b. paper color.
   c. initial temperature.
   d. change in temperature over time.

22. Over which time period did the yellow paper absorb the most heat?
   a. 0–20 minutes
   b. 20–40 minutes
   c. 40–60 minutes
   d. The same amount of heat was absorbed during each time period.

23. Which of the following statements draws the most support from the evidence in this experiment?

    a. Lighter colors tend to absorb more heat over time than darker colors when placed in sunlight.

    b. Darker colors tend to absorb more heat over time than lighter colors when placed in sunlight.

    c. Light and dark colors tend not to absorb any heat when placed in sunlight.

    d. Light and dark colors absorb significant and comparable amounts of heat when placed in sunlight.

24. If you were making a winter coat and wanted to maximize heat absorption, the fabric color you should use, based on the evidence collected here, is

    a. white.

    b. yellow.

    c. blue.

    d. black.

25. If the students were to repeat the experiment, variations in which of the following conditions during data collection would be least likely to affect the appearance of the graph?

    a. the temperature outside

    b. the time of day

    c. the barometric pressure

    d. the paper colors used

Questions 26–30 are based on the following information.

A petroleum reservoir is an oil pool contained in porous rock formations. Rocks that contain such resources are called reservoir rocks. Learning about the reservoir capacity of particular rock types could provide insights into where one might find naturally occurring crude oil or natural gas reservoirs. A group of students decided to do a simple test to get an idea of the reservoir capacity of several different kinds of rocks, opting to test mudstone, sandstone, limestone, and slate. The students obtained two samples of each kind of rock, all of the same approximate shape, size, and mass. The students separated each rock onto its own plate and used a Pasteur pipette to administer six drops of mineral oil to each rock. The students used a stopwatch to measure the time, in minutes, that it took for all of the mineral oil to be soaked up into each rock sample. Their results are shown in the table.

ROCK TYPE	TIME NEEDED TO SOAK UP OIL (min.)		
	TRIAL 1	TRIAL 2	AVERAGE
Mudstone	16.76	16.80	16.78
Sandstone	2.17	2.25	2.21
Limestone	4.40	4.20	4.30
Slate	17.23	16.11	16.67

26. The most precise data were obtained for

    a. mudstone.

    b. sandstone.

    c. limestone.

    d. slate.

27. Sedimentary rocks tend to be very porous, like a sponge, because they are formed from compacted sand and sediments. The two tested rock types that most strongly exhibit this specific feature of sedimentary rocks, based on the data, are

    a. mudstone and sandstone.

    b. sandstone and limestone.

    c. limestone and slate.

    d. slate and mudstone.

28. How does the evidence gathered in this experiment relate to the following statement?

Limestone and sandstone would make for better reservoir rocks than mudstone and slate.

   a. The evidence disproves the statement.
   b. The evidence proves the statement to be true.
   c. The evidence conflicts with the statement but does not disprove it.
   d. The evidence supports the statement but does not prove it to be true.

29. A constant in all trials of this experiment was
   a. the number of drops of oil applied to the rock.
   b. the type of rock.
   c. the rock density.
   d. the time it took for the rock to soak up the oil.

30. The longest soaking time was observed for slate, yet the longest average soaking time was observed for mudstone. Which of the following options would help to confirm which of the two rock types has the longer soaking time?
   a. Repeat the experiment using natural gas rather than oil.
   b. Perform additional trials of the same experiment.
   c. Test two additional rock types, like marble and shale.
   d. Convert all times from minutes to seconds.

Questions 31–35 are based on the following information.

Sodium (Na) reacts with chlorine gas (Cl_2) to produce solid sodium chloride (NaCl). The balanced chemical equation for this process is the following:

$$2Na(s) + Cl_2(g) \rightarrow 2NaCl(s)$$

A group of scientists wanted to look into the stoichiometry, a method that quantifies the relationship between reactants and products, for this particular reaction. The group constructed a sealed reaction chamber and filled it with an excess of chlorine gas. Then the scientists added a carefully measured mass of solid sodium to the reaction chamber and allowed the reaction to run to completion. The reactions were controlled to ensure that Na is the limiting reactant and is completely used up in the reaction. Upon completion of the reaction, the mass of solid sodium chloride produced in the reaction was measured. Two trials were performed per reaction. The results of their work are shown in the table.

MASS OF INPUT Na(g)	MASS OF NaCl PRODUCED (g)		
	TRIAL 1	TRIAL 2	AVERAGE
1.00	5.07	5.09	5.08
2.00	10.25	10.09	10.17
4.00	20.22	20.48	20.35

31. The independent variable in this experiment is
   a. the mass of NaCl produced during the reaction.
   b. the mass of Na used in the reaction.
   c. the mass of Cl_2 added to the chamber for the reaction.
   d. the sealed reaction chamber.

32. The scientists decide to graph the average measured product masses as a function of the input reactant masses. Which of the following graphs most closely reflects this relationship?

a.

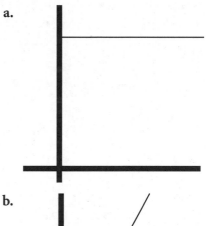

b.

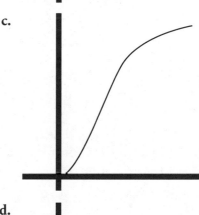

c.

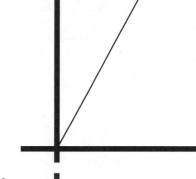

d.

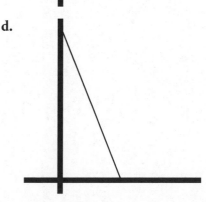

33. When the scientists perform a theoretical stoichiometry calculation, they find that their experimentally determined value for NaCl mass produced from a given Na mass is nearly identical to the theoretical calculation. This means that the data from this particular set of trials are

a. precise.

b. not precise.

c. accurate.

d. inaccurate.

34. If 1.50 g Na are reacted with excess Cl_2, how much NaCl should be produced, based on the collected data?

a. less than 5.08 g

b. between 5.08 g and 10.17 g

c. between 10.17 g and 20.35 g

d. more than 20.35 g

35. To conversely test the effect of Cl_2 mass on NaCl production, the scientists could measure NaCl production after setting up a reaction chamber with initial conditions in which

a. Na is in excess relative to Cl_2.

b. Na is in excess relative to NaCl.

c. Cl_2 is in excess relative to Na.

d. Cl_2 is in excess relative to NaCl.

Questions 36–40 are based on the following information.

A team of scientists wanted to investigate the effects of water levels on species richness and seed density in wetlands. Using a Tibetan plateau as a wetland source, the scientists examined a typical wetland (T), a drying wetland (D), and a saline-alkaline wetland (S). The scientists tracked species richness and seed density in 0 to 5 cm and 5 to 10 cm soil depths per plot, in the presence of 0 cm, 5 cm, and 10 cm water levels. Their results are shown in the following charts.

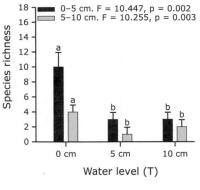

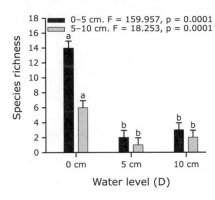

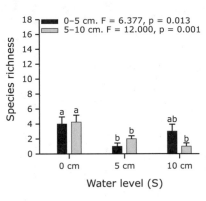

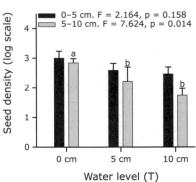

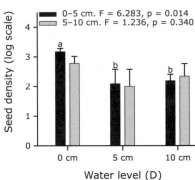

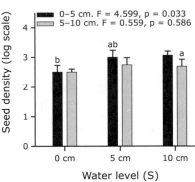

Source: http://journals.plos.org/plosone/article?id=10.1371/journal.pone.0101458

36. Throughout this study, how many different dependent variables are used?

   a. 1

   b. 2

   c. 3

   d. 4

37. Which of the following is a constant in all measured trials during the study?

   a. geographical region

   b. water level

   c. soil depth

   d. water alkalinity

38. Which of the following conclusions can be drawn about species richness in a typical wetland?

a. As water level increases, species richness decreases.

b. As water level increases, species richness increases.

c. As soil depth increases, species richness decreases.

d. As soil depth increases, species richness increases.

39. The largest observed seed density in any of the wetlands occurs in the

a. drying wetland at a 0 cm water depth.

b. drying wetland at a 5 cm water depth.

c. typical wetland at a 0 cm water depth.

d. typical wetland at a 10 cm water depth.

40. Larger error bars on the graph represent

a. increased accuracy.

b. decreased accuracy.

c. increased precision.

d. decreased precision.

Questions 41–45 are based on the following information.

To gain insight into how long a cell spends in each phase of the cell cycle, Elizabeth decided to use the squashing method to make a microscope slide using a small piece of an onion root tip. HCl and Carnoy's fixative were used to make the cells dye susceptible, and blue toluidine dye was used to track the chromosomes in the cells, allowing for distinction between the phases. After preparing a slide, Elizabeth examined the cells under a compound microscope and counted the number of cells in each phase out of a random pool of 50 cells that appeared in focus in the microscope's field of view. She then repeated this process three more times. Elizabeth's cell counts are displayed in the data table.

	INTERPHASE	PROPHASE	METAPHASE	ANAPHASE	TELOPHASE
Slide 1	42	4	1	2	1
Slide 2	40	3	2	3	2
Slide 3	40	4	4	2	0
Slide 4	39	5	3	2	1

41. What is the average number of cells, out of 50, that Elizabeth found in telophase in her four microscope slides?

a. 0

b. 1

c. 2

d. 3

42. Why were chemicals needed to make these particular cells, as opposed to animal or bacterial cells, dye susceptible?

a. Plant cells store their chromosomes in vacuoles that are difficult to access.

b. Plant cells have nuclear envelopes that tend to be difficult to penetrate.

c. Plant cells are surrounded by rigid cell walls that are difficult to cross.

d. Plant cells have thick cytosol that must be broken down for the dye to access the chromosomes.

43. What is the dependent variable in this experiment?

    a. the phases of mitosis

    b. the number of cells counted per phase

    c. the number of seconds the cells spent in each phase

    d. the total number of cells studied per trial

44. Based on the data collected, cells appear to spend the greatest amount of time in

    a. interphase.

    b. prophase.

    c. anaphase.

    d. telophase.

45. To distinguish between interphase and prophase, Elizabeth noted that the nucleus appeared darker in color from the dye in prophase relative to interphase. This difference could be attributed to

    a. chromosome disintegration.

    b. chromosome duplication.

    c. vesicle fusion.

    d. nuclear envelope dissolution.

Questions 46–50 are based on the following information.

A group of scientists wanted to study the effect of acute exercise on prostate cancer cell growth. The scientists focused on the growth of the prostate cancer cell line LNCaP, which has been well characterized. A known number of LNCaP cells were incubated in media supplemented with 10% fetal bovine serum (FBS) growth supplement (normal conditions), media supplemented with a pool of human serum from 10 resting male individuals ("rest"), or media supplemented with a pool of human serum from the same 10 individuals after an hour of bicycling at increasing intensity ("exercise"). All tests were done at room temperature. The scientists detected "cell proliferation" by marking and counting the number of cells after each incubation. Their results are shown in Figure 1.

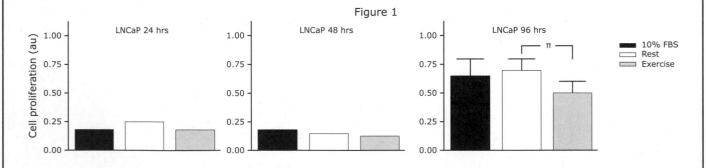

Figure 1

The scientists then repeated the test for 48 hours using the rest and exercise sera for 10 different individuals, marked on the *x*-axis by a random identifying number (1, 13, 25, etc.). The results are shown in Figure 2.

Figure 2

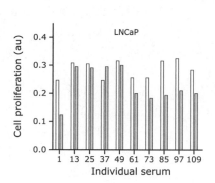
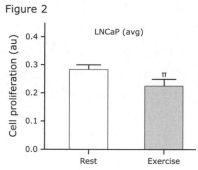

46. Which of the following would serve as a valid control for this set of experiments?
  a. Test a wider range of incubation times for all the tests.
  b. Repeat all experiments at a warmer temperature to reflect body temperature.
  c. Repeat all experiments using a non-cancerous cell line.
  d. Repeat all experiments using only female exercise serum donors.

47. The individual test subject whose exercise serum did not follow the trend observed in the others was
  a. individual 1.
  b. individual 13.
  c. individual 37.
  d. individual 73.

48. Based on the data, the most significant LNCaP cell proliferation in any media type occurred
  a. during the first 24 hours.
  b. between 24 and 48 hours.
  c. between 48 and 96 hours.
  d. after 96 hours.

49. How does the evidence gathered in this experiment relate to the following statement?

Physical activity reduces the proliferation of prostate cancer cells.

  a. The evidence disproves the statement.
  b. The evidence proves the statement to be true.
  c. The evidence conflicts with the statement but does not disprove it.
  d. The evidence supports the statement but does not prove it to be true.

50. The scientists want to see if longer durations of exercise more significantly affect prostate cancer cell growth. As such, the part of the experiment they would need to change to answer this scientific question is the
  a. test subject preparation.
  b. cell/serum incubation time lengths.
  c. cancer cell line used.
  d. type of exercise performed by the test subjects.

Social Studies

70 Minutes
50 Questions

This practice test is modeled on the content and timing of the official HiSET® Social Studies test and, like the official test, presents a series of questions that assess your ability to use social studies content knowledge and analyze and evaluate various kinds of social studies information.

Questions 1–5 are based on the following information.

When the American Civil War ended in 1865, tens of thousands of newly freed African Americans had left their former plantation homes and become refugees. To address this growing crisis, Congress established the Bureau of Refugees, Freedmen, and Abandoned Lands, better known as the Freedmen's Bureau. The bureau aided African Americans in their transition from slavery to freedom and helped them make new lives for themselves. The Bureau provided food, clothing, and medical care. From 1865 to 1872, more than 21 million food rations were distributed. Perhaps the most enduring aspect of the Freedmen's Bureau was its contribution to education. The bureau helped establish more 1,000 schools, greatly increasing literacy among African Americans.

Attempts to provide land ownership to African Americans proved difficult. Many Northerners proposed the idea of seizing Confederate land and distributing it to the freed African Americans. President Andrew Johnson and many in Congress rejected the idea because it violated individual property rights. Congress eventually rejected the idea altogether. Consequently, the Freedmen's Bureau was forced to manage sharecropping arrangements. Sharecroppers were tenant farmers, living and working on former plantations. Instead of paying their rent in cash, sharecroppers paid a share of their crops, often an exceedingly large portion. This often led to oppressive living conditions for African American sharecroppers.

1. Which of the following would best summarize the main goal of the Freedmen's Bureau?
   a. a method to punish the former Confederate states
   b. provide economic stimulus to the devastated Southern states
   c. help freed African Americans make new lives for themselves
   d. return African Americans to the Southern states

2. Which of the following best justifies the viewpoints of many Americans who opposed the seizing of Confederate lands?
   a. religious beliefs
   b. a strict interpretation of Constitutional rights
   c. the concept of "states' rights"
   d. the principle of separation of powers

3. Consider this statement from the passage.

   Perhaps the most enduring aspect of the Freedmen's Bureau was its contribution to education.

   This statement is best classified as

   a. an opinion.
   b. an observation.
   c. a scientific conclusion.
   d. an established fact.

4. Which of the following titles would best represent the main idea of this passage?

a. Policy Successes of the Freedmen's Bureau

b. The Emergence of Sharecropping in Reconstruction America

c. Political Conflict within the Freedmen's Bureau

d. The Role of the Freemen's Bureau in Post–Civil War America

5. According to the passage, which of the following best explains the emergence of the sharecropping system?

a. Adequate amounts of fertile land were not available.

b. Effective policies to provide African Americans with land could not be established.

c. The Freedmen's Bureau worked to move African Americans back to their former homes in the South.

d. Congress was strongly opposed to land ownership for African Americans.

Questions 6–9 are based on the following information.

In 1777, the Continental Congress created the Articles of Confederation. These articles were the first constitution of the United States of America. The Articles of Confederation established a system for the 13 states to cooperate and band together for a common purpose—winning the Revolutionary War. The Articles set up a one-house legislature in which each state had one vote. This governing body was given control over the Continental Army and the authority to conduct foreign policy with other nations. However, state representatives were keenly aware of the unfair treatment they experienced as a colony of the British government. Consequently, the states placed strict limitations on the Confederation Congress. The Confederation Congress could not enforce the laws it passed, and it did not have the power to tax.

In effect, the Congress could not require the states to do anything.

Following victory in the Revolutionary War, the United States and the state governments were in deep debt. Individual states imposed heavy taxes on their citizens, which created widespread resentment and in some cases armed rebellions. The Confederation Congress could not tax citizens and had no method to prevent citizens from rebelling. In 1786, George Washington wrote:

"I do not conceive we can exist long as a nation, without having lodged somewhere a power which will pervade the whole Union."
—George Washington, letter to John Jay, August 1786

6. According to information in the passage, which of the following best expresses why the states restricted the power of the Confederation Congress?

a. State governments thought citizens had the right to actively rebel against central governments.

b. The states were fearful of an unaccountable and tyrannical central government, such as the British government.

c. Each state wished to have complete control over wartime powers.

d. State representatives wished to abandon all forms of taxation.

7. Which of the following scenarios would have most likely resulted in a continuation of the Articles of Confederation?

a. the breakup of the United States into separately ruled states

b. the return of British rule in America

c. the appointment of an American monarchy

d. the eventual adoption of a bicameral, or two-house, legislature

8. Based on information in the passage, which of the following was the most pressing issue facing the United States at that time?
   a. an overbearing Congress
   b. debt
   c. a lack of a coherent foreign policy
   d. armed rebellions

9. The quote from George Washington expresses his opinion that
   a. a strong dictatorial government or leader was necessary to preserve the country.
   b. a large and violent citizen uprising was imminent.
   c. the Articles of Confederation had granted too much power to Congress.
   d. a central government with authorities over all states was needed to hold the country together.

Questions 10–13 are based on the following information.

The U.S. Constitution serves as the framework of national, or federal, government. The framers created a strong federal government, but they did not deprive states of all authority. In ratifying the Constitution, the states granted powers to the federal government but retained others. This sharing of powers and responsibilities is called federalism. States have some authority to handle their specific needs but also must work with the federal government and the other states in matters of national importance.

Article VI of the Constitution explicitly states that the Constitution is the "supreme Law of the Land." The Constitution and the laws created by Congress take priority over state and local laws. This is called the "supremacy clause." However, the Tenth Amendment, which was added to the Constitution as part of the Bill of Rights, protects the states and

citizens from a too-powerful federal government. This amendment establishes that powers not given to the federal government and not denied to the states in the Constitution belong to the states or to the people.

10. Which of the following would be considered a "check," or limit, on the federal government's power?
    a. the "supremacy clause"
    b. the amendment process
    c. the Tenth Amendment
    d. the limiting of state government powers

11. Which of the following statements is an opinion about federalism?
    a. Federalism is the most effective system of governance.
    b. Federalism is the concept through which power is shared between national and state governments.
    c. Federalism requires state governments to be just as powerful as the federal government.
    d. Federalism was abandoned in the United States with the ratification of the Bill of Rights.

12. Which of the following best explains the insertion of the supremacy clause in Article VI of the Constitution?
    a. to prevent the states and citizens from challenging federal laws
    b. to prevent conflicts between federal, state, and local laws
    c. to prevent states from becoming too powerful
    d. to prevent states from writing laws similar to federal laws

13. Based on information in the passage, which of the following conclusions is most plausible concerning the Tenth Amendment?
   a. Proponents of a strong federal government wanted the Tenth Amendment included in the Bill of Rights.
   b. The Tenth Amendment was included to negate the powers granted to Congress in Article VI.
   c. The Framers added the Tenth Amendment to limit the voices of common citizens.
   d. The Framers added the Tenth Amendment to appease those who supported states' rights and individual liberties.

Questions 14–17 are based on the following information.

As part of a report about technology in the United States at the end of the twentieth century, a journalist included the following timeline.

1982	First use of the emoticons :-) and :-(in a computer message
1983	Music CDs go on sale; the first American cell phone system goes into operation
1984	Apple releases the first Macintosh computer
1985	Nintendo Entertainment System enters U.S. market
1989	Tim Berners-Lee invents the World Wide Web
1991	The World Wide Web is opened to public access
1995	Release of the first DVDs

14. Which of the following titles would best represent the theme of this timeline?
   a. U.S. Government Support of High-Tech Industries in the 1980s and 1990s
   b. Innovations in Communications Technologies in the 1980s and 1990s
   c. Development of Digital Music in the 1980s and 1990s
   d. Key Computer Innovations in the 1980s and 1990s

15. Based on information in the timeline, which of the following statements is most plausible?
   a. American cell phone companies did not contribute any technological innovations.
   b. Apple computers led the development of computer-based e-mail systems and the use of emoticons.
   c. The World Wide Web borrowed technology from the Nintendo game consoles.
   d. Entertainment industries played a role in communications innovations in the 1980s and 1990s.

16. Which of the following factors was probably the primary reason for the rapid growth of the World Wide Web?
   a. the rise of multinational corporations
   b. government funding for start-up companies
   c. the spread of personal computers
   d. the growth of computer science schools and classes

17. Using the information in the timeline, which time period produced the most communication innovations?
   a. 1982–1985
   b. 1984–1989
   c. 1985–1991
   d. 1989–1995

Questions 18–21 are based on the following information.

Occupations with the Most Job Growth, 2014 and Projected 2024
(Numbers in Thousands)

OCCUPATION	EMPLOYMENT			MEDIAN ANNUAL WAGE, 2014
	2014	2024	% CHANGE	
Personal care aides	1,768.4	2,226.5	25.9	$35,540
Registered nurses	2,751	3,190.3	16	$66,640
Home health aides	913.5	1,261.9	38.1	$21,380
Construction laborers	1,159.1	1,306.5	12.7	$31,090
Office clerks—general	3,062.5	3,158.2	3.1	$28,670
Computer systems analysts	567.8	686.3	20.9	$82,710

Data is from the Occupational Employment Statistics program, U.S. Department of Labor, U.S. Bureau of Labor Statistics. Source: Employment Projections program, U.S. Bureau of Labor Statistics

18. Using information from the chart, which occupation does the government project to increase the greatest by 2024?
a. construction laborers
b. home health aides
c. office clerks
d. computer systems analysts

19. Of the occupations detailed on the chart, which will have the fewest workers in 2024?
a. registered nurses
b. personal care aides
c. computer systems analysts
d. construction laborers

20. Which of the following CANNOT be verified by information on the graph?
a. None of the occupations on the chart will show a decline from 2014 and 2024.
b. By 2024, the average wage for home health aides will be the lowest.
c. The increase in the number of construction laborers by 2024 will be less than 15%.
d. Registered nurses earned triple the annual wage of home health aides in 2014.

21. A job seeker shows the chart to an employment counselor and asks for the best advice for pursuing a new occupation. The job seeker's criteria are strong job hiring potential and a high annual salary. Which of the following occupations would be the counselor's best recommendation?
a. computer systems analyst
b. personal care aide
c. construction laborer
d. registered nurse

Questions 22–25 are based on the following information.

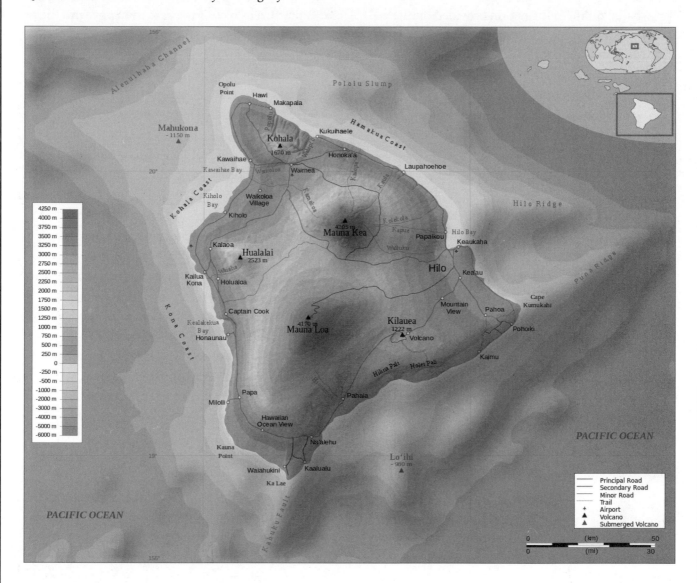

22. Using information from the map, the distance from Opolu Point in the north to Ka Lae in the south is approximately

a. 60 miles.

b. 120 miles.

c. 190 miles.

d. 90 miles.

23. Which of the following most accurately describes the interior of the island of Hawaii?

a. flat and gently rolling plains

b. valleys that are below sea level

c. hilly and dominated by two large mountains

d. highly developed with urban centers

24. Which of the following is a valid conclusion based on the information provided on the map?
   a. Key industrial centers are located on the southern coast.
   b. Kawaihae Bay is the center of Hawaii's tourism industry.
   c. Hawaii is major transportation center for the Hawaiian Islands.
   d. Hawaii is not densely populated.

25. Using all the information presented in the map, which of the following is a valid conclusion?
   a. This island is located in the middle of the North Pacific Ocean, between Asia and North America.
   b. This island is the smallest in its group.
   c. This island is located in the southern Indian Ocean.
   d. This island is a major shipping center for trans-Pacific trade.

Questions 26 and 27 are based on the following information.

On March 4, 1861, Abraham Lincoln delivered his first inaugural address. Just one month later, war would break out. In the speech, Lincoln stated the following:

> This country, with its institutions, belongs to the people, who inhabit it. Whenever they shall grow weary of the existing government, they can exercise their constitutional right of amending it, or their revolutionary right to dismember, or overthrow it.

26. According to President Lincoln, what options do citizens have if they are unhappy with their government?
   a. Their only option is to start a new country.
   b. They can rewrite the Constitution to give the people expanded rights.
   c. They can change the government through the democratic process or start a revolution.
   d. Citizens can reorganize government institutions to make them more agreeable.

27. Which of the following can best be described as the most important concept of American government underscored by Lincoln's words?
   a. The people, not the government, hold true power.
   b. Americans do not have an inherent right to rebel against their government.
   c. The Constitution should never be amended without government approval first.
   d. The people are only as strong as their government's institutions.

Questions 28–32 are based on the following information.

Before the 1950s, the fight for African Americans' civil rights had limited success. The Great Migration, a time when large populations of African Americans moved from the South to northern regions, helped bring them greater political power. Voting was less restrictive in the North, and politicians listened to and helped address African Americans' concerns.

The Civil Rights movement gained momentum rapidly after World War II. The federal government began to take a firmer stand for civil rights. In addition, several court victories granted greater legal and social equality for African Americans, but Southern segregationists vigorously opposed these gains.

During the 1950s, the Civil Rights movement became more powerful. Civil rights leaders protested unfair laws. They promoted sit-ins at segregated businesses that refused to serve African Americans. At the sit-ins, protesters entered businesses and refused to leave unless they were served. Many civil rights activists boycotted segregated public services like buses. They also gathered for peaceful marches. Some white Southerners resisted these efforts and used violence and fear against civil rights supporters. Civil rights leaders pushed the movement forward anyway.

28. What does the first paragraph imply about the African American participation in the political process in the South prior to the Great Migration?
   a. Southern African Americans were not interested in political participation.
   b. African American political participation in the South was limited or restricted.
   c. Southern politicians were ineffective in registering African Americans to vote.
   d. Southern states banned African Americans from voting.

29. According to the passage, which of the following was primarily responsible for the Civil Rights movement gaining strength after World War II?
   a. the defeat of powerful pro-segregation Southern politicians
   b. the success of violent protests against unfair laws
   c. growing public acceptance of African American equality
   d. actions of the federal government, including legal decisions

30. The style of protests used by civil rights leaders could be most accurately described as
   a. passive.
   b. violent walkouts.
   c. civil disobedience.
   d. collective revolution.

31. The information in the passage supports which of the following conclusions?
   a. Civil rights leaders lost public support following World War II.
   b. Only African Americans in the North benefited from advances in civil rights legislation.
   c. Opposition to civil rights for African Americans quickly disappeared in the 1950s.
   d. Civil rights leaders were determined and consistent in how to fight for civil rights.

32. Which of the following is the best definition of the word *segregate* as used in the passage?
   a. to outlaw specific people because of historical reasons
   b. to use violence as a means to influence legislation
   c. to separate or divide people along racial lines
   d. to forcibly relocate large populations of people

Questions 33–35 are based on the following information.

In some state and local level elections, voters may decide on issues and candidates. The *initiative*, for example, is a process through which citizens can propose new laws or amendments to state constitutions. The process begins by citizens or organizations gathering signatures of qualified voters to place on a petition. If enough qualified voters sign the petition, the proposed law, or proposition, is placed on the ballot at the next general election.

The *referendum* is a process through which citizens either approve or reject a state or local law. As with the initiative process, supporters of a referendum must gather a determined number of signatures of qualified voters to place on a petition. Currently, about half of the states allow citizens the right to petition to have a law referred, or sent back, to the voters for their approval at the next general election.

33. Which of the following statements best explains the difference between an initiative and a referendum?

    a. A referendum makes a decision on an existing law, and an initiative proposes a potential law.

    b. Unlike an initiative, a referendum must first be approved by the state's Supreme Court before being placed on the ballot.

    c. An initiative must always be issued by a state governor.

    d. A referendum does not require supporters to go through the petition process.

34. Which of the following illustrates the use of a ballot initiative?

    a. A presidential candidate endorses a policy for use by his or her political party's platform.

    b. A group of concerned parents gathers signatures to try to raise the minimum drinking age law in the state.

    c. A city council polls citizens about a proposal to build a new park.

    d. An environmental organization lobbies the state legislature to create a new wildlife sanctuary.

35. Which of the following assumptions can be made based on the information in the passage?

    a. Initiatives are almost always likely to succeed.

    b. Initiatives and referendums provide citizens the means to counterbalance the political power held by local and state governments.

    c. Referendums are not popular, since only about half of all states allow them.

    d. Local, state, and federal lawmakers often make mistakes that need to be corrected by the citizens.

Questions 36–38 are based on the following information.

In economics, the price of a product or service is related to supply and demand. *Supply* means the quantity of a specific product or service that is available. *Demand* describes the amount of that product or service that consumers want to purchase. Sellers need to earn money on the goods they produce. Buyers want to spend as little as possible. These factors also influence the price of goods. When there is a large supply of a product, buyers can shop around for the best price. Consequently, sellers lower their prices to sell their products. As the price goes down, demand usually increases because consumers want to spend as little as possible. Conversely, if a product or service is scarce, buyers cannot shop around. Therefore, sellers can raise their prices. Eventually, an optimum price is set when the quantity of goods available is equal to the quantity demanded. When this happens, supply and demand have reached equilibrium.

36. Using information in the passage, which of the following statements best describes what would happen to the price of pecans if a drought drastically reduced the pecan crop yet demand for pecans increased?
  a. The price would go down.
  b. The price would reach equilibrium.
  c. The price would most likely stay the same.
  d. The price would go up.

37. A technology manufacturer introduced a new smartphone in January with a price of $500. By December of that year, however, the phones had a price of $250. According to the principles of supply and demand, which of the following is likely to be true about the new smartphone?
  a. Supply for the phone was high but the demand was low.
  b. Both the supply and demand for the phone were low.
  c. Supply for the phone was low but demand was high.
  d. Both the supply and demand for the phone were high.

38. The optimum price of a product or service clears the market. This is the price at which
  a. consumers spend all of their money.
  b. every product is sold at lower than projected prices.
  c. quantity demanded equals quantity supplied.
  d. excess demand is twice the quantity of supply.

Questions 39–42 are based on the following information.

The property tax is a major source of funding for public safety, schools, roads, libraries, and other services in most American communities. Local governments use property tax revenues mostly to pay the salaries of local government employees, such as police officers, firefighters, and teachers. Some communities also use these revenues for road and school construction, park maintenance, and human services. Generally, an individual's property tax bill is determined by multiplying the local property tax rate by the assessed value of his or her property.

The cost of all these items increases from year to year because of inflation, population growth, and sometimes other factors, such as changes in state law. Concern over rising property tax bills has led a number of states to implement limits on the amount of property tax revenue that counties, municipalities, and school districts can collect. Some other states are considering property tax caps. Property tax "rate caps" place a limit on the rate of property taxes. Another kind of tax cap is an "assessment cap." Assessment caps limit the annual increase in the assessed value of an individual's property. A "total levy cap" is the most restrictive type of tax cap. This type limits the annual increase in a locality's total property tax revenue.

39. A new assessment cap was recently imposed on the town of Fairview. In addition, just before the tax cap went into effect, a large subdivision broke ground on the south side of town. The subdivision is made up of very large single-family homes. Which of the following entities would be most affected by the tax cap?
  a. the Fairview Parks Department
  b. the Fairview Police Department
  c. the Fairview Fire Department
  d. the Fairview School District

40. Which of the following statements would most likely be the opinion of Fairview's director of human resources?

a. Property tax rates should be raised to help attract more businesses and potential employees.

b. Property tax rates should not be capped so that the town can offer salaries that are competitive with the private sector to attract qualified workers.

c. Property tax rates should be capped because that will allow the town to hire more employees.

d. Property tax rates have very little effect on the hiring process in Fairview.

41. Which of the following statements might best explain why the Fairview Chamber of Commerce supported a tax cap?

a. A tax cap improves the economic competitiveness of local businesses and reduces the chances that they will relocate to other communities.

b. Tax caps could lead to cuts in municipal services and may negatively impact the school system.

c. Tax caps will force the town to protect more land by not rezoning it for development.

d. A tax cap will force struggling businesses to close, opening new opportunities for other businesses.

42. A citizen of Fairview who is a strong supporter of smaller and more limited government might argue which of the following in support of a total levy cap?

a. A tax cap could lead to increased state aid to the town to make up lost property tax revenue, leading to loss of local control over policies and programs.

b. A tax cap may disproportionately benefit wealthier residents.

c. A tax cap will force Fairview to exercise discipline over budget and tax practices and force the town to find more efficient ways to deliver services.

d. A tax cap will pressure the town to make up revenue by increasing local fees.

Questions 43 and 44 are based on the following information.

The academic field of economics did not really exist until the Scottish philosopher Adam Smith wrote *Inquiry into the Nature and Causes of the Wealth of Nations* in 1776. Smith's work is still used by economists today. Smith argued that individuals left on their own would work for their own self-interest. In doing so, they would be guided as if by an "invisible hand" to use resources efficiently. Consumers, all acting in their own self-interest, would naturally point the national economy in a direction that would benefit the greatest number of people. From the writings of Smith and others came the idea of laissez-faire economics. *Laissez-faire* is a French term that means "to let alone." According to Smith and others who hold similar ideas, governments should not interfere in the marketplace. The government's role is confined to those actions necessary to ensure free competition.

43. According to Adam Smith, what are the results of individuals working for their own self-interest?
   a. Governments will eventually be needed to support the economy.
   b. Resources will soon be depleted.
   c. Only a few individuals will benefit.
   d. Individuals will use resources efficiently.

44. Which of the following policies is an example of laissez-faire?
   a. large government taxes on exports
   b. removal of all tariffs on imports and exports
   c. government regulations placed on some businesses but not others
   d. a minimum wage law

Questions 45–47 are based on the following information.

This editorial cartoon was created in 1909 by E.W. Gustin. The image shows a housewife preparing to vote on Election Day. The cartoon actually predates the ratification of the Nineteenth Amendment, which guaranteed the women the right to vote, by 11 years.

45. Which of the following best describes what the artist thinks will happen once women are allowed to vote?
  a. Women will leave their families.
  b. The traditional family structure will break down.
  c. Women will still be treated unequally.
  d. Men's ability to find work outside the home will be restricted.

46. Based on the content of the cartoon, which best captures the artist's opinion of guaranteeing women the right to vote?
  a. The artist supports giving women the right to vote.
  b. The artist opposes giving women the right to vote.
  c. The artist is indifferent to the idea of women voting.
  d. There is not enough information in the cartoon to draw a conclusion.

47. Which of the following is the most valid conclusion one can draw based on the cartoon?
  a. Women gaining the right to vote will lead to greater equality.
  b. Women will be denied the right to vote because American men will resist the Nineteenth Amendment.
  c. The movement to gain women's voting rights was disorganized and had very little power.
  d. Divorce rates in the United States will rise dramatically following women gaining the right to vote.

Questions 48–50 are based on the following information.

Although the Constitution makes no mention of political parties, the first parties formed just a few years after the founding of the country. The parties were created because Americans have different ideas and opinions about how to govern the nation. People join political parties because they share similar values and ideas about the leadership of the government. Today, the United States has several political parties, with two—the Democratic and the Republican parties—dominating American politics.

Both political parties and members of political parties can be classified based on their ideas about government. The Democratic Party tends to be liberal. Liberals, who are often referred to as being on the left of the political spectrum, generally advocate political change and social progress. To accomplish this, they tend to favor a robust federal government that is more directly involved in regulating the economy and in providing services for the citizens. Conservatives, who have generally moved to the Republican Party, are said to be on the right of the political spectrum. Republicans tend to prefer slow or no political and social changes in the country. Republicans believe that less government regulation of the economy is the best way to promote the growth of production. Individuals who fall somewhere in between liberal and conservative are often called moderates.

48. Which of the following statements would NOT be a reason for joining a political party?
  a. to help promote and elect a specific political candidate
  b. to learn about views and concepts that are different from their own political views
  c. to associate with other Americans who share similar political ideas about government
  d. to vote in a closed primary election

49. Which of the following best reflects the views of a person who is on the right of the political spectrum?

   a. tax breaks for small businesses that work with poor urban and rural families

   b. support for significant changes to the U.S. Constitution

   c. endorsement of a political candidate who promotes evolving American values

   d. creation of 50 new government state agencies to help poor American families

50. Which of the following activities would be the best way to determine the accuracy of the descriptions of the Democratic and Republican parties in the passage?

   a. Investigate and learn what the parties say about each other.

   b. Review historical documents that explain why each party was first established.

   c. Review the statements and viewpoints of one Republican and one Democratic representative.

   d. Read the official platforms of each party.

Practice Test 1
Answers and Explanations

Language Arts—Reading

To calculate your HiSET® score on the Language Arts—Reading section, first take a look at the correct answer for each of the 40 questions of the exam. Count up your **correct answers** only, and give yourself 1 point for each. Then, add up all of your points. This is your **raw score**.

Find your raw score and your **scaled score** in the following table. Remember, for each test section, a passing score is 8. (For the essay, a passing score is 2.)

You need a scaled score of 45 to pass the complete HiSET® exam.

LANGUAGE ARTS—READING SCORING			
RAW	SCALED	RAW	SCALED
0	1	21	12
1	2	22	12
2	3	23	13
3	4	24	13
4	5	25	13
5	6	26	14
6	7	27	14
7	7	28	14
8	8	29	15
9	8	30	15
10	9	31	15
11	9	32	15
12	9	33	16
13	10	34	17
14	10	35	17
15	10	36	18
16	11	37	18
17	11	38	19
18	11	39	20
19	11	40	20
20	12		

1. **The correct answer is choice c.** At this point in the story, the reader can only predict that Max Alben will use the time machine to travel back through time, but there is no indication of where, exactly, he will travel. Choice **a** is incorrect because the passage does not indicate what time period Max Alben will travel to. Choice **b** is incorrect because paragraph 4 states that it will be a "backward journey," not a forward one into the future. Choice **d** is incorrect because if Max travels back in time, it is possible he will meet his great-grandfather, but since the period to which he will travel is unknown, that is not the best prediction to make.

2. **The correct answer is choice a.** The word "authorities" makes the most sense if used in place of "powers" in paragraph 7, since the word is used in reference to people. Choice **b** is incorrect because "strengths" is a synonym for "powers," but does not refer to people and does not make as much sense as "authorities" does in this context. Choice **c** is incorrect because "abilities" is a synonym for "powers," but does not refer to people and does not make as much sense as "authorities" does in this context. Choice **d** is incorrect because "resources" is a synonym for "powers," but does not refer to people and does not make as much sense as "authorities" does in this context.

3. **The correct answer is choice c.** The possibility that Max Abden's journey through time could kill him creates a tone of tension since he cannot relax in the knowledge that he will be safe. Choice **a** is incorrect because Max's death is not a sure thing; if it were, his journey would be sad. Choice **b** is incorrect because the tone would be horrifying only if Max was sure to die during his journey. Choice **d** is incorrect because there is nothing humorous about the possibility that Max could die during his journey.

4. **The correct answer is choice b.** Max Abden decides to follow in his great-grandfather's footsteps to become a time traveler, which means he likely thinks of his great-grandfather as a role model to follow. Choice **a** is incorrect because although Max seems to have affection for his great-grandfather, that alone is not evidence that his great-grandfather was a gentle person. Choice **c** is incorrect because the author reveals that it was Max's great-grandfather's special physical traits, not any exceptional level of intelligence, that made him an ideal time traveler. Choice **d** is incorrect because nothing in the passage indicates that Max thinks his great-grandfather was a foolish man.

5. **The correct answer is choice a.** Earlier in the passage, the narrator reveals that Max's great-grandfather "possessed a great deal of immunity to extra-temporal blackout," but it is not perfectly clear what that means until that idea is refined in this line in paragraph 8. Choice **b** is incorrect because this line does not refine any information from paragraph 6, which deals with Max's great-grandfather's special abilities, not the black marketeers. Choice **c** is incorrect because this line does not refine any information from paragraph 6, which deals with Max's great-grandfather's special abilities, not the black marketeers. Choice **d** is incorrect because this line does not refine any information from paragraph 6, which deals with Max's great-grandfather's special abilities, not Abd Sadha.

6. **The correct answer is choice d.** Based on the passage, you can conclude that Abd Sadha is not a scientist, and he may not fully understand why the scientists have added an extra precaution to Max's time travel journey. Choice **a** is incorrect because Abd Sadha says the scientists suggested the precaution, which makes it clear that he did not forget that he did not suggest the precaution. Choice **b** is incorrect because there is no evidence that Abd Sadha does not have faith in the scientists. Choice **c** is incorrect because there is no evidence that the precaution is intended to protect Max Abden since Abd Sadha has not explained what that precaution is yet.

7. **The correct answer is choice d.** The main purpose of the Bill of Rights is to establish the specific rights and freedoms Americans are due. Choice **a** is incorrect because the author of the Bill of Rights does not compare American rights to those of any other nation. Choice **b** is incorrect because the author never indicates that the rights the Bill of Rights established are not enjoyed by other citizens of the world. Choice **c** is incorrect because the author of the Bill of Rights does not compare American rights to those of any other nation.

8. **The correct answer is choice a.** The sixth amendment goes into some detail about how a fair criminal prosecution and trial should be conducted. Choice **b** is incorrect because although the eighth amendment mentions a basic point about the cost of bail, it does not indicate how that cost should be determined. Choice **c** is incorrect because although the third amendment discusses soldiers, it is more concerned with the rights of homeowners than soldiers. Choice **d** is incorrect because although the first amendment briefly mentions that people have the right to belong to any religion, it does not go into any detail about how a new religion is established.

9. **The correct answer is choice b.** The first amendment protects the freedom of speech, which indicates that the author believed this was a right to value. Choice **a** is incorrect because the Bill of Rights does not indicate that soldiers deserve special rights that other people do not enjoy. Choice **c** is incorrect because although the fourth amendment sets limits on the reasons a person can be searched or arrested, the Bill of Rights does not indicate that people rarely committed the crimes of which they have been accused. Choice **d** is incorrect because although the author has ideas of how to improve the American legal system, he does not indicate that he does not support the system overall.

10. **The correct answer is choice b.** According to the tenth amendment, both the states and the people may exercise powers when those powers are not "delegated to the United States by the Constitution, nor prohibited by it to the States." Choice **a** is incorrect because the Bill of Rights never indicates whose duty it is to enforce its amendments. Choice **c** is incorrect because a state government cannot be subjected to a trial by jury; only an individual can, and the Bill of Rights indicates nothing that contradicts this fact. Choice **d** is incorrect because the formation of militias is a right, not a duty.

11. The correct answer is choice c. In the preamble to the Bill of Rights, the author mentions that the document's point was to "prevent misconstruction or abuse of [the Constitution's] powers." This expresses the assumption that the Constitution required clarification on certain points, which the Bill of Rights provides. Choice **a** is incorrect because it is a fact, not an assumption, that the United States Constitution applied to all states. Choice **b** is incorrect because it is an opinion, not an assumption, and is not indicated in the passage. Choice **d** is incorrect because although the document assumes that the Constitution requires clarification to prevent misunderstanding, it does not indicate that such misunderstandings have already been widespread.

12. The correct answer is choice a. According to the first paragraph, Fanny did not possess "striking beauty." According to the second paragraph, she also felt different from her good-looking cousins, as well as unhappy and ashamed. Therefore, it is reasonable to conclude that their beauty in contrast to her perceived lack of beauty made her feel self-conscious. Choice **b** is incorrect because the cousins did not behave in a way that suggests they rejected her, and their good looks would be less likely to make Fanny feel rejected than self-conscious. Choice **c** is incorrect because although the cousins' good looks probably stirred negative feelings in Fanny, those feelings would be closer to shame than irritation. Choice **d** is incorrect because it suggests that the cousins' good looks made Fanny feel positive, and there is no evidence of this in the passage.

13. The correct answer is choice d. In this passage, Fanny must adjust to a new situation: living with her cousins, aunt, and uncle. Her discomfort with this new situation is one of the passage's themes. Choice **a** is incorrect because this passage is more about the difficulty of adjusting to an entirely new living situation than merely meeting one's family. Choice **b** is incorrect because although Fanny is a young person and having difficulties, it is not her youth that is causing her problems. Choice **c** is incorrect because the passage focuses more on Fanny's difficulty relating to her cousins, who are relatively close to her age, and not her much older aunt and uncle.

14. The correct answer is choice b. Shortly before his behavior is described as "conciliating," Sir Thomas is described as kindly and aware that Fanny needs encouragement. Based on that information, it makes the most sense that "conciliating" is a positive word, such as "soothing." Choice **a** is incorrect because "terrifying" is a negative word, whereas Sir Thomas's "conciliating" behavior is described in positive terms. Choice **c** is incorrect because "horrible" is a negative word, whereas Sir Thomas's "conciliating" behavior is described in positive terms. Choice **d** is incorrect because although "wonderful" is a positive word, and Sir Thomas's "conciliating" behavior is described in positive terms, "wonderful" is too extreme to fit the situation.

15. The correct answer is choice d. At the beginning of the passage, the reader learns of how sharp, or acute, Fanny's feelings are when she meets her new family. This line sums up those feelings by describing them as "acute" overall. Choice **a** is incorrect because this line spoken by Mrs. Norris does not relate to information introduced earlier in the passage. Choice **b** is incorrect because this line spoken by Mrs. Norris does not relate to information introduced earlier in the passage. Choice **c** is incorrect because this line provides new information; it does not summarize previous information.

16. The correct answer is choice b. In paragraph 3, Mrs. Norris expresses both disappointment in Fanny's sulky behavior and understanding of why Fanny feels this way, so Mrs. Norris seems to have conflicting feelings about the newest member of the household. Choice **a** is incorrect because paragraph 4 reveals that Mrs. Norris allowed Fanny time to get used to Mansfield Park, which she probably would not have done if she had no faith that Fanny would get used to it. Choice **c** is incorrect because Mrs. Norris understands why Fanny feels sulky. Choice **d** is incorrect because it does not account for Mrs. Norris's disappointment in Fanny's behavior.

17. The correct answer is choice a. The reader usually learns more about the central character's feelings and impressions than those of any other character in a story. Choice **b** is incorrect because although Fanny is clearly the central character of this story, she does not actually narrate it, nor does any other character in the story. Choice **c** is incorrect because Fanny makes observations about her family but does not really seem to be judging them. Choice **d** is incorrect because Fanny is the central, or most important, character in the story.

18. The correct answer is choice d. As a whole, the author describes a variety of things about tea in ancient Chinese culture: its evolution across several periods, the ways it was made, and its use in botany, medicine, religious ceremonies, and more. Choice **a** is incorrect because it only focuses on specific details in the passage and not the overall purpose of the passage. Choice **b** is incorrect because the author mentions non-Chinese cultures at the end of the final paragraph but does not make any comparisons. Choice **c** is incorrect because Chinese religious ceremonies are mentioned in the second paragraph but are not the overall focus of the entire passage.

19. The correct answer is choice b. As it is used to describe an approach toward making tea in paragraph 1, the word "school" is used to mean a "specific approach." Choice **a** is incorrect because although it is a correct definition of "school," it does not apply to the way "school" is used in this particular context. Choice **c** is incorrect because although it is a correct definition of "school," it does not apply to the way "school" is used in this particular context. Choice **d** is incorrect because although it is a correct definition of "school," it does not apply to the way "school" is used in this particular context.

20. The correct answer is choice b. Of the four possible choices, only this one is an opinion rather than a fact. Not everyone may agree that the terminology of art classification is often abused. Choice **a** is incorrect because it is a fact, not an opinion. Choice **c** is incorrect because it is a fact, not an opinion. Choice **d** is incorrect because it is a fact, not an opinion.

21. The correct answer is choice c. Kakuzo Okakura's passage describes the essential role tea played across the history of Chinese culture, and the paragraph expresses the same idea as it pertains to wedding traditions. Choice **a** is incorrect because only Kakuzo Okakura's passage discusses Taoist and Buddhist traditions. Choice **b** is incorrect because only the paragraph discusses how tea is used to represent the respect between two groups of people, which are two different families in this particular case. Choice **d** is incorrect because only the paragraph specifically discusses the twenty-first century.

22. The correct answer is choice a. According to the second paragraph, Taoists expected tea to make them immortal, whereas Buddhists merely used its caffeine to stay awake while meditating for long periods. Choice **b** is incorrect because although Taoist and Buddhist uses of tea are mentioned one after the other, there is no indication that one tradition inspired the other. Choice **c** is incorrect because a person does not need to be sensitive to the properties of tea for its caffeine to help her or him stay awake. Choice **d** is incorrect because the passage only reveals that Buddhists used tea as a means to stay awake while meditating; there is no indication that drinking it was an especially important tradition in and of itself.

23. The correct answer is choice b. The poet explains that the poem takes place "far back in swallow-time" and that the sounds of Sunday bells can be heard to establish the poem's setting. Choice **a** is incorrect because these details are not particularly important in the poem. Choice **c** is incorrect because these details describe the character's present, not his memories. Choice **d** is incorrect because these details do more to establish setting than mood.

24. The correct answer is choice c. The poem is mainly about a boy from Baghdad who is now living elsewhere and thinking about how much he misses his homeland. Choice **a** is incorrect because the boy is sad while he listens to the sound of bells. Choice **b** is incorrect because although a greenhouse is mentioned in the poem, there is no indication that he works in the greenhouse. Choice **d** is incorrect because the boy's encounter with the swallow is not the most important idea in the poem despite the poem's title. Also, the swallow does not sing, it screams.

25. The correct answer is choice b. The poem refers to the boy being aboard a ship, and since he is living in a new place in the poem, the reader can conclude that the boy traveled to that new home aboard a ship. Choice **a** is incorrect because although a swallow bothers the boy in the poem, there is no evidence that he has a terrible fear of birds. Choice **c** is incorrect because there is no evidence that he kept a garden when he lived in Baghdad. Choice **d** is incorrect because although the boy does not seem to have friends in his new home, there is no evidence that shyness is the reason for this.

26. The correct answer is choice c. The poet uses the word "stagnant," which means stale and lacking flow, to reflect the boy's mood of sadness in a new country. Choice **a** is incorrect because there is no indication that it is the boy's job to replace the water in the greenhouse tank. Choice **b** is incorrect because the boy's use of the word "stagnant" merely reflects a mood; it does not prove anything. Choice **d** is incorrect because water can go stagnant in a greenhouse tank in any country.

27. The correct answer is choice c. The second stanza reveals that the swallow screamed at the boy, while the following stanzas show that he had been thinking about his life in Baghdad. When the swallow screams, it breaks the boy's concentration on those thoughts. Choice **a** is incorrect because the conclusion that the swallow ruined the boy's life is too extreme. Choice **b** is incorrect because the boy was not actually sleeping; he was deep in memory. Choice **d** is incorrect because the swallow stopped the boy from dreaming; it did not cause him to have dreams.

28. The correct answer is choice d. The poem mainly focuses on how the boy misses his home country and does not have friends in his new country. Choice **a** is incorrect because the poem is not about someone doing a job. Choice **b** is incorrect because although the poem takes place on a Sunday, the poem's tone is not relaxed. Choice **c** is incorrect because although a bird bothers the boy while he is in a garden, this is not the most important detail in the poem.

29. The correct answer is choice d. That Lincoln valued friendship as well as success is shown by his delaying a political speech to help a friend who was losing a fight. Choice **a** is incorrect because nothing in the passage indicates that Lincoln announced he was not humble. Choice **b** is incorrect because Lincoln makes his political policies clear in the first paragraph. Choice **c** is incorrect because although Lincoln was a strong speech maker, nothing in the passage indicates that he was at his strongest while making speeches.

30. The correct answer is choice b. Browne and Lewis acknowledge that Lincoln failed to be elected to the state legislature, but only Browne explains why this happened in any detail. Choice **a** is incorrect because Lewis illustrates Lincoln's honesty through his nickname "Honest Abe" and reputation for treating people fairly while working at a store. Browne illustrates his honesty through the plain and direct way he spoke and dressed. Choice **c** is incorrect because both the Lewis and Browne refer to Lincoln's failure to be elected to the state legislature. Choice **d** is incorrect because Lewis, not Browne, describes how Lincoln opened a store with a partner.

31. The correct answer is choice b. The passage indicates that Lincoln needed income. Choice **a** is incorrect because "purposes" is a synonym of "means," but it does not match how "means" is used in the context of paragraph 3 and would not make sense if used in place of "means" in that paragraph. Choice **c** is incorrect because "indicates" is a synonym of "means," but it would not make sense if used in place of "means" in the paragraph. Choice **d** is incorrect because "certainties" is a synonym of "means," but it would not make sense if used in place of "means" in the paragraph.

32. The correct answer is choice d. The author includes this extended quote from Mr. A.Y. Ellis to support his impartial details about Lincoln's life with more personal observations from a friend. Choice **a** is incorrect because the quote is not especially humorous. Choice **b** is incorrect because although the quote does vary the style of the writing a little, it has a more important purpose than this. Choice **c** is incorrect because the author could easily have given the reader the information outside the confines of a quote.

33. **The correct answer is choice c.** According to the final paragraph of the passage, Lincoln was not known well outside of New Salem before the election, but he won so many votes in the election that his profile must have been higher by the time the election was over. Choice **a** is incorrect because Lincoln considered getting involved in a business outside of politics after the election. Choice **b** is incorrect because Lincoln was already aggressive, which his physical removal of a fighting man in the first paragraph supports. Choice **d** is incorrect because the introduction to the passage explains that Lincoln went on to become president of the United States after his loss in the state legislature election.

34. **The correct answer is choice d.** Lincoln uses the expression "short and sweet" to describe his politics in paragraph 1, and he goes on to make several statements that suggest his politics are simple. Choice **a** is incorrect because Although something "sweet" might be "delightful," one would not describe stances on banking, tariffs, or other basic yet serious political matters as "delightful." Choice **b** is incorrect because Although something "short" might be inadequate, it is unlikely that Lincoln would announce that his politics were inadequate in a speech intended to win him political office. Choice **c** is incorrect because it is unlikely Lincoln would announce his politics as "common."

35. **The correct answer is choice d.** The author uses Watson's discussion of his postponed holiday to discuss how holidays have no interest for Holmes, who prefers to absorb himself in his work above all else. Choice **a** is incorrect because a holiday is not the setting of this story; in fact, the holiday Watson mentions has been postponed. Choice **b** is incorrect because although Watson's holiday has been postponed, he talks at length about Holmes's feelings about holidays, not his own personal life. Choice **c** is incorrect because the paragraph indicates that Holmes has very little interest in travel.

36. **The correct answer is choice a.** Holmes previously said he noticed that Watson had "expressed incredulity," and this line from paragraph 9 clarifies what Watson did to express incredulity. Choice **b** is incorrect because it does not clarify anything stated earlier in the passage. Choice **c** is incorrect because it does not clarify anything stated earlier in the passage. Choice **d** is incorrect because it does not clarify anything stated earlier in the passage.

37. **The correct answer is choice d.** Watson reacts to Holmes's study of Watson's behavior by exclaiming, "You have followed me wonderfully!" which seems like a delighted reaction to Holmes's insights. Choice **a** is incorrect because if Watson had felt such a negative reaction to Holmes, he probably would not have exclaimed, "You have followed me wonderfully!" Choice **b** is incorrect because if Watson had felt such a negative reaction to Holmes, he probably would not have exclaimed, "You have followed me wonderfully!" Choice **c** is incorrect because Watson's exclamation of "You have followed me wonderfully!" indicates that he probably understood Holmes's observations without confusion.

38. The correct answer is choice c. Holmes is as interested in analyzing Watson's behavior as Watson is in hearing Holmes's analysis, which indicates that both men share a fascination with human behavior. Choice **a** is incorrect because only Holmes seems to have a particular knack in actually studying body language. Choice **b** is incorrect because only Watson seems interested in taking holidays. Choice **d** is incorrect because although there is a portrait of Henry Ward Beecher atop Watson's books, there is no strong indication that either Watson or Holmes is especially fascinated by him.

39. The correct answer is choice a. Watson does not seem to realize he had made his incredulity clear, which is why Holmes then explains in detail how Watson had done this. Choice **b** is incorrect because Watson likely realized he'd felt incredulous even if he was not aware of how Holmes knew this. Choice **c** is incorrect because Watson seems to react more to Holmes's observation than to Holmes's feelings about Watson's incredulity. Choice **d** is incorrect because Watson likely realized he'd felt incredulous, which means he was capable of feeling incredulous.

40. The correct answer is choice b. In the first paragraph, Watson explains that Holmes always has his mind on either the evildoer of the town or his brother of the country, so Holmes's search for such criminals will likely be an important event as the story continues. Choice **a** is incorrect because Holmes and Watson's previous discussion of Edgar Allan Poe was just a means to allow Holmes to show off his powers of insight, so Poe's writing is unlikely to be important as the story continues. Choice **c** is incorrect because the matter of Watson's expression of incredulity is settled in this passage and will not likely be important as the story continues. Choice **d** is incorrect because although Watson's holiday has been postponed, suggesting he will go on holiday eventually, this matter seems less important than Holmes's search for wrongdoers.

Language Arts—Writing Part 1

To calculate your HiSET® score on the Language Arts—Writing section, first take a look at the correct answer for each of the 50 questions of the exam. Count up your **correct answers** only, and give yourself 1 point for each. Then, add up all of your points. This is your **raw score**.

Find your raw score and your **scaled score** in the following table. Remember, for each test section, a passing score is 8. (For the essay, a passing score is 2.)

You need a scaled score of 45 to pass the complete HiSET® exam.

LANGUAGE ARTS—WRITING SCORING			
RAW	SCALED	RAW	SCALED
0	1	26	9
1	2	27	9
2	3	28	9
3	3	29	9
4	4	30	9
5	4	31	10
6	5	32	10
7	5	33	10
8	5	34	10
9	6	35	10
10	6	36	11
11	6	37	11
12	6	38	11
13	6	39	11
14	7	40	11
15	7	41	12
16	7	42	12
17	7	43	12
18	7	44	12
19	8	45	13
20	8	46	13
21	8	47	13
22	8	48	14
23	8	49	14
24	8	50	14
25	9		

1. **The correct answer is choice c.** The possessive form of "it" doesn't need an apostrophe. Choice **a** is incorrect because "it's" it is a contraction of "it is," not a possessive pronoun, which is what the sentence requires. Choice **b** is incorrect because the pronoun "it" here is possessive. If you try to replace it with "it is," the sentence doesn't work. Choice **d** is incorrect because this sentence requires the possessive form of the pronoun "it," which is "its." "Its'" is not a word.

2. **The correct answer is choice b.** The original sentence is confusing because the modifier "food scraps and plant matter" is misplaced. Placing the modifier after the word it modifies ("garbage") and adding "such as" makes it clear that the clause is modifying the beginning of the sentence. Choice **a** is incorrect because as it stands, the sentence is confusing because the modifier "food scraps and plant matter" is misplaced, making it seem as though the natural waste would go into food scraps and plant matter. Choice **c** is incorrect because it presents the three objects as though they were items in a list, which they are not. Choice **d** is incorrect because "food scraps and plant matter" are supposed to modify "garbage," and this answer choice deletes the word they should be modifying.

3. **The correct answer is choice c.** The writer intends to use an idiom indicating a policy by which the first person who comes is the first person who is served, and this phrase conveys that meaning correctly. Choice **a** is incorrect because the writer intends to use an idiom indicating a policy by which the first person who comes is the first person who is served, and the phrase used in the sentence does not convey that meaning correctly. Choice **b** is incorrect because the writer intends to use an idiom indicating a policy by which the first person who comes is the first person who is served, and this phrase does not convey that meaning correctly. Choice **d** is incorrect because the writer intends to use an idiom indicating a policy by which the first person who comes is the first person who is served, and this phrase does not convey that meaning correctly.

4. **The correct answer is choice d.** The second sentence is a list of items that can be composted, so a colon is needed to show that a list follows. Choice **a** is incorrect because this combination deletes necessary information; without the phrase "can be composted," the sentence seems like a random list of items. Choice **b** is incorrect because it uses a comma to join the two sentences and set up the list of items. Choice **c** is incorrect because the list of items is not introduced by "such as" or "including."

5. **The correct answer is choice a.** The paragraph's topic is specific information about what materials are included in the program and where you can drop them off for composting, and this sentence wraps up the information given in the paragraph. Choice **b** is incorrect because material is to be dropped off at 35 locations, not at the city landfill, so its hours would be an irrelevant addition to the paragraph. Choice **c** is incorrect because it introduces extra information that does not relate to the rest of the paragraph. Choice **d** is incorrect because this answer choice restates information given in the paragraph's first sentence. The reader already knows this information, so it is unnecessary to repeat it at the end of the paragraph.

6. **The correct answer is choice d.** It uses quotation marks to show the reader where the second part of the interrupted quote begins and ends. Choice **a** is incorrect because the underlined sentence is a part of Marguerite Cobb's quote, so the sentence should start with punctuation that shows that Marguerite is speaking. Choice **b** is incorrect because it removes all quotation marks, so the reader can't tell whether the text is part of the quote or the article. Choice **c** is incorrect because the ellipsis points are unnecessary and a quotation mark is missing.

7. **The correct answer is choice c.** Matthews' political affiliation has nothing to do with composting or his reaction to it, so it is not relevant to the rest of the paragraph. Choice **a** is incorrect because Matthews' politics do not seem to have anything to do with his position on the composting program. Choice **b** is incorrect because the composting program is not really a political issue and there is no reason for the author to make it one. Choice **d** is incorrect because while it is entirely possible that some readers might disagree with Matthews' position on the recycling program if they dislike his politics, there is a more logical reason to delete the sentence than the reason given in this answer choice.

8. **The correct answer is choice c.** The writer intends to use an idiom meaning "to leave behind evidence," and "leaving a trace" conveys this meaning. Choice **a** is incorrect because the writer intends to use an idiom meaning "to leave behind evidence," but "leaving a bit" is not an accepted idiom, so the sentence's meaning is confusing. Choice **b** is incorrect because the writer intends to use an idiom meaning "to leave behind evidence," but "leaving a sample" is not an accepted idiom, so the reader probably does not understand what the sample in question is. Choice **d** is incorrect because the writer intends to use an idiom meaning "to leave behind evidence," but "leaving an evidence" is not an accepted idiom, nor does it make grammatical sense.

9. **The correct answer is choice b.** The pronoun needs to agree with the plural noun "thieves," and "they" refers to more than one person. Choice **a** is incorrect because the pronoun needs to agree with the plural noun "thieves," but "he" is in the singular form. Choice **c** is incorrect because the pronoun needs to agree with the plural noun "thieves," but "he" is in the singular form. This answer choice does not correct the original problem; it merely converts the words into a contraction. Choice **d** is incorrect because the pronoun needs to agree with "thieves," which is more than one person, but "it" refers to a single object or non-human creature.

10. **The correct answer is choice b.** Because this is an article, the writer should use a source with extensive knowledge on the subject. An officer who worked directly on the case would likely have accurate information. Choice **a** is incorrect because it is unlikely that a current volunteer at the museum has any firsthand knowledge of what happened 25 years ago. Choice **c** is incorrect because it can be difficult for the writer to verify whether the secondhand information is accurate. Choice **d** is incorrect because anyone can post information online without having to prove its accuracy.

11. **The correct answer is choice a.** It specifically transitions from the basic "what happened and who did it" questions in paragraph 2 to paragraph 3's topic: why the thieves did it. This sentence tells the reader what to expect in paragraph 3. Choice **b** is incorrect because the transition is too informal ("Anyway"), and "nobody really knows anything" is misleading. It has little to do with the rest of the paragraph. Choice **c** is incorrect because it has little information that tells the reader what the paragraph will be discussing. Choice **d** is incorrect because it has little information that tells the reader what the paragraph will be discussing.

12. The correct answer is choice d. It is a compound sentence with two independent clauses ("police were never able to trace it directly, and since then all 13 pieces have gone back underground") and a dependent clause with a coordinating conjunction ("Although they believe the artwork was offered for sale in Philadelphia in the 2000s"). Choice **a** is incorrect because the underlined sentence has three independent clauses. The writer needs to connect them in a way that makes sense and tells the reader how they're related. Choice **b** is incorrect because it turns the first two clauses into a run-on sentence. Choice **c** is incorrect because it sets up a cause-and-effect relationship that doesn't make sense.

13. The correct answer is choice c. The word "heist" means theft. From the sentence, the reader knows that the underlined noun is most likely related to the crime. Choice **a** is incorrect because although the sentence does refer to something that has been stolen, "stealing" is not typically used as a noun. There is a synonym of "theft" that would work better in this particular context. Choice **b** is incorrect because while the sentence does refer to something that has been stolen, "stolen" is not typically used as a noun. There is a synonym of "theft" that would work better in this particular context. Choice **d** is incorrect because there is a more specific word choice that denotes a crime has taken place.

14. The correct answer is choice d. It summarizes the piece and ties it back to the movie reference in the first paragraph without creating any shifts in tone or perspective. Choice **a** is incorrect because the underlined sentence is inappropriate because it doesn't match the tone or the perspective of the article. The writer has stayed neutral up to this point and hasn't inserted his or her own direct opinion. Choice **b** is incorrect because it inserts the writer's personal perspective into an article that is otherwise impartial and impersonal. Choice **c** is incorrect because the tone is sarcastic, which doesn't fit with the informative tone of the piece.

15. The correct answer is choice c. In the original paragraph, every sentence in this paragraph begins with "I am." This answer choice adds a subordinate clause that shifts away from the "I am" pattern without changing the meaning of the sentence. Choice **a** is incorrect because all of the other sentences in this paragraph start with "I am." The writer should vary the sentence structure to make it more interesting to the reader. Choice **b** is incorrect because all of the other sentences in this paragraph start with "I am." The writer should vary the sentence structure to make it more interesting to the reader. Choice **d** is incorrect because the sentence has information that the writer wants to convey to the reader.

16. The correct answer is choice b. This sentence needs a superlative adjective, and "earliest" is the most appropriate choice. Choice **a** is incorrect because the writer is comparing many things (his memories of the past), so this sentence needs a superlative adjective instead of a comparative one. Choice **c** is incorrect because this sentence needs a superlative adjective, but "most early" is not the correct superlative form of "early." Choice **d** is incorrect because it means the opposite of what the writer is trying to say.

17. The correct answer is choice d. The sentence calls for a past-tense verb, and "spent" is the correct past tense of "spend." Choice **a** is incorrect because the verb is in the present tense. The writer is talking about his previous experience, so the verb should be in the past tense. Choice **b** is incorrect because the verb is in the present tense. The writer is talking about his previous experience, so the verb should be in the past tense. Choice **c** is incorrect because it is in the future progressive tense. The sentence requires the past tense because the writer is describing something that has already happened.

18. The correct answer is choice c. "Honing" means "sharpening" and correctly completes the idiomatic phrase "honing my skills." Choice **a** is incorrect because the sentence as it originally stands contains a common idiom mistake. "Homing" means "zeroing in on something," which doesn't make sense in context. Choice **b** is incorrect because the writer seems to intend to use an idiomatic expression meaning "improving skills." This answer choice results in an awkward phrase. Choice **d** is incorrect because while one might in a sense "find" one's skills during a class, this would make the sentence awkward. There is a common idiomatic phrase the writer intends to use that would be more appropriate in this context.

19. The correct answer is choice a. It indicates that the writer will be talking about a different set of skills. Choice **b** is incorrect because it gives redundant information about the Arturo circus that is repeated later in the sentence. Choice **c** is incorrect because the tone is too informal. Choice **d** is incorrect because it is unclear for what the author is thankful.

20. The correct answer is choice d. It changes the possessive into a plural noun. Choice **a** is incorrect because the underlined text should be a plural noun, not a singular possessive noun, but the apostrophe indicates possession. Choice **b** is incorrect because the underlined text should be a plural noun, not a possessive noun, but the apostrophe here indicates possession. Choice **c** is incorrect because there are multiple Arturo brothers.

21. The correct answer is choice b. It converts the fragment into a subordinate clause that supports "I'm ready to pack my suitcase and take my show on the road." Choice **a** is incorrect because the text is a fragment. Choice **c** is incorrect because although it is a complete sentence, it makes little sense in the context of the paragraph. It's unclear exactly which stage the writer is talking about. Choice **d** is incorrect because it replaces the fragment with another fragment.

22. The correct answer is choice c. It keeps the adverb at the front of the sentence and "with your rodeo" correctly follows the phrase it modifies, "job opening." Choice **a** is incorrect because the text is confusing because the modifier "with your rodeo" is supposed to modify "job opening" but is dropped in the middle of the sentence. It seem as though the writer will be receiving assistance from the rodeo to learn more about the job. Choice **b** is incorrect because "Your rodeo" is placed at the beginning of the sentence, making it seem as though the writer is addressing a rodeo rather than a human being. Choice **d** is incorrect because it misplaces the adverb "therefore." It is confusing to move the adverb to the end of the sentence because it suggests that more information will follow, which is not the case here.

23. **The correct answer is choice c.** "Outweigh" makes sense because it means that risks are more important than social benefits, which expresses the difference of opinion the writer is trying to describe. Choice **a** is incorrect because the gist of this sentence is that potential risks prevail over social benefits, but without the preposition "over," the sentence does not make grammatical sense. Another word makes more logical and grammatical sense in this context. Choice **b** is incorrect because "sway" means to move and does not make sense in this context. Choice **d** is incorrect because "outplay" doesn't work because it seems as though the risks and the benefits are playing against each other, and that doesn't convey the writer's meaning clearly.

24. **The correct answer is choice b.** It is grammatically correct and supports the previous sentence. Choice **a** is incorrect because there is a clearer and more grammatically correct way to combine the sentences. Choice **c** is incorrect because it is a fragment. Choice **d** is incorrect because "likewise" is misleading. It should be used when introducing an idea similar to the previous one, which is not what this sentence is doing.

25. **The correct answer is choice d.** It correctly separates the subordinate clause with commas. Choice **a** is incorrect because the subordinate clause ("who include parents") should be set off from the independent clause ("These advocates stress . . .") rather than combined with no punctuation. Choice **b** is incorrect because it makes the sentence grammatically incorrect by removing a necessary pronoun to set off the subordinate clause ("who include parents") from the independent clause ("These advocates stress . . ."). Choice **c** is incorrect because it makes the sentence grammatically incorrect by removing a necessary pronoun to set off the subordinate clause ("who include parents") from the independent clause ("These advocates stress . . .").

26. **The correct answer is choice c.** It corrects the original fragment by adding a subject ("They") to the sentence. Choice **a** is incorrect because the sentence is a fragment because it lacks a subject. Choice **b** is incorrect because it changes the tense of the verb without introducing the necessary subject. Choice **d** is incorrect because it is the same as the original fragment.

27. **The correct answer is choice d.** The people the writer is discussing are expressing strong opinions that are in opposition to other opinions, so "argue" is the best word to use in this context. Choice **a** is incorrect because "say" is not the best word for this context since the writer is discussing people who are making an argument. Choice **b** is incorrect because "admit" is not the best word for this context since the writer is discussing people who are making an argument. Choice **c** is incorrect because "pretend" is not the best word for this context since the writer is discussing people who are making an argument.

28. **The correct answer is choice d.** "Require" is plural to match the plural subject and in the present tense to suit the context of the paragraph. Choice **a** is incorrect because the sentence needs a plural verb form to match the plural subject "Both Facebook and Instagram." Choice **b** is incorrect because the rest of the paragraph makes it clear that this sentence should be in the present tense, whereas "required" is a past-tense form. Choice **c** is incorrect because "requiring" is a gerund form, not the standard present tense. With a gerund here, the sentence is a fragment.

29. The correct answer is choice b. The original sentence fails to indicate that one clause ("some youth advocates believe that these guidelines don't go far enough to protect kids' privacy") provides a contrasting opinion to the previous clause ("They also recommend that any users under the age of 16 have parental permission"). The conjunction "but" indicates that contrast correctly. Choice **a** is incorrect because the sentence fails to indicate that one clause ("some youth advocates believe that these guidelines don't go far enough to protect kids' privacy") provides a contrasting opinion to the previous clause ("They also recommend that any users under the age of 16 have parental permission"). A different conjunction than "and" is needed to indicate this contrast. Choice **c** is incorrect because the sentence needs a coordinating conjunction to join its two clauses and is a run-on sentence without one. Choice **d** is incorrect because punctuation is missing.

30. The correct answer is choice c. The adverb "below" belongs after the noun. Choice **a** is incorrect because "below" should follow the noun. Choice **b** is incorrect because it removes the noun, leaving the sentence unclear. Choice **d** is incorrect because it removes the adverb that specifies the policies to which the writer is referring. The sentence is unclear without the adverb.

31. The correct answer is choice d. The writer intends to use an idiomatic phrase meaning "in operation," and "in effect" conveys that meaning. Choice **a** is incorrect because the writer intends to use an idiomatic phrase meaning "in operation," but "in affect" does not make grammatical sense. It should be "in effect." Choice **b** is incorrect because the writer intends to use an idiomatic phrase meaning "in operation," but "in the effective" does not make sense. Choice **c** is incorrect because the writer intends to use an idiomatic phrase meaning "in operation," but changing "in affect" to "affecting" does not clarify the meaning of this sentence.

32. The correct answer is choice c. It moves the verb into the present tense. The adverb "currently" indicates the sentence takes place in the present. Choice **a** is incorrect because it uses the past tense of "live." The adverb "currently" indicates that this sentence needs a verb in the present tense. Choice **b** is incorrect because it changes "currently" to "previously," which doesn't make sense for the audience of the letter. Choice **d** is incorrect because the adverb "currently" indicates the sentence takes place in the present but "will" refers to the future.

33. The correct answer is choice d. It includes all the necessary information, while making it clear that "including dogs over 35 pounds" modifies "large animals." Choice **a** is incorrect because although this combination is grammatically correct, it is reads awkwardly. There is a more effective way to combine the sentences. Choice **b** is incorrect because it eliminates information that could be useful to the reader (that dogs over 35 pounds count as large animals). Choice **c** is incorrect because it creates a confusing compound sentence with the modifying phrase at its beginning. The fact that "including animals over 35 pounds" is modifying "large animals" needs to be clear immediately.

34. The correct answer is choice c. As originally written, the pronouns in the sentence failed to agree. This choice fixes that error by maintaining use of the second-person pronoun "you." Choice **a** is incorrect because as written, the pronouns in this sentence do not agree. The plural third-person pronoun "they" is used before switching to the singular second-person pronoun "you." Choice **b** is incorrect because It causes the sentence to switch from the plural first-person pronoun "we" to the singular second-person pronoun "you." The pronouns in this sentence need to agree. Choice **d** is incorrect because this memo is directed at a human being, and it is incorrect to indicate a human with the pronoun "it."

35. The correct answer is choice a. Tenants have the right to know the full extent of the penalties they will incur if they continue to be negligent in paying the pet deposit fee. Choice **b** is incorrect because this information is not really intended to frighten tenants; it is merely intended to clarify the consequences of not paying the pet deposit. Choice **c** is incorrect because whether or not the additional fees are necessary is irrelevant; as long as those fees are required, they deserve to be indicated in the memo. Choice **d** is incorrect because the full extent of the fees a negligent tenant could incur is hardly a minor piece of information. Tenants have the right to know the full extent of the penalties they will incur if they continue to be negligent in paying the pet deposit fee.

36. The correct answer is choice c. This sentence belongs immediately after the rules for refuse disposal are discussed, and those rules are detailed in sentences 1 and 2 of the paragraph. Choice **a** is incorrect because this sentence would not make sense if introduced before the rules regarding where refuse should be placed are detailed. Choice **b** is incorrect because this sentence belongs after the rules regarding refuse disposal are detailed; it does not belong in the middle of that discussion. Choice **d** is incorrect because this sentence belongs immediately after all the rules for refuse disposal are discussed, and those rules are detailed in sentences 1 and 2 of the paragraph. By sentence 3, the memo has moved on to another topic.

37. The correct answer is choice d. This is the correct answer because it adds the friendly information about the block party while maintaining a formal tone. Choice **a** is incorrect because this is a formal letter to the building's tenants, and the closing should reflect that as well. The underlined text is too informal. Choice **b** is incorrect because this is a formal letter to the building's tenants, and the closing should reflect that as well. This text is too informal. Choice **c** is incorrect because it is at once too informal and too threatening for an informative memo.

38. **The correct answer is choice d.** Billy Buddy's Old Town Grill is the proper name of a restaurant, and therefore each word should be capitalized. Choice **a** is incorrect because Billy Buddy's Old Town Grill is the proper name of a restaurant, and therefore each word should be capitalized. Choice **b** is incorrect because Billy Buddy's Old Town Grill is the proper name of a restaurant, and therefore each word should be capitalized. Choice **c** is incorrect because Billy Buddy's Old Town Grill is the proper name of a restaurant, and therefore each word should be capitalized. However, the word "restaurant" is not part of that proper name, so it should begin with a lowercase letter.

39. **The correct answer is choice c.** The closing sentence for this paragraph should relate to the information presented in the first paragraph and help to cement the tone for the next paragraphs. This choice does both by comparing the listed restaurants (Pizza Town and McDonald's) to Billy Budd's Old Town Grill and setting up the main topic: why her experience was bad. Choice **a** is incorrect because the information presented here is irrelevant both to this paragraph and to the review as a whole. Choice **b** is incorrect because the review talks about the bad experiences, not the positive ones, so a closing sentence like this one goes against the theme of this paragraph and the passage as a whole. Choice **d** is incorrect because the information presented here is irrelevant to this paragraph and the review as a whole.

40. **The correct answer is choice d.** The first sentence of paragraph 2 states the writer's conclusion that her experience at the restaurant was terrible, and the second sentence moves back before she had reached that conclusion. This transitional phrase establishes that backward movement through time. Choice **a** is incorrect because paragraph 2 states the writer's conclusion that her experience at the restaurant was terrible, and the second sentence moves back before she had even arrived at the restaurant. Therefore, a transitional phrase establishing that the writer has finished her meal does not make sense in this context. Choice **b** is incorrect because the transitional phrase between the opening sentence, which establishes a conclusion reached in the present, and the second sentence, which refers to the past, needs to indicate that backward movement in time. However, this transitional phrase suggests that something is being done very quickly, which does not make sense in this context. Choice **c** is incorrect because the first sentence of paragraph 2 states the writer's conclusion that her experience at the restaurant was terrible, and the second sentence moves back before she had reached that conclusion. However, this transitional phrase suggests that her conclusion is still in the process of being made.

41. **The correct answer is choice c.** This sentence should be deleted because it's irrelevant to the restaurant review. Choice **a** is incorrect because the setting of this passage is the restaurant the writer is reviewing, not the gym and the places where she ran errands. Choice **b** is incorrect because whether the author was hungry before arriving at the restaurant is not relevant in this passage. Choice **d** is incorrect because although the writer had a bad experience at the restaurant, she is not mainly concerned with having the reader feel sorry for her.

42. The correct answer is choice b. It combines the two redundant sentences into a single clearly stated sentence. Choice **a** is incorrect because the opening sentences for this paragraph are awkward and redundant. Using a semicolon to join them into a single sentence does not correct that problem. Choice **c** is incorrect because it is awkward and unclear about the order of events. Choice **d** is incorrect because although each individual clause is clear, the sentence is choppy and awkward.

43. The correct answer is choice d. It condenses the information into a clear statement. Choice **a** is incorrect because the original sentences were awkwardly constructed. Combining the unaltered sentences into a single sentence is not the most effective way to correct that awkwardness. Choice **b** is incorrect because this sentence is clearer than the original sentences, but it deletes necessary information. What exactly did the waitress help? Choice **c** is incorrect because it changes the tense to present when the rest of the writer's review is in past tense.

44. The correct answer is choice a. The underlined phrase is correct as written. The singular pronoun phrase "his or her" agrees with the subject "each person." Choice **b** is incorrect because the subject of the sentence is the singular "each person," but "their" is a plural pronoun. Choice **c** is incorrect because the subject of the sentence is the singular "each person," but "our" is a plural pronoun. Furthermore, it implies that everyone at the table shared the same dinner. Choice **d** is incorrect because although a singular pronoun is needed to agree with the singular subject of the sentence ("each person"), the masculine pronoun "his" suggests that every person at the table was male, which is not the case.

45. The correct answer is choice b. A "desert" is a dry, sandy environment. This word should be spelled "dessert," which is a sweet treat eaten after a meal. Choice **a** is incorrect because "desert" is misspelled. Choice **c** is incorrect because "preorder," which means "order at an earlier date," is spelled correctly here. Choice **d** is incorrect because "prior," which means "at an earlier time," is spelled correctly here.

46. The correct answer is choice d. Both words are lowercase since they are not part of the title in a proper name. Choice **a** is incorrect because "Mayor" isn't used here with a specific name, so it should begin with a lowercase letter. Choice **b** is incorrect because "The" should be lowercase since it is not at the beginning of the sentence, and "Mayor" should be lowercase unless it's used as a title in a proper name. Choice **c** is incorrect because the article "The" should not be uppercase unless it begins a sentence.

47. The correct answer is choice b. It replaces the conjunction with a conjunctive adverb that doesn't require a second clause. Choice **a** is incorrect because the underlined text starts with a conjunction, which results in a fragment. Choice **c** is incorrect because it results in a fragment. Choice **d** is incorrect because it does not make sense in the context of the sentence.

48. The correct answer is choice d. The author intends to use an idiomatic phrase meaning "completely genuine" here, and that is what "as good as gold" means. Choice **a** is incorrect because the author intends to use an idiomatic phrase meaning "completely genuine" here, but "as good as money" is not a common idiom. Choice **b** is incorrect because the author intends to use an idiomatic phrase meaning "completely genuine" here, but "as solid as silver" is not a common idiom. Choice **c** is incorrect because the author intends to use an idiomatic phrase meaning "completely genuine" here, but "completely ironclad" is not a common idiom.

49. **The correct answer is choice c.** It lets the reader know that the speaker will be talking more specifically about a plan to correct the city's tourism problems. Choice **a** is incorrect because the reader already knows that this person is running for mayor, and this has little to do with the rest of the paragraph. Choice **b** is incorrect because the writer has already established that there is a problem with tourism, so this sentence is redundant. Choice **d** is incorrect because the writer has already established that the beaches are "some of the best," so this sentence would contradict that assertion. It also fails to transition into the following sentence smoothly.

50. **The correct answer is choice c.** It suits the positive tone of the rest of the speech while wrapping it up effectively. Choice **a** is incorrect because this sentence is too informal for a professional political speech. There is a better way to phrase this information that suits the style and tone of the rest of the speech. Choice **b** is incorrect because earlier in the speech, the writer specified an intention not to dwell on the previous mayor. This concluding statement contradicts that while wallowing in negativity the rest of the speech avoids. Choice **d** is incorrect because this would end the speech on a weak tone. Another choice uses strong and positive language that matches the rest of the speech.

Language Arts—Writing Part 2

On test day, your essay will be scored by two graders. Each will read over your essay, and assign it a score from 1 to 6 using the following grading criteria. Using this table, assign your own essay a score from 1 to 6. Then, read the provided sample essays and explanations to get a sense of what an essay at every level looks like. You need a score of 2 to pass this portion of the exam.

SCORE	EXPLANATION
1	*Essays at this score point do not sufficiently support an argument. They do not take a stance on the given question and do not provide solid evidence or reasoning to back up any claims.* These essays: • do not offer a clear opinion, as requested by the given prompt. The topic at hand might be mentioned, but there is no context for the information and no main idea to tie any information together into a cohesive thought. • are not structured: There is no introduction, conclusion, or main thesis. They often are not separated into paragraphs, and if they are, they lack smooth transitions from one paragraph to the next. • feature very simple vocabulary and sentence structure throughout. There is often a misuse of grammar, along with frequent errors in capitalization, punctuation, and spelling.
2	*Essays at this score point might bring up points related to the given prompt, but they do not sufficiently support an argument with a well-thought-out stance, backed by evidence. Thoughts are often jumbled and unrelated, and there is not a firm grasp of language rules or sentence and paragraph structure.* These essays: • do not fully develop a clear stance on the given issue. Often, if an opinion is given, either it is not developed or expanded on with examples from the given texts or it relies too heavily on pulling information from the given texts. • often do not feature an introduction, conclusion, or paragraphs—if they do, these elements are not cohesive and do not flow properly. • do not have a solid command of sentence structure—sentences are either short and choppy or long and run-on. Sentences do not flow into one another, and there is no cohesive tone throughout the piece. • have limited command of grammar, usage, spelling, capitalization, and punctuation rules.
3	*Essays at this score point take a solid stance on the given issue and show partial command of developing an argument using proper usage rules.* These essays: • take a definitive stance on the given issue but do not fully develop this point of view with sufficient evidence—from the given texts and from the writer's personal experiences. Several points are presented to clarify the author's point of view, but a cohesive and well-rounded argument is not presented. • might feature an introduction, supporting paragraphs, and a conclusion, although one or all of these may be underdeveloped. If present, transitions are simple and used inconsistently. • begin to feature a command of language, although word choice and sentence structure are often unvaried or repetitive. Sentences in score 3 essays also might be too long and uncontrolled. Essays often feature errors in capitalization, punctuation, and spelling.
4	*Essays at this score point adequately take a stance on the argument presented and back it up with some evidence and reasoning. Basic writing rules are followed, but mistakes are often presented and can be too casual.* These essays: • begin to develop a point of view in response to the given topic. The writer has a clear stance on the issue. Essays bring in personal examples and examples from the given essays, along with some discussion of alternate claims and/or counterclaims. • usually contain a clear introduction and conclusion but often lack sufficient development of supporting paragraphs within. Transitions are used, although they may be simple, and organization of sentences within paragraphs is often jumbled and awkward. • feature an adequate command of grammar, usage, sentence structure, and punctuation. Word choice and sentence format are somewhat varied, and a cohesive tone is used throughout. Errors are often present, but they do not interfere with the essay's clarity in message.

5   Essays at this score point take a definitive stance on the argument presented, backing it up with solid examples, reasoning, and presentation of counterarguments. While these essays may feature minor mistakes, they show a good command of language, usage, and variety of word choice and sentence structure. These essays:

- solidly present and back up a central position or claim on the given prompt. These essays also include a balanced discussion of counterclaims. Several ideas to back up a point of view are provided and expanded on, along with evidence from real life and the provided texts.
- feature a clear introduction, conclusion, and supporting paragraphs. Transitions are used throughout to unify ideas and create a cohesive point of view.
- show a very solid command of grammar, usage, spelling, punctuation, and sentence structure. Words are used correctly and varied throughout, and sentences vary in length and complexity. Thee essay may contain some errors in usage and some deviations in tone, but nothing detracts from the overall stance and content of the essay.

6   Essays at this score point present a strongly written and defended argument using sufficient evidence from varied sources, presentation of counterarguments, and a solid command of language and grammar conventions. These essays:

- expertly present, develop, and defend a point of view on a given topic. They explore the topic from all sides and present arguments countering differing opinions. Writers have a clear point of view and defend it with many examples taken from real life and from the given texts in the prompt.
- feature a definitive and well-written introduction, conclusion, and set of supporting paragraphs to back up all claims made. Strong transitions are used to connect thoughts and link together all claims and evidence made.
- demonstrate extremely strong command of language and grammar. Vocabulary and sentence structure throughout are varied in length and complexity. These essays have very few, if any, errors in spelling, punctuation, and usage. Essays feature a cohesive tone throughout that is appropriate for the topic at hand.

Sample Score 1 Essay:

Basicaly riding a bike is ok for kids but theres no point if your old enough to drive a car. I mean who cares. ride a bicycle in the street. cars are in the street. and that's were you'll find me driving my car. I havent' even had a bike since I was like a little kid. Pretty soon there will be special lains for tricycles. ha ha.

About This Essay

While this essay does talk about bike riding, it does not address the essay prompt, use evidence from the passages, or acknowledge alternate or opposing ideas. A broad opinion on bicycles themselves is given ("but theres no point if your old enough to drive a car"), but the proposal to construct a bike lane in the city is not mentioned. There is no introduction or conclusion, and there are no transitions or main thesis to this essay. Most glaringly, this essay is filled with errors in grammar ("if *your* old enough to drive a car"), punctuation ("*theres* no point"), and spelling ("special *lains* for tricycles").

Sample Score 2 Essay:

Some people want special lanes for bikes. I get it. They ride bikes and don't want to risk hit by a car. So they ride in special lanes for bikes which is probably a good thing. Cars can really be dangerus. A lot of people get into car accidents every year. People should not ride bikes on roads that are meant for cars. At leest if they doesn't have too. The department of transportation says so. If they have no choice, well then, there you are. So bike lanes are usually good.

About This Essay

While this essay does take a stance on bike lanes ("So bike lanes are usually good"), it does not use evidence from the passages to back up its point or acknowledge alternate or opposing ideas. It offers some personal opinions ("Cars can really be dangerus."), but it does not expand on these opinions in a clear and argumentative manner. While this essay has a loose thesis, it lacks an introduction, a conclusion, and transitions to build on the opening statements.

Finally, this essay has many errors in grammar ("They ride bikes and don't want to risk hit by a car."), punctuation ("At leest if they *doesn't* have too."), and spelling ("Cars can really be *dangerus*.").

Sample Score 3 Essay:

I recently heard about the plans to build a bike lane in the community. Not a bad idea! Actualy why would anybody not support this plan? Maybe they don't like the noise of road work. Maybe they think it will cost higher taxes. I don't know. all I know is those people are completely wrong. Why is this even being debated. Let's get started on those new bike lanes right away!

Riding on the same roads as cars is not safe. Everybody knows that. So many people who ride bikes say they do not feel safe riding the same roads that cars do. Those people will probably ride more if they have there own bike lanes. So please start building these bike lanes RIGHT AWAY! I'm all for them. I might even buy a new bike if there was a great new bike lane in my very own neghborhood!

About This Essay

This essay takes a firm stance on bike lanes and begins to back it up with some reasoning and examples. However, it does not sufficiently cite examples from the texts or give counter-examples of the opposing points of view and why they are incorrect. There is a brief introduction, but there is not a proper conclusion or paragraphs within that expand on a point of view. Finally, there are evident errors in spelling ("*Actualy* why would anybody not support this plan?"), capitalization ("*all* I know is those people are completely wrong."), and punctuation ("Why is this even being debated.")

Sample Score 4 Essay:

Please build a bike lane in our town. It is an amazing idea! As a concerned citizen who cares about the environment and safety, a bike lane will be a great solution to those two problems. Nearly half of people have bikes. A quarter of the population have bike paths and lanes. But our town is not part of that population and I believe we need to be.

Riding bikes on roads meant for cars is very dangerous, and you can't blame 13% of people for being afraid to ride their bikes on those roads. A lot of people are terrible drivers. Some people may say that bike lanes are not good for getting to work and that people will still drive cars most of the time. Others may complain about the cost of creating new bike lanes, which is pretty high at a total cost of $2,600,000. But should we be putting a price tag on the value of human life? Also, think of the money people will save on car maintenence and gasoline.

New bike lanes could really improve our city. They can make them safer. People with bikes would be very grateful using them! So like I said before please use public funds to make a new bike path and not something no one really needs.

About This Essay

This essay addresses the given prompt, takes a stance on the issue, and offers evidence from the given texts to support its stance ("Nearly half of people . . ." and "A quarter of the population have . . ."). This essay also has an introduction, a body, and a conclusion. To attain a higher score, the author should further develop his or her stance with smoother integration of facts. The tone of the essay is often awkward ("So like I said before please use public funds to make a new bike path and not something no one really needs."), and although grammar and usage are generally correct, ideas can be presented in a more formal, professional tone.

Sample Score 5 Essay:

News of a possible bike lane in our town has really caught my attention. I read that public funds will be used to pay for this bike lane if it happens. I bet all the bike riders in our city are really enthusiastic about that bike lane. But I think public funds could be used better.

First of all, people seem to want bike lanes because they are frightened. The U.S. Department of

Transportation says that 13% of people who ride bikes are scared of riding alongside cars. However 10% are still scared when there is a bike lane around. That is not a big difference. Clearly people won't be that much more confident of their safety just by creating a bike lane in our town. Furthermore, the recent report from the U.S. Department of Transportation has no concrete data arguing that bike lanes actually improve road safety.

Another reason people want a bike lane is the environment. But I don't think people are going to sell their cars just for this reason. Most of the people I know drive even though nearly half of adults have access to bikes. I bet some might use the bike lanes for recreational rides on the weekends, but they will still use their cars to get to work and school. I don't think the beleif that the environmental situation will get better just by installing a bike lane justifies the expence.

Instead, I think we should use the public funds that would have been used to create bike lanes on improving the roads we already have. There are pot holes and cracks everywhere. They don't just damage car tires. They are also dangerous for people who use them for bike riding. Riding a bike through a pot hole or over a crack is much more dangerous than just sharing the road with cars.

So instead of wasting public funds on building totally new paths just for one kind of vehicle, I think we should spend less money to simply improve the roads we already have that cars and bikes use every day.

About This Essay

This essay takes a solid stance on the given prompt and backs it up with evidence from real life ("Most of the people I know drive . . .") and from the given essays ("The U.S. Department of Transportation says that 13% of people . . ."). The writer looks at both points of view and carefully responds to the alternative point of view with carefully reasoned counterarguments. There is a solid introduction and there are backing paragraphs, but there could be a more definitive conclusion. Although there are a few spelling mistakes ("a bike lane justifies the *expence*"),

the essay shows a solid command of grammar and usage.

Sample Score 6 Essay:

As a bicyclist myself, I believe that installing bike lanes would be an excellent way to encourage the health, safety, and environmental benefits of bicycling. We have the opportunity to use these public funds in a positive and productive way, and building dedicated bike lanes in our city is a great first step toward a safer (and greener) future for our city.

With so many health issues caused by obesity and being connected to our phones and tablets 24/7, bicycling lets people take some time out of their day to get exercise while also commuting to work, running errands, or spending time with their families. According to a U.S. Department of Transportation survey, nearly half of all American adults have household access to a bike; and more than half of those people rode their bikes in the month before the survey was taken. If half of our community has access to a bike, think of how many people we can get out and riding in the fresh air.

However, there are more benefits than just exercise. A recent editorial that is clearly not in favor of the proposal takes issue with the fact that the U.S. Department of Transportation has failed to provide concrete data about the actual safety benefits of bike lanes. Having ridden through the city on my own bike, I can vouch for the fact that the roads are very dangerous. Bicyclists have to share the roads with cars, and quite frankly, when a few pounds of metal come up against several tons of steel, which one do you think is going to win? The Department of Transportation report suggests that the most important part of bike lanes is not how many people ride, but rather how safe those people are. People will feel more encouraged and confident about using their bikes if they do not have to worry as much about getting hurt in a car wreck. Bike lanes keep car traffic and bike traffic separate, and as long as everyone follows the rules of the road, everyone is safer.

Our city deserves transportation options that allow us to make the best decisions for ourselves and our *families. Granted, the cost is something we have to consider, but a one-time $2,600,000 bill is worth the well being of our fellow citizens, even if it is only the psychological well being that comes with a new sense of confidence. If even half of the community takes advantage of the bike lanes, I believe it's a very worthy project for the city to adopt.*

About This Essay

This essay takes a stance on the given topic ("As a bicyclist myself, I believe that installing bike lanes would be an excellent way to encourage the health, safety, and environmental benefits of bicycling."), presents a clear and definitive introduction and conclusion, and backs up the point of view with strong, well-written supporting paragraphs. The author shows a strong command of English grammar and usage—sentences throughout differ in length and tone, and word choice and vocabulary vary. Transitions are used effectively ("However, there are more benefits than just exercise."), along with evidence from real life and from the given texts to establish and defend a point of view.

Mathematics

To calculate your HiSET® score on the Mathematics section, first take a look at the correct answer for each of the 50 questions of the exam. Count up your **correct answers** only, and give yourself 1 point for each. Then, add up all of your points. This is your **raw score**.

Find your raw score and your **scaled score** in the following table. Remember, for each test section, a passing score is 8. (For the essay, a passing score is 2.)

You need a scaled score of 45 to pass the complete HiSET® exam.

MATHEMATICS SCORING			
RAW	SCALED	RAW	SCALED
0	1	26	12
1	1	27	12
2	2	28	12
3	2	29	13
4	3	30	13
5	3	31	13
6	4	32	13
7	5	33	14
8	6	34	14
9	7	35	14
10	8	36	14
11	8	37	15
12	8	38	15
13	9	39	15
14	9	40	15
15	9	41	16
16	10	42	16
17	10	43	16
18	10	44	17
19	10	45	17
20	10	46	18
21	11	47	18
22	11	48	19
23	11	49	20
24	11	50	20
25	12		

1. **The correct answer is choice b.** $3\frac{3}{4}$ cups $= \frac{15}{4}$ cups. Let x be the number of cups of flour needed for 90 cookies and set up the proportion $\frac{\frac{15}{4}}{36} = \frac{x}{90}$. Solving for x yields $90(\frac{15}{4}) = 36x \Rightarrow x = \frac{75}{8} = 9\frac{3}{8}$ cups. Choice **a** is incorrect because $3\frac{3}{4} \neq \frac{9}{4}$. Choice **c** seems to be the result of estimating. Set up a proportion to find the exact amount needed. Choice **d** is incorrect because it is the amount needed for 72 cookies, not 90. Choice **e** is incorrect because it would be the amount for 108 cookies, not 90.

2. **The correct answer is choice e.** Since the diameter is 16 cm, the radius is 8 cm. So, the radius of the desired circle is 24 cm. Its area is $\pi(24)^2 = 576\pi$ square centimeters. Choice **a** is incorrect because you forgot to square the radius. Choice **b** is incorrect because it is the circumference, not the area. Choice **c** is incorrect because you computed the circumference using the diameter instead of finding the area. Choice **d** is incorrect because you squared the diameter, not the radius.

3. **The correct answer is choice c.** The description suggests that the plant and rabbit populations decrease and increase together, which is indicated by the graph. Choice **a** is incorrect. The graph suggests that the plants and rabbits have an inverse relationship, which is not true. Choice **b** is incorrect because there is no cyclic behavior present in the graph; it suggests that the plant population dies and the rabbits continue to flourish. Choice **d** is incorrect because the graph suggests that both the plant and rabbit populations remain constant over time, which is not suggested in the description. Choice **e** is incorrect because both populations should be cyclic; the graph suggests that the plant population eventually dies out.

4. **The correct answer is choice c.** Observe that $\left(\frac{1}{2}\right)^{-t} = 2^t$, and so, with every increase in t by one minute, the population doubles. Choice **a** is incorrect because 68 is the initial population only and does not affect the actual growth rate; here, the population doubles every minute. Choice **b** is incorrect because this is an example of exponential growth. Choice **d** is incorrect because while the population size starts at 68, it continues to increase with time, so this is not the maximum size. Choice **e** is incorrect because $\left(\frac{1}{2}\right)^{-t} = 2^t$, so it grows rather than diminishing.

5. **The correct answer is choice b.** First write the system as $\begin{cases} y = ax - 3 \\ y = \frac{1}{a}x + \frac{1}{a} \end{cases}$

The only way for such a system to have no solution is for the slopes to be equal but the y-intercepts to differ. Here, the slopes are equal when $a = \frac{1}{a}$, which occurs when $a = -1$ or 1. Choice **a** is incorrect because the slopes of the lines are different for this value of a, so the lines will intersect at least once, thereby giving a solution of the system. Choice **c** is incorrect because the slopes of the lines are different for this value of a, so the lines will intersect at least once, thereby giving a solution of the system. Choice **d** is incorrect because the slopes of the lines are different for this value of a, so the lines will intersect at least once, thereby giving a solution of the system. Choice **e** is incorrect because the slopes of the lines are different for this value of a, so the lines will intersect at least once, thereby giving a solution of the system.

6. The correct answer is choice b. The number 2 must be excluded from the domain because it makes the denominator of the first term equal to zero, so that it would be undefined. The radicand must be nonnegative, so that $x \geq -1$. Taking those two conditions together results in the number line in this choice. Choice **a** is incorrect because x must be greater than or equal to -1, and the radicand must be nonnegative. Choice **c** is incorrect because you need to exclude 2 from the domain, since it makes the first term undefined. Choice **d** is incorrect because you should not exclude 0 from the domain because it makes the numerator equal to zero, which is permissible. Choice **e** is incorrect because for the radicand to be nonnegative, x must be greater than or equal to -1, not less than or equal to -1.

7. The correct answer is choice e. There is a total of 150 attendees. Those whose age is greater than 40 are those in the bottom two rows, which gives 52 out of 150 attendees. So the probability of randomly choosing an attendee whose age is greater than 40 is $\frac{52}{150} = \frac{26}{75}$. Choice **a** is incorrect because you divided the correct number (52) by 100 instead of the total number of attendees, 150. Choice **b** is incorrect because this uses only the last row; you should use the bottom *two* rows. Choice **c** is incorrect because this is the probability that a randomly selected attendee's age is *not* greater than 40. Choice **d** is incorrect because you used only the second to last row in your calculation; you should also use the *last* row.

8. The correct answer is choice c. The sine of an angle is the length of the side opposite the angle divided by the hypotenuse. This results in the given equation. Choice **a** is incorrect because you cannot use cosine since you do not have the side adjacent to the given angle; cosine is adjacent divided by hypotenuse. Choice **b** is incorrect because you cannot use tangent since you do not have the side adjacent to the given angle; tangent is opposite divided by adjacent. Choice **d** is incorrect because you cannot use cosine since you do not have the side adjacent to the given angle; cosine is adjacent divided by hypotenuse. Choice **e** is incorrect because the right side should be the reciprocal of what it is; sine is opposite divided by hypotenuse.

9. The correct answer is choice b. This expression equals $(\frac{1}{6}) \cdot (\frac{2}{3})^4 = \frac{1}{6} \cdot \frac{16}{81} = \frac{8}{243}$, which is a rational number. Choice **a** is incorrect because while this is written as a fraction, the numerator and denominator are not integers. Choice **c** is incorrect because this product equals $2^{\frac{1}{3}} \cdot 2^{\frac{1}{2}} = 2^{\frac{5}{8}}$, which is irrational. Choice **d** is incorrect because this equals $9\pi^2$, which is a product of a rational number and an irrational number and so must be irrational. Choice **e** is incorrect because the sum of two positive irrational numbers is irrational.

10. The correct answer is choice e. The translation rule is "add 4 to the x-coordinate and add 5 to the y-coordinate." Doing so to A and F, respectively, yields the points $A' = (2,6)$ and $F' = (7,6)$. Choice **a** is incorrect because you reversed the amounts to be added to the x- and y-coordinates. Choice **b** is incorrect because you only moved in the x-direction. Choice **c** is incorrect because you only moved in the y-direction. Choice **d** is incorrect because you moved 4 left and 5 down but should have moved 4 right and 5 up.

11. **The correct answer is choice e.** Use the two labeled points to determine the slope of the best fit line is $\frac{8-4}{28-12} = \frac{1}{4}$. Using the point $(12,4)$ with this slope, we can write the equation of the best fit line in slope-intercept form as $y - 4 = \frac{1}{4}(x - 12)$, so that $y = \frac{1}{4}x + 1$. Now we must determine the value of x for which $y = 10$: $\frac{1}{4}x + 1 = 10$, so that $x = 36$. Choice **a** is incorrect because you divided the desired rating by the slope of the best fit line, but this is not how you use the best fit line to determine a rating. Choice **b** is incorrect because 30 is too low, as can be seen on the best fit line. Choice **c** is incorrect because 32 is too low, as can be seen on the best fit line. Choice **d** is incorrect because it would yield a rating less than 10.

12. **The correct answer is choice c.** The height of the new cylinder is $2(30 \text{ in.}) = 60$ in. The diameter of the base of the new cylinder is $\frac{D}{3}$ in., so its radius is $\frac{D}{6}$ in. So the volume of the new cylinder is $\pi(\frac{D}{6})^2(60) = \frac{5}{3}\pi D^2$ cubic inches. Choice **a** is incorrect because you mistakenly used the volume formula for a right circular cone. Choice **b** is incorrect because you mistakenly used the volume formula for a sphere. Choice **d** is incorrect because you did not square the radius in the volume formula. Choice **e** is incorrect because you did not double the height.

13. **The correct answer is choice c.** First write all fractions using the least common denominator: $(x - 1)(x + 1)$ and then simply $\frac{2(x+1)}{(x-1)(x-1)} - \frac{3}{(x+1)(x-1)} - \frac{2(x-1)}{(x+1)(x-1)} = \frac{2x+2-3-2x+2}{(x+1)(x-1)} = \frac{1}{x^2-1}$. Choice **a** is incorrect because you cannot add fractions by simply adding the numerators and denominators in this manner; first get a least common denominator. Choice **b** is incorrect because you changed the subtraction signs to addition signs. Choice **d** is incorrect because when rewriting each fraction using the least common denominator, you only multiplied the first term of each binomial in the numerator by the number, but you should distribute it to both terms. Choice **e** is incorrect because this is the negative of the correct answer.

14. **The correct answer is choice a.** The remaining amount to be deposited into the savings account is $6,500 - x$. Multiply each of these amounts by the respective interest rate, add the resulting expressions, and set it equal to $100.50. Doing so yields this expression. Choice **b** is incorrect because the right side should equal $100.50. Choice **c** is incorrect because the coefficients on the left side show the interest rates but should show the total of the principal and the interest. Choice **d** is incorrect because the quantity $x - 6,500$ should be $6,500 - x$. The coefficients on the left side show the interest rates but should show the total of the principal and the interest. Choice **e** is incorrect because you do not add percentages like this and then apply them to a total sum; rather, apply the appropriate percentage to each quantity *separately* and then add those amounts together.

15. The correct answer is choice c. Factor the left side as $(3x + 1)(3x + 2)$. Setting each of these factors equal to zero yields $x = -\frac{1}{3}, -\frac{2}{3}$. So, this equation has two negative real solutions. Choice **a** is incorrect because one of the solutions of this equation is zero and the second is the positive real number 2. Choice **b** is incorrect because the left side factors as $(5x + 1)^2$, so that this equation has a repeated negative real solution, not two different negative real solutions. Choice **d** is incorrect because this equation has two complex conjugate solutions. Choice **e** is incorrect because the left side factors as $(2x - 1)(4x - 1)$. Setting each of these factors equal to zero yields $x = \frac{1}{2}, \frac{1}{4}$, which are not negative.

16. The correct answer is choice a. The median of this data set is the average of the 12th and 13th outcomes, namely $\frac{6 + 8}{2} = 7$. Choice **b** is incorrect because this middle number listed in the left column is not automatically the median; you must account for the different frequencies. Choice **c** is incorrect because this is the average of the 13th and 14th outcomes, but since there are 24 outcomes, you should have averaged the 12th and 13th outcomes. Choice **d** is incorrect because this is the mode, not the median. Choice **e** is incorrect because this is the mean, not the median.

17. The correct answer is choice e. Use the exponent rules to simplify as follows:

$$\frac{x^{\frac{3}{2}}}{x^{\frac{1}{4}}} = x^{\frac{3}{2} - \frac{1}{4}} = x^{\frac{5}{4}}$$

So, $\frac{5}{4}$ should be inserted in the box. Choice **a** is incorrect; $\frac{x^a}{x^b} = x^{a-b}$, not $x^{\frac{a}{b}}$. Choice **b** is incorrect because $\frac{x^a}{x^b} = x^{a-b}$, not x^{a+b}, and $\sqrt[m]{x^n} = x^{\frac{n}{m}}$, not $x^{\frac{m}{n}}$. Choice **c** is incorrect because $\sqrt[m]{x^n} = x^{\frac{n}{m}}$, not $x^{\frac{m}{n}}$. Choice **d** is incorrect because $\frac{x^a}{x^b} = x^{a-b}$, not x^{a+b}.

18. The correct answer is choice e. Let H be the height of the highest geyser. Set up a proportion: $\frac{H}{13} = \frac{x}{y}$. Solving for H then yields $H = \frac{13x}{y}$. Choice **a** is incorrect. You should multiply by 13, not divide by it. Choice **b** is incorrect because when solving a proportion for a specific quantity, you should cross-multiply, not cross-add. Choice **c** is incorrect because you should divide by y, not multiply by it. Choice **d** is incorrect because you interchanged x and y.

19. The correct answer is choice a. Let x be the number of quarters in the collection. There are $x - 2$ nickels and $2x + 1$ dimes. Multiply each quantity by the value of the type of coin, sum these totals, and set it equal to 3.50:

$$0.05(x - 2) + 0.10(2x + 1) + 0.25x = 3.50$$
$$0.50x - 0.10 + 0.10 = 3.50$$
$$x = 7$$

There are $7 - 2 = 5$ nickels. Choice **b** is incorrect because this is the number of quarters. Choice **c** is incorrect because this is twice the number of quarters; the number of nickels is two less than the number of quarters. Choice **d** is incorrect because this is the number of dimes. Choice **e** is incorrect because the monetary value of 5 nickels is 25 cents, but there are not 25 nickels in the collection.

20. **The correct answer is choice a.** Start by multiplying the two binomials inside the brackets, and then square the resulting quantity: $[(1 - 3x^2)(1 + 3x^2)]^2 = [1 - 9x^4]^2 = 1 - 9x^4 - 9x^4 + 81x^8 = 1 - 18x^4 + 81x^8$. Choice **b** is incorrect because you forgot to include the middle term (involving the x^4 terms), and the sign of the x^8 term should be positive. Choice **c** is incorrect because the exponent of the highest degree term should be 8, not 6. Choice **d** is incorrect because when you FOIL the binomials inside the brackets, you should get $1 - 9x^4$, not $1 - 6x^4$. Then, when you squared $1 - 6x^4$, you forgot the middle term. Choice **e** is incorrect because when you FOIL the binomials inside the brackets, you should get $1 - 9x^4$, not $1 - 6x^4$.

21. **The correct answer is choice b.** The number of hearts in one deck is 13, so there are 26 in the combined deck. The number of aces in one deck is 4, so there are 8 in the combined deck. There are two aces of hearts in the combined deck, and we do not want to count them twice. Hence, the desired probability is $\frac{26 + 8 - 2}{104} = \frac{32}{104} = \frac{4}{13}$. Choice **a** is incorrect because this is the probability of selecting neither a heart nor an ace. Choice **c** is incorrect because you counted the two aces of hearts twice. Choice **d** is incorrect because this is the probability of getting a heart, but you did not account for the possibility of getting an ace. Choice **e** is incorrect because this is the probability of getting an ace, but you did not account for the possibility of getting a heart.

22. **The correct answer is choice b.** The middle binomial factors as $(x - 1)(x + 1)$. So this function equals zero only when $x = -2, -1, 1,$ or 3. Choice **a** is incorrect. The zeros of the first and last factors are 2 and –3, respectively, and these are not among the given set of zeros. Choice **c** is incorrect because the first binomial factors as $(x - 2)(x + 2)$ and the first of these two linear factors is zero when $x = 2$. So the complete set of zeros for this polynomial includes 2. Choice **d** is incorrect because this polynomial has 0 as one of its zeros. Choice **e** is incorrect because this polynomial has –3 and 2 as zeros, but these are not included in the given set of zeros.

23. **The correct answer is choice c.** Solve the equation as follows:

$$2\sqrt{1 - x} - 10 = 0$$
$$2\sqrt{1 - x} = 10$$
$$\sqrt{1 - x} = 5$$
$$1 - x = 25$$
$$x = -24$$

Since this value satisfies the original equation, it is the one and only solution. Choice **a** is incorrect. When solving a linear equation $ax + b = c$, subtract b from both sides; do not add it. Choice **b** is incorrect because $\sqrt{a - b} \neq \sqrt{a} - \sqrt{b}$. Choice **d** is incorrect because you dropped the radical sign in the middle of the solution. Once you take 10 to the right side and divide by 2, the equation should be $\sqrt{1 - x} = 5$, not $1 - x = 5$. Choice **e** is incorrect because once you isolate the radical term and square both sides, you get an x-value that actually satisfies the original equation.

24. The correct answer is choice c. To find the midpoint, average the x- and y-coordinates: $(\frac{a+(a=6)}{2},\frac{(b-1)+(b-3)}{2})=(\frac{2a+6}{2},\frac{2b-4}{2})=(a+3,b-2)$. Choice **a** is incorrect because you seem to have eyeballed the location of the midpoint, but you must use the formula to find its exact coordinates. Choice **b** is incorrect because you subtracted the x- and y-coordinates instead of adding them. Choice **d** is incorrect because you cannot simplify fractions in this manner: $\frac{a+b}{a} \neq \frac{\cancel{a}+b}{\cancel{a}}$. Choice **e** is incorrect because you forgot to divide by 2 in each coordinate.

25. The correct answer is choice d. Apply the Pythagorean theorem using the lengths of the legs as 60 and 150. The length of the bridge is $\sqrt{60^2+150^2}$ feet. Choice **a** is incorrect because you should add the squares of the legs, not subtract them. Choice **b** is incorrect because you forgot the square root. Choice **c** is incorrect because you cannot simplify a square root of a sum in this manner: $\sqrt{a^2+b^2} \neq a+b$. Or you might have incorrectly assumed that the longest side is equal to the sum of the shorter sides. Choice **e** is incorrect because you must use the Pythagorean theorem, not simply subtract the lengths of the legs.

26. The correct answer is choice e. Suppose, for instance, that $a=\sqrt{2}$. Then $a^2=2$, which is rational. Choice **a** is incorrect because the sum of an irrational number and a rational number is irrational. Choice **b** is incorrect; since b is nonzero rational and a is irrational, the product must be irrational. Choice **c** is incorrect because $2b$ is rational and a is irrational, and the difference of a rational number and an irrational one is irrational. Choice **d** is incorrect because $\frac{a}{b}=\frac{1}{b}\cdot a$; here, $\frac{1}{b}$ is rational and a is irrational, and the product is therefore irrational.

27. The correct answer is choice b. Apply the distributive property and then combine terms like this:
$$3x(1-2x)+4x^2(x-3)-2x^3$$
$$=3x-6x^2+4x^3-12x^2-2x^3$$
$$=2x^3-18x^2+3x$$
Choice **a** is incorrect. You only multiplied the first term of each binomial by the expression outside; you must use the distributive property to correctly perform this multiplication. Choice **c** is incorrect because you only multiplied the first term of each binomial by the expression outside; you must use the distributive property to correctly perform this multiplication. You also ignored the $-2x^3$ term at the end. Choice **d** is incorrect because the sign of $18x^2$ is incorrect. Choice **e** is incorrect because the signs of the first and last terms are incorrect.

28. The correct answer is choice d. The first expression is the cost of the salad and the second term is the 6% tax on this cost; the sum is the total cost of the salad. Choice **a** is incorrect because you did not convert 6% to 0.06 before applying it to the cost of the salad. Choice **b** is incorrect because you forgot to include the tax. Choice **c** is incorrect because you did not apply 6% to the cost of the salad; you don't simply add 0.06 as a term by itself without applying it to a quantity. Choice **e** is incorrect because the initial cost (pretax) of the salad is wrong; you should only multiply the cost of a topping (0.80) by x, not also by the base price of the salad.

29. The correct answer is choice b. Solve the inequality as follows:

$$-x - 3[4(1 - 2x) + 5] > x$$
$$-x - 3[4 - 8x + 5] > x$$
$$-x - 12 + 24x - 15 > x$$
$$23x - 27 > x$$
$$22x > 27$$
$$x > \frac{27}{22}$$

So the solution set is $\{x \mid x > \frac{27}{22}\}$.

Choice **a** is incorrect because you canceled $-x$ on the left side with x on the right side and divided in the wrong manner: if $ax > b$, then $x > \frac{b}{a}$, not $x > \frac{a}{b}$. Choice **c** is incorrect because you only multiplied the first term in brackets by the -3 outside; you must apply the distributive property to perform this multiplication. Choice **d** is incorrect because this is the reciprocal of the correct answer. Choice **e** is incorrect because you canceled $-x$ on the left side with x on the right side.

30. The correct answer is choice a. Gather the terms without a y on one side, simplify, and then isolate y:

$$\frac{7}{x} - \frac{3}{y} = \frac{4}{2x}$$
$$\frac{7}{x} - \frac{4}{2x} = \frac{3}{y}$$
$$\frac{14 - 4}{2x} = \frac{3}{y}$$
$$\frac{5}{x} = \frac{3}{y}$$
$$5y = 3x$$
$$y = \frac{3}{5}x$$

Choice **b** is incorrect because you cannot flip fractions of a sum in this manner: $\frac{a}{b} + \frac{c}{d} \neq \frac{b}{a} + \frac{d}{c}$. Get a least common denominator and combine the fractions. Choice **c** is incorrect because you divided in the wrong manner: if $ax \leq b$, then $x \leq \frac{b}{a}$, not $x \geq \frac{a}{b}$. Choice **d** is incorrect because you cannot add fractions by simply adding their numerators and denominators; you need to get a least common denominator. Choice **e** is incorrect because you cannot flip fractions of a sum in this manner: $\frac{a}{b} + \frac{c}{d} \neq \frac{b}{a} + \frac{d}{c}$. Get a least common denominator and combine the fractions. Also, you divided in the wrong manner: if $ax \leq b$, then $x \leq \frac{b}{a}$, not $x \geq \frac{a}{b}$.

31. **The correct answer is choice d.** First, convert the quantities to ones involving the same power of 10. Note that $3.1 \times 10^5 = 31 \times 10^4$. So the difference is $(31 \times 10^4) - (2.3 \times 10^4) = (31 - 2.3) \times 10^4 = 28.7 \times 10^4 = 2.87 \times 10^5$. Choice **a** is incorrect. You added instead of subtracting and did so incorrectly; make certain that when adding or subtracting quantities expressed using scientific notation that you first represent them all using a common power of 10. Choice **b** is incorrect because you subtracted incorrectly. When adding or subtracting quantities expressed using scientific notation, you first represent them all using a common power of 10, and you cannot simply subtract exponents. Choice **c** is incorrect because you added instead of subtracting. Choice **e** is incorrect because you subtracted in the wrong order.

32. **The correct answer is choice b.** The equation is the standard form of a circle with center $(3,-1)$ and radius 2. The graph shown in this choice is such a circle. Choices **a** and **c** are incorrect because the circle's center should be $(3,-1)$. Choice **d** is incorrect because the circle's radius should be 2, not 4. Choice **e** is incorrect because the circle's center should be $(3,-1)$, and its radius should be 2, not 4.

33. **The correct answer is choice b.** Let x represent the number of points he must score in the seventh game. Compute the average as follows:

$$\frac{48 + 38 + 38 + 34 + 44 + 44 + x}{7} = 40$$

$$\frac{246 + x}{7} = 40$$

$$x = 280 - 246 = 34$$

So he must score 34 points.

Choice **a** is incorrect. This is the average of the first six games; scoring this many points in the seventh game would yield an average of 41, not 40. Choice **c** is incorrect because this would ensure that the mode is 44, but the mean would be higher than 40. Choice **d** is incorrect because this would ensure that the mode is 38, but the mean would be slightly higher than 40. Choice **e** is incorrect because this would require the average of the first six games to be 40, which it is not.

34. **The correct answer is choice e.** Forty people were asked the question and 11 of them responded that they prefer receiving a text message. This gives $\frac{11}{40} = 27.5\%$. So, you would expect 27.5% of 8,000 = 2,200 alumni to prefer receiving a text message. Choice **a** is incorrect because this is the number you would expect to prefer e-mail. Choice **b** is incorrect because this is the number you would expect to prefer a newsletter. Choice **c** is incorrect because this is the number you would expect to NOT prefer a text message. Choice **d** is incorrect because this is the number you would expect to prefer a phone call.

35. The correct answer is choice c. Let x = number of turkey sandwiches and y = number of roast beef sandwiches. The first equation of this system is the sum of the number of each type of sandwich, which is 12. The second equation gives the total cost as a sum of costs for each type of sandwich bought, which is also correct. Choice **a** is incorrect. The right sides of these equations should be interchanged. Choice **b** is incorrect because the cost equation (the first one) is wrong; multiply the number of each type of sandwich by the cost of that type of sandwich and add those two quantities. Choice **d** is incorrect because the right side of the first equation should be multiplied by 100. Choice **e** is incorrect because the first equation is wrong; this would require there to be at least 12 of one type of sandwich, which is not possible based on the information given.

36. The correct answer is choice d. These are the only x-values of points where the graph crosses or touches the x-axis. The x-coordinate of every such point is included in this set. So it is a complete set of zeros. Choice **a** is incorrect. You should not include in this set those x-values at which there is a maximum or a minimum value of the graph that does not sit on the x-axis. Choice **b** is incorrect because since the graph touches the x-axis at –6, –6 is a zero of the function. Choice **c** is incorrect because these are the x-values at which the graph has a maximum or a minimum, not the zeros. Choice **e** is incorrect because this is the y-value of the y-intercept, but the zeros are the x-values of the points at which the graph crosses the x-axis.

37. The correct answer is choice c. You must first complete the square to find the vertex:

$$y(x) = 2x^2 - 20x + 47$$
$$y(x) = 2(x^2 - 10x) + 47$$
$$y(x) = 2(x^2 - 10x + 25) + 47 - 50$$
$$y(x) = 2(x - 5)^2 - 3$$

The vertex is $(5, -3)$. Since the coefficient of the squared term is positive, the parabola opens up. So, the range includes all values starting at –3 and going up; that is, the range is $\{y \mid y \geq -3\}$. Choice **a** is incorrect because you must first complete the square to put the parabola into standard form; specifically, 47 is not the y-coordinate of the vertex. Also, since the coefficient of the squared term is positive, the range will extend to positive infinity, not negative infinity. Choice **b** is incorrect because this is the domain. No quadratic function has a range consisting of all real numbers because it has a maximum or minimum value at the vertex. Choice **d** is incorrect because you must first complete the square to put the parabola into standard form; specifically, 47 is not the y-coordinate of the vertex. Choice **e** is incorrect because the parabola opens up, not down.

38. The correct answer is choice b. Use the exponent rules to simplify, as follows:

$$2^4 \times 25^2 = 2^4 \times (5^2)^2 = 2^4 \times 5^4 = (2 \times 5)^4$$

Choice **a** is incorrect because you cannot combine the terms like this because the bases and exponents are both different in the given form. Choice **c** is incorrect because the bases are different so you cannot combine the terms by simply adding the exponents. Choice **d** is incorrect because $a^b \cdot c^b = (a \cdot c)^b$, not $a^b \cdot c^b = (a \cdot c)^{b+b}$. Choice **e** is incorrect because $a^b \cdot c^b = (a \cdot c)^b$, not $a^b \cdot c^b = (a \cdot c)^{b \cdot b}$.

39. **The correct answer is choice d.** The radius is 10 cm, so using the formula $S = r \cdot (\theta \cdot \frac{\pi}{180})$ yields

$$S = (10 \text{ cm}) \cdot (150 \cdot \tfrac{\pi}{180}) = \tfrac{25}{3}\pi \text{ cm}$$

Choice **a** is incorrect because this is the circumference of the entire circle, not just the arc of the shaded sector. Choice **b** is incorrect because you used the diameter instead of the radius in the arc length formula. Choice **c** is incorrect because you used the diameter instead of the radius in the arc length formula, and you did not multiply the angle by $\frac{\pi}{180}$. Choice **e** is incorrect because you did not multiply the angle by $\frac{\pi}{180}$.

40. **The correct answer is choice e.** Spins are independent of each other. So no matter how many times you were to spin the spinner, the probability would always be the same. Choice **a** is incorrect because this is the probability of getting red. Choice **b** is incorrect because there are not equal numbers of red and green spaces, so red and green are not equally likely. Choice **c** is incorrect because this is the probability of getting two greens in two spins, which is not the event for which the probability was asked. Choice **d** is incorrect because this event can happen.

41. **The correct answer is choice b.** Since y increases as x increases for this collection of points, the best fit line will rise from left to right and hence have a positive slope. Choice **a** is incorrect because there is always a best fit line, even for sporadically placed points. Choice **c** is incorrect because as x increases, y increases for this collection of points. A horizontal line would suggest no change in y. Choice **d** is incorrect because as x increases, y increases for this collection of points. A negative slope would suggest the y values decreased. Choice **e** is incorrect because as x increases, y increases for this collection of points. A vertical line would suggest no change in x.

42. **The correct answer is choice a.** Divide 2,871.46 by 31.2 to get 92.03397436. The zero is a significant digit, so rounding to three significant digits yields 92.0. Choice **b** is incorrect because you rounded to the ones digit incorrectly. The digit to its immediate right would need to be 5 or greater. Choice **c** is incorrect because the zero is a significant digit, so you rounded to four significant digits. Choice **d** is incorrect because the zero is a significant digit, so you rounded to four significant digits and did so incorrectly. Choice **e** is incorrect because the digits before the decimal point count toward the number of significant digits.

43. The correct answer is choice b. You can easily compare this option with option **c**, since they are both expressed in terms of $(\frac{2}{3})^t$, and see that the two options cannot be the same ($\frac{171}{2} \neq 38$). This option is the only one that cannot be transformed to look exactly like option **c**. Choice **a** is incorrect because if you change this equation so that it's expressed in terms of $(\frac{2}{3})^t$, you get $C = 57(\frac{2}{3})^{t+1} = 57 \cdot (\frac{2}{3}) \cdot (\frac{2}{3})^t = 38(\frac{2}{3})^t$, which is the same as option **c**. Options **d** and **e** can be transformed in the same way. Choice **c** is incorrect because when options **a**, **d**, and **e** are transformed so that they are also expressed in terms of $(\frac{2}{3})^t$, they look just like this option and are therefore equivalent to it. Only **b** cannot be made to look just like this option. Choice **d** is incorrect because if you change this equation so that it's expressed in terms of $(\frac{2}{3})^t$, you get

$C = 38\left(\frac{3}{2}\right)^{-t} = 38\left[\left(\frac{3}{2}\right)^{-1}\right]^t = 38\left(\frac{2}{3}\right)^t$, which is the same as option **c**. Options **a** and **e** can be transformed in the same way. Choice **e** is incorrect because if you change this equation so that it's expressed in terms of $(\frac{2}{3})^t$, you get

$C = \frac{76}{3}\left(\frac{3}{2}\right)^{1-t} = \frac{76}{3} \cdot \left(\frac{3}{2}\right) \cdot \left(\frac{3}{2}\right)^{-t} = 38\left(\frac{3}{2}\right)^{-t} = 38\left[\left(\frac{3}{2}\right)^{-1}\right]^t = 38\left(\frac{2}{3}\right)^t$. This expression is the same as option **c**. Options **a** and **e** can be transformed in the same way.

44. The correct answer is choice b. First get a least common denominator on the left side and combine the fractions. Then set the resulting numerator equal to zero and solve for x:

$$\frac{2}{x-3} - \frac{2}{2x-1} = 0$$
$$\frac{2(2x-1)}{(x-3)(2x-1)} - \frac{3(x-3)}{(x-3)(2x-1)} = 0$$
$$\frac{2(2x-1) - 3(x-3)}{(x-3)(2x-1)} = 0$$
$$\frac{4x - 2 - 3x + 9}{(x-3)(2x-1)} = 0$$
$$4x - 2 - 3x + 9 = 0$$
$$x + 7 = 0$$
$$x = -7$$

Since the solution is not extraneous, the solution set is {-7}.

Choice **a** is incorrect because you did not distribute the negative correctly through the second binomial when getting a least common denominator on the left side. Choice **c** is incorrect because this is the set of values that make the original expression in the equation undefined, not the solutions of the equation. A solution would make the numerator equal to zero and NOT the denominator. Choice **d** is incorrect because you did not distribute the quantities outside each binomial to both terms after getting a least common denominator. Choice **e** is incorrect because once you get a least common denominator, simplify, and set the resulting numerator equal to zero, the value you get, namely −7, is a solution of the original equation.

45. **The correct answer is choice d.** The diagonals are congruent. Use the Pythagorean theorem to determine the length of $\overline{SQ}$: $\sqrt{a^2 + x^2}$. Double this to get the desired sum. Choice **a** is incorrect because the lengths of the diagonals of a rectangle are the same, so they should be expressed using the same expression. Choice **b** is incorrect because the length of each diagonal is given by the Pythagorean theorem, which requires a square root. Choice **c** is incorrect because this is the perimeter of the rectangle, not the sum of the lengths of the diagonals. Choice **e** is incorrect because since both a and x are legs of a right triangle, their squares should be added inside the square root.

46. **The correct answer is choice d.** Let S be the original price. Then $x = S - \frac{p}{100}S = S\left(\frac{100 - p}{100}\right)$ dollars. So $S = \frac{100x}{100 - p}$. Choice **a** is incorrect because the denominator is wrong here. This would mean that the price was marked up by p percent, not down by p percent. Choice **b** is incorrect because this is the sale price, expressed as a percentage of the original price. Choice **c** is incorrect because you cannot cancel in fractions like this: $\frac{100x}{100 - p} \neq \frac{\cancel{100}x}{\cancel{100} - p}$. Choice **e** is incorrect because this is the price you would get by applying a discount of $p\%$ to the discounted price x.

47. **The correct answer is choice b.** First rewrite the system in standard form:
$$\begin{cases} 2x - y = 1 \\ x + 2y = 1 \end{cases}$$
Multiply the first equation by 2: $4x - 2y = 2$. Add this equation to the second one to cancel the y terms: $5x = 3$, so $x = \frac{3}{5}$. Now substitute this into the first equation to get $2\left(\frac{3}{5}\right) - y = 1$, so $y = \frac{1}{5}$. So the solution of the system is $x = \frac{3}{5}$, $y = \frac{1}{5}$. Choice **a** is incorrect because this satisfies the second equation, but not the first. So it is not a solution of the system. Choice **c** is incorrect because when you multiplied the first equation of the system by 2 (to eliminate the terms), you forgot to multiply the constant term by 2. Choice **d** is incorrect because it satisfies the first equation but not the second one. So it is not a solution of the system. Choice **e** is incorrect because you added the left and right sides, but you cannot combine $2x$ and $-2y$ to get zero since they are not like terms.

48. **The correct answer is choice b.** The statement is false. When you reflect the graph over the line $y = x$, the resulting graph is not of a function, since it would not pass the vertical line test. There is no inverse. Choice **a** is incorrect because the statement is true. There are points associated with every x-value in this interval. Choice **c** is incorrect because the statement is true. The smallest y-value is –4, and this occurs when $x = 4$. Choice **d** is incorrect because the statement is true. Every y-value in this interval is the output for at least one x-value. Choice **e** is incorrect because the statement is true. The graph rises from left to right as x moves through this interval.

49. The correct answer is choice b. The average value of a function on a given interval (a,b) is $\frac{f(b)-f(a)}{b-a}$. Applying this gives $\frac{5-1}{1-(-1)}=2$, which is the largest of all average values listed in the other choices. Choice **a** is incorrect because this average value is negative, which is smaller than $(-1,1)$. Choice **c** is incorrect because this average value is 1, which is smaller than $(-1,1)$. Choice **d** is incorrect because this average value is 0, which is smaller than $(-1,1)$. Choice **e** is incorrect because this average value is negative, which is smaller than $(-1,1)$.

50. The correct answer is choice c. Solve the following equation for v_0:

$$140 = \tfrac{1}{2}g(3)^2 + v_0(3) + 205$$
$$\tfrac{1}{3}\left(140 - \tfrac{9}{2}g - 205\right) = v_0$$
$$\tfrac{1}{3}\left(-65 - \tfrac{9}{2}g\right) = v_0$$
$$-\tfrac{1}{6}(130 + 9g) = v_0$$

Choice **a** is incorrect. When solving the equation $140 = \tfrac{1}{2}g(3)^2 + v_0(3) + 205$, note that $3^2 = 9$, not 6. Choice **b** is incorrect because this expression results from interchanging the meanings of s_0 and v_0. Choice **d** is incorrect because this expression results from using $v_0 = 140$ instead of $s_0 = 140$. Choice **e** is incorrect because you used $v_0 = 140$ instead of $s_0 = 140$ and mistakenly computed 3^2 as 6.

Science

To calculate your HiSET® score on the Science section, first take a look at the correct answer for each of the 50 questions of the exam. Count up your **correct answers** only, and give yourself 1 point for each. Then, add up all of your points. This is your **raw score**.

Find your raw score and your **scaled score** in the following table. Remember, for each test section, a passing score is 8. (For the essay, a passing score is 2.)

You need a scaled score of 45 to pass the complete HiSET® exam.

SCIENCE SCORING			
RAW	SCALED	RAW	SCALED
0	1	26	12
1	1	27	12
2	2	28	12
3	2	29	13
4	3	30	13
5	3	31	13
6	4	32	13
7	5	33	14
8	6	34	14
9	7	35	14
10	8	36	14
11	8	37	15
12	8	38	15
13	9	39	15
14	9	40	15
15	9	41	16
16	10	42	16
17	10	43	16
18	10	44	17
19	10	45	17
20	10	46	18
21	11	47	18
22	11	48	19
23	11	49	20
24	11	50	20
25	12		

1. **The correct answer is choice b.** The tested variable in this experiment is the presence or absence of light, which the experimenter changed by applying the black paper; this is the independent variable. The dependent variable that was measured in this experiment was the color change on the leaf. Choice **a** is incorrect because the tested variable in this experiment is the presence or absence of light, which the experimenter changed by applying the black paper; this is the independent variable. The dependent variable that was measured in this experiment was the color change on the leaf. Choice **c** is incorrect because the tested variable in this experiment is the presence or absence of light, which the experimenter changed by applying the black paper; this is the independent variable. The dependent variable that was measured in this experiment was the color change on the leaf. Choice **d** is incorrect because the tested variable in this experiment is the presence or absence of light, which the experimenter changed by applying the black paper; this is the independent variable. The dependent variable that was measured in this experiment was the color change on the leaf.

2. **The correct answer is choice a.** Since the parts of the leaf blocked from the light did not undergo photosynthesis to produce starch, while those that were exposed to the light did perform photosynthesis to produce starch, it can be concluded that the presence of light is essential for photosynthesis.

3. **The correct answer is choice b.** The purpose of the plant incubation in the dark is to remove all starch (glucose) so that there is no glucose in the plant at the start of the experiment. Skipping the incubation in the dark means that the entire leaf will have starch initially, and even the parts of the leaf that are not undergoing photosynthesis will still contain starch as a result. Since iodine detects starch, the addition of iodine would cause the entire leaf to turn bluish black because starch would be present everywhere.

4. **The correct answer is choice d.** By removing the chlorophyll, the experimenter was able to halt any photosynthesis in its tracks and detect the produced starch based on its presence immediately upon removal from the light incubation step.

5. **The correct answer is choice a.** Only this procedure appropriately uses the noted detection method to determine photosynthetic production via starch detection while also testing dryness in comparison with a wet trial. Choice **b** is incorrect because this procedure appropriately uses the noted detection method to determine photosynthetic production via starch detection, but it addresses the effect of water presence in overload instead of dryness. It also lacks a control. Choices **c** and **d** are incorrect because these procedures appropriately use the noted detection method to determine photosynthetic production via starch detection, but do not address the presence of water.

6. **The correct answer is choice b.** This hypothesis correctly focuses on temperature as the independent variable and makes the reasonable assumption that increased interactions among molecules will allow for the reaction to occur more frequently and therefore more rapidly. Choices **a** and **c** are incorrect because these hypotheses focus on pressure as the independent variable rather than temperature. Choice **d** is incorrect because this hypothesis correctly focuses on temperature as the independent variable, but it is not reasonable to assume that increased interactions between molecules will cause the reaction to occur more slowly.

7. **The correct answer is choice d.** According to the passage, R^2 values close to 1 indicate that the best-fit line was very close to the data points, while lower R^2 values indicate increased deviation of the line from the data. The lowest R^2 value would therefore describe the line that most deviated from the data, and this occurred at 70°C.

8. **The correct answer is choice c.** Based on the data, and logically, as the reaction rate increases for a chemical reaction, it will take less time for the concentration of reactant to be halved.

9. **The correct answer is choice d.** You can never say that data evidence proves or disproves a conclusion; you can only state that it supports or does not support a given hypothesis or prediction. In this case, the data provide support for the given statement because reaction rate appears to increase as temperature increases. Choices **a** and **b** are incorrect because you can never say that data evidence proves or disproves a conclusion; you can only state that it supports or does not support a given hypothesis or prediction. Choice **c** is incorrect because in this case, the data provide support for the given statement because reaction rate appears to increase as temperature increases.

10. **The correct answer is choice a.** As with many biomolecules, high temperature causes denaturation, compromising the structure and function of PhzO. Choice **b** is incorrect because the same dependent variable—reaction rate—is being measured in this hypothetical experiment since the same setup is being used. Choice **c** is incorrect because this kind of R^2 trend does not have any support from the data. Choice **d** is incorrect because the procedure indicates that initial rate data were taken over the first hour, so it would not take days to collect that data, even though the half-lives of the reactions are relatively long.

11. The correct answer is choice c. Nowhere in this study do the scientists control for the average number of predators who normally visited each location. Choice **a** is incorrect because the total bar sizes in the graphs provide the total number of predators who visited each location. Choice **b** is incorrect because the bar graph bars are broken down into the types of predators who visited each location. Choice **d** is incorrect because the comparison of each bar for the "2 mice" and "6 mice" locations provides a proportion of predators who visited locations with stronger versus weaker scents.

12. The correct answer is choice c. Neither snakes nor cats visited the unscented control locations. Choices **a**, **b**, and **d** are incorrect because foxes regularly visited both scented and unscented locations throughout the duration of the experiment.

13. The correct answer is choice b. The function of a control is to serve as an unaffected point of comparison for the test groups. Here, the unscented control shows the predators typically attracted to unscented locations for comparison to the predators typically attracted to scented locations. Choice **a** is incorrect because only one prey type (mice) was tested. Choice **c** is incorrect because the control location was unscented. Choice **d** is incorrect because the control is a negative control; a positive control might attract a more complete array of predators to show the diversity of a region.

14. The correct answer is choice c. You can never say that data evidence proves or disproves a conclusion; you can only state that it supports or does not support a given hypothesis or prediction. In this case, the data do not support the given statement because the locations with weaker scents (2 mice) attracted more predators than locations with stronger scents (6 mice).

15. The correct answer is choice a. For the "2 mice" scented group, the total number of visiting predators was 7 after the first two days, but only 2 more visited over the next four days. For the "6 mice" scented group, the total number of visiting predators was 5 after the first two days, but only 2 more visited over the next four days. For the unscented control plot, 1 predator visited after the first two days, and 3 more visited over the next four days. Therefore, the number of visiting predators was highest over the first two days for the scented locations and highest over the latter four days for the unscented locations.

16. The correct answer is choice d. Reflex time is the dependent variable, and hours slept is the independent variable. Choices **a** and **b** are incorrect because reflex time is one of the variables, but gender and sleep location are irrelevant to the study of interest. Choice **c** is incorrect because reflex time and hours slept are the variables, but this question has them swapped. Reflex time is the dependent variable, and hours slept is the independent variable.

17. The correct answer is choice d. The smallest effect between the trials would be the trial with the two numbers that are closest together. The differences in measurements between the trials were 2.0 inches for Subject #1, 2.8 inches for Subject #2, 1.3 inches for Subject #3, and 0.1 inches for Subject #4. The smallest number of this bunch, by far, is 0.1 for Subject #4, so Subject #4 was least affected by the difference in sleep times between the trials.

18. The correct answer is choice a. For all four trials, the reflex times after no sleep were slower than the reflex times after 9+ hours of sleep. Therefore, less sleep results in slower reflex times. Choices **c** and **d** are incorrect because since reflex times are the dependent variable, differences in reflex times are not the cause of the sleep times; the opposite is true.

19. The correct answer is choice b. Increasing the number of trials is usually a surefire way to increase the reliability of experimental results. Choice **a** is incorrect because using only male subjects limits the scope of the experiment and decreases its reliability. Choice **c** is incorrect because measuring in feet with a yardstick would give the same results with larger, less exact units. Choice **d** is incorrect because using fewer test subjects limits the scope of the experiment and decreases its reliability.

20. The correct answer is choice b. The ruler's starting point relative to each test subject's hand was the same for all experimental trials. Choice **a** is incorrect because reflex time is the dependent variable. Choice **c** is incorrect because four different test subjects were used throughout the experiment. Choice **d** is incorrect because the number of hours slept is the independent variable.

21. The correct answer is choice d. A larger change in temperature is indicative of greater heat absorption. Choice **a** is incorrect because time spent in sunlight may correlate with heat absorption, but it is not the independent variable. Measuring time is not the way heat absorption is detected. Choice **b** is incorrect because paper color may correlate with heat absorption, but it is not the way heat absorption is detected. Choice **c** is incorrect because initial temperature does not provide any information about heat absorption; it simply indicates the temperature at which measurements were first taken.

22. The correct answer is choice a. The slope is steeper in the first time period line segment for the yellow line than for the other two time periods. Alternatively, reading the temperatures on the y-axis indicates that the temperature increased by twice as much during the first time period compared with either of the other two time periods.

23. The correct answer is choice b. The black paper saw the greatest temperature increase, while the white paper saw the smallest temperature increase, with yellow and blue falling in between. A greater increase in temperature indicates more heat absorbed, so the conclusion that can be drawn is that darker colors tend to absorb more heat over time than lighter colors when placed in sunlight.

24. The correct answer is choice d. Black absorbed more heat than any other tested color, based on the data.

25. The correct answer is choice c. The barometric pressure does not really affect any aspect of this experiment. Choice **a** is incorrect because variations in the outdoor temperature would affect both the initial temperature and temperature change. Choice **b** is incorrect because variations in the time of day would affect the amount of sunlight directed at the paper. Choice **d** is incorrect because variations in the paper colors would give completely different data.

26. The correct answer is choice a. *Precision* refers to how close repeated trials in a data set are to one another, so the rock type with the most precise data will be the one with numbers that are closest to one another.

27. The correct answer is choice b. Porous rocks will exhibit small times for soaking up the oil because they have larger holes into which liquid can seep. Therefore, sandstone and limestone are likely sedimentary because their soaking times are significantly lower than those of mudstone and slate.

28. **The correct answer is choice d.** Reservoir rocks are porous rocks that may contain resources in those pores. Based on the data, sandstone and limestone are more porous than mudstone or slate, as their soaking times are much smaller than those of mudstone or slate, so sandstone and limestone would make for better reservoir rocks than the other two rock types. Choices **a** and **b** are incorrect because you can never say that data evidence proves or disproves a conclusion; you can only state that it supports or does not support a given hypothesis or prediction. Choice **c** is incorrect because reservoir rocks are porous rocks that may contain resources in those pores. Based on the data, sandstone and limestone are more porous than mudstone or slate, as their soaking times are much smaller than those of mudstone or slate, so sandstone and limestone would make for better reservoir rocks than the other two rock types.

29. **The correct answer is choice a.** Six drops of oil were applied to each rock in every trial. Choice **b** is incorrect because the type of rock is varied and is the independent variable. Choice **c** is incorrect because the rock mass was the same in each trial, but it cannot be stated definitely that the volume was the same in every trial due to internal porosity, so the density was not a constant among the trials. Choice **d** is incorrect because the soaking time is the dependent variable.

30. **The correct answer is choice b.** Performing additional trials of the same experiment would give additional information about both slate and mudstone, and this might either confirm the higher soaking time recorded for slate or suggest that it is an outlier. Choice **a** is incorrect because using natural gas would test a different phenomenon: gas absorption rather than oil absorption. Choice **c** is incorrect because while testing additional rock types would provide additional soaking data, these additional data would not provide any further insight into whether slate or mudstone has the longer soaking time. Choice **d** is incorrect because converting the times from minutes to seconds does not provide any new information.

31. **The correct answer is choice b.** The mass of Na is varied and is the independent variable. Choice **a** is incorrect because the mass of NaCl produced in the reaction is the dependent variable, not the independent variable. Choice **c** is incorrect because the mass of Cl_2 is a constant in the experiment because it is always the same for every trial. Choice **d** is incorrect because the sealed reaction chamber is a constant in the experiment because it is always the same for every trial.

32. The correct answer is choice b. The data show that increasing the mass of input Na increases the mass of NaCl produced in the reaction. Doubling the input Na mass doubles the output NaCl mass, so this is an increasing linear relationship. Choice **a** is incorrect because the data show that increasing the mass of input Na increases the mass of NaCl produced in the reaction. Since the graph does not correspond with this relationship, it can be ruled out. Choice **c** is incorrect because doubling the input Na mass doubles the output NaCl mass, so this is an increasing linear relationship. This graph does not represent a linear relationship. Choice **d** is incorrect because the data show that increasing the mass of input Na increases the mass of NaCl produced in the reaction. Since this graph does not correspond with this relationship, it can be ruled out.

33. The correct answer is choice c. Accuracy describes how close an experimental value is to theoretical value. Choices **a** and **b** are incorrect because precision describes how close values for various repeated trials are to one another.

34. The correct answer is choice b. 1.50 g falls between 1.00 and 2.00 g, which are two Na masses tested during this experiment. The mass of NaCl produced by 1.50 g Na should therefore fall between the corresponding masses of NaCl produced by 1.00 and 2.00 g Na, which are 5.08 g and 10.17 g, respectively.

35. The correct answer is choice a. To test the effect of Na mass on NaCl production, the setup was arranged with Na as the limiting reactant and Cl_2 as the excess reactant. Therefore, to test the effect of Cl_2 mass on NaCl production, the setup must be arranged with Cl_2 as the limiting reactant and Na as the excess reactant.

36. The correct answer is choice b. Species richness and seed density are the two variables that are measured, so they are the two dependent variables in the study.

37. The correct answer is choice a. Because all measurements occur on the same Tibetan plateau, the geographical region is constant throughout the study. Choice **b** is incorrect because the water level is an independent variable because it is varied over the course of the experiment. Choice **c** is incorrect because the soil depth is an independent variable because it is varied over the course of the experiment. Choice **d** is incorrect because water alkalinity may be considered an independent variable because one of the environments is a saline-alkaline wetland.

38. The correct answer is choice a. For nearly every soil depth in the typical wetland (T), a higher water level correlates with decreased species richness. Choices **c** and **d** are incorrect because there are no really clear-cut patterns of correlation between soil depth and species richness because the data plateau, particularly between 5 and 10 cm, or diverge at some point from a potential consistent trend.

39. The correct answer is choice a. Of the four options, choice **a** is the largest; it is the only one that significantly exceeds 3 on the seed density axis (log scale), with or without error bars.

40. The correct answer is choice d. Error bars encompass the data points that contribute to the mean/average represented in the bar graph. Therefore, larger bars represent decreased precision because they indicate that the contributing values are further away from one another.

41. The correct answer is choice b. Average number of cells in telophase = $\frac{1+2+0+1}{4} = 1$.

42. The correct answer is choice c. The key distinction between plant and animal cells that accounts for the need for HCl and Carnoy's fixative is the cell wall, which is made of cellulose and is tough to penetrate. The breakdown of the cell wall by the chemicals allows for dye entry so that the chromosomes can be marked by the dye.

43. The correct answer is choice b. The dependent variable, which is the measured variable, is the number of cells counted per phase. Choice **a** is incorrect because the phases of mitosis are the independent variable. Choice **c** is incorrect because the number of seconds spent in each phase is not relevant to this experiment, but it describes another potential experiment that could provide further insight into the scientific question. Choice **d** is incorrect because the total number of cells is a constant, not a dependent variable.

44. The correct answer is choice a. The largest numbers of cells by far on each slide are seen in interphase; this indicates that cells more often than not tend to be found in interphase.

45. The correct answer is choice b. Since the dye specifically colors chromosomes, the intensification of the color of the nucleus must be due to an increase in chromosome concentration, and only chromosome duplicates satisfy this criterion.

46. The correct answer is choice c. The scientific question asks whether exercise serum affects cancerous cell lines, so a solid point of comparison would be to repeat the experiment with a non-cancerous cell line to show that the behavior of the cancerous cells is actually specific to cancerous cells. Choice **a** is incorrect because testing a wider range of times would provide significantly more data, but it would not serve as a control. Choice **b** is incorrect because another trial at warmer temperature is a possible additional experiment to perform, but it would not be a valid control because temperature is not a relevant independent variable. Choice **d** is incorrect because a trial using only female donors is a possible additional experiment to perform, but it would not be a valid control because test subject sex is not a relevant independent variable. Additionally, it would not be especially relevant to test a prostate cancer cell line using female serum samples since females do not have prostate glands.

47. The correct answer is choice c. Individual 37 is the only one in which the cell proliferation in the cells incubated with the "exercise" serum exceeded that in the cells incubated with the "rest" serum.

48. The correct answer is choice c. Based on Figure 1, the bars on the graphs grew most drastically between 48 and 96 hours. Choices **a** and **b** are incorrect because this time period showed much less growth than the last 48 hours. Choice **d** is incorrect because the time period after 96 hours was not tested, so there are no data to support this conclusion.

49. The correct answer is choice d. You can never say that data evidence proves or disproves a conclusion; you can only state that it supports or does not support a given hypothesis or prediction. In this case, the data provide support for the given statement because incubations that occurred in the presence of the "exercise" serum in Figures 1 and 2 exhibited lower levels of cell proliferation than those that occurred in the presence of the "rest" serum or in the presence of no serum. Choices **a** and **b** are incorrect because you can never say that data evidence proves or disproves a conclusion; you can only state that it supports or does not support a given hypothesis or prediction.

50. The correct answer is choice a. Changing the exercise duration only affects the test subject preparation and therefore the serum, so choices **b** and **c** are incorrect because the cell incubation and cell type should not be changed. Choice **d** is incorrect because the scientists want to switch the duration of exercise, not the type of exercise.

Social Studies

To calculate your HiSET® score on the Social Studies section, first take a look at the correct answer for each of the 50 questions of the exam. Count up your **correct answers** only, and give yourself 1 point for each. Then, add up all of your points. This is your **raw score**.

Find your raw score and your **scaled score** in the following table. Remember, for each test section, a passing score is 8. (For the essay, a passing score is 2.)

You need a scaled score of 45 to pass the complete HiSET® exam.

SOCIAL STUDIES SCORING			
RAW	SCALED	RAW	SCALED
0	1	26	12
1	1	27	12
2	2	28	12
3	2	29	13
4	3	30	13
5	3	31	13
6	4	32	13
7	5	33	14
8	6	34	14
9	7	35	14
10	8	36	14
11	8	37	15
12	8	38	15
13	9	39	15
14	9	40	15
15	9	41	16
16	10	42	16
17	10	43	16
18	10	44	17
19	10	45	17
20	10	46	18
21	11	47	18
22	11	48	19
23	11	49	20
24	11	50	20
25	12		

1. **The correct answer is choice c.** Freed African Americans faced uncertain futures when the Civil War ended. Most had lost their homes and the means to support themselves and their families. By establishing the Freedmen's Bureau, Congress believed it could provide immediate aid to those in need and a foundation upon which freed African Americans could build new lives. Choice **a** is incorrect because it cannot be validated from information in the passage. Choice **b** is incorrect because although the Freedmen's Bureau may have provided some economic stimulus in the South, there is nothing in the passage that states it was the main goal of the bureau. Choice **d** is incorrect because the passage does not mention the Freedmen's Bureau trying to return African Americans to the South.

2. **The correct answer is choice b.** Among the rights provided in the Bill of Rights to the U.S. Constitution is the right of American citizens to be "secure in their persons, houses, papers, and effects, against unreasonable searches and seizures." President Andrew Johnson and many in Congress rejected the idea because it violated individual property rights. Choice **a** is incorrect because the passage makes no mention of religious beliefs influencing some Americans to think that seizing the lands was wrong. Choice **c** is incorrect because the concept of "states' rights" was a key concern for many Southerners, but this claim is not supported by information in the passage. Choice **d** is incorrect because separation of powers is a system in which branches of government balance power and is not relevant to the situation described.

3. **The correct answer is choice a.** The key word in this statement is *perhaps*. Definitions for *perhaps* include possibly, conceivably, and imaginably. Beginning the statement with this word signifies that the writer is presenting an opinion about the Freedmen's Bureau's role in education. Choice **b** is incorrect because an observation is a statement about something a person notices, which could be an opinion or a fact. In this context, "observation" is not the best answer. Choice **c** is incorrect because the idea expressed in the statement could not have been reached through scientific methods. Choice **d** is incorrect because the statement cannot be proven true.

4. **The correct answer is choice d.** Identifying the main idea of the entire passage requires understanding the key concepts from both paragraphs. Only this title reflects those key concepts. Choice **a** is incorrect because policy successes are mentioned in the passage, but this title does not accurately reflect the key ideas and descriptions in both paragraphs. Choice **b** is incorrect because the emergence of sharecropping during Reconstruction is mentioned in the passage, but this title does not accurately reflect the key ideas and descriptions in both paragraphs. Choice **c** is incorrect because political conflict is mentioned in the passage, but this title does not accurately reflect the key ideas and descriptions in both paragraphs.

5. **The correct answer is choice b.** Based on information in the passage, Congress, the president, and the Freedmen's Bureau were unable to agree on the most effective policies to provide freed African Americans with their own land. Choice **a** is incorrect because the passage makes no statement suggesting that the amount of fertile land was insufficient. Choice **c** is incorrect because nowhere in the passage is it stated that the Freedmen's Bureau worked to return African Americans to their former homes. Choice **d** is incorrect because although many in Congress opposed the seizing of former Confederate lands, they did so on the basis of individual property rights, not because the land would be given to African Americans.

6. **The correct answer is choice b.** Most citizens and representatives of the states had lived through the colonial rule of the British government. They had fought a bloody war to win their independence and the right of self-government. The states did not want to risk the possibility of another strong central government that might oppress and restrict their rights and liberty. Choice **a** is incorrect because there is no information in the passage to support this statement. Choice **c** is incorrect because although state leaders wanted to retain as much power as possible to govern themselves, they realized that wartime powers were best left to a central government. Choice **d** is incorrect because state leaders did not want to discard all forms of taxation. Taxes were needed to fund governments.

7. **The correct answer is choice a.** The most likely result would have been the breakup of the states, with power reverting back to the individual states. Choice **b** is incorrect because the Revolutionary War proved very expensive and difficult for the British. There was no support for the return of British rule either from the English or the victorious colonists. Choice **c** is incorrect because the passage describes the fear and contempt Americans held for the colonial British government, which was controlled by the English king. The passage offers no reason to think Americans would embrace an American monarchy. Choice **d** is incorrect because the passage says that state representatives at the time believed that a one-house legislature was a sound way of limiting power of the Confederation Congress. The states most likely would not have supported a bicameral legislature at that time.

8. **The correct answer is choice b.** The most serious issue facing the country was the inability of the Confederation Congress to impose taxes to pay off the debts incurred from the war against Great Britain. Choice **a** is incorrect because leadership and governing issues facing the new country were mainly caused by a weak and ineffective Congress, not an overbearing one. Choice **c** is incorrect because the Articles of Confederation granted the Confederation Congress the power to deal with foreign nations. Choice **d** is incorrect because although armed rebellions did occur, the root causes were usually financial and often led back to the inability of Congress to tax and secure revenue from the states.

9. **The correct answer is choice d.** One legislature that set laws for all the states was needed to maintain the Union. Choice **a** is incorrect because Washington would have no doubt desired a strong leader but would not have advocated a dictatorial government or leader. Choice **b** is incorrect because there is no support in Washington's statement to back up potential citizen uprisings. Choice **c** is incorrect because Washington and other Americans thought exactly the opposite. Washington's statement expresses his opinion that the Confederation Congress was too limited and weak to effectively govern the entire country.

10. **The correct answer is choice c.** The Tenth Amendment grants powers to the states that were not given to the federal government. These powers are "checks" on the "necessary and proper" power of the federal government, which is provided for in Article I, Section 8 of the Constitution. Choice **a** is incorrect because the supremacy clause does not limit the federal government; it recognizes the Constitution and federal laws as supreme. Choice **b** is incorrect because the amendment process does not limit the federal government. Amendments might restrict or expand the powers of the federal government, but the process does not. Choice **d** is incorrect because limiting state powers would grant the federal government even more power.

11. **The correct answer is choice a.** This statement cannot be either proved or disproved.

12. **The correct answer is choice b.** The "supremacy clause" prevents conflicts between state, local, and federal laws by placing federal, or constitutional, laws above the others. Choice **a** is incorrect because the Constitution protects the rights of Americans to challenge federal laws. Choice **c** is incorrect because this statement cannot be supported by the passage. Choice **d** is incorrect because the supremacy clause is relevant in situations where state and federal laws are in conflict, not the same.

13. **The correct answer is choice d.** Written after the ratification of the Constitution, the Tenth Amendment protects civil liberties and places limits on the power of the federal government. The Bill of Rights was written in response to concerns many Americans had about protecting civil liberties. Choice **a** is incorrect because proponents of a strong federal government would not want the states to retain more powers. Choice **b** is incorrect because the Tenth Amendment does not negate the powers of Congress granted in Article IV. Choice **c** is incorrect because the Tenth Amendment does not limit the voices of common citizens; it gives citizens powers that are not specifically given to Congress.

14. **The correct answer is choice b.** Each item on the timeline describes an innovation or aspect of communications technologies. Choices **a**, **c**, and **d** are incorrect because each item on the timeline describes an innovation or aspect of communications technologies, and these choices describe only specific areas within the communications field.

15. **The correct answer is choice d.** Three of the eight items listed on the timeline involve entertainment innovations. Based on this evidence, this statement is the most plausible of the answers. Choice **a** is incorrect because the timeline states that American phone companies developed a cell phone system in 1983. Choice **b** is incorrect because information in the timeline does not support this claim. Choice **c** is incorrect because the items listed on the timeline do not support this statement.

16. **The correct answer is choice c.** Considering all the answers, the spread of personal computers is the most plausible. To use the World Wide Web initially, people needed computers. As personal computers became more common, more and more people accessed the Web. Choice **a** is incorrect because although the number of multinational corporations may have increased, one cannot make the correlation between them and the rise of the World Wide Web. Choice **b** is incorrect because start-up companies more than likely helped advance the spread of the World Wide Web, but they were not the primary reason for the growth. Choice **d** is incorrect because computer science education drove interest and expertise in computer technologies, but it did not have the impact of the spread of personal computers, many used by people without formal computer education.

17. **The correct answer is choice a.** Within the time period of 1982–1985, the timeline lists four communication innovations. Choices **b**, **c**, and **d** are incorrect because these time periods contain only three innovations each.

18. **The correct answer is choice b.** The government projects that the number of home health aides will increase by 38.1% from 2014 to 2024—considerably more than the other occupations. Choice **a** is incorrect because the government projects that the number of construction laborers will increase by only 12.7% from 2014 to 2024. Choice **c** is incorrect because office clerks are projected to show the slowest growth of the occupations on the chart. Choice **d** is incorrect because computer systems analysts will increase at a 20.9% rate, but still lower than home health aides.

19. **The correct answer is choice c.** By 2024, there will be 686,300 computer systems analysts. This is over a half million fewer workers than the next lowest occupation. Choice **a** is incorrect because by 2024, there will be more registered nurses than any other occupation on the chart. Choice **b** is incorrect because personal care aides, as one of the fastest growing occupations, will top several other occupations in total workers by 2024. Choice **d** is incorrect because the increase in the number of construction laborers is slowing but still producing more workers than the computer systems analyst occupation.

20. **The correct answer is choice b.** Median annual wage data only covers wages reported in 2014. Wages for 2024 cannot be verified by the information on this chart. Choice **a** is incorrect because this statement can be verified in the "% Change" column; no occupation shows a decline. Choice **c** is incorrect because the percent change in construction workers can be confirmed in the "% Change" column. Choice **d** is incorrect because the salary figures in the far-right column show the salaries of registered nurses and home health aides.

21. **The correct answer is choice a.** Of the possible choices, computer systems analyst would be the strongest recommendation. This occupation is projected to grow significantly by 2024, and the annual median wage is the highest. Choice **b** is incorrect because the median annual wage for personal care aides is considerably less than for computer systems analysts. Choice **c** is incorrect because construction laborers will see relatively slow growth and a fairly low median annual wage. Choice **d** is incorrect because registered nurses would be the second best recommendation.

22. **The correct answer is choice d.** Using the scale at the bottom right, one can measure the approximate distant between the two points to be around 90 miles. Choice **a** is incorrect because this distance is too short. Choice **b** is incorrect because this distance is considerably off, according to the scale. Choice **c** is incorrect because this distance is considerably off, according to the scale.

23. **The correct answer is choice c.** The interior of Hawaii is hilly and rises to two large mountains, Mauna Loa and Mauna Kea. Choice **a** is incorrect because the color-coded elevation scale clearly shows the interior is not flat. Choice **b** is incorrect because there are no valleys in the interior that are shown on the map. Choice **d** is incorrect because very few roads traverse the interior, and according to the map, no cities or communities are located in the interior.

24. **The correct answer is choice d.** The map shows the communities on the island, with Hilo identified as the only large community. In addition, there are no cities, villages, or communities identified in the interior of the island. Choice **a** is incorrect because the map does not show industrial centers. Choice **b** is incorrect because the map does not show information about the tourism industry. Choice **c** is incorrect because there is no information on the map that can support this claim.

25. **The correct answer is choice a.** The small projection map in the upper right corner identifies the location of the Hawaiian Islands. Choice **b** is incorrect because the island of Hawaii is identified with a box around it in the insert map, showing that it is the largest of the Hawaiian Islands. Choice **c** is incorrect because the projection map in the upper right corner identifies the location of the Hawaiian Islands. In addition, labels on the main map identify the surrounding water as the Pacific Ocean. Choice **d** is incorrect because shipping and trade information is not presented on the map.

26. **The correct answer is choice c.** Lincoln states that American citizens have the right to amend, or change, the government through the constitutional and democratic process. If that fails, citizens also have the right to rebel and overthrow the government. Choice **a** is incorrect because Lincoln suggests two possible options. Choice **b** is incorrect because Lincoln is not recommending scrapping the Constitution, but rather working within it. Choice **d** is incorrect because Lincoln does not suggest reorganizing institutions.

27. **The correct answer is choice a.** By describing the processes through which citizens can change their government, Lincoln is reinforcing the American democratic concept that the people hold the true power in the United States. Choice **b** is incorrect because Lincoln outlines a "right" of citizens to rebel. Choice **c** is incorrect because the idea that the Constitution should never be amended without government approval first is incorrect. The Constitution provides a process for changing it. Choice **d** is incorrect because, as Lincoln stated, the institutions of government ultimately belong to and are shaped by the citizens, not the other way around.

28. The correct answer is choice b. The passage states that voting in the North was less restrictive than in the South. The implication is that Southern states limited or made it difficult for African Americans to vote. Choice **a** is incorrect because this statement is not supported by information in the passage. Choice **c** is incorrect because nowhere is it stated that voting registration efforts by politicians were ineffective in Southern states. Choice **d** is incorrect because the Fifteenth Amendment guaranteed the right to vote to African American men prior to the Great Migration. States often made it difficult to vote, but they could not ban African American men from voting.

29. The correct answer is choice d. The passage states that the federal government took a firmer stand for civil rights and the court decisions helped African Americans win greater equality. Choice **a** is incorrect because the passage does not discuss elections in which pro-segregation politicians were defeated. Choice **b** is incorrect because the passage does not present evidence of violent protests. Choice **c** is incorrect because the passage does not present evidence of the growing public acceptance of equality.

30. The correct answer is choice c. The strategy major civil rights leaders employed is known as civil disobedience. Civil disobedience is a symbolic violation of a law, rather than a rejection of the system as a whole. Supporters of civil disobedience advocated disobeying laws on moral grounds. Choice **a** is incorrect because the methods used by civil rights leaders were not passive. Choice **b** is incorrect because civil rights leaders did not employ violent tactics. Also, the demonstrations mentioned in the passage were sit-ins, not walkouts. Choice **d** is incorrect because although civil rights leaders were well organized and often worked together for the common goal, they did not advocate a revolution.

31. The correct answer is choice d. Despite facing violence from those who disagreed with equal rights for African Americans, civil rights leaders kept the movement going using civil disobedience. Choice **a** is incorrect because information in the passage contradicts the statement that the movement lost momentum following the war. Choice **b** is incorrect because this claim is not supported by the passage. Choice **c** is incorrect because it is contradicted by information in the passage.

32. The correct answer is choice c. The best clue for the meaning of *segregate* is in the second paragraph: "They promoted sit-ins at segregated businesses that refused to serve African Americans." From this, the reader can understand that it must mean to divide or exclude people because of race. The two other uses of variants of the word *segregate* also indicate that the word means to separate people because of race. Choice **a** is incorrect because it may be true that segregation and racism were prevalent in the past, but this does not mean that segregation was based on historical reasons. Choice **b** is incorrect because the information in the passage does not directly link segregation, violence, and legislation. Choice **d** is incorrect because in the passage *segregate* is not used in a context that would link the practice to the idea of relocating people.

33. The correct answer is choice a. Initiatives seek to create new laws or state constitutional amendments. Referendums seek to either approve or reject an existing state or local law. Choice **b** is incorrect because approval by the state's Supreme Court is not described in the passage. Choice **c** is incorrect because the process of an initiative does not require a governor's approval or actions. Choice **d** is incorrect because the passage clearly states that referendums must also be built upon the petition process.

34. The correct answer is choice b. Initiatives concern proposed state or local laws or state constitutional amendments. Choice **a** is incorrect because a political party's platform is based on policy or viewpoints, not initiatives. Choice **c** is incorrect because this is an example of a public poll, not an initiative. Choice **d** is incorrect because this is an example of a public interest group lobbying a legislature, which does not require a ballot initiative.

35. The correct answer is choice b. Regardless of the specific issue or the success or failure of individual initiatives and referendums, the processes give citizens a voice in the political workings of their communities. Choice **a** is incorrect because this claim cannot be supported by the information in the passage. Choice **c** is incorrect because this statement is not supported by information in the passage. Choice **d** is incorrect because although this claim might very well be true, it is an opinion that is not verified by the passage.

36. The correct answer is choice d. As the passage describes, if a product or service is scarce, consumers have fewer options to shop around. Therefore, sellers usually raise their prices. Choice **a** is incorrect because it is the reverse result. Choice **b** is incorrect because equilibrium is reached when the supply and demand are the same. Choice **c** is incorrect because according to the law of supply and demand, an item's scarcity will always have some effect on its price.

37. The correct answer is choice a. The phone manufacturer has cut the price of the phone in half from what it initially charged. This reflects a situation in which the consumer demand for the phone is much lower than the available supply. The manufacturer therefore lowered the price. Choice **b** is incorrect because this scenario does not reflect an accurate reaction to the principles of supply and demand. Choice **c** is incorrect because this scenario does not reflect an accurate reaction to the principles of supply and demand. Choice **d** is incorrect because this scenario does not reflect an accurate reaction to the principles of supply and demand.

38. The correct answer is choice c. The optimum price is set when the quantity of goods available is equal to the quantity demanded. Choice **a** is incorrect because it reflects a situation that is not consistent with consumer behavior or the information in the passage. Choice **b** is incorrect because sellers would not be able to stay in business if they had to sell their products at prices that did not earn them a profit. Choice **d** is incorrect because it reflects a scenario that is not supported by information in the passage.

39. **The correct answer is choice d.** The new subdivision is looking to attract families, so the school district would be greatly affected because many of the home buyers would likely have children. An assessment cap would limit the amount of revenue that could be collected to help support the school system. In addition, the homes in the subdivision are very large. Larger homes are usually assessed at a higher value than smaller homes. This will force the school district to serve many more students with a lower-than-expected budget because of the limit on assessed property taxes. Choices **a**, **b**, and **c** are incorrect because although the Fairview Parks, Police, and Fire Departments would be affected by the tax cap because they are funded through taxes, they would not be affected as much as the School District.

40. **The correct answer is choice b.** Not capping tax rates will provide a human resources director the money to hire employees. Pay rates are usually important to job seekers. If the town of Fairview cannot offer competitive salaries, many job seekers will look elsewhere. Choice **a** is incorrect because raising property tax rates will not help attract new businesses. Rate raises usually make it more difficult to attract businesses. Choice **c** is incorrect because capping tax rates will limit the amount of money that can be used to hire new employees. Choice **d** is incorrect—because all town units are funded through taxes, tax rates have a huge effect on the hiring of town employees.

41. **The correct answer is choice a.** As an organization that promotes the local businesses in the community, the Chamber of Commerce would actively support policies that strengthen and protect the businesses in town. Choices **b**, **c**, and **d** are incorrect because they describe a policy that would hurt local businesses and thus thwart the work and goals of the Chamber of Commerce.

42. **The correct answer is choice c.** A supporter of smaller, limited government would argue for policies that decrease the size and influence of government, as well as promote a more efficient government. Choice **a** is incorrect because a proponent of smaller, limited government would not want the state to take control of local issues because of a tax cap. Choice **b** is incorrect because most citizens would not defend a tax policy that does not treat citizens equally. Choice **d** is incorrect because a proponent of smaller, limited government would not want to be hit by fee increases because of a tax cap.

43. **The correct answer is choice d.** Smith thought that individuals working in their own self-interest would do everything in their power to use their resources as efficiently as possible. Choice **a** is incorrect because Smith argued that self-interest would reduce the need for government intervention in the economy. Choice **b** is incorrect because Smith thought that individuals working in their own self-interest would do everything in their power to protect their resources. Choice **c** is incorrect because Smith thought that individuals working in their own self-interest would benefit the greatest number of people.

44. **The correct answer is choice b.** A laissez-faire policy would be one that produces minimal government influence in the market. Choice **a** is incorrect because this policy is an example of an active government. Choices **c** and **d** are incorrect because these policies are examples of an active government influencing the economy, which is not what Smith advocated.

45. **The correct answer is choice b.** The artist includes various elements in the cartoon that imply the traditional roles of women and men will change once women gain the right to vote. These include the husband taking care of the children and wearing an apron while surrounded by dishes and clothes on the line outside. Choice **a** is incorrect because this claim cannot be confirmed by the details in the cartoon. Choice **c** is incorrect because there are no details in the cartoon that support this idea. Choice **d** is incorrect because although the traditional roles may change, the ability of men to find work is not addressed in the details of the cartoon.

46. **The correct answer is choice b.** The depiction of the home in disarray suggests that the artist does not support giving women the vote. Choice **a** is incorrect because the depiction of the home in disarray suggests that the artist does not support giving women the vote. Choices **c** and **d** are incorrect because there are details in the cartoon that reveal that the artist has strong feelings about the subject.

47. **The correct answer is choice a.** Details in the cartoon imply that women taking on roles outside the home will more than likely require men and women to share duties and lead to more equality and opportunities for women. Choice **b** is incorrect because the husband in the cartoon is depicted as bewildered and unable to prevent his wife from leaving the home. Choice **c** is incorrect because the wife is shown as organized and determined and the wall hanging also shows thought and effort put into the movement. In addition, the small leaflet at the bottom right lists members of the "Hen Party," a slang term for a women's social gathering. This shows that women were working together to further the cause. Choice **d** is incorrect because there are no details in the cartoon that support this conclusion.

48. **The correct answer is choice b.** This is an illogical reason to join a political party. People join political parties because they share similar political opinions and viewpoints, not to learn about different or conflicting opinions and viewpoints. Choice **a** is incorrect because this is one of the main reasons why a person might join a political party. Choices **c** and **d** are incorrect because they are good reasons for joining a political party.

49. **The correct answer is choice a.** A person on the right of the political spectrum is most likely conservative. As the passage states, conservatives have gravitated toward the Republican Party, which advocates for minimal government involvement. Tax breaks for small businesses are consistent with the Republican idea of promoting the private sector. Choice **b** is incorrect because a person on the right would not support significant changes to the Constitution. Choice **c** is incorrect because a person on the right would most likely resist social changes. Choice **d** is incorrect because a conservative would support tax breaks that advocate for the private sector rather than additional government agencies solving social issues.

50. **The correct answer is choice d.** Of the possible activities, reading the official platforms of each party is the best method to judge the accuracy of the information in the passage. Choice **a** is incorrect because relying on information based on what the parties say about each other is unreliable. Choice **b** is incorrect because political parties change over time, so using historical documents will not provide appropriate or relevant information. Choice **c** is incorrect because relying on the opinions of just two political representatives will not provide enough information to accurately judge the descriptions.

3 ▶ HiSET®
PRACTICE TEST 2

This practice test is modeled on the format, content, and timing of the official HiSET® test.

You can choose either to take each test separately, or to take all five tests together. However you decide to use this practice test, try to take each part under the most test-like conditions you can.

Try to take your test in a quiet spot, as free from distraction as possible. At the beginning of each test section, you will find test information, including the actual time liimts you will be given on your exam day. If you want to work under testing conditions, set a timer and aim to complete each test section within the given time limit.

You should work carefully, but not spend too much time on any one question. And remember—be sure you answer every question! You *are not* penalized for incorrect answers; you are only rewarded for correct ones!

When you complete this entire practice exam, you will find complete answer explanations for every question that explain not only why correct answers are right, but also why incorrect answers are wrong. You will also find sample essays at every level, and information on scoring your exam.

Good luck!

Language Arts—Reading

65 Minutes
40 Questions

This practice test is modeled on the content and timing of the official HiSET® Language Arts—Reading test and, like the official test, presents a series of questions that assess your ability to understand, interpret, and analyze a broad range of literary and informational texts. Refer to the passages as often as necessary when answering the questions.

Use the following information to answer questions 1–6.

Jonathan Harker is a British lawyer who travels to Transylvania to do business with the mysterious Count Dracula. In this excerpt from *Dracula* by Bram Stoker, Harker makes a terrible discovery.

(1)

I only slept a few hours when I went to bed, and feeling that I could not sleep any more, got up. I had hung my shaving glass by the window, and was just beginning to shave. Suddenly I felt a hand on my shoulder, and heard the Count's voice saying to me, "Good morning." I started, for it amazed me that I had not seen him, since the reflection of the glass covered the whole room behind me. In starting I had cut myself slightly, but did not notice it at the moment. Having answered the Count's salutation, I turned to the glass again to see how I had been mistaken. This time there could be no error, for the man was close to me, and I could see him over my shoulder. But there was no reflection of him in the mirror! The whole room behind me was displayed, but there was no sign of a man in it, except myself.

(2)

This was startling, and coming on the top of so many strange things, was beginning to increase that vague feeling of uneasiness which I always have when the Count is near. But at the instant I saw that the cut had bled a little, and the blood was trickling over my chin. I laid down the razor, turning as I did so half round to look for some sticking plaster. When the Count saw my face, his eyes blazed with a sort of demoniac fury, and he suddenly made a grab at my throat. I drew away and his hand touched the string of beads which held the crucifix. It made an instant change in him, for the fury passed so quickly that I could hardly believe that it was ever there.

(3)

"Take care," he said, "take care how you cut yourself. It is more dangerous than you think in this country." Then seizing the shaving glass, he went on, "And this is the wretched thing that has done the mischief. It is a foul bauble of man's vanity. Away with it!" And opening the window with one wrench of his terrible hand, he flung out the glass, which was shattered into a thousand pieces on the stones of the courtyard far below. Then he withdrew without a word. It is very annoying, for I do not see how I am to shave, unless in my watch-case or the bottom of the shaving pot, which is fortunately of metal.

(4)

When I went into the dining room, breakfast was prepared, but I could not find the Count anywhere. So I breakfasted alone. It is strange that as yet I have not seen the Count eat or drink. He must be a very peculiar man! After breakfast I did a little exploring in the castle. I went out on the stairs, and found a room looking towards the South.

(5)

The view was magnificent, and from where I stood there was every opportunity of seeing it. The castle is on the very edge of a terrific precipice. A stone falling from the window would fall a thousand feet without touching anything! As far as the eye can reach is a sea of green tree tops, with occasionally a deep rift where there is a chasm. Here and there are silver threads where the rivers wind in deep gorges through the forests.

(6)

But I am not in heart to describe beauty, for when I had seen the view I explored further. Doors, doors, doors everywhere, and all locked and bolted. In no place save from the windows in the castle walls is there an available exit. The castle is a veritable prison, and I am a prisoner!

1. The Count most likely destroys the mirror because
  a. he does not cast a reflection in it.
  b. human vanity disgusts him.
  c. he is angry at Harker for using it.
  d. he is repelled by the sight of blood in it.

2. In what way is Harker the same before his encounter with the Count as he is after the encounter?
  a. He realizes he is a prisoner.
  b. He is annoyed.
  c. He knows the Count is inhuman.
  d. He feels unsettled.

3. When Harker says that he felt the Count's hand on his shoulder, his use of the word "suddenly" (paragraph 1) creates a tone that is
  a. horrific.
  b. exhilarating.
  c. joyful.
  d. thrilling.

4. After discovering that he is a prisoner in the Count's castle, Harker will most likely
  a. ask the Count to let him go free.
  b. search for a way out of the castle.
  c. attempt to find other prisoners.
  c. learn to enjoy living there.

5. When Harker sees the view out of the castle window, it most likely
  a. makes him feel better about staying with the Count.
  b. causes him to feel even more upset than he already does.
  c. has little effect on his feelings about staying with the Count.
  d. gives him a moment of peace in the middle of unsettling events.

6. Which of the following meanings associated with the word "terrific" seems most intended in paragraph 5?
  a. supreme
  b. wonderful
  c. talented
  d. extreme

Use the following information to answer questions 7–12.

Theodore Roosevelt was the twenty-sixth president of the United States. In this excerpt from *Theodore Roosevelt: An Autobiography*, he included the following letter he wrote addressing matters of conservation during his time as governor of New York.

(1)

". . . I have had very many complaints before this as to the inefficiency of the game wardens and game protectors, the complaints usually taking the form that the men have been appointed and are retained without due regard to the duties to be performed. I do not wish a man to be retained or appointed who is not thoroughly fit to perform the duties of game protector. The Adirondacks are entitled to a peculiar share of the Commission's attention, both from the standpoint of forestry, and from the less important, but still very important, standpoint of game and fish protection. The men who do duty as game protectors in the Adirondacks should, by preference, be appointed from the locality itself, and should in all cases be thorough woodsmen. The mere fact that a game protector has to hire a guide to pilot him through the woods is enough to show his unfitness for the position. I want as game protectors men of courage, resolution, and hardihood . . . who can camp out in summer or winter; who can go on snow-shoes, if necessary; who can go through the woods by day or by night without regard to trails.

(2)

"I should like full information about all your employees, as to their capacities, as to the labor they perform, as to their distribution from and where they do their work."

(3)

Many of the men hitherto appointed owed their positions principally to political preference. The changes I recommended were promptly made, and much to the good of the public service. In my Annual Message, in January, 1900, I said:

(4)

"Great progress has been made through the fish hatcheries in the propagation of valuable food and sporting fish. The laws for the protection of deer have resulted in their increase. Nevertheless, as railroads tend to encroach on the wilderness, the temptation to illegal hunting becomes greater, and the danger from forest fires increases. There is need of great improvement both in our laws and in their administration. The game wardens have been too few in number. More should be provided. None save fit men must be appointed; and their retention in office must depend purely upon the zeal, ability, and efficiency with which they perform their duties. The game wardens in the forests must be woodsmen; and they should have no outside business. In short, there should be a thorough reorganization of the work of the Commission. A careful study of the resources and condition of the forests on State land must be made. It is certainly not too much to expect that the State forests should be managed as efficiently as the forests on private lands in the same neighborhoods. And the measure of difference in efficiency of management must be the measure of condemnation or praise of the way the public forests have been managed.

(5)

"The subject of forest preservation is of the utmost importance to the State. The Adirondacks and Catskills should be great parks kept in perpetuity for the benefit and enjoyment of our people. Much has been done of late years towards their preservation, but very much remains to be done. The provisions of law in reference to sawmills and wood-pulp mills are defective and should be changed so as to prohibit dumping dye-stuff, sawdust, or tan-bark, in any amount whatsoever, into the streams. Reservoirs should be made, but not where they will tend to destroy large sections of the forest, and only after a careful and scientific study of the water resources of the region. The people of the forest regions are themselves growing more and more to realize the necessity of preserving both the trees and the game."

7. Information in this passage would be most useful to argue that
   a. industry should be allowed to expand without obstacles.
   b. environmental protection is not a recent idea.
   c. climate change is one of today's most important issues.
   d. Roosevelt was America's most conscientious politician.

8. Read the following paragraph.

Our natural environment is undeniably extraordinary. Its verdant beauty invites all who stroll through it to enjoy it. It provides natural resources such as wood, game, and water. When we use those resources, they replenish naturally without the need for human actions of any sort.

Which idea in this paragraph differs from the ideas in the main passage?
   a. The natural environment is full of essential resources.
   b. The natural environment does not need human action.
   c. The natural environment is undeniably extraordinary.
   d. The natural environment should be enjoyed by people.

9. Roosevelt seems to believe that woodsmen
   a. possess a particular skill for dealing with game.
   b. are to blame for the destruction of the environment.
   c. know less about game than they know about trees.
   d. are not educated enough to do anything but work as woodsmen.

10. According to the passage, both fish and deer
   a. have benefited from recent actions.
   b. are in danger of extinction.
   c. have proven to be great resources.
   d. are jeopardized by railroads.

11. In paragraph 1, Roosevelt most likely states that game and fish protection is less important than forestry protection because forestry protection
   a. has better resources than game and fish protection does.
   b. is more difficult than game and fish protection.
   c. affects more factors than game and fish protection does.
   d. is more popular among voters than game and fish protection.

12. Roosevelt most likely believes that the encroachment of railroads on forests will increase instances of illegal hunting because
   a. trains distract game wardens.
   b. more people will be in the forests.
   c. railroads attract criminal behavior.
   d. hunters often travel by train.

Use the following information to answer questions 13–18.

Paul Dombey owns a shipping company and dreams of having his son join him in the business one day. This excerpt from *Dombey and Son* by Charles Dickens reveals Dombey's thoughts about his newborn son.

(1)
Dombey sat in the corner of the darkened room in the great arm-chair by the bedside, and Son lay tucked up warm in a little basket bedstead, carefully disposed on a low settee immediately in front of the fire and close to it, as if his constitution were analogous to that of a

muffin, and it was essential to toast him brown while he was very new.

(2)

Dombey was about eight-and-forty years of age. Son about eight-and-forty minutes. Dombey was rather bald, rather red, and though a handsome well-made man, too stern and pompous in appearance, to be prepossessing. Son was very bald, and very red, and though (of course) an undeniably fine infant, somewhat crushed and spotty in his general effect, as yet. On the brow of Dombey, Time and his brother Care had set some marks, as on a tree that was to come down in good time—remorseless twins they are for striding through their human forests, notching as they go—while the countenance of Son was crossed with a thousand little creases, which the same deceitful Time would take delight in smoothing out and wearing away with the flat part of his scythe, as a preparation of the surface for his deeper operations.

(3)

Dombey, exulting in the long-looked-for event, jingled and jingled the heavy gold watch-chain that depended from below his trim blue coat, whereof the buttons sparkled phosphorescently in the feeble rays of the distant fire. Son, with his little fists curled up and clenched, seemed, in his feeble way, to be squaring at existence for having come upon him so unexpectedly.

(4)

"The House will once again, Mrs Dombey," said Mr Dombey, "be not only in name but in fact Dombey and Son;" and he added, in a tone of luxurious satisfaction, with his eyes half-closed as if he were reading the name in a device of flowers, and inhaling their fragrance at the same time; "Dom-bey and Son!"

(5)

The words had such a softening influence, that he appended a term of endearment to Mrs Dombey's name (though not without some hesitation, as being a man but little used to that form of address): and said, "Mrs Dombey, my—my dear."

(6)

A transient flush of faint surprise overspread the sick lady's face as she raised her eyes towards him.

(7)

"He will be christened Paul, my—Mrs Dombey—of course."

(8)

She feebly echoed, "Of course," or rather expressed it by the motion of her lips, and closed her eyes again.

(9)

"His father's name, Mrs Dombey, and his grandfather's! I wish his grandfather were alive this day! There is some inconvenience in the necessity of writing Junior," said Mr Dombey, making a fictitious autograph on his knee; "but it is merely of a private and personal complexion. It doesn't enter into the correspondence of the House. Its signature remains the same." And again he said "Dombey and Son," in exactly the same tone as before.

(10)

Those three words conveyed the one idea of Mr Dombey's life. The earth was made for Dombey and Son to trade in, and the sun and moon were made to give them light. Rivers and seas were formed to float their ships; rainbows gave them promise of fair weather; winds blew for or against their enterprises; stars and planets circled in their orbits, to preserve inviolate a system of which they were the centre. Common abbreviations took new meanings in his eyes, and had sole reference to them. A. D. had no concern with Anno Domini, but stood for anno Dombei—and Son.

13. As the story continues, Dombey will most likely
   a. try to get his son involved in the family business.
   b. have great success doing business with his son.
   c. spend a lot of time taking care of his infant son.
   d. send his son to study at an excellent university.

14. Dombey most likely says, "The House will once again . . . be not only in name but in fact Dombey and Son" because he had
   a. another son with whom he did business.
   b. been in business with his own father.
   c. used the business name while running it alone.
   d. purchased the business from another Dombey.

15. The author most likely states that "The earth was made for Dombey and Son to trade in" (paragraph 10) in order to
   a. prove that Dombey is an extremely powerful man.
   b. show that Dombey knows very little about the earth.
   c. illustrate that business is all that matters to Dombey.
   d. explain how Dombey first became a businessman.

16. Which of the following lines from paragraph 2 restates information from earlier in the passage?
   a. "Dombey was about eight-and-forty years of age."
   b. "Dombey was rather bald, rather red, and though a handsome well-made man, too stern"
   c. "the countenance of Son was crossed with a thousand little creases"
   d. "Time would take delight in smoothing out and wearing away with the flat part of his scythe"

17. In paragraph 1, the author most likely compares Dombey's son to a muffin to create a tone that is
   a. humorous.
   b. fantastical.
   c. grim.
   d. romantic.

18. Based on the way she behaves in the passage, Mrs. Dombey most likely
   a. has no respect for her husband.
   b. had problems during childbirth.
   c. allows her husband to make all decisions.
   d. is very important to her husband.

Use the following information to answer questions 19–23.

Mark Twain is widely regarded as one of literature's wittiest writers. In the following passage from "How to Tell a Story," Twain explains some of his secrets for writing funny stories.

(1)
I do not claim that I can tell a story as it ought to be told. I only claim to know how a story ought to be told, for I have been almost daily in the company of the most expert story-tellers for many years.

(2)

There are several kinds of stories, but only one difficult kind—the humorous. I will talk mainly about that one. The humorous story is American, the comic story is English, the witty story is French. The humorous story depends for its effect upon the manner of the telling; the comic story and the witty story upon the matter.

(3)

The humorous story may be spun out to great length, and may wander around as much as it pleases, and arrive nowhere in particular; but the comic and witty stories must be brief and end with a point. The humorous story bubbles gently along, the others burst.

(4)

The humorous story is strictly a work of art—high and delicate art—and only an artist can tell it; but no art is necessary in telling the comic and the witty story; anybody can do it. The art of telling a humorous story—understand, I mean by word of mouth, not print—was created in America, and has remained at home.

(5)

The humorous story is told gravely; the teller does his best to conceal the fact that he even dimly suspects that there is anything funny about it; but the teller of the comic story tells you beforehand that it is one of the funniest things he has ever heard, then tells it with eager delight, and is the first person to laugh when he gets through. And sometimes, if he has had good success, he is so glad and happy that he will repeat the "nub" of it and glance around from face to face, collecting applause, and then repeat it again. It is a pathetic thing to see.

(6)

Very often, of course, the rambling and disjointed humorous story finishes with a nub, point, snapper, or whatever you like to call it. Then the listener must be alert, for in many cases the teller will divert attention from that nub by dropping it in a carefully casual and indifferent way, with the pretence that he does not know it is a nub.

(7)

Artemus Ward used that trick a good deal; then when the belated audience presently caught the joke he would look up with innocent surprise, as if wondering what they had found to laugh at. Dan Setchell used it before him, Nye and Riley and others use it to-day.

(8)

But the teller of the comic story does not slur the nub; he shouts it at you—every time. And when he prints it, in England, France, Germany, and Italy, he italicizes it, puts some whooping exclamation-points after it, and sometimes explains it in a parenthesis. All of which is very depressing, and makes one want to renounce joking and lead a better life.

19. The author believes that telling a humorous story
a. is the best way to tell a story.
b. requires great attention to details.
c. is something anyone can do successfully.
d. requires a natural gift for storytelling.

20. What does "gravely" (paragraph 5) mean?
a. frighteningly
b. seriously
c. angrily
d. amusingly

21. The author expresses an opinion when he states that
a. a humorous story is a work of art.
b. humorous storytelling originated in America.
c. the "nub" is the point of a story.
d. Artemus Ward pretended his stories were not funny.

22. Read the following paragraph.

There is an art to public speaking. One never rambles when addressing others in any way, shape, or form. There is a point to every discussion, and the audience must understand that point by any means short of shouting it at them. Never leave an audience confused about your ideas, opinions, or intentions.

Both the writer of this paragraph and the author of the passage agree that someone addressing an audience should never
a. leave the audience confused.
b. ramble in any way, shape, or form.
c. shout his or her point.
d. fail to make a point.

23. Twain most likely does NOT
a. repeat the nub when telling humorous stories.
b. have experience telling humorous stories.
c. think Artemus Ward told humorous stories well.
d. believe Americans are the best humorous storytellers.

Use the following information to answer questions 24–29.

A man discovers that a raven has settled in his bedroom in this excerpt from "The Raven" by Edgar Allan Poe.

(1) Once upon a midnight dreary, while I pondered, weak and weary,
Over many a quaint and curious volume of forgotten lore,
While I nodded, nearly napping, suddenly there came a tapping,
As of some one gently rapping, rapping at my chamber door.
"'Tis some visitor," I muttered, "tapping at my chamber door—
Only this, and nothing more."

(2) Ah, distinctly I remember it was in the bleak December,
And each separate dying ember wrought its ghost upon the floor.
Eagerly I wished the morrow;—vainly I had sought to borrow
From my books surcease of sorrow—sorrow for the lost Lenore—
For the rare and radiant maiden whom the angels name Lenore—
Nameless here for evermore.

(3) And the silken sad uncertain rustling of each purple curtain
Thrilled me—filled me with fantastic terrors never felt before;
So that now, to still the beating of my heart, I stood repeating,
"'Tis some visitor entreating entrance at my chamber door—
Some late visitor entreating entrance at my chamber door;—
This it is, and nothing more."

(4) Presently my soul grew stronger; hesitating then no longer,
"Sir," said I, "or Madam, truly your forgiveness I implore;
But the fact is I was napping, and so gently you came rapping,
And so faintly you came tapping, tapping at my chamber door,
That I scarce was sure I heard you,"—here I opened wide the door;—
Darkness there, and nothing more.

(5) Deep into that darkness peering, long I stood there wondering, fearing,
Doubting, dreaming dreams no mortals ever dared to dream before;
But the silence was unbroken, and the stillness gave no token,
And the only word there spoken was the whispered word, "Lenore!"
This I whispered, and an echo murmured back the word, "Lenore!"—
Merely this, and nothing more.

(6) Back into the chamber turning, all my soul within me burning,
    Soon again I heard a tapping somewhat louder than before.
    "Surely," said I, "surely that is something at my window lattice:
    Let me see, then, what threat is, and this mystery explore—
    Let my heart be still a moment and this mystery explore;—
    'Tis the wind and nothing more."

(7) Open here I flung the shutter, when, with many a flirt and flutter,
    In there stepped a stately raven of the saintly days of yore;
    Not the least obeisance made he; not a minute stopped or stayed he;
    But, with mien of lord or lady, perched above my chamber door—
    Perched upon a bust of Pallas just above my chamber door—
    Perched, and sat, and nothing more . . .

(8) But the raven, sitting lonely on the placid bust, spoke only
    That one word, as if his soul in that one word he did outpour.
    Nothing further then he uttered—not a feather then he fluttered—
    Till I scarcely more than muttered, "other friends have flown before—
    On the morrow *he* will leave me, as my hopes have flown before."
    Then the bird said, "Nevermore." . . .

(9) "Be that word our sign in parting, bird or fiend," I shrieked, upstarting—
    "Get thee back into the tempest and the Night's Plutonian shore!
    Leave no black plume as a token of that lie thy soul hath spoken!
    Leave my loneliness unbroken!—quit the bust above my door!
    Take thy beak from out my heart, and take thy form from off my door!"
    Quoth the Raven, "Nevermore."

(10) And the Raven, never flitting, still is sitting, still is sitting
    On the pallid bust of Pallas just above my chamber door;
    And his eyes have all the seeming of a demon's that is dreaming,
    And the lamplight o'er him streaming throws his shadow on the floor;
    And my soul from out that shadow that lies floating on the floor
    Shall be lifted—nevermore!

24. In stanza 2, the phrase "each separate dying ember wrought its ghost upon the floor" means that
a. a ghost came floating out of the fire's embers.
b. the fire's dying embers looked like a ghost.
c. the fire was dying, just as a ghost is dead.
d. the fire's embers cast lights and shapes on the floor.

25. This poem is mainly about the narrator
a. becoming irritated by a raven that is loose in his home.
b. remembering a lost love as a raven appears in his home.
c. feeling sad because he lost the woman that he loved.
d. hearing a rapping sound on the door of his chamber.

26. What does "radiant" (stanza 2) mean?
a. shining
b. healthy
c. beautiful
d. heat giving

27. The poet most likely begins the poem with words such as "dreary," "weak," and "weary" in order to set a tone that is
a. frightening.
b. thrilling.
c. boring.
d. gloomy.

28. The raven most likely repeats the word "nevermore" because
a. it will never reveal its secrets.
b. it will never return after this night.
c. Lenore will never return.
d. the narrator never really knew Lenore.

29. This poem would have the greatest meaning to people who are
a. living by themselves.
b. unhappy during the winter.
c. having trouble sleeping.
d. mourning a loved one.

Use the following information to answer questions 30–34.

The Articles of Confederation were the first constitution of the United States' original 13 states. In this excerpt from *The Federalist No. 1* by Alexander Hamilton, the founder of the Federalist party reacts to the Articles of Confederation.

To the People of the State of New York:

(1)

After an unequivocal experience of the inefficacy of the subsisting federal government, you are called upon to deliberate on a new Constitution for the United States of America. The subject speaks its own importance; comprehending in its consequences nothing less than the existence of the UNION, the safety and welfare of the parts of which it is composed, the fate of an empire in many respects the most interesting in the world. It has been frequently remarked that it seems to have been reserved to the people of this country, by their conduct and example, to decide the important question, whether societies of men are really capable or not of establishing good government from reflection and choice, or whether they are forever destined to depend for their political constitutions on accident and force. If there be any truth in the remark, the crisis at which we are arrived may with propriety be regarded as the era in which that decision is to be made; and a wrong election of the part we shall act may, in this view, deserve to be considered as the general misfortune of mankind.

(2)

This idea will add the inducements of philanthropy to those of patriotism, to heighten the solicitude which all considerate and good men must feel for the event. Happy will it be if our choice should be directed by a judicious estimate of our true interests, unperplexed and unbiased by considerations not connected with the public good. But this is a thing more ardently to be wished than seriously to be expected. The plan offered to our deliberations affects too many particular interests, innovates upon too many local institutions, not to involve in its discussion a variety of objects foreign to its merits, and of views, passions and prejudices little favorable to the discovery of truth.

(3)

Among the most formidable of the obstacles which the new Constitution will have to encounter may readily be distinguished the obvious interest of a certain class of men in every State to resist all changes which may hazard a diminution of the power, emolument, and consequence of the offices they hold under the State establishments; and the perverted ambition of another class of men, who will either hope to aggrandize themselves by the confusions of their country, or will flatter themselves with fairer prospects of elevation from the subdivision of the empire into several partial confederacies than from its union under one government.

30. Which of the following states the primary purpose of this passage?
   a. to propose a new constitution for the United States
   b. to criticize the failure of the Articles of Confederation
   c. to argue against passions and prejudices
   d. to make sure that Americans remain patriotic

31. The author makes the assumption that adopting a new constitution will
   a. replace the Articles of Confederation.
   b. promote philanthropy as much as patriotism.
   c. make some politicians afraid they will lose their jobs.
   d. make the United States the most interesting empire in the world.

32. What is the most likely reason that the author discusses possible reactions to a new constitution in paragraph 3?
   a. to build support for his proposal for a new constitution
   b. to argue that a new constitution may not be worth the trouble
   c. to prove that he understands how his ideas will affect the United States
   d. to prepare his audience for possible problems that may arise.

33. According to the author, how would the United States be different after replacing the Articles of Confederation with a new constitution?
   a. There would be an end to human misfortune.
   b. Americans would be freer to express themselves.
   c. Politicians would be more trustworthy.
   d. Philanthropy would be stronger in the United States.

34. The author describes the United States as in a state of crisis in paragraph 1 to
   a. suggest that he is losing faith in the United States.
   b. show how much work will be required to adopt a new constitution.
   c. imply that everyone in the country will not agree to a new constitution.
   d. emphasize that it is a crucial time to adopt a new constitution.

Use the following information to answer questions 35–40.

Australia is the setting of this excerpt from *An Australian Girl* by Mrs. Alick Macleod.

(1)

It was one Sunday afternoon in the middle of December and in the province of South Australia. The grass was withered almost to the roots, fast turning gray and brown. Indeed, along the barer ridges of the beautiful hills that rise in serried ranks to the east of Adelaide, the herbage was already as dry and bleached as carded flax. In the gullies, thickly timbered and lying in perpetual shade, the ground still retained the faint graying green distinctive of Australian herbage in a state of transition from spring verdure to summer drought.

(2)

But soon even the shadiest recesses would bear witness to the scorching dryness of the season. For even before the middle of this first month of summer, two or three of those phenomenal days had come which furnish anecdotes for many successive months alike to the weather statist and the numerous class who cultivate community of soul by comparing experiences of those dreadful days on which 'the hall thermometer stood at 104° before noon.' This Sunday had not quite been one of the days that make the oldest residents turn over heat averages extending to the early dawn of the country's history. But, nevertheless, it was a very hot, still day, without a breath of wind stirring, and in the distance that faint shimmering bluish haze which, to the experienced eye, tells its own tale of days to come.

(3)

The masses of white, silver and messmate gum-trees that clothe these same Adelaide hills so thickly, formed a grateful resting-place for the eye, wearied with the steadfast glare of sunshine. So did the vineyards that dot their declining slopes, and the gardens and orchards that are scattered broadcast to the east of the town. But even Adelaide itself is interwoven with the foliage of trees, which do so much to mitigate, both for eye and body, the severities of a semi-tropical climate. This fascinating embroidery of trees is more especially observable in glancing over North Adelaide. This extensive and important suburb, which is divided from Adelaide proper by the Torrens Lake and Park Lands, lies considerably above the city and adjacent suburbs. So large a proportion of the houses are surrounded by gardens, that from some points of view North Adelaide looks like a well-trimmed wood, thickly studded with houses.

(4)

And these gardens are, as a rule, neither suburban slips, with precocious trees selected for their speedy power of growth, nor the painfully pretentious enclosures which auctioneers delight to term 'grounds.' No, they are genuine gardens—roomy, shadowy, well planted, well watered; rich in flowers and many fruit-trees, bending in due season under their fertile loads; haunted with the hum of rifling bees, fragrant with the perfume of old-world blossoms. In such a garden on this Sunday afternoon a young man and woman were slowly pacing up and down a broad central walk, thickly trellised with vines. The gadding tendrils, the wealth of wide emerald leaves, the countless oval clusters of ripening grapes—Crystal, Black Prince, and delicate Ladies' Fingers—which clothed the trellis on the sides and overhead, made a delightful picture. So did the great rose-trees hard by, garlanded after their kind with pale pink, yellow, white and blood-red roses.

35. Based on the fact that this passage takes place in December, South Australia most likely
  a. is undergoing a bizarre event in this story.
  b. does not have a winter season.
  c. is not intended to be realistically described in this story.
  d. experiences summer at a different time than the United States does.

36. What is the most likely reason that the author describes the heat in paragraph 2 before describing the trees and gardens in the following paragraphs?
  a. to create a sense of contrast
  b. to describe a confusing setting
  c. to provide important plot details
  d. to show that nothing is what it seems

37. In paragraph 2, the author describes days that are 104° before noon as an opportunity to do which of the following?
  a. to suggest that something bad is going to happen
  b. to prove that people can endure anything
  c. to establish that the weather is not as bad as it could be
  d. to imply that a major change is about to occur

38. Which of the following lines from paragraph 4 refines information from earlier in the paragraph?
  a. "And these gardens are, as a rule, neither suburban slips, with precocious trees selected for their speedy power of growth"
  b. "No, they are genuine gardens—roomy, shadowy, well planted, well watered; rich in flowers and many fruit-trees"
  c. "In such a garden on this Sunday afternoon a young man and woman were slowly pacing up and down a broad central walk"
  d. "Crystal, Black Prince, and delicate Ladies' Fingers—which clothed the trellis on the sides and overhead, made a delightful picture."

39. The main idea of paragraph 4 is that
  a. a young man and woman walk through a lush garden.
  b. gardens in Adelaide contain several varieties of grapes.
  c. grounds are much more pretentious than gardens are.
  d. bees fly around the gardens in Adelaide.

40. Which of the following meanings associated with the word "phenomenal" seems most intended in paragraph 2?
  a. absolutely wonderful
  b. able to be sensed
  c. highly unusual
  d. without precedent

Language Arts—Writing

Part 1: Multiple Choice
50 Questions
75 Minutes

This practice test is modeled on the content and timing of the official HiSET® Language Arts—Writing test and, like the official test, presents a series of questions that assess your ability to recognize and produce effective standard American written English. Like the official test, this practice is broken up into two parts: Part 1 consists of multiple-choice questions; Part 2 consists of an essay.

Part 1 is a test of skills involved in revising written materials that contain grammatical and stylistic errors. In this section, you will find the types of passages you come across in everyday life—letters, memos, articles, and so on.

You will find each passage presented twice: first in a box without any marks so you can read it uninterrupted, and then in a spread-out format with certain parts underlined and numbered.

For each numbered portion of the passage, you will be asked to choose the alternative that fixes the writing to make it correct, clear, organized, and free of grammatical errors. If you think the original underlined version is best, choose "No change."

Read through the draft blog entry. Then go on to the suggestions for revision that follow.

Another year, another bake-off in the books! The Duck Hollow Community Volunteers Association would love to thank everyone who came out and baked, ate, or helping set up our favorite annual event.

Now on to the important part: the desserts! This year's theme was "old family recipes," and judging from the entries, Duck Hollow has some great family traditions. There were some very creative entries this year. There was Mark Jackson's savory pork empanadas (from his mother's native Argentina). There was also Jill Gibbons's mock apple pie (hold the apples!). It was originally Jill's grandmothers bake-off-winning recipe from 1964.

There were so many great dishes on the tables, and how did the judges manage to pick just one winner? Our judges this year were: Mayor Lindy Rodriguez, Police Chief Tony Marco, and Fire Captain Dennis Hopkins. Dennis has assured me that the deliberations were feirce and it was a very tough call to make.

Yet, the "best in show" prize went to Nakiesha Sanders's heavenly angel food cake with fresh berries. Following closely behind her in second and third place, respectfully, were Marnie Swenson with her peach cobbler and Mike Felton with his German chocolate cake. The winners were well rewarded for their fabulous efforts. However, everyone who entered is a winner in my (cook)book, and I'm already looking forward to next year.

---

(1)

Another year, another bake-off in the books! The Duck Hollow Community Volunteers Association would love to thank everyone who came out and baked, ate, or helping set up our favorite annual event. [1]

(2)

Now on to the important part: the desserts! This year's theme was "old family recipes," and judging from the entries, Duck Hollow has some great family traditions. There were some very creative entries this year. There was Mark Jackson's savory pork empanadas (from his mother's native Argentina). There was also Jill Gibbons's mock apple pie (hold the apples!). [2] It was originally Jill's grandmothers [3] bake-off-winning recipe from 1964.

(3)

There were so many great dishes on the tables, and how did the judges manage to pick just one winner? [4] Our judges this year were: Mayor Lindy Rodriguez, Police Chief Tony Marco, and Fire Captain Dennis Hopkins. Dennis has assured me that the deliberations were feirce [5] and it was a very tough call to make.

(4)

(1) Yet, [6] the "best in show" prize went to Nakiesha Sanders's heavenly angel food cake with fresh berries. (2) Following closely behind her in second and third place, respectfully, were Marnie Swenson with her peach cobbler and Mike Felton with his German chocolate cake. (3) The winners were well rewarded for their fabulous efforts. (4) However, everyone who entered is a winner in my (cook)book, and I'm already looking forward to next year. [7]

1. **a.** *(No change)*
   b. came out and baked, eating, or helping set up our favorite annual event
   c. came out and baked, ate, or help setting up our favorite annual event
   d. came out and baked, ate, or helped set up our favorite annual event

2. Which of the following would be the best way to combine the indicated sentences?
   a. There were some very creative entries this year, there was Mark Jackson's savory pork empanadas (from his mother's native Argentina), and there was also Jill Gibbons's mock apple pie (hold the apples!).
   b. There were some very creative entries this year, such as Mark Jackson's savory pork empanadas (from his mother's native Argentina) and Jill Gibbons's mock apple pie (hold the apples!).
   c. Very creative entries this year, such as Mark Jackson's savory pork empanadas (from his mother's native Argentina) and Jill Gibbons's mock apple pie (hold the apples!).
   d. There were some very creative entries this year, that were Mark Jackson's savory pork empanadas (from his mother's native Argentina) and Jill Gibbons's mock apple pie (hold the apples!).

3. **a.** *(No change)*
   b. Jills grandmothers
   c. Jill's grandmothers'
   d. Jill's grandmother's

4. a. (No change)

   b. Were there many great dishes on the tables, and how did the judges manage to pick just one winner?

   c. With so many great dishes on the tables, how did the judges manage to pick just one winner?

   d. The judges, how did they manage to pick just one winner, there were so many great dishes on the tables.

5. Which of the words is misspelled?

   a. (None)

   b. assured

   c. deliberations

   d. feirce

6. a. (No change)

   b. Basically

   c. Someday

   d. Ultimately

7. The writer wants to add the following information to paragraph 4:

The first-prize winner received a $50 gift certificate to the Bargain Barn, and the runners-up received certificates of smaller values.

For the most logical organization of ideas, where should this sentence be placed?

   a. after sentence 1

   b. after sentence 2

   c. after sentence 3

   d. after sentence 4

Read through the draft recipe. Then go on to the suggestions for revision that follow.

You will need the following ingredients to make chocolate chip cookies, 1 cup butter, 1 cup brown sugar, 2 eggs, 1 teaspoon salt, 1 teaspoon baking soda, 3 cups flour, and 2 cups chocolate chips.

Start by preheating your oven to 350 degrees. While the oven is heated, soften the butter and circle up the rest of the ingredients. Add the brown and white sugar to the softened butter. Once combined, add one at a time the eggs. Mix well. Now, hey, you're ready to add the dry ingredients!

Sift the flour, baking soda, and salt together so that they are blended. Stir them into the butter/sugar mixture. Allow the dough to rest in the refrigerator for 30 minutes.

After the dough freezes, stir in the chocolate chips. Mold the dough into one-tablespoon balls, and drop each onto a cookie sheet. Do this in batches of 12. Put the cookie sheet in the oven, and bake the cookies for 10 to 12 minutes, or until they are golden brown. Move the cookies to a wire rack and let them cool before serving.

(1)

You will need the following ingredients to make chocolate chip <u>cookies, 1 cup butter</u>, [8] 1 cup brown sugar, 2 eggs, 1 teaspoon salt, 1 teaspoon baking soda, 3 cups flour, and 2 cups chocolate chips.

(2)

Start by preheating your oven to 350 degrees. While the oven is <u>heated</u>, [9] soften the butter and <u>circle up</u> [10] the rest of the ingredients. Add the brown and white sugar to the softened butter. <u>Once combined, add one at a time the eggs.</u> [11] Mix well. <u>Now, hey, you're ready to add the dry ingredients!</u> [12]

(3)

(1) Sift the flour, baking soda, and salt together so that they are blended. (2) Stir them into the butter/sugar mixture. (3) Allow the dough to rest in the refrigerator for 30 minutes. [13]

(4)

After the dough <u>freezes</u> [14], stir in the chocolate chips. Mold the dough into one-tablespoon balls, and drop each onto a cookie sheet. Do this in batches of 12. Put the cookie sheet in the oven, and bake the cookies for 10 to 12 minutes, or until they are golden brown. Move the cookies to a wire rack and let them cool before serving.

8. a. (*No change*)
   b. cookies; 1 cup butter
   c. cookies: 1 cup butter
   d. cookies. 1 cup butter

9. a. (*No change*)
   b. heating
   c. heats
   d. heat

10. a. (*No change*)
   b. gather through
   c. round up
   d. bunch around

11. a. (*No change*)
   b. Add the combined eggs one at a time.
   c. Once combined, add one egg.
   d. Once combined, add the eggs one at a time.

12. a. (*No change*)
   b. Get ready to add those dry ingredients, my friend.
   c. You will add the dry ingredients now!
   d. Now you're ready to add the dry ingredients.

13. The writer would like to add the following information to paragraph 3:

Now you have cookie dough.

For the most logical organization of ideas, where should this sentence be placed?
   a. before sentence 1
   b. after sentence 1
   c. after sentence 2
   d. after sentence 3

14. a. (*No change*)
   b. chills
   c. colds
   d. ices

Read through the draft job description. Then go on to the suggestions for revision that follow.

Do you love the great outside? Would you like to have an office that features visits from wildlife and all the fresh air you could want? If so, the Parks Department has a great opportunity for you. We're seeking a park ranger based in Deep Woods State Park to start immediately.

Applicants should have a Bachelor's degree in forestry at a minimum. They can also have a degree in environmental science or biology. If an applicant has equivalent education or work history, a degree may not be necessary. Applicants should also be in good physical shape, as the job may require significant walking, hiking, and lifting.

The park ranger would be responsible for protection and supervising Deep Woods State Park. The park ranger would provide information to park guests in the Visitor's Center and supervise the grounds. He or she would enforce all legal and safety rules for the park and work with law enforcement as necessary. The park ranger would also be responsible for coordinating the park's Junior Ranger program, which educates 4 to 12 children about the park's history, environment, and safety rules.

If this sounds like the job for you, hit us up at our website. Please be prepared to send a full resume and list of references.

(1)

Do you love the <u>great outside?</u> [15] Would you like to have an office that features visits from wildlife and all the fresh air you could want? If so, the Parks Department has a great opportunity for you. We're seeking a park ranger based in Deep Woods State Park to start immediately.

(2)

<u>Applicants should have a bachelor's degree in forestry at a minimum. They can also have a degree in environmental science or biology.</u> [16] If an applicant has equivalent education or work history, a degree may not be necessary. Applicants should also be in good physical shape, as the job may require significant walking, hiking, and lifting. [17]

(3)

The park ranger would be responsible <u>for protection and supervising Deep Woods State Park.</u> [18] The park ranger would provide information to park guests in the Visitor's Center and supervise the grounds. He or she would enforce all legal and safety rules for the park and work with law enforcement as necessary. The park ranger would also be responsible for coordinating the park's Junior Ranger program, which educates <u>4 to 12 children</u> [19] about the park's history, environment, and safety rules.

(4)

If this sounds like the job for you, <u>hit us up at our website.</u> [20] Please be prepared to send a full resume and list of references.

15. **a.** *(No change)*
   b. huge outside
   c. great out of doors
   d. great outdoors

16. Which of the following would be the best way to combine the indicated sentences?
   a. Applicants should have a bachelor's degree in forestry at a minimum: they can also have a degree in environmental science, or biology.
   b. At a minimum, applicants should have a bachelor's degree in forestry, biology, or environmental science.
   c. Applicants should have a minimum bachelor's degree in: forestry, environmental science, or biology.
   d. Minimum applicants have a bachelor's degree in forestry, environmental science, or biology.

17. Which of the following sentences, added to the end of paragraph 2, would provide the best conclusion to the paragraph?
   a. Applicants should also be trained and certified in CPR and first aid.
   b. The park ranger may encounter animals while on duty.
   c. The most recent park ranger retired after 25 years on the job.
   d. Deep Woods State Park is 10,000 acres.

18. **a.** (*No change*)
   b. for protection and supervision Deep Woods State Park
   c. for protecting and supervising Deep Woods State Park
   d. for having protected and supervised Deep Woods State Park

19. **a.** (*No change*)
   b. aged children 4 to 12
   c. 4 years old to 12 years old
   d. 4- to 12-year-old children

20. **a.** (*No change*)
   b. If this sounds like the job for you, give us a shout at our website.
   c. If this sounds like the job for you, please visit our website.
   d. If you are of the belief that you are qualified to accept this position, a website visit is for you.

Read through the draft travel article. Then go on to the suggestions for revision that follow.

Find yourself on the Outer Banks, in North Carolina, during the summer, there's a nightly event you shouldn't miss, or you'll regret it. Every night when the weather is temperate, the ghost crabs come out to play, whether there are people on the beach or not.

They're only about two inches wide when they're fully grown. They're also so light in color that they blend in with the sand. Because they're so small and light, you might only see a wisp of movement before they disappear into small holes in the beach. If you blink, you might miss them as they scuttle over the sand toward their burrows.

Ghost crabs may also seem ghostly because they come out at only sunset. Most beachgoers have packed up and gone home for dinner by then, so the crabs are able to muster the courage to scurry out on the beach, moving from their homes to the water and from the water to their homes. Ghost crabs mostly keep to themselves, but if you try to catch one, you might be on the receiving end of a sharp pinch! You may want to check out other Outer Banks wildlife the wild horses in Corolla and the clusters of dolphins that often frolic near the shores.

(1)

Find yourself on the Outer Banks, in North Carolina, during the summer, there's a nightly event you shouldn't miss, or you'll regret it. [21] Every night when the weather is temperate, the ghost crabs come out to play, whether [22] there are people on the beach or not.

(2)

[23] They're only about two inches wide when they're fully grown. They're also so light in color that they blend in with the sand. Because they're so small and light, you might only see a wisp of movement before they disappear into small holes in the beach. If you blink, you might miss them as they scuttle over the sand toward their burrows. [24]

(3)

Ghost crabs may also seem ghostly because they come out at only sunset. [25] Most beachgoers have packed up and gone home for dinner by then, so the crabs are able to muster the courage to scurry out on the beach, moving from their homes to the water and from the water to their homes. Ghost crabs mostly keep to themselves, but if you try to catch one, you might be on the receiving end of a sharp pinch! [26] You may want to check out other Outer Banks wildlife the wild horses in Corolla and the clusters of dolphins that often frolic near the shores. [27]

21. a. *(No change)*
   b. This summer, in the Outer Banks in North Carolina: a nightly even you won't want to miss.
   c. Finding yourself in North Carolina's Outer Banks this summer, there's a nightly event you shouldn't miss.
   d. If you find yourself in North Carolina's Outer Banks this summer, there's a nightly event you shouldn't miss.

22. Which of the following words, if any, is misspelled?
   a. *(None)*
   b. weather
   c. temperate
   d. whether

23. Which of the following sentences, added to the beginning of paragraph 2, would provide the best introduction to the paragraph?
  a. Now, these crabs aren't "ghosts" exactly— they are very real and very much alive!
  b. Some species of ghost crabs actually have very bright colors.
  c. Ghost crabs' eyeballs sit at the end of long and swollen eyestalks.
  d. Ghost crabs are found mostly in the Atlantic Ocean along the North and South American coasts.

24. The writer is considering deleting the indicated information. Should the writer delete this material?
  a. No, because it provides relevant information about the topic of the passage.
  b. No, because it introduces the topic of the following paragraph.
  c. Yes, because it basically restates the information in the sentence before it.
  d. Yes, because it veers too far from the topic of the passage.

25. **a.** (*No change*)
  b. only come out at sunset
  c. come only out at sunset
  d. come out only at sunset

26. Which of the following would be the best transitional phrase to begin the sentence?
  a. When you are on the Outer Banks,
  b. After you've visited the ghost crabs,
  c. Before you visit North Carolina,
  d. Check it out:

27. **a.** (*No change*)
  b. The wild horses in Corolla and the clusters of dolphins that often frolic near the shores, they are other Outer Banks wildlife for you to check out.
  c. Check out other Outer Banks wildlife, the wild horses in Corolla, and the clusters of dolphins that often frolic near the shores.
  d. Check out other Outer Banks wildlife: the wild horses in Corolla and the clusters of dolphins that often frolic near the shores.

Read through the draft letter. Then go on to the suggestions for revision that follow.

Dear Editors of the *Tribune*,

I've been perusing your periodicul for more than forty years, and in those decades I've never felt the need to write a letter to the editors before. However, things change, and your article on the school board meeting June 15 was so full of inaccuracies and slanted opinions that I had to speak up.

First of all, I think that your reporter, Missy Palmer-Florick, was out of line when she called supporters of the new school yoga initiative "overgrown flower children." Wanting to teach relaxation techniques to our overstimulated kids is not some joke. It is not on the same level as running around barefoot at Woodstock.

The information you printed about the vote on the high school Harvest Day dance was incorrect. I was at the meeting, and I remember the vote. Six votes for keeping the dance and four votes against it. If you'll recall, the police had to be called twice. There were also two non-votes, as board members Joseph Franklin and Mamie Gunderson were not at the meeting. Yet your reporter who wrote that the vote was "tied at 6–6." Was Ms. Palmer-Florick even at the meeting?

As a member of this community, I have expect better from our local newspaper. I hope you'll print a retraction of all the wrong information and give your reporters a refresher course on how to report the news.

---

(1)

Dear Editors of the *Tribune*,

I've been <u>perusing your periodicul for more than forty</u> [28] years, and in those decades I've never felt the need to write a letter to the editors before. However, things change, and <u>your article on the school board meeting June 15</u> [29] was so full of inaccuracies and slanted opinions that I had to speak up.

(2)

First of all, I think that your reporter, Missy Palmer-Florick, was <u>out of line</u> [30] when she called supporters of the new school yoga initiative "overgrown flower children." <u>Wanting to teach relaxation techniques to our overstimulated kids is not some joke. It is not on the same level as running around barefoot at Woodstock.</u> [31]

(3)

[32] The information you printed about the vote on the high school Harvest Day dance was incorrect. I was at the meeting, and <u>I remember the vote. Six votes for keeping the dance and four votes against it.</u> [33] If you'll recall, the police had to be called twice. There were also two non-votes, as board members Joseph Franklin and Mamie Gunderson were not at the meeting. <u>Yet your reporter who wrote that the vote was "tied at 6–6."</u> [34] Was Ms. Palmer-Florick even at the meeting?

(4)

As a member of this community, I <u>have expect</u> [35] better from our local newspaper. I hope you'll print a retraction of all the wrong information and give your reporters a refresher course on how to report the news.

28. Which of the following words, if any, is misspelled?
   a. *(None)*
   b. perusing
   c. periodicul
   d. forty

29. a. *(No change)*
   b. your article on the June 15 school board meeting
   c. your June 15 school board meeting article on
   d. your school board meeting June 15 article

30. a. *(No change)*
   b. off the hook
   c. under the radar
   d. beyond the pale

31. Which of the following would be the best way to combine the indicated sentences?
   a. Wanting to teach relaxation techniques to our overstimulated kids is not some joke; it is not some joke on the same level as running around barefoot at Woodstock.
   b. Wanting to teach relaxation techniques to our overstimulated kids is not some joke it is not on the same level as running around barefoot at Woodstock.
   c. Wanting to teach relaxation techniques to our overstimulated kids is not some joke; it is not some joke on the same level as running around.
   d. Wanting to teach relaxation techniques to our overstimulated kids is not on the same level as running around barefoot at Woodstock.

32. Which of the following would be the best transitional word or phrase to begin the sentence?
   a. Similarly,
   b. In contrast,
   c. Therefore,
   d. Second,

33. Which of the following would be the best way to combine the indicated sentences?
   a. I remember the vote there were six votes for keeping the dance and four votes against it.
   b. I remember the vote; four votes for keeping the dance and six votes against it.
   c. I remember the vote: six votes for keeping (the dance) and four votes against it.
   d. I remember the vote: six votes for keeping the dance and four votes against it.

34. a. *(No change)*
   b. Yet your reporter wrote that the vote was "tied at 6–6."
   c. Your reporter who yet wrote that the vote was "tied at 6–6."
   d. Yet your reporter, who wrote that the vote was "tied."

35. a. *(No change)*
   b. expects
   c. expect
   d. will expect

Read through the biographical report. Then go on to the suggestions for revision that follow.

> If you wrote one of the most famous and beloved novels in the world, what would you do next, would you capitalize on your success and keep publishing books? Would you bask in your fame and become a professional celebrity? If you were author Harper Lee, you would choose another option altogether: quietly live and never write another book.
>
> When Harper Lee published her *To Kill a Mockingbird* novel in July 1960, it became a sensation. The book—a coming-of-age story about a young girl living in Civil Rights–era Alabama—was a major bestseller. It won one of the most prestigious literary prizes, the Pulitzer, that same year. Within two years, it was adapted into a blockbuster Academy Award–winning movie. The public couldn't get enough of Ms. Lee and her writing.
>
> Despite this, Harper Lee did not take well to being a celebrity author. She once described feeling overwhelmed by the big lights.
>
> She withdrew from the literary world. We lost a truly unique voice. Perhaps the biggest loss of all was that she never writes another novel.

(1)

If you wrote one of the most famous and beloved novels in the world, <u>what would you do next, would you capitalize on your success and keep publishing books?</u> [36] Would you bask in your fame and become a professional celebrity? If you were author Harper Lee, you would choose another option altogether: <u>quietly live and never write another book.</u> [37]

(2)

<u>When Harper Lee published her *To Kill a Mockingbird* novel in July 1960,</u> [38] it became a sensation. The book—a coming-of-age story about a young girl living in Civil Rights–era Alabama—was a major bestseller. It won one of the most prestigious literary prizes, the Pulitzer, that same year. Within two years, it was adapted into a blockbuster Academy Award–winning movie. The public couldn't get enough of Ms. Lee and her writing.

(3)

Despite this, Harper Lee did not take well to being a celebrity author. She once described feeling overwhelmed by the <u>big lights</u> [39]. [40]

(4)

[41] She withdrew from the literary world. We lost a truly unique voice. [42] Perhaps the biggest loss of all was that <u>she never writes another novel</u> [43].

36. a. *(No change)*
   b. what would you do next: would you capitalize on your success and keep publishing books?
   c. what would you do next? Would you capitalize on your success and keep publishing books?
   d. what would you do next would you capitalize on your success and keep publishing books?

37. **a.** *(No change)*
    b. live and quietly never write another book.
    c. quietly live and quietly never write another book.
    d. live quietly and never write another book.

38. **a.** *(No change)*
    b. When Harper Lee published *To Kill a Mockingbird* her novel in July 1960
    c. When Harper Lee published her novel, *To Kill a Mockingbird*, in July 1960
    d. When Harper Lee published her novel in July 1960 *To Kill a Mockingbird*

39. **a.** *(No change)*
    b. stage lights
    c. spotlight
    d. lights

40. Which of these would be an appropriate source for the writer to use and mention here?
    a. an excerpt from a biography theorizing about why Lee did not want to be a celebrity
    b. a first-person anecdote from a close friend of Lee about Lee's feelings about being a celebrity
    c. a newspaper editorial about how *To Kill a Mockingbird* made Lee a celebrity
    d. a quote from an interview in which Lee explains her feelings about being a celebrity

41. Which of the following sentences, added at the beginning of paragraph 4, would provide the best opening for the paragraph?
    a. In 2015, HarperCollins published Lee's first draft of *To Kill a Mockingbird* under the title *Go Set a Watchman*.
    b. The movie version of *To Kill a Mockingbird* went on to win several Academy Awards.
    c. Lee never quite recovered from her fear of fame, and she remained intensely private for the rest of her life.
    d. Harper Lee was the childhood friend of another famous writer: Truman Capote.

42. Which of the following would be the best way to combine the indicated sentences?
    a. When she withdrew from the literary world, we lost a truly unique voice.
    b. She withdrew from the literary world we lost a truly unique voice.
    c. She withdrew from the literary world then we lost a truly unique voice.
    d. She withdrew from the literary world and lost a truly unique voice.

43. **a.** *(No change)*
    b. she never wrote another novel
    c. she will never write another novel
    d. she is never writing another novel

Read through the personal narrative. Then go on to the suggestions for revision that follow.

When you're a couch potato, training to run a 5K race is one of the hardest things I've ever done. I wasn't sure if I could do it, but now I know.

It began when my best friend started babbling about running the big marathon. All I knew about marathoners was that they were very devoted to running all the time. Jeff told me it had been a lifelong goal and he had recently decided to go for it. Okay, more power to you, Jeff. It got me thinking: why shouldn't I try something like this as well? I was pretty sure a marathon would kill me, but maybe a 5K race would be possible.

After making my decision, I had to deal with the hard part: the training. The last time I'd run any distance farther than the bus stop, I was in school. I needed to take baby steps, so I took small jogs every morning. Then I thought about quitting every day for that first week. Then I forgot about quitting. Then I even started liking it. Within a few weeks, I was actually looking *forward* to my morning run! I went ahead and signed up for the Memorial Day 5K.

On race day, I was nervous but ready. I barely noticed the other runners stretching and chatting at the starting line around me. By mile 3, I was struggling. Somehow, I found the adrenaline to keep going, and I crossed that finish line. Amazingly, I finished ten seconds under my best training time.

(1)

When you're a couch potato, training to run a 5K race is one of the hardest things I've ever done. [44] I wasn't sure if I could do it, but now I know.

(2)

It began when my best friend started babbling [45] about running the big marathon. All I knew about marathoners was that they were very devoted to running all the time. Jeff told me it had been a lifelong goal and he had recently decided to go for it. Okay, more power to you, Jeff. [46] It got me thinking: why shouldn't I try something like this as well? I was pretty sure a marathon would kill me, but maybe a 5K race would be possible.

(3)

After making my decision, I had to deal with the hard part: the training. [47] The last time I'd run any distance farther than the bus stop, I was in school. I needed to take baby steps, so I took small jogs every morning. Then I thought about quitting every day for that first week. Then I forgot about quitting. Then I even started liking it. [48] Within a few weeks, I was actually looking *forward* to my morning run! I went ahead and signed up for the Memorial Day 5K.

(4)

(1) On race day, I was nervous but ready. (2) I barely noticed the other runners stretching and chatting at the starting line around me. (3) By mile 3, I was struggling. (4) Somehow, I found the adrenaline to keep going, and I crossed that finish line. Amazingly, I finished ten seconds under my best training time. [49] [50]

44. **a.** *(No change)*

    b. I am a couch potato. Training to run a 5K race is one of the hardest things I've ever done.

    c. Training to run a 5K race is one of the hardest things I've ever done, especially since I'm a couch potato.

    d. When you're a couch potato, training to run a 5K race is one of the hardest things you'll ever do.

45. **a.** *(No change)*

    b. echoing

    c. pronouncing

    d. boasting

46. The writer is considering deleting the indicated information. Should the writer delete this material?

    a. No, because it adds some needed humor to an otherwise serious narrative.

    b. No, because it introduces information that is important to the passage.

    c. Yes, because it is unnecessary and shifts the perspective of the passage.

    d. Yes, because it is a sentence fragment, which is grammatically incorrect.

47. **a.** *(No change)*

    b. After making my decision came the hard part.

    c. After I'd made my decision (the easy part) then came the hard part; the training.

    d. Then came the hard part (after I'd made my decision).

48. Which of the following would be the best way to combine the indicated sentences?

    a. Then I thought about quitting every day for that first week—then I forgot about quitting—then I even started liking it.

    b. Then I thought about quitting every day for that first week then I forgot about quitting then I even started liking it.

    c. I thought about quitting every day for that first week, but I soon forgot about quitting and even started liking it.

    d. Then I thought about quitting every day for that first week . . . I forgot about quitting . . . I even started liking it.

49. Which of the following sentences, added at the end of paragraph 4, would provide the best closing sentence for the paragraph?

    a. Not too bad for a couch potato.

    b. Take that, Jeff!

    c. It was my best running time ever.

    d. The marathon is scheduled for next month.

50. The writer wants to add the following information to paragraph 4:

I heard the "pow" of the starter pistol, and I was off!

For the most logical organization of ideas, where should this sentence be placed?

    a. after sentence 1

    b. after sentence 2

    c. after sentence 3

    d. after sentence 4

Part 2: Essay Question
45 Minutes

This part of the practice test will assess your writing skills. On the official exam, you will have a 45-minute limit to plan and write your essay. Your essay will be scored on how well you

- develop a main idea and support it with strong reasons, examples, and details
- clearly organize your ideas, including the use of an introduction and conclusion, logical paragraphs, and effective transitions

- use language, including varied word choice and sentence constructions and appropriate voice
- clearly and correctly use writing conventions

Each passage offers a different perspective on the same important issue. Read both passages carefully, taking note of the strengths and weaknesses of each author's discussion. Then write an essay that explains your own opinion on the important issue discussed in both passages.

The following excerpt includes Federal Aviation Administration (FAA) drone guidelines.

Unmanned Aircraft Systems, also known as drones, are small flying vehicles without pilots that are becoming popular for personal use, such as hobby flying or photography. However, they can also serve recreational functions. Drones can be used to conduct illegal surveillance. If improperly piloted, they can also prove to be extremely dangerous. Therefore, the Federal Aviation Administration has recently put forth guidelines for ownership and operation of drones that will help guarantee the legal and safe use of these recent occupiers of American airspace. The FAA's guidelines include the following specifications:

Model aircraft operations are for hobby or recreational purposes only.

The FAA has partnered with several industry associations to promote Know Before You Fly, a campaign to educate the public about using unmanned aircraft safely and responsibly. Individuals flying for hobby or recreation are strongly encouraged to follow safety guidelines, which include:

- Fly below 400 feet and remain clear of surrounding obstacles.
- Keep the aircraft within visual line of sight at all times.
- Remain well clear of and do not interfere with manned aircraft operations.
- Don't fly within 5 miles of an airport unless you contact the airport and control tower before flying.
- Don't fly near people or stadiums.
- Don't fly an aircraft that weighs more than 55 lbs.
- Don't be careless or reckless with your unmanned aircraft—you could be fined for endangering people or other aircraft.

The statutory parameters of a model aircraft operation are outlined in Section 336 of Public Law 112-95 (the FAA Modernization and Reform Act of 2012). Individuals who fly within the scope of these parameters do not require permission to operate their UAS; any flight outside these parameters (including any non-hobby, non-recreational operation) requires FAA authorization. For example, using a UAS to take photos for your personal use is recreational; using the same device to take photographs or videos for compensation or sale to another individual would be considered a non-recreational operation.

Furthermore, the FAA has proposed a new system by which state government can enact mandatory drone registration. Registration is intended to reduce dangerous piloting errors by forcing drone owners to consider the consequences of improper drone use. They also protect the owners themselves by proving ownership in case of theft. At the cost of $5, registration is an inexpensive and simple way to protect your drone and the privacy and safety of others. The FAA has made a wise decision in calling for drone registration.

The following excerpt comes from a newspaper editorial about the FAA's requiring all drone owners to register their drones.

A homemaker is not expected to register an oven even though it could prove to be a deadly device. A teenager is not expected to register an iPhone even though it can be used as a surveillance device. A child is not expected to register her teddy bear. So why has the FAA singled out the drone as a device that poses such a great risk that it needs to be registered?

According to this new registration program, the FAA allows state governments to require all drones over 0.55 lbs and below 55 lbs to be registered. The registration fee is a mere $5. The fine for failing to register can be as much as a whopping $27,500. In the most extreme cases, those who fail to register their drones may face a three-year prison stay. So if little Johnny forgets to register that drone he got for his birthday and it is now buzzing through a park as if it were a kite, he could suffer some serious consequences.

Every day, we use devices that can be employed for potentially nefarious purposes. However, only the most dangerous ones—such as cars—tend to require registration. Having to register something as innocuous as a drone seems oddly heavy-handed, and the penalties tumble over the precipice of absurdity. With such penalties in place, The FAA may be teetering at the top of a slippery slope that could lead to even heavier fines and prison sentences.

The FAA is not only targeting children with its new drone registration program, it is treating all Americans like children. The FAA is overreaching in a bid to line its pockets with fine-generated income and line prisons with people who have committed no greater offense than flying a model airplane. It is our duty as Americans to take a stand against the FAA's new drone registration program.

Write an essay in which you explain your own position on the issue of whether or not the state government should require drone owners to register their drones.

Be sure to use evidence from the text passages provided as well as specific reasons and examples from your own experience and knowledge to support your position. Remember that every position exists within the context of a larger discussion of the issue, so your essay should, at minimum, acknowledge alternate and/or opposing ideas. When you have finished your essay, review your writing to check for correct spelling, punctuation, and grammar.

_____

_____

_____

_____

_____

_____

_____

_____

_____

_____

_____

_____

_____

_____

_____

_____

_____

_____

_____

_____

_____

_____

Mathematics

90 Minutes
50 Questions

This practice test is modeled on the content and timing of the official HiSET® Mathematics test and, like the official test, presents a series of questions that assess your ability to solve quantitative problems using fundamental concepts and reasoning skills.

1. Assuming that b is a positive real number, solve this system:
$$\begin{cases} bx - y = 2b^2 \\ bx + 2y = 3b^2 \end{cases}$$
   a. $x = 7b, y = 5b^2$
   b. $x = 1, y = b - 2b^2$
   c. $x = b, y = b^2$
   d. $x = \frac{7}{3}b, y = \frac{1}{3}b^2$
   e. $x = \frac{7}{3}b, y = \frac{5}{3}b$

2. Suppose that a polynomial $p(x)$ satisfies the following conditions:
   - $(x + 4)^2$ divides $p(x)$ evenly.
   - $-4, 3, 0,$ and 1 are the only x-intercepts.
   - $p(x)$ has degree 6.

   Which of the following functions could be $p(x)$?
   a. $p(x) = x(x + 4)^2(x - 3)(x - 1)$
   b. $p(x) = x^3(x + 4)^2(x - 3)(x - 1)$
   c. $p(x) = x^2(x - 3)(x - 1)(x + 4)^2$
   d. $p(x) = x(x^2 - 9)(x + 4)^2(x - 1)$
   e. $p(x) = (x + 4)^3(x - 3)(x - 1)$

3. Downtown Wheels has different varieties of bikes available and on sale. There are four colors (red, green, black, and silver), two types of seats (large and standard), and three types of structures (beach cruiser, mountain bikes, and 10-speed). If a selection is drawn at random, what is the probability that it is a mountain bike?
   a. $\frac{1}{24}$
   b. $\frac{1}{12}$
   c. $\frac{1}{6}$
   d. $\frac{1}{4}$
   e. $\frac{1}{3}$

4. The diameter of Sphere A is 4 centimeters. What is the volume (in cubic centimeters) of a sphere whose radius is triple that of Sphere A?
   a. $2{,}304\pi$
   b. $6{,}912\pi$
   c. 576π
   d. 288π
   e. 864π

5. Which of the following expressions is equivalent to $(2x^2 + 3)(2 - 4x^2)$?
   a. $-8x^2$
   b. $8x^4 + 6$
   c. $-8x^4 - 8x^2 + 6$
   d. $8x^4 + 8x^2 - 6$
   e. $-8x^2 + 6$

6. Consider the following diagram:

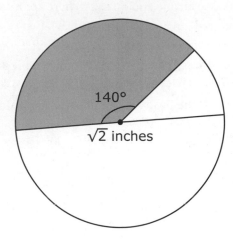

140°

√2 inches

What is the area (in square inches) of the shaded sector?

a. $\frac{7}{36}\pi$

b. $\frac{1}{2}\pi$

c. $\frac{7}{9}\pi$

d. $\frac{7\sqrt{2}}{36}\pi$

e. $\frac{11}{36}\pi$

7. Fill in the box with the correct exponent:
$$\sqrt[3]{x^2} \cdot \sqrt{x^5} = x^{\square}$$

a. $\frac{5}{3}$

b. $\frac{19}{6}$

c. $\frac{19}{10}$

d. $\frac{3}{5}$

e. $-\frac{11}{6}$

8. A furniture store manager decides to mark up the price of a living room set by $q\%$ in anticipation of increased interest during the holiday gift-buying season. If the new price is $\$z$ before tax, what was the price of the set before the markup?

a. $\frac{100}{100+q}z$

b. $\frac{100+q}{100}z$

c. $z+q$

d. $\frac{100}{q}z$

e. $(1+\frac{100}{q})z$

9. Two different groups, each consisting of 20 people from the audience of a rock concert, are asked to choose their favorite song from a list of four: song A, song B, song C, and song D. The results are as follows:

	SONG A	SONG B	SONG C	SONG D	TOTAL
Group 1	4	4	12	0	20
Group 2	4	6	10	0	20
TOTAL	8	10	22	0	40

Which of the following is an accurate inference regarding the entire audience?
a. Exactly 25% of the audience has song B as their favorite song on this list.
b. One expects that song C would be listed as the favorite by most audience members.
c. More than half of the audience has song C as their favorite on the list.
d. Song C must be the most modern hit based on the number who identified it as their favorite.
e. Nobody in the audience identifies song D as their favorite on the list.

10. Solve for x: $-2(x + 2) - 1 = 2(2 - x)$.

   a. -3

   b. $\frac{1}{4}$

   c. 9

   d. $-\frac{4}{9}$

   e. no solution

11. The fuel efficiency of a car is measured using the equation $F = \frac{M}{g}$, where M is the number of miles and g is the number of gallons used to travel that number of miles. If Sam's fuel efficiency is 56.1 miles per gallon and he drove 151.47 miles, how many gallons of fuel did he use?

   a. 95.4

   b. 0.37

   c. 27.0

   d. 3.70

   e. 2.70

12. Consider the following sequence of numbers: $-7, -15, -23, \ldots$

Which of the following is the formula for the nth term of this sequence?

   a. $f(n) = n - 8, n \geq 1$

   b. $f(n) = -7 + 8n, n \geq 0$

   c. $f(n) = -7 - 8n, n \geq 0$

   d. $f(n) = 7 - 8n, n \geq 0$

   e. $f(n) = -7n - 8n, n \geq 0$

13. A homeowner needs to anchor an 8-foot-tall inflatable snowman to the ground, as shown in the diagram:

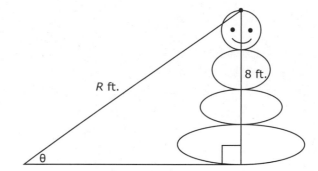

If a rope that is R feet long is fastened to the top of the snowman's head, which of the following equations can be used to determine the angle θ that the rope makes with the ground?

   a. $\sin \theta = \frac{8}{R}$

   b. $\tan \theta = \frac{8}{R}$

   c. $\cos \theta = \frac{R}{8}$

   d. $\sin \theta = \frac{R}{8}$

   e. $\cos \theta = \frac{8}{R}$

14. Consider the ordered pairs (x, y) given in the table:

x	-3	2	5	8	11	14
y	7	5	4	-1	-2	-5

Which of the following best describes the line of best fit for this data?

   a. The best fit line passes through all of these points.

   b. The best fit line is horizontal.

   c. The slope of the best fit line is negative.

   d. The slope of the best fit line is positive.

   e. There is no best fit line.

15. Light travels at an approximate rate of 3.2×10^8 meters per second. How far does light travel in one day?

a. 7.68×10^9 meters

b. 1.92×10^{10} meters

c. 1.935×10^{14} meters

d. 1.152×10^{12} meters

e. 2.7648×10^{13} meters

16. Consider the line segment $\overline{AB}$:

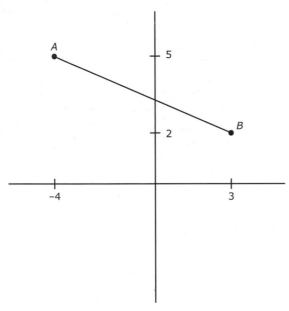

What are the endpoints of the image $\overline{A'B'}$ of this line segment obtained after reflecting $\overline{AB}$ over the line $x = -6$?

a. $A'(16,5)$, $B'(9,2)$

b. $A'(-4,7)$, $B'(3,10)$

c. $A'(-8,5)$, $B'(-15,2)$

d. $A'(-4,-17)$, $B'(3,-14)$

e. $A'(5,-4)$, $B'(3,2)$

17. Which of the following expressions is NOT equivalent to $x(2x - 3) - 3(4 - 2x^2) + 6x^2$?

a. $6x^2 + x(2x - 3) - 3(4 - 2x^2)$

b. $-[3(4 - 2x^2) - 6x^2 - x(2x - 3)]$

c. $14x^2 - 3(x + 4)$

d. $2x^2 - 3x - 12$

e. $x(2x - 3) - 3(4 - 4x^2)$

18. Which of the following quadratic equations has the solution set $\{\pm 4i\}$?

a. $x^2 + 16 = 0$

b. $x^2 = 16$

c. $x^2 = 16x$

d. $x(x + 16) = 0$

e. $16x^2 + 1 = 0$

19. Micah's tennis record suggests that whenever he serves the ball, the probability that he will score the point is 0.35, the probability that he will have one fault is 0.47, and the probability that he will do neither is 0.61. What is the probability that Micah either scores the point or has one fault?

a. 0.82

b. 0.66

c. 0.35

d. 0.47

e. 0.49

20. What is the perimeter (in feet) of the shaded sector?

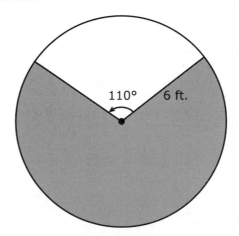

a. $\frac{50}{3}\pi + 12$

b. $\frac{25}{3}\pi$

c. 1,512

d. 1,500

e. $12 + \frac{25}{3}\pi$

21. Assuming that a, b, c, d, and e are real numbers, what property of the real numbers is illustrated?

$$(a + b) + (c + d) = a + (b + c + d)$$

a. associative property
b. additive identity
c. commutative property
d. additive inverse
e. distributive property

22. The profit (in hundreds of dollars) that each member of the chess club earns by selling rolls of holiday gift wrap over the course of six weeks depends on the amount, a, that they charge per roll. From which of the following equivalent forms could you immediately determine the maximum profit?
a. $-3(a - 4)^2 + 8$
b. $-3(a - 2)(a - 6)$
c. $-3a^2 + 24a - 36$
d. $-(36 - 24a + 3a^2)$
e. $-3(a^2 - 8a + 16) + 8$

23. If the domain of a function $y = f(x)$ is $[-2,6]$ and its range is $[-1,8]$, what are the domain and range of the function $g(x) = f(x + 3) - 2$?
a. domain = $[-2,6]$ and range = $[-3,6]$
b. domain = $[1,9]$ and range = $[-3,6]$
c. domain = $[-5,3]$ and range = $[1,10]$
d. domain = $[-5,3]$ and range = $[-3,6]$
e. domain = $[1,9]$ and range = $[1,10]$

24. A merchant at the farmer's market sells plums and peaches. If the cost for 5 plums and 6 peaches is $6.75 and the cost of 8 plums and 3 peaches is $7.50, which system can be used to determine the price of one plum and one peach?

a. $\begin{cases} x + y = 11 \\ 8x + 3y = 14.25 \end{cases}$

b. $\begin{cases} 5x + 6y = 7.50 \\ 8x + 3y = 6.75 \end{cases}$

c. $\begin{cases} 5x + 3y = 6.75 \\ 8x + 6y = 7.50 \end{cases}$

d. $\begin{cases} 8x + 6y = 6.75 \\ 5x + 3y = 7.50 \end{cases}$

e. $\begin{cases} 5x + 6y = 6.75 \\ 8x + 3y = 7.50 \end{cases}$

25. Fill in the box with the correct exponent:

$$\sqrt[3]{\sqrt{\tfrac{1}{5}}} = 5^{\square}.$$

a. $\frac{1}{6}$
b. $-\frac{5}{6}$
c. -6
d. $-\frac{2}{3}$
e. $-\frac{1}{6}$

26. What is the equation of the circle shown, whose center is O?

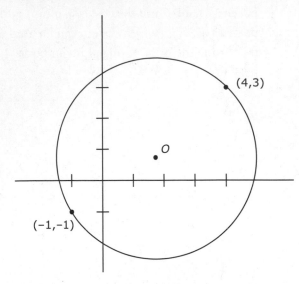

a. $(x - \frac{3}{2})^2 + (y - 1)^2 = \frac{41}{4}$

b. $(x - \frac{3}{2})^2 + (y - 1)^2 = 41$

c. $(x + \frac{3}{2})^2 + (y + 1)^2 = \frac{41}{4}$

d. $(x - \frac{3}{2})^2 + (y - 1)^2 = \sqrt{\frac{41}{2}}$

e. $(x - \frac{3}{2})^2 + (y - 1)^2 = \sqrt{41}$

27. A player spins the following spinner:

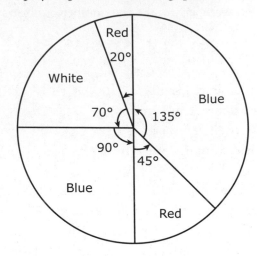

What is the probability that the spinner does not land on red or white?

a. 0.375

b. 0.750

c. 0.806

d. 0.625

e. 0.600

28. Suppose that P_1 and P_2 represent two populations of sea turtles and $P_1 > P_2$. Which of the following inequalities is true?

a. $\frac{P_1}{P_1 + P_2} < \frac{P_2}{P_1 + P_2}$

b. $\frac{P_2}{P_1 + P_2} > \frac{1}{2}$

c. $\frac{P_1}{P_2} = \frac{P_2}{P_1}$

d. $2P_1 > P_1 + P_2$

e. $\frac{P_2}{P_1 + P_2} > \frac{P_1 + P_2}{P_2}$

29. Which of the following systems has no solution?

a. $\begin{cases} 4x = 2y - 1 \\ 6x = 3y + 4 \end{cases}$

b. $\begin{cases} 2x = 7y - 3 \\ 4x = 14y - 6 \end{cases}$

c. $\begin{cases} 2x - 7 = 1 \\ 3y + 5 = 2 \end{cases}$

d. $\begin{cases} 5y - x = 0 \\ 10y = 2x \end{cases}$

e. $\begin{cases} y = \frac{1}{2}x + 1 \\ y = -2x - 1 \end{cases}$

30. Compute the average value for the function $g(x) = x^2 - 3x$ on the interval $[-1,2]$.

a. -6

b. 0

c. $\frac{2}{3}$

d. -1

e. -2

31. Which of the following data sets has a mean of 6, median of 7, and mode of 2?

a. 2, 2, 2, 2, 7, 8, 8, 8, 10

b. 2, 2, 6, 9, 15

c. 2, 2, 2, 7, 7, 11, 11

d. 2, 6, 6, 6, 15

e. 1, 2, 2, 6, 7, 7, 24

32. A building casts a shadow that is a feet long. In the same sunlight, a scale model of the building that is c feet tall casts a shadow that is b feet long. How tall (in feet) is the actual building?

a. $\frac{b}{a \cdot c}$

b. $\frac{b}{a + c}$

c. $a + b + c$

d. $\frac{a + c}{b}$

e. $\frac{a \cdot c}{b}$

33. If Sam jogs at a rate of 6 miles per hour, approximately how many minutes would it take him to jog 5,000 feet?

a. 833

b. 1,704.6

c. 28.4

d. 9.5

e. 568

34. A dinner bill comes to $75.50 before applying the 6% tax. You have a coupon for 15% off the bill before tax and intend to tip 20% on the taxed amount after the coupon is applied. What is the total amount you will pay?

a. $81.64

b. $77.02

c. $64.18

d. $68.03

e. $90.60

35. The following graph shows the frequency of finding certain types of coins on the beach during a scavenger hunt:

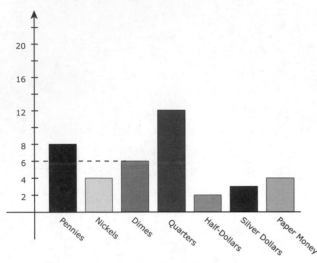

Assuming this is typical of such scavenger hunts, what percentage of the findings obtained in a hunt would you expect to be attributed to either quarters or silver dollars?

a. 40%

b. 30%

c. 10%

d. 20%

e. 60%

36. Which of the following expressions is equivalent to $\frac{5x^3 + x^2}{2x - 5} \div \frac{75x^3 + 30x^2 + 3x}{4x^2 - 8x - 5}$?

a. $\frac{x^2(2x + 1)}{15x + 1}$

b. $\frac{3x^3(5x + 1)^3}{(2x + 1)(2x - 5)^2}$

c. $\frac{x(2x - 1)}{3(5x - 1)}$

d. $\frac{2x + 1}{18}$

e. $\frac{2x^2 + x}{15x + 3}$

37. What is the solution set of the equation $\frac{x}{1 - x} + \frac{2}{x} = -1$?

a. $\left\{\frac{3}{2}\right\}$

b. $\{0,1\}$

c. $\{\ \}$

d. $\{2\}$

e. $\{-1,3\}$

38. The area of a rectangle is 88 square feet, and its perimeter is 38 feet. Which of the following equations can be used to determine the length of the sides of the rectangle?

a. $2x + 2(88 - x) = 38$

b. $2x + \frac{176}{x} = 38$

c. $x + \frac{88}{x} = 38$

d. $2x + \frac{x}{44} = 38$

e. $x + \frac{88}{x} = 44$

39. In a psychology experiment, the following information shows the number of hours slept versus the number of errors made during a 10-minute driving simulation.

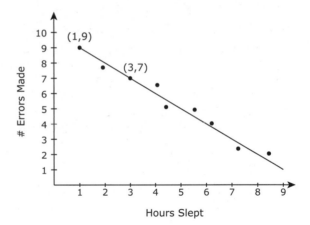

Suppose the best fit line is as shown in the diagram. Use it to predict the number of errors you would expect to make if you had 4 hours of sleep prior to completing the simulation.

a. 10

b. 6

c. 1

d. 5

e. 8

40. What is the domain of the function
$j(x) = \frac{x}{x^2 + 16}$?

a. $\{x \mid x \neq 0\}$

b. $\{x \mid x \neq -4,4\}$

c. $\{x \mid x \neq 4\}$

d. $\{x \mid x \neq -4,0,4\}$

e. all real numbers

41. Which of the following real numbers is irrational?

a. $(\frac{3}{5})^{-4}$

b. $0.32\overline{1}$

c. $\sqrt[3]{2} \cdot \sqrt[3]{32}$

d. $\sqrt{36} - \sqrt{20}$

e. $(\frac{1}{\pi})^0$

42. An airline allows rectangular carry-on bags whose maximum diagonal measurement of a side of the bag is 20 inches and maximum height of that side is 9 inches. Which of the following gives the dimensions of the maximum length (in inches) allowed?

a. $20^2 - 9^2$

b. $\sqrt{9^2 + 20^2}$

c. $\sqrt{20^2 - 9^2}$

d. $20^2 + 9^2$

e. $20 - 9$

43. Which of the following points lies on the line containing the segment shown here?

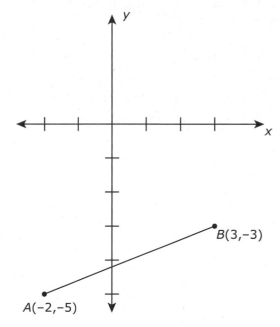

a. $(0,-4)$

b. $(-4,-10)$

c. $(5,2)$

d. $(-7,-6)$

e. $(-12,-9)$

44. The following chart shows the product ratings for a new smart home electronic device:

RATING (NUMBER OF STARS)	FREQUENCY
0	6
1	3
2	5
3	25
4	12
5	28

What is the median product rating?

a. 3.5 stars

b. 4.0 stars

c. 3.0 stars

d. 3.4875 stars

e. 3.77 stars

45. For which of the following inequalities is the solution set all real numbers?

   a. $x^2 - 4 \geq 0$

   b. $x(x + 5) < 0$

   c. $x^2 > -9$

   d. $(x - 3)^2 < 0$

   e. $-1 - x^2 \geq 0$

46. What is the solution set for the equation $x\sqrt{4x} - 1 = 0$?

   a. $\{\frac{1}{3}\}$

   b. $\{0\}$

   c. $\left\{\dfrac{1}{2^{\frac{3}{2}}}\right\}$

   d. $\left\{2^{-\frac{2}{3}}\right\}$

   e. $\left\{2^{\frac{2}{3}}\right\}$

47. You measure the amount of rainfall during the spring season. The function $r(x)$ gives the cumulative inches of rainfall, where x is measured in days. Which of the following can be solved to find the number of days it takes to get 7 inches of rain?

   a. $r(7) = x$

   b. $r(7) = 7$

   c. $7r(x) = 1$

   d. $r(x) = 1$

   e. $r(x) = 7$

48. Aaron measures the length of his MP3 player with a ruler. Which of the following is the most likely measurement?

   a. 30 mm

   b. 0.5 in.

   c. 0.34 m

   d. 8.2 cm

   e. 0.016 ft.

49. Consider the following graph of the polynomial $p(x)$:

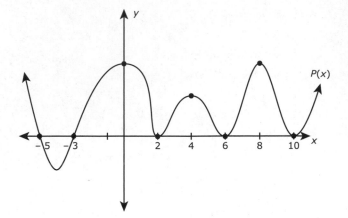

Which of the following is NOT a factor of $p(x)$?

   a. $x + 5$

   b. $x - 2$

   c. $x - 6$

   d. $x - 10$

   e. $x - 3$

50. What is the range of the function $f(t) = 3 \cdot 2^t$, when t is restricted to the interval $[1,4]$?

   a. $\{y \mid 1 \leq y \leq 4\}$

   b. $\{y \mid y > 0\}$

   c. all real numbers

   d. $\{y \mid 6 \leq y \leq 24\}$

   e. $\{y \mid 6 \leq y \leq 48\}$

Science

80 Minutes
50 Questions

This practice test is modeled on the content and timing of the official HiSET® Science test and, like the official test, presents a series of questions that assess your ability to use science content knowledge, apply principles of scientific inquiry, and interpret and evaluate scientific information.

Questions 1–5 are based on the following information.

Liming is an agricultural strategy that involves adding calcium- and magnesium-rich materials to neutralize soil acidity, increase bacterial activity, and promote soil particle aggregation. Several students were interested in comparing soil samples that were unaffected and soil samples that had been supplemented via liming. The students located a farm that uses liming on its soil, and they marked off one 4 × 4 m plot of unaffected soil and one 4 × 4 m plot of limed soil. Before the experiment and each week during the three-week experiment, the students reacted a 1.0 g soil sample with potassium permanganate and took an absorbance reading at 565 nm as an indicator of relative carbon biomass in the soil. The students tested three samples and took the average, including standard deviation–based error. The results are shown in the table.

| TIME (WEEKS) | ABSORBANCE AT 565 NM | |
	UNAFFECTED SOIL	LIMED SOIL
0	0.921 ± 0.001	0.927 ± 0.004
1	0.915 ± 0.002	0.813 ± 0.002
2	0.907 ± 0.003	0.783 ± 0.001
3	0.897 ± 0.002	0.699 ± 0.001

1. Given the function of liming, it can be concluded that lime is, relative to the original soil before liming, more
   a. hydrophobic.
   b. acidic.
   c. basic.
   d. neutral.

2. The lowest standard deviations included on the table are indicative of
   a. high precision.
   b. low precision.
   c. high accuracy.
   d. low accuracy.

3. The dependent variable in this experiment is
   a. the time points at which the readings were taken.
   b. the presence or absence of liming in the soil.
   c. the concentration of magnesium ions in the soil.
   d. relative carbon biomass, as tracked by the absorbance at 565 nm.

4. How does the evidence gathered in this experiment relate to the following statement?

   Soil liming reduces carbon sequestration in the soil over time.

   a. The evidence disproves the statement.
   b. The evidence proves the statement to be true.
   c. The evidence conflicts with the statement but does not disprove it.
   d. The evidence supports the statement but does not prove it to be true.

5. The scientists want to determine if the differences in carbon biomass changes observed between the same unaffected and limed soil plots are due to changes in bacterial population diversity over time. Which of the following procedures would test this scientific question?

a. Dilute and plate 1.0 g of unaffected and limed soil samples, from three weeks of study, onto agar plates and count the numbers and types of bacteria that grow overnight.

b. Dilute and plate 1.0 g of unaffected soil samples, from three weeks of study, onto agar plates containing magnesium and calcium and then count the numbers and types of bacteria that grow overnight.

c. Strain the unaffected and limed soil samples, from three weeks of study, to remove large soil aggregates and weigh the soil aggregates to determine the mass percentage of aggregates in the samples.

d. Dilute 1.0 g of unaffected and limed soil samples, carefully remove the soil, and determine the biomass relative to the overall sample mass.

Questions 6–10 are based on the following information.

Rhiannon was interested in investigating the correlation of the average distance of each planet from the sun with its average surface temperature. She wondered whether the proximity from the sun was the most important determinant of surface temperature. After doing some literature research, Rhiannon organized her data:

PLANET	AVERAGE DISTANCE FROM SUN (km)	AVERAGE SURFACE TEMPERATURE (°C)
Mercury	57 million	167
Venus	108 million	457
Earth	150 million	14
Mars	228 million	−55
Jupiter	779 million	−145
Saturn	1.43 billion	−168
Uranus	2.88 billion	−224
Neptune	4.50 billion	−200

6. Which of the following hypotheses might be posed to predict the outcome of the scientific question of interest?

a. If sunlight is more intense on planetary surfaces at closer distances than at farther distances, then closer planets should be brighter in appearance in the night sky than more distant planets.

b. If sunlight is more intense on planetary surfaces at closer distances than at farther distances, then closer planets should receive more intense light and experience warmer surface temperatures.

c. If sunlight is more intense on planetary surfaces at closer distances than at farther distances, then the atmospheres on planets at closer distances should be thinner than the atmospheres on planets at farther distances.

d. If sunlight is more intense on planetary surfaces at closer distances than at farther distances, then closer planets should experience warmer temperatures in their uppermost atmospheric layers than more distant planets.

7. Which of the following conclusions accurately responds to the scientific question, according to the collected evidence?
  a. In general, the average surface temperature increases for a planet as its distance from the sun increases.
  b. In general, the average surface temperature decreases for a planet as its distance from the sun increases.
  c. In general, the diameter of a planet increases as its distance from the sun increases.
  d. In general, the diameter of a planet decreases as its distance from the sun increases.

8. Data points used to calculate planetary distances from the sun are not precise because
  a. planet diameters vary widely.
  b. planets have elliptical orbits.
  c. some planets are rock and others are gaseous.
  d. planets vary in their numbers of moons.

9. Unexpected surface temperature variations may be attributed to differences in
  a. distances from nearby first-magnitude stars.
  b. revolution times.
  c. planet diameters.
  d. atmospheric conditions.

10. If planetary surface temperatures were plotted as a function of distances from the sun, the graph would appear to be
  a. positive and linear.
  b. negative and linear.
  c. positive and exponential.
  d. negative and exponential.

Questions 11–15 are based on the following information.

In the Namib Desert, fog-basking beetles and Namib dune bushman grass are able to collect water directly from fog. The beetles position themselves on dune ridges, optimally located, while the grass mostly grows at dune bases where less fog water is available. A group of scientists decided to test the amount of water each collected over time. The scientists collected beetles and grass from the Namib Desert. The beetles were killed by light freezing, and the grass was cut into 100-mm-long pieces. The beetles and grass were placed in a fog chamber, a 50 L refrigerator, at 10 to 15°C, comparable to temperatures during a fog in the Namib Desert. Beetles were placed at a 23-degree angle, the angle of their basking stance, and the grass was placed at the same angle. Fog was generated mechanically. Eppendorf tubes were used to catch water that ran off of the organisms. As a means of comparison for any special surface properties of the grass, a metal wire made of galvanized iron was also tested; this wire had the same dimensions as the grass, and it was also placed at a 23-degree angle. Twelve trials were performed, but none of the experiment objects were reused. The scientists recorded water collection per mm^2 based on the upper surface area of each experimental object.

The results are shown in Figure 1, including standard deviation–based error bars.

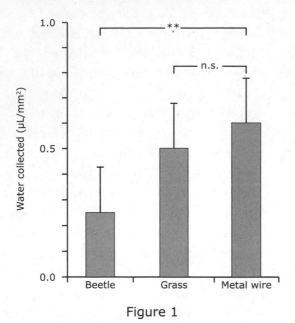

Figure 1

The experiment was run again with beetles and grass over two hours, with water volume measured every 20 minutes throughout the experiment, and the results are shown in Figure 2. The black line represents the beetles, and the gray line represents the grass.

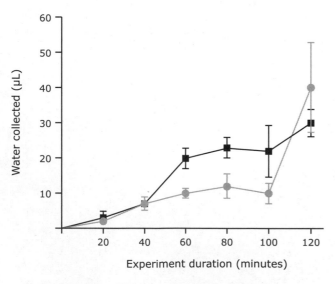

Source: http://www.plosone.org/article/fetchObject.action?uri= info:doi/10.1371/journal.pone.0034603&representation=PDF

Figure 2

11. In the first experiment, which of the following conditions was NOT a constant for all trials?
    a. the positioned angle of the test object per trial
    b. the temperature in the fog chamber per trial
    c. the identity of the test object per trial
    d. the size of the fog chamber per trial

12. According to Figure 2, the average volume of water collected by the grass after one hour was approximately
    a. 10 µL.
    b. 20 µL.
    c. 30 µL.
    d. 45 µL.

13. In Figure 1, the "n.s." abbreviation that marks the bars for the grass and wire stands for "not significant." These bars are labeled as such because
    a. there was too much experimental error during data collection.
    b. the obtained data values are far from the known "true" values.
    c. not enough trials were performed for the data sets to be considered significant.
    d. their error bars overlap, indicating that the difference between them is insignificant.

14. In order from most to least efficient water collectors over two hours, based on average values in Figure 1, the three objects are
    a. beetle, grass, and metal wire.
    b. grass, beetle, and metal wire.
    c. metal wire, beetle, and grass.
    d. metal wire, grass, and beetle.

15. Which of the following conclusions can be drawn about the water collection of the beetles and grass based on the average data in Figure 2?

  a. The beetle collected water more steadily over the course of two hours, but the grass collected a greater volume of water.

  b. The grass collected water more steadily over the course of two hours, but the beetle collected a greater volume of water.

  c. The beetle and grass collected lower volumes of water than the metal wire.

  d. The grass and metal wire collected lower volumes of water than the beetle.

Questions 16–20 are based on the following information.

Kory's friends employ the so-called "5-second rule" if they drop food on the ground, claiming it will be safe to eat if it is removed from the dirty surface before five seconds are up. Kory decided to test this rule in the lab using jellybeans and cold cut turkey. Using sterile gloves to avoid contamination, Kory placed each food item on the laboratory floor for five seconds, timed using a stopwatch. After five seconds, Kory removed each item from the ground, swabbed the item with a sterile swab, and gently streaked the swab onto a petri dish containing growth medium. Kory then repeated the test with the same two types of food items, but on the sidewalk outside. Finally, Kory swabbed samples of the food items that had not touched a surface and plated those samples as a control. Kory placed the six petri dishes at 37°C to allow any bacteria in the samples to grow. After 24, 48, and 72 hours, he checked the plates and counted the number of distinct bacterial colonies he saw. Kory then repeated the whole experiment two more times. His data are shown in the following graph.

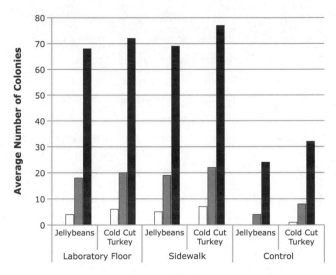

Tested Surfaces & Food Samples

☐ Average Number of Colonies 24 h
◼ Average Number of Colonies 48 h (gray)
■ Average Number of Colonies 72 h

16. The use of a sterile swab is important because

  a. it helps to prevent the introduction of bacterial contamination onto the plates from outside sources.

  b. it removes the excess nutrient growth medium from the plates.

  c. it helps to kill off any bacteria that may already be present on the plates.

  d. it specifically prevents the growth of fungi while allowing the growth of the bacteria under investigation.

17. The purpose of the control trials was to

  a. confirm that no bacteria grow from the unaffected food samples.

  b. demonstrate the diversity of bacteria that can grow on the plates.

  c. quantify bacterial colonies that grow from unaffected food samples.

  d. show that fungi will not grow on the plates.

18. In general, which surface conferred more bacteria to the food items over any time period?
   a. the laboratory floor
   b. the sidewalk
   c. Both surfaces conferred equal numbers of colonies to the food.
   d. Neither surface conferred any colonies to the food.

19. How does the evidence gathered in this experiment relate to the following statement?

The "5-second" rule holds, as surface contact did not significantly increase the amount of bacteria swabbed from the food items.

   a. The evidence disproves the statement.
   b. The evidence proves the statement to be true.
   c. The evidence conflicts with the statement but does not disprove it.
   d. The evidence supports the statement but does not prove it to be true.

20. If the number of bacterial colonies observed for any food item on a given surface is graphed as a function of time, the resulting graph would generally be
   a. positive and linear.
   b. negative and linear.
   c. positive and exponential.
   d. negative and exponential.

Questions 21–25 are based on the following information.

A factory was built along the Running River. The factory owner claimed that safe waste disposal practices were being followed, but a group of students wanted to use invertebrate species sampling along the Running River to make sure this was indeed the case. The students chose two locations on the river to acquire samples: Location 1 was located just downstream of the factory, where water pollution from the factory might be expected to run, while Location 2 was located well upstream of the factory, where any water pollution from the factory would not be expected to be present. The students made invertebrate collections in both locations one month before the factory opened, one month after it opened, and six months after it opened. From their collections, the students specifically identified pollution-sensitive species (e.g., mayflies, stoneflies, and caddisflies), moderately pollution-tolerant species (e.g., dragonflies, damselflies, and scuds), and pollution-tolerant organisms (e.g., midge larva and aquatic worms). Pollution-sensitive organisms function best at neutral pH, require dissolved oxygen, and prefer colder water, while pollution-tolerant organisms can handle the former conditions as well as low oxygen, variations in pH, and warmer water. For each type of organism, the students calculated the relative abundance, equal to the percentage of that specific organism group relative to the total number of collected organisms. Their results are shown in the table.

| | | RELATIVE ABUNDANCES (%) | |
		LOCATION 1	LOCATION 2
One Month before Opening	Pollution-sensitive species	45.2	48.0
	Somewhat pollution-tolerant species	49.6	47.5
	Pollution-tolerant species	5.2	4.5
One Month after Opening	Pollution-sensitive species	48.0	49.2
	Somewhat pollution-tolerant species	47.0	46.4
	Pollution-tolerant species	5.0	4.4
Six Months after Opening	Pollution-sensitive species	50.5	52.0
	Somewhat pollution-tolerant species	44.4	43.3
	Pollution-tolerant species	5.1	4.7

21. The purpose of sampling invertebrates from each of the two locations is to
   a. allow for comparison between organisms in slow-moving and fast-moving water.
   b. provide a positive control by sampling water that is definitely polluted and water that could potentially be polluted by the factory.
   c. gather data for water that would and would not be affected by potential factory pollution.
   d. collect pH values from two portions of the river so that an average pH value can be calculated.

22. The greatest relative abundance of pollution-tolerant organisms was observed at
   a. Location 1 one month before the factory opened.
   b. Location 1 one month after the factory opened.
   c. Location 2 one month after the factory opened.
   d. Location 2 six months after the factory opened.

23. The reason for gathering data points one month prior to the factory opening is to
   a. serve as a negative control by exhibiting typical invertebrate abundances in both locations prior to human interference.
   b. serve as a positive control by exhibiting typical invertebrate abundances in a polluted environment.
   c. allow for water quality comparisons of the two locations with a still body of water.
   d. provide a seasonal comparison of dissolved oxygen in both locations.

24. How does the evidence gathered in this experiment relate to the following statement?

Despite its claims to the contrary, the factory is contributing significant pollution to Running River at Location 1.

   a. The evidence disproves the statement.
   b. The evidence proves the statement to be true.
   c. The evidence conflicts with the statement but does not disprove it.
   d. The evidence supports the statement but does not prove it to be true.

25. Based on the description of pollution-sensitive and pollution-tolerant species, the key distinction between the two types of species is that
   a. pollution-sensitive species are generalists, while pollution-tolerant species are specialists.
   b. pollution-sensitive species are specialists, while pollution-tolerant species are generalists.
   c. pollution-sensitive species are herbivores, while pollution-tolerant species are omnivores.
   d. pollution-sensitive species are omnivores, while pollution-tolerant species are herbivores.

Questions 26–30 are based on the following information.

Kylie's dad, a fantastic cook, always told her that adding salt to water makes it boil faster. Kylie decided to test it for herself. She added 5 cups of water each into three identical cooking pots. She then added 1 tablespoon of salt to one pot and two tablespoons of salt to another pot and added no salt to the third pot. All three pots were placed on the stovetop and set at the same medium heat level. Kylie added a cooking thermometer to each pot to keep track of the temperature, recording the temperature at which water boils. She also used a stopwatch and recorded how long it took for each pot to reach its boiling point. Kylie's data are shown in the following graph.

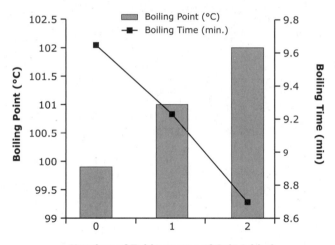

Number of Tablespoons of Salt Added

26. Which of the following choices provides the experimental question posed in this experiment?
   a. How does boiling point affect boiling time in water?
   b. How does boiling time affect boiling point in water?
   c. How do boiling point and boiling time affect the salt concentration in water?
   d. How does the addition of salt affect boiling point and boiling time in water?

27. What was the boiling time, in minutes, for pure water in this experiment?
  a. 8.91 min.
  b. 9.65 min.
  c. 99.8 min.
  d. 102.2 min.

28. A constant among all three trials of this experiment was
  a. the number of tablespoons of salt added to the water.
  b. the volume of water used in the pot.
  c. the boiling point of the water.
  d. the time it took the water sample to reach its boiling point.

29. According to the data, increasing the number of tablespoons of salt in the water
  a. decreases the boiling point and increases the boiling time.
  b. increases the boiling point and increases the boiling time.
  c. increases the boiling point and decreases the boiling time.
  d. decreases the boiling point and decreases the boiling time.

30. If the same experiment was repeated with 0.5 tablespoons of salt added to the water, the best estimate for the boiling point of the sample, based on the collected data, is
  a. 99.5°C.
  b. 100.5°C.
  c. 101.5°C.
  d. 102.5°C.

Questions 31–35 are based on the following information.

Carbon (C) reacts with fluorine gas (F_2) to produce gaseous carbon tetrafluoride (CF_4). The balanced chemical equation for this process is the following:

$$C(s) + 2F_2(g) \rightarrow CF_4(g)$$

A group of scientists wanted to look into the stoichiometry, a method that quantifies the relationship between reactants and products, for this particular reaction. The group constructed a sealed reaction chamber and filled it with varying quantities of fluorine gas. Then the scientists added a carefully measured mass of 5.00 g solid carbon, in excess to the fluorine gas, to the reaction chamber and allowed the reaction to run to completion such that the fluorine gas was completely used up. Upon completion of the reaction, the mass of solid carbon remaining was measured. The results of their work are shown in the table.

INPUT MASS OF $F_2(g)$	INITIAL MASS OF $C(g)$	FINAL MASS OF $C(g)$	DECREASE IN MASS OF $C(g)$
10.00	5.00	3.42	1.58
20.00	5.00	1.84	3.16
30.00	5.00	0.26	4.74

31. The independent variable in this experiment is
  a. the input mass of F_2.
  b. the initial mass of C.
  c. the final mass of C.
  d. the decrease in mass of C.

32. Which of the following states the experimental question posed in this investigation?
  a. How does the initial mass of C as a limiting reagent affect the mass of CCl_4 produced?
  b. How does the initial mass of F_2 as a limiting reagent affect the mass of CCl_4 produced?
  c. How does the initial mass of C as a limiting reagent affect the mass of F_2 used up in the reaction?
  d. How does the initial mass of F_2 as a limiting reagent affect the mass of C used up in the reaction?

33. If the scientists plotted the mass of the excess reactant used up in the reaction as a function of the mass of the limiting reactant used in the reaction, which of the following graphs most resembles the appearance of this plot?

a.

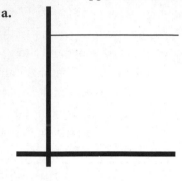

b.

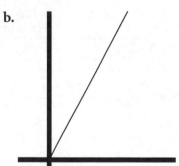

c.

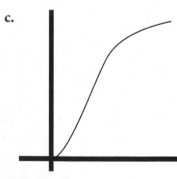

d.

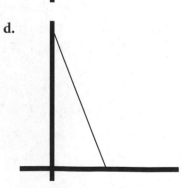

34. If 40.00 g F_2 reacted with 5.00 g C, what mass of C would remain after the reaction is complete?

a. 0.00 g

b. 0.13 g

c. 4.87 g

d. 5.00 g

35. Which of the following experiments would additionally provide stoichiometric data about this reaction?

a. Track the appearance of CF_4 as a function of mass of limiting C or F_2.

b. Track the disappearance of CF_4 as a function of mass of limiting C or F_2.

c. Track the appearance of CF_4 as a function of time.

d. Track the disappearance of CF_4 as a function of time.

Questions 36–40 are based on the following information.

Noah wanted to investigate oscillatory motion by studying the way a pendulum moves back and forth around a pivot point. He decided to study the effects of the bob mass and pendulum length on period length. The period length is defined as the time it takes for the bob of a pendulum to complete a single full cycle, swinging to the left and then back to the right. Noah set up a pendulum, as shown:

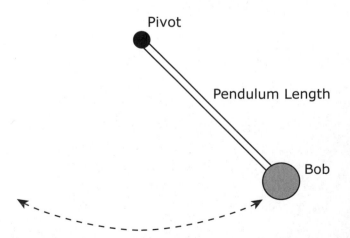

Noah then performed a number of trials exactly the same way, only varying bob masses and pendulum lengths, and used a stopwatch to measure the period length for each trial. He used the same pendulum setup throughout the experiment, only altering the aforementioned variables. His data are shown in the table.

BOB MASS (g)	PENDULUM LENGTH (cm)	PENDULUM PERIOD (SECONDS)		
		TRIAL 1	TRIAL 2	AVERAGE
100	50	1.333	1.335	1.334
100	100	1.699	1.690	1.695
100	150	1.808	1.908	1.858
200	150	1.800	1.918	1.859
400	150	1.799	1.917	1.858

36. A constant in every trial in this experiment is
    a. the mass of the bob.
    b. the angle of bob release.
    c. the length of the pendulum rod.
    d. the period length of the pendulum.

37. The most precise pair of trials in this experiment is the trial using
    a. the 100 g bob and the 50 cm pendulum length.
    b. the 100 g bob and the 150 cm pendulum length.
    c. the 200 g bob and the 150 cm pendulum length.
    d. the 400 g bob and the 150 cm pendulum length.

38. Noah wants to graph average pendulum period length as a function of bob mass. Which of the following graphs best displays the plot he would observe?

    a.

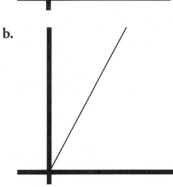

    b.

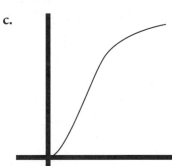

    c.

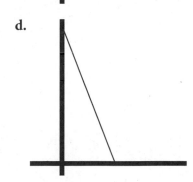

    d.

39. Which conclusion can be drawn about the effect of pendulum length on pendulum period?

    a. Period length decreases as pendulum length increases.

    b. Period length increases as pendulum length increases.

    c. Period length does not change as pendulum length increases.

    d. Period length fluctuates as pendulum length increases.

40. If the same experiment were performed on the moon, the length of each period of oscillation would

    a. increase due to increased gravitational acceleration.

    b. decrease due to increased gravitational acceleration.

    c. increase due to decreased gravitational acceleration.

    d. decrease due to decreased gravitational acceleration.

Questions 41–45 are based on the following information.

A group of students were interested in studying the effect of temperature on respiration in cold-blooded organisms. The balanced chemical equation for aerobic respiration—the reaction of glucose and oxygen to form carbon dioxide, water, and energy—is the following:

$$C_6H_{12}O_6 + 6O_2 \rightarrow 6CO_2 + 6H_2O + \text{energy}$$

The students focused on crickets and decided to track respiration using an O_2 gas sensor to detect oxygen gas concentrations. The students prepared three water baths, at 10°C, 20°C, and 30°C, with a thermometer in each to ensure that the desired temperatures were maintained. The students weighed several immobilized crickets and chose three that were equal in mass. The students chose one of these crickets and placed it into a respiration chamber in the 10°C water bath. After securing the gas sensor into the top of the respiration chamber, the students waited two minutes and then collected data for five minutes. The students then repeated the experiment in the 20°C and 30°C water baths. Their data for the three trials are shown.

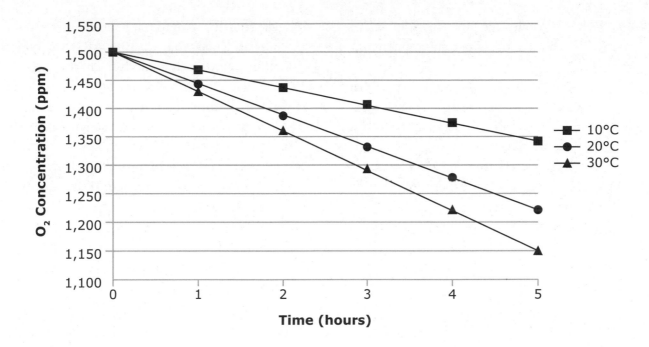

41. The dependent variable in this experiment is
   a. CO_2 concentration.
   b. time.
   c. O_2 concentration.
   d. temperature.

42. The purpose of waiting two minutes before collecting data is to
   a. allow for other physiological processes to halt so that they do not interfere with the respiration readings.
   b. equilibrate each of the respiration temperatures to their respective target temperatures.
   c. give the crickets time to move around so that they achieve maximal respiration rates for more accurate detection.
   d. prevent heat exchange between the water bath and the respiration chamber.

43. Based on the provided data, which of the following conclusions can be drawn about cellular processes in cold-blooded organisms?
   a. As temperature increases, the rate of photosynthesis increases in cold-blooded organisms.
   b. As temperature increases, the rate of photosynthesis decreases in cold-blooded organisms.
   c. As temperature increases, the rate of respiration increases in cold-blooded organisms.
   d. As temperature increases, the rate of respiration decreases in cold-blooded organisms.

44. Which of the following procedures provides another means of tracking respiration in the crickets?

a. Measure the consumption of CO_2 gas during the process.

b. Measure the release of energy in the form of heat during the process.

c. Detect the increase in fluorescence of the cricket throughout the experiment.

d. Measure light output from the cricket throughout the experiment.

45. The students want to test photosynthesis in peas using the same experimental setup. Which of the following limitations might they experience with this new experiment?

a. Peas perform photosynthesis in addition to respiration, so only a net change in O_2 could be measured.

b. Peas do not perform respiration because they do not have mitochondria, so no signal would be obtained.

c. Peas cannot withstand the low 10°C temperature and will not perform any cellular processes at this temperature.

d. Peas will not respire unless they have germinated.

Questions 46–50 are based on the following information.

Coral disease in the Indo-Pacific has increased dramatically of late, especially *Montipora* white syndrome, a tissue-loss disease found on *Montipora capitata* corals near Hawaii. A group of scientists wanted to identify the causative agent of this disease, so they sampled bacteria from a diseased fragment of *M. capitata* and isolated a *Vibrio* strain, OCN002, which indeed caused the disease. The scientists decided to measure the abundance of bacteria among treatment groups in infection trials, using OCN002, by detecting the average number of colony-forming units (CFUs) that grew on culture plates per milliliter of mucus plated.

The scientists plated a "Pre-inoculation" group based on numerous fragments of untreated *M. capitata* corals. They then plated a "Seawater" group based on coral fragments exposed to filtered seawater. The group "OCN002—Healthy" refers to CFUs from coral fragments that were exposed to the OCN002 bacterial strain but remained healthy, while the group "OCN002—Diseased" refers to CFUs from coral fragments that were exposed to the OCN002 bacterial strain and developed tissue loss. The group's results are shown in the graph. The light gray bars represent CFUs detected on a general growth medium, on which all bacteria grow, while the dark gray bars represent CFUs detected on a medium that only allows the growth of *Vibrio* strains. Standard deviation error bars are included for each bar.

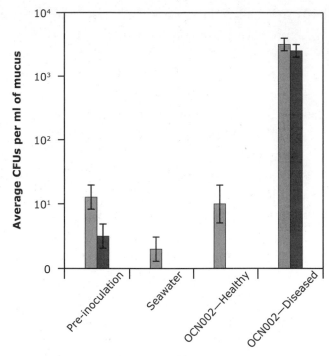

Source: http://journals.plos.org/plosone/article?id=10.1371/journal.pone.0046717

46. Numerous *M. capitata* fragments were used per treatment in order to
    a. confirm replicable results and identify outlier data points.
    b. include corals from a wide array of species for more universally applicable evidence.
    c. determine the accuracy of each trial for the data set.
    d. provide a "healthy" coral control to which the diseased corals may be compared.

47. For a particular trial set, dividing the value of the dark gray bar by the value of its corresponding light gray bar provides
    a. the total number of bacteria found in the mucus for that trial set.
    b. the fraction of total coral fragments that were found to be diseased.
    c. the fraction of total bacteria that were *Vibrio*.
    d. the total number of coral fragments tested for that trial set.

48. What effect does seawater addition have on the presence of bacteria in the coral fragment mucus, based on the data?

   a. Seawater promotes general bacterial growth.

   b. Seawater decreases general bacterial growth.

   c. Seawater promotes *Vibrio* growth only.

   d. Seawater has no effect on general bacterial growth.

49. What conclusion can be drawn about the bacterial presence in the mucus of healthy and diseased cells that have been exposed to OCN002?

   a. The healthy coral mucus contained no bacteria at all, while the diseased coral mucus contained a significant amount of bacteria.

   b. Most of the bacteria in the healthy coral mucus were *Vibrio*, while most of the bacteria in the diseased coral mucus were not *Vibrio*.

   c. The amounts and types of bacteria in the mucus of the healthy and diseased coral fragments were comparable and significant in quantity.

   d. The diseased coral mucus contained a significant quantity of bacteria, most of which were *Vibrio*, while the healthy coral mucus contained far fewer bacteria.

50. Which set of trials on general growth plates provided the most precise set of data?

   a. Pre-inoculation

   b. Seawater

   c. OCN002—Healthy

   d. OCN002—Diseased

Social Studies

70 Minutes
50 Questions

This practice test is modeled on the content and timing of the official HiSET® Social Studies test and, like the official test, presents a series of questions that assess your ability to use social studies content knowledge and analyze and evaluate various kinds of social studies information.

Questions 1–3 are based on the following information.

Societies have developed different broad economic approaches to manage the production and distribution of goods and services. Economists generally recognize four basic types of economic systems:

Traditional economies are systems in which economic decisions are based on what has been done in the past. The standards of living are often static in traditional economies, and individuals do not enjoy much financial or occupational mobility. Traditional economic systems are usually found in smaller, poorer societies.

Command economies are controlled by the government or state. The government owns the means of production, sets economic goals through central planning, regulates prices and wages, and ultimately decides how to use and distribute resources.

Market economies are those in which the means of production are privately owned and economic decisions are made by individuals. Individuals and companies in the marketplace decide how resources are allocated, how goods are distributed, and how best to set market prices and distribute income.

Mixed economies combine some elements of the market economy, such as private ownership of property, with some elements of the command economy,

such as limited government regulation. Many economic decisions are made in the market by individuals. However, the government may play a role in the distribution of resources.

1. Canada's agricultural industry is dominated by privately owned enterprises. However, the industry as a whole has become increasingly reliant on government subsidies to compete with other countries. This is an example of which type of economic system?
   a. command economy
   b. market economy
   c. mixed economy
   d. traditional economy

2. North Korean authorities placed price controls on non-food items in the country's farmers' markets and monitored sales of sought-after household goods, such as spoons, toothbrushes, and candles. What type of economy is represented here?
   a. command economy
   b. market economy
   c. mixed economy
   d. traditional economy

3. In the first century B.C.E., China was divided into scattered feudal states. These states were highly stratified societies. The vast majority of people were peasants, who were too poor or incapable of changing jobs or social and wealth status. Feudalism is an example of which of the four types of economic systems?
   a. command economy
   b. market economy
   c. mixed economy
   d. traditional economy

Questions 4–7 are based on the following information.

Discovered in Ethiopia in 1974, Lucy is one of the most famous fossil discoveries to date. Scientists found enough bones to put together nearly 40% of a skeleton of a hominid, or humanlike creature, that lived around 3.2 million years ago. The man who discovered the fossil named the find *Lucy* and her species *Australopithecus afarensis*, which means "southern ape of Afar."

Alive, Lucy would have been about 3 feet 7 inches tall and weighed around 64 pounds. She would have looked somewhat similar to a chimpanzee. Like a chimpanzee, Lucy had a small brain, long, dangly arms, short legs, and a large belly. However, unlike a chimpanzee, Lucy's knees and pelvis show that she routinely walked upright on two legs, as humans do. This form of locomotion, known as "bipedalism," is the single most important difference between humans and apes, placing Lucy firmly within the hominin, or human, family. Lucy's discovery meant that scientists who had previously believed that bipedalism occurred after the brain grew larger and more developed had to rethink everything they thought they knew about human evolution.

4. Which of the following statements is NOT supported by information in the passage?
   a. Lucy is the oldest known human ancestor.
   b. Lucy shares traits with humans and chimpanzees.
   c. Lucy might be described as a transitional fossil.
   d. Lucy was the size of a modern-day human child.

5. According to the passage, how did scientists conclude that Lucy walked upright on two legs?
   a. They compared Lucy's arms to how chimpanzees use their arms in moving.
   b. They studied Lucy's pelvis and knees and compared them to humans'.
   c. They determined that Lucy's size would have made her more likely to walk upright.
   d. They found that Lucy's large belly would have prevented her from walking on four limbs.

6. Which of the following best summarizes the writer's opinion of the importance of Lucy?
   a. Lucy represented a new lineage of apes that had not yet been discovered.
   b. Lucy's discovery forced scientists to reevaluate what they knew about how humans first became bipedal.
   c. Reconstructing Lucy's skeleton forced scientists to develop new theories about where to locate early hominins.
   d. Lucy's discovery confirmed Ethiopia as the best location to search for early hominins.

7. Which of the following statements might best reflect the main theme of the passage?
   a. Scientists can now reveal incredible insights into human evolution with very few fossils.
   b. Lucy's discovery illustrates that chimpanzees have not stopped evolving.
   c. Lucy reveals that hominins became bipedal before their brains enlarged and developed.
   d. Lucy has forced scientists to conclude that humans and chimpanzees are not as closely related as previously thought.

Questions 8–10 are based on the following information.

The following bar graph shows how many Americans voted in the three presidential elections in 2004, 2008, and 2012.

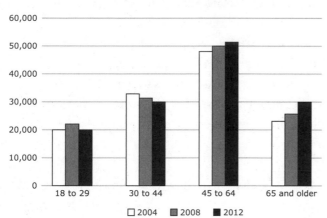

Voter Turnout, by Age: 2004–2012
(numbers in thousands)

Source: U.S. Census Bureau, Current Population Survey, November Select Years.
https://www.census.gov/prod/2014pubs/p20-573.pdf

8. Which voter age range has a decreased participation rate in each presidential election from 2004 to 2012?
   a. 18 to 29
   b. 30 to 44
   c. 45 to 64
   d. 65 and older

9. According the graph, which age group produces the most voters?
   a. 18 to 29
   b. 30 to 44
   c. 45 to 64
   d. 65 and older

10. Based on information on the graph, which of the following conclusions is most plausible?
   a. More 18- to 29-year-old Americans will vote in 2016.
   b. Fewer 45- to 64-year-old Americans will vote in 2016.
   c. The same number of voters 65 and older will vote in 2016.
   d. Fewer 30- to 44-year-old Americans will vote in the 2016 election.

Questions 11–14 are based on the following information.

The Industrial Revolution began in Great Britain in the 18th century and spread to other parts of the world soon after. The Industrial Revolution brought about great changes that were technological, socio-economic, and cultural. Along with changes in transportation, a revolution occurred in business and industry. Manufacturing shifted from using hand tools to using large, complex machines. Skilled artisans were replaced by unskilled workers. Manufacturing processes were often separated into a number of tasks that were completed by specific workers. Industrialists built large factories, many of which contained hundreds of machines and employed many workers. These factories often replaced the traditional home-based workshops. The great changes in manufacturing and transportation allowed producers to sell their goods countrywide, and even abroad, instead of just locally.

11. Which of the following is the most likely outcome to a small family who wove handmade sweaters in their home?
   a. The family's business would have been bought out by a large manufacturer.
   b. The family would have been forced to upgrade its production capacity.
   c. The family would have been forced to reduce its production capacity.
   d. The family would have been driven out of business.

12. Which of the following is the best example of a socioeconomic change created by the Industrial Revolution?

    a. Transportation efficiency provided manufacturers with greater profits.

    b. Taxes were lowered to spur even more industrialization.

    c. Young adult children left their family homes to move to find jobs in large urban areas.

    d. New technological advancements kicked off a wave of research and development in even newer technologies.

13. Based on information in the passage, it could be concluded that one of the chief effects of the Industrial Revolution was in

    a. manufacturing processes.

    b. new applications of hand tools.

    c. the development of new home-based industries.

    d. factory labor laws.

14. Which of the following would be the most plausible reason why a manufacturer would employ unskilled workers rather than skilled workers?

    a. Unskilled workers could work longer hours than skilled workers.

    b. Unskilled workers could be paid less than skilled workers.

    c. Unskilled workers could be trained to learn more tasks.

    d. Unskilled workers were more willing to relocate.

Questions 15 and 16 are based on the following information.

All American citizens play a part in making the country and their communities safe and productive. Each citizen has certain responsibilities to fulfill. Responsibilities are things citizens should do—obligations that they do voluntarily. These actions are positive actions that benefit society as a whole. American citizens also have legal duties that they are required to perform. National, state, and local governments require Americans to perform certain duties established by laws. If they fail to perform them, they are subject to legal penalties, such as fines or imprisonment.

15. Which of the following actions is NOT a legal duty required of American citizens?

    a. obey laws

    b. serve on a jury if notified

    c. vote

    d. pay taxes

16. Which of the following actions would be considered a civic responsibility?

    a. attending and participating in a local school board meeting

    b. renewing a driver's license

    c. obeying local trespassing laws

    d. attending school until the age of 16

Questions 17–21 are based on the following information.

City Budget
(in millions of dollars)

Projected Income: $8.23 Million

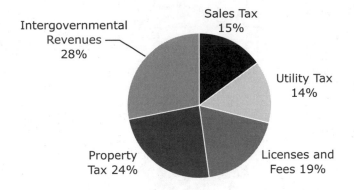

Projected Expenditures
$8.64 Million

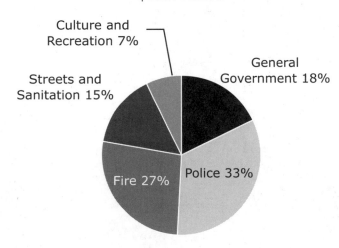

17. According to the charts, where does the city get most of its revenue?
   a. licenses and fees
   b. property taxes
   c. utility taxes
   d. intergovernmental revenues

18. According to the charts, where does the city spend the most money?
   a. fire department
   b. streets and sanitation
   c. police department
   d. general government

19. Which of the following terms best describes the relationship between the city's projected income and projected expenditures?
   a. bankrupt
   b. in the black
   c. deficit
   d. surplus

20. Which of the following actions would city leaders most likely take if the relationship between its projected income and expenses is accurate?
   a. Raise taxes
   b. Hire additional city hall employees to work on the problem
   c. Create additional services to provide for citizens' needs
   d. Eliminate the streets and sanitation department

21. Intergovernmental revenues is money that one level of government receives from another level. If the government of the state in which this city is located has a budget crisis, which of the following is the most likely effect the city will feel?
   a. Revenues and expenditures will remain the same.
   b. City revenues will decrease.
   c. The city will develop a surplus.
   d. City expenditures will have to increase.

Questions 22–24 are based on the following information.

The following political cartoon was created in 1920 by David Orro. The cartoon depicts Chicago Mayor William "Big Bill" Thompson.

22. What is the subject of the cartoon?
  a. political revenge
  b. government response to the Great Depression
  c. political corruption
  d. government attempts to weaken union workers

23. Using details from the cartoon, which of the following best describes how the cartoonist illustrates Mayor Thompson's political power?
  a. Thompson is portrayed as much larger than the men in the line.
  b. Thompson is well liked by city workers.
  c. Thompson holds a bag of money.
  d. Thompson has support from New York, as reflected by the tiger that represents Tammany Hall.

24. Which of the following best supports the cartoonist's point of view?

a. Thompson is very unpopular.

b. All Chicago city workers are corrupt.

c. Thompson lacks the political skills required to hold on to power.

d. Thompson maintains his power by buying off city workers.

Questions 25–28 are based on the following information.

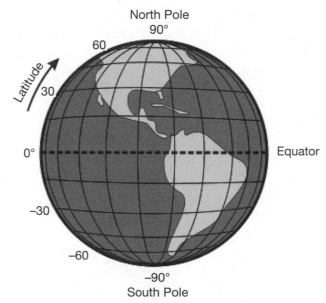

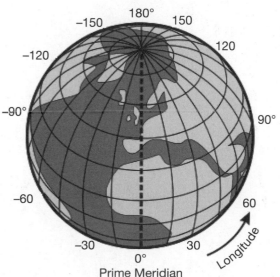

25. Which of the following is the key line of longitude?

a. Equator

b. North Pole

c. South Pole

d. Prime Meridian

26. Based on the information in the globe diagrams, how many degrees of longitude are represented on the globe?

a. 180

b. 90

c. 360

d. 270

27. Which of the following marks the location of the Equator on Earth?

a. 90 degrees latitude

b. 180 degrees longitude

c. 0 degrees latitude

d. 0 degrees longitude

28. European explorers and navigators sailing west across the Atlantic Ocean to the New World in the 15th and 16th centuries could calculate their positions of latitude by taking measurements of the sun's location in the sky. They were unable to determine how far west they had come, however. Which of the following statements is the most plausible account for this?

a. The length of voyages across the Atlantic was too great to accurately determine location.

b. Accurate measurements of longitude had not yet been developed.

c. Taking measurements west of the Prime Meridian was not as accurate.

d. The west-to-east prevailing winds over the Atlantic made navigation extremely difficult.

Questions 29–31 are based on the following information.

Amendment XXII
Section 1

No person shall be elected to the office of the President more than twice and no person who had held the office of President, or acted as President, for more than two years of a term to which some other person was elected president shall be elected to the office of President more than once.

—U.S. Constitution

29. Based on information in the 22nd Amendment, what is the longest time one person may serve as president?
   a. 8 years
   b. 6 years
   c. 10 years
   d. 4 years

30. Which of the following is the most likely reason the 22nd Amendment was added to the Constitution?
   a. American citizens wanted the right to change presidents whenever they felt like it.
   b. Political leaders were concerned that a person could wield too much power and influence if in office too long.
   c. It had been the position of the Constitution Framers that two limits were the maximum.
   d. Political leaders did not want presidents serving into old age.

31. Which of the following is the most valid reason for opposing the 22nd Amendment?
   a. It prevents voters from democratically electing the president of their choice.
   b. Politicians require more time to gather experience to carry out the duties of the presidency.
   c. It fosters gridlock in Congress.
   d. It undermines the concept of separation of powers.

Questions 32–35 are based on the following information.

A shadow has fallen upon the scenes so lately lighted by the Allied victory. . . . From Stettin in the Baltic to Trieste in the Adriatic, an iron curtain has descended across the continent. Behind that line lie all the capitals of the ancient states of Central and Eastern Europe. Warsaw, Berlin, Prague, Vienna, Budapest, Belgrade, Bucharest and Sofia, all these famous cities and the populations around them lie in what I must call the Soviet sphere, and all are subject in one form or another, not only to Soviet influence, but to a very high and, in some cases, increasing measure of control from Moscow. . . .

In front of the iron curtain which lies across Europe are other causes for anxiety . . . in a great number of countries, far from the Russian frontiers and throughout the world, Communist fifth columns are established and work in . . . absolute obedience to the directions they receive from the Communist center. . . . I do not believe that Soviet Russia desires war. What they desire is the fruits of war and the indefinite expansion of their power and doctrines. . . .

The safety of the world requires a new unity in Europe, from which no nation should be permanently outcast. . . . Surely we should work with conscious purpose for a grand pacification of Europe, within the structure of the United Nations and in accordance with its Charter. That I feel is an open cause of policy of very great importance.

—Winston Churchill, excerpts from "The Sinews of Peace," Fulton, Missouri, March 5, 1946

32. Which of the following best summarizes Churchill's view of Europe in 1946?
   a. Europe has entered an era of tranquility and imminent peace.
   b. Only a small portion of Europe has been disrupted.
   c. Communism is not expanding throughout Europe.
   d. Europe has become divided.

33. Using information from the passage, which of the following best summarizes what Churchill meant by "iron curtain"?
   a. a metal wall that separated Soviet Russia and its satellite countries from Western Europe
   b. an impenetrable barrier between Eastern and Western Europe that shut off Soviet areas from the West
   c. an irreconcilable difference in social ideologies between Soviet Russia and the West
   d. the oppressive ideas of Communism that Soviet Russia forced on Eastern European countries

34. According to Churchill, what is the ultimate goal of Soviet Russia?
   a. to militarily conquer the world
   b. to control Eastern Europe from the Baltic Sea to the Adriatic Sea
   c. to expand their power and spread communism
   d. to dismantle the United Nations

35. Based on information in the speech, which of the following is most likely Churchill's purpose for giving it?
   a. to raise awareness of the potential dangers of the Soviet Union in Eastern Europe
   b. a justification to kick the Soviet Union out of the United Nations
   c. to present evidence to prepare for war with Soviet Russia
   d. to build support for Western Europe's own "iron curtain"

Questions 36–39 are based on the following information.

Baron de Montesquieu was an 18th-century French political philosopher whose writings had great influence on the leaders who wrote the U.S. Constitution. Montesquieu proposed that governments could and should govern with honor rather than through fear. Governments could also respect and advance human dignity.

In order to have this liberty, it is necessary the government be so constituted as one man need not be afraid of another. . . . When the legislative and executive power are united in the same body of magistrates, there can be no liberty. . . .

Again there is no liberty, if the judiciary power be not separated from the legislative and executive. Were it joined with the legislative, the life and liberty of the subject would be exposed to arbitrary [control], for the judge would be then the legislator. Were it joined to the executive power, the judge might behave with violence and oppression.

—Baron de Montesquieu,
from *The Spirit of Laws*

36. Montesquieu thought that for people to have liberty and individual rights, a government should not get too much power. Which choice best describes Montesquieu's idea of how to make sure a government doesn't get too much power?
   a. A government should be divided into branches to separate and balance power.
   b. Governments should be divided into as many levels as possible.
   c. Judges should have absolute control over the law-making body.
   d. Violence and oppression can be used by individuals to intimidate government leaders.

37. Which of the following is the key to maintaining liberty, according to Montesquieu?
   a. a judicial branch of government
   b. separation of legislative and executive powers
   c. a strong executive power
   d. combined judiciary and legislative powers

38. Which principle of American democracy did the Constitution framers adapt from the ideas Montesquieu presented in the passage?
   a. popular sovereignty
   b. rule of law
   c. limited judicial power
   d. separation of powers

39. Baron de Montesquieu's ideas are best illustrative of the ideals of
   a. the Protestant Reformation.
   b. the Enlightenment.
   c. the Abolitionist Movement.
   d. the First Great Awakening.

Questions 40–43 are based on the following information.

Students for a Democratic Society, or SDS, was an American student organization that flourished in the mid to late 1960s and was known for its activism against the Vietnam War.

INTRODUCTION:
AGENDA FOR A GENERATION

We are people of this generation, bred in at least modest comfort, housed now in universities, looking uncomfortably to the world we inherit. . . . When we were kids the United States was the wealthiest and strongest country in the world. . . . Freedom and equality for each individual, government of, by, and for the people—these American values we found good. . . .

As we grew, however, our comfort was penetrated by events too troubling to dismiss. First, the permeating and victimizing fact of human degradation, symbolized by the Southern struggle against racial bigotry, compelled most of us from silence to activism. Second, the enclosing fact of the Cold War, symbolized by the presence of the Bomb, brought awareness that we ourselves, and our friends, and millions of abstract "others" we knew more directly because of our common peril, might die at any time. . . .

Our work is guided by the sense that we may be the last generation in the experiment with living. . . . The search for truly democratic alternatives to the present, and a commitment to social experimentation with them, is a worthy and fulfilling human enterprise, one which moves us and, we hope, others today.

—from the *Port Huron Statement*, 1962

40. Which of the following issues led to the activism of the members of the SDS?
   a. poverty and economic decline
   b. slavery and social disorder
   c. racial bigotry and the Cold War
   d. loss of individual rights and tougher university requirements

41. Based on information in the passage, why do SDS members have such a sense of urgency about their activism?
   a. The threat of nuclear destruction is very great.
   b. The United States is on the verge of economic collapse.
   c. Racial strife is destroying the American social system.
   d. There is likelihood of war in Vietnam.

42. Which of the following best indicates the goals of members of SDS?

    a. to return to a modest, comfortable lifestyle and traditional political systems of earlier decades

    b. to overthrow the Southern states that still protect racial bigotry

    c. to return the United States to its former military and economic strength

    d. the search for truly democratic alternatives to the present and a commitment to social experimentation with them

43. The views expressed by the SDS *Port Huron Statement* were probably most similar to those of

    a. an official of a conservative organization.

    b. a high-ranking officer in the U.S. military.

    c. an official of a liberal organization.

    d. an opponent of affirmative action and equal rights for all.

Questions 44–46 are based on the following information.

Brenda Jackson saved money to purchase her first new car and found a great deal at a car dealership. Problems started soon after she drove the car off the lot. The car stalled whenever she stopped at stop signs or traffic lights. Brenda returned the car to the dealer for repair. In most cases, the warranty the car maker gives will cover the repairs the car needs at no cost to the owner. Brenda wondered what would happen if the car ended up spending more time in the repair shop than on the road. Would the dealer be able to fix Brenda's car's problem, or did she buy a "lemon"?

    A "lemon" is a vehicle that has a defect that the dealer has not fixed within a reasonable number of chances. State lemon laws provide some protection.

In most states, to qualify as a lemon, the problem has to be serious enough that it "substantially impairs the use, value, or safety" of the vehicle and the vehicle has not been properly repaired within a "reasonable number of attempts." Generally, if the car has been repaired three to four (or more) times for the same defect within the warranty period and the defect has not been fixed, the car qualifies as a "lemon."

44. Which of the following is the most likely reason lemon laws are enacted?

    a. Lemon laws protect the car manufacturers from lawsuits brought by consumers.

    b. Lemon laws protect consumers who have purchased faulty vehicles.

    c. Lemon laws protect dealers from claims made by poor drivers.

    d. Lemon laws increase the safety of state roads.

45. Which of the following is the most plausible reason that a defective car that cannot be fixed is called a "lemon"?

    a. Most people love to eat lemons, which suggests that everyone will eventually buy a "lemon" car.

    b. Lemons are a hearty fruit, reflecting a good or strong purchase.

    c. Dealers coined the phrase because, like lemons, which are renewable, "lemon" vehicles keep coming back for repairs.

    d. Lemons have a sour taste, so they are used to describe bad, or sour, purchases.

46. What is/are the main criterion/criteria for determining if Brenda's vehicle is a lemon?
  a. the length of Brenda's warranty period
  b. the seriousness of the defect and the inability to fix it after a certain number of opportunities
  c. the amount of money required to fix the vehicle's defects
  d. if Brenda cannot use the vehicle for 20 days

Questions 47–50 are based on the following information.

Article 1, Section 7, of the U.S. Constitution outlines how bills are passed.

> [1] All Bills for raising Revenue shall originate in the House of Representatives; but the Senate may propose or concur with Amendments as on other Bills.
> [2] Every bill which shall have passed the House of Representatives and the Senate, shall, before it become a Law, be presented to the President of the United States; If he approve he shall sign it, but if not he shall return it. . . .
> [3] Every order, resolution, or vote to which the concurrence of the Senate and House of Representatives may be necessary (except on a question of Adjournment) shall be presented to the President of the United States; and before the Same shall take Effect, shall be approved by him, or being disapproved by him, shall be repassed by two thirds of the Senate and House of Representatives. . . .
>   —Article 1, Section 7, U.S. Constitution

47. Which of the following reasons best explains why the Framers required the House of Representatives, the Senate, and the president to all be involved in the passing of legislation?
  a. The process creates more bureaucracy and makes it impossible to pass laws.
  b. The process eliminates unpopular and unnecessary laws and acts as a form of checks and balances.
  c. This process requires everyone in Congress and the president to agree on legislation.
  d. This process gives more power to the House and Senate than to the president.

48. What issue is the exception to this process?
  a. Presidential veto
  b. if the House and Senate can't come to agreement
  c. adjournment of Congress
  d. vacancy in the presidency

49. Given the fact that members of the House of Representatives face elections every two years and Senators every six years, which of the following is the most plausible explanation for why all bills that raise revenue must originate in the House?
  a. The Constitution forbids the Senate from being involved in revenue bills.
  b. The Senate's only focus is on foreign affairs and judicial appointments.
  c. House members must have backgrounds and experience in financial matters.
  d. Voters have more input in electing or rejecting those who write tax bills.

50. From 1789 through 2015, presidents have vetoed 2,571 bills, but Congress has overturned only 110 of them. Based on this information and the process described in Article 1, Section 7, it could be concluded that

a. getting a two-thirds majority in both houses of Congress is very difficult.

b. the House and Senate can never reach a consensus.

c. the president's legislative power has been reduced.

d. the Constitution makes it impossible for Congress to override a presidential veto.

Practice Test 2
Answers and Explanations

Language Arts—Reading

To calculate your HiSET® score on the Language Arts—Reading section, first take a look at the correct answer for each of the 40 questions of the exam. Count up your **correct answers** only, and give yourself 1 point for each. Then, add up all of your points. This is your **raw score**.

Find your raw score and your **scaled score** in the following table. Remember, for each test section, a passing score is 8. (For the essay, a passing score is 2.)

You need a scaled score of 45 to pass the complete HiSET® exam.

LANGUAGE ARTS—READING SCORING			
RAW	SCALED	RAW	SCALED
0	1	21	12
1	2	22	12
2	3	23	13
3	4	24	13
4	5	25	13
5	6	26	14
6	7	27	14
7	7	28	14
8	8	29	15
9	8	30	15
10	9	31	15
11	9	32	15
12	9	33	16
13	10	34	17
14	10	35	17
15	10	36	18
16	11	37	18
17	11	38	19
18	11	39	20
19	11	40	20
20	12		

1. **The correct answer is choice a.** In the first paragraph, Harker explains that the Count does not cast a reflection in the mirror. Choice **b** is incorrect because the Count only calls the mirror "a foul bauble of man's vanity" as an excuse for destroying it. Choice **c** is incorrect because Dracula has a more important reason for destroying the mirror. Choice **d** is incorrect because the Count probably would not reach for Harker's throat if the Count was repelled by the sight of blood.

2. **The correct answer is choice d.** In the first paragraph, Harker says that he had trouble sleeping the night before and goes on to say that he has always felt uneasy in the Count's presence. His strange encounter with the Count does nothing to ease that unsettled feeling. Choice **a** is incorrect because Harker does not discover that he is a prisoner until after his encounter with the Count. Choice **b** is incorrect because Harker only says that he feels annoyed after the Count breaks his mirror. Choice **c** is incorrect because Harker only gets a clue that the Count is inhuman during his encounter with the Count.

3. **The correct answer is choice d.** Since the Count's behavior is so strange and unpleasant, the use of the word "suddenly" contributes to the story's thrilling tone. Choice **a** is incorrect because even though there are horrific elements in this story, the word "suddenly" does not create a horrific tone. Choice **b** is incorrect because "exhilarating" has positive connotations that are not present in this story. Choice **c** is incorrect because the passage does not have a joyful tone.

4. **The correct answer is choice b.** Paragraph 6 suggests that Harker is already thinking about exit possibilities. Choice **a** is incorrect because there is nothing in the passage to suggest that the Count is likely to allow Harker to go free just because he asks to go free. Choice **c** is incorrect because Harker likely has greater concerns than looking for other prisoners. Choice **d** is incorrect because the Count's castle is so strange and creepy that Harker is more likely to search for a way out of it than to try to enjoy living there.

5. **The correct answer is choice c.** Harker is unsettled before seeing the view, and when he sees it, he focuses on how far away the ground is as much as he does the view's beauty, so it is unlikely that seeing the view makes him feel any less unsettled than he already felt. Choice **a** is incorrect because even though Harker notices the view's beauty, he does not seem any less unsettled about staying with the Count. Choice **b** is incorrect because there is no evidence that seeing the view makes him feel more unsettled; he does not become more unsettled until he realizes that all of the doors are locked. Choice **d** is incorrect because although Harker notices the view's beauty, he also notices how high up he is, which probably does not make him feel very peaceful.

6. The correct answer is choice d. After describing the precipice as "terrific," Harker indicates how high up it is, which means the precipice is of extreme height. Choice **a** is incorrect because although "supreme" can be used as a synonym for "terrific," it would not make sense if used in place of "terrific" in this particular context. Choice **b** is incorrect because although "wonderful" can be used as a synonym for "terrific," it would not make sense if used in place of "terrific" in this particular context. Choice **c** is incorrect because although "talented" can be used as a synonym for "terrific," it would not make sense if used in place of "terrific" in this particular context.

7. The correct answer is choice b. Environmental protection is one of the most important and discussed issues today, but the fact that Theodore Roosevelt was arguing in favor of environmental protection more than 100 years ago shows that it is hardly a recent idea. Choice **a** is incorrect because Roosevelt is arguing that people need to protect the natural environment, which is counter to the idea that industry should be allowed to expand without obstacles. Choice **c** is incorrect because even though climate change is an environmental issue, there is nothing in this passage about climate change. Choice **d** is incorrect because the fact that Roosevelt was conscientious about a particular issue is not enough evidence to argue that he was America's *most* conscientious politician.

8. The correct answer is choice b. This paragraph argues that human intervention is unnecessary to replenish the natural resources people use, while the passage argues that people need to change the way they use natural resources or those resources will disappear, which indicates the need for human actions. Choice **a** is incorrect because Roosevelt never denies that the natural environment is full of resources. Choice **c** is incorrect because both pieces seem to agree that the natural environment is extraordinary. Choice **d** is incorrect because both pieces indicate that people should be allowed to enjoy the natural environment.

9. The correct answer is choice a. Roosevelt states that game wardens should be woodsmen, which indicates that he believes they have a particular skill for dealing with game. Choice **b** is incorrect because Roosevelt would not likely want to appoint people he believes are destroying the environment to serve as game wardens. Choice **c** is incorrect because Roosevelt would not likely want to appoint people he believes know little about game to serve as game wardens. Choice **d** is incorrect because Roosevelt believes woodsmen should serve as game wardens.

10. The correct answer is choice a. In paragraph 4, Roosevelt discusses recent actions to create fish hatcheries and deer-protection laws that have been beneficial to those particular animals. Choice **b** is incorrect because the fact that those animals have benefited from recent actions does not suggest that they are in danger of extinction. Choice **c** is incorrect because Roosevelt discusses how fish and deer have benefited from recent actions but does not try to prove that they are great resources for humans. Choice **d** is incorrect because Roosevelt says that the railroads create dangers of illegal hunting and forest fires, not that they are putting fish and deer in jeopardy.

11. The correct answer is choice c. If forests are destroyed, game and fish will have no place to live, which means the destruction of game and fish. Allowing game and fish to be overhunted will not have as extreme an effect on game and fish as the destruction of their homes. There is no evidence in the passage that supports choices **a**, **b**, and **d**.

12. The correct answer is choice b. Human activity increases as the presence of humans increases, so if more people are in the forests because of the railroads, it makes sense that there will be more illegal hunting. Choices **a**, **c**, and **d** are incorrect because there is no evidence in the passage that supports these inferences.

13. The correct answer is choice a. Even though his son is only an infant, Dombey is already talking about doing business as "Dombey and Son." Choice **b** is incorrect because it is too specific a prediction to make; while it is likely that Dombey will try to get his son involved in the family business, there is no reason to believe that partnership will be a "great success." Choice **c** is incorrect because Dombey seems more concerned about his business future with his son than caring for the infant. Choice **d** is incorrect because there is no evidence in the passage that Dombey's son will require a university education to take part in the family business.

14. The correct answer is choice b. Later in the passage, Dombey refers to his son's grandfather, and that the grandfather is no longer alive, so this is the most likely conclusion to draw. Choice **a** is incorrect because there is no indication that Dombey had another son. Choice **c** is incorrect because the fact that he will be using that business name again means he went through a period in which he did not use it—most likely the period in which he ran the business alone. Choice **d** is incorrect because there is no indication in the passage that Dombey purchased his business from another person named Dombey.

15. The correct answer is choice c. The author is suggesting that Dombey thinks that the earth's only purpose is to give him a place to do business because Dombey is only interested in doing business. Choice **a** is incorrect because the author is using the line to illustrate how Dombey felt about the world and himself, not how the rest of the world actually saw him. Choice **b** is incorrect because the line is not making a point about the earth; it is illustrating something about Dombey's approach to life. Choice **d** is incorrect because the line does not explain anything about how Dombey first became a businessman.

16. The correct answer is choice c. The author had already described Dombey's son as "crushed," and these lines use different words to make a similar description of the child's appearance. Choices **a**, **b**, and **d** are incorrect because these lines do not restate information from earlier in the passage.

17. The correct answer is choice a. The author's comparison of Dombey's son to a muffin is supposed to be humorous. Choice **b** is incorrect because although a human cannot actually be similar to a muffin, the author's comparison of Dombey's son to a muffin is supposed to be humorous. Choice **c** is incorrect because although there are grim aspects to this story, a muffin is not a grim image. Choice **d** is incorrect because there is nothing romantic about this story.

18. The correct answer is choice b. Mrs. Dombey is sickly in this passage, and her son is less than an hour old, so it is reasonable to conclude that she had problems during childbirth that caused her condition. Choice **a** is incorrect because Mrs. Dombey does not say or do anything disrespectful toward her husband. Choice **c** is incorrect because the fact that Mrs. Dombey lets her husband make one decision—the naming of their child—is not enough evidence to conclude that she allows him to make all decisions. Choice **d** is incorrect because Dombey does not seem to take much notice of his wife's sickly condition, and she is surprised when he uses an endearing term for her, which indicates that she may not be very important to him.

19. The correct answer is choice b. Since the author goes into great detail about the best way to tell a humorous story, he clearly believes that humorous stories need to be told with great attention to such details. Choice **a** is incorrect because the author states that telling humorous stories is the most difficult form of storytelling, not that it is the best form. Choice **c** is incorrect because if humorous storytelling is so difficult, it probably is not something anyone can do successfully. Choice **d** is incorrect because if natural gifts were all that was needed to tell humorous stories, the author probably would not go to such lengths to explain how to tell humorous stories.

20. The correct answer is choice b. Because the author goes on to say that "the teller does his best to conceal the fact that he even dimly suspects that there is anything funny about it," the reader can deduce that "gravely" means "seriously." Choices **a**, **c**, and **d** are incorrect because they do not accurately explain the meaning of "gravely."

21. The correct answer is choice a. This is an opinion because not everyone may agree that telling a humorous story is a work of art. Choices **b**, **c**, and **d** are incorrect because they are facts, not opinions.

22. The correct answer is choice c. The author of the paragraph states that a speaker should make the audience understand his or her point "short of shouting it at them," and Twain refers to the act of shouting the point, or "nub," of a story as "depressing." Choice **a** is incorrect because Twain suggests that leaving the audience confused can be done to humorous effect. Choice **b** is incorrect because Twain suggests that rambling can be humorous. Choice **d** is incorrect because Twain says that humorous stories may have a point, but he does not insist that they must have one.

23. The correct answer is choice a. Twain says that he thinks it is "pathetic" when storytellers repeat the nub of their stories, so it is logical to conclude that he would not do this when telling his own stories. Choice **b** is incorrect because someone who knows so much about humorous storytelling probably tells humorous stories. Choice **c** is incorrect because Twain mentions how Artemus Ward used a particular trick when telling humorous stories but does not express any opinions about those stories. Choice **d** is incorrect because Twain explains that "The humorous story is American" and criticizes how humorous stories are sometimes told in other countries.

24. The correct answer is choice d. With this phrase, the author is using non-literal language to convey the image of a fire's dying embers casting ghostly lights and shapes on the floor. Choice **a** is incorrect because the phrase is not meant literally; there is not actually a ghost in the room. Choice **b** is incorrect because the phrase describes the effect the embers are creating, not the fire or the embers themselves. Choice **c** is incorrect because the phrase describes the effect the embers are creating, not the fire or the embers themselves.

25. The correct answer is choice b. It accounts for the most important details in the poem. Choices **a** and **c** are incorrect because they leave out an important detail. Choice **d** is incorrect because it does not account for the main idea of the poem.

26. The correct answer is choice c. The narrator uses the word "radiant" to describe Lenore, the woman he loves. Choice **a** is incorrect because one would not typically use the word "shining" to describe a person. Choice **b** is incorrect because the passage suggests that Lenore is dead, so she likely would not be described as "healthy." Choice **D** is incorrect because one would not typically say that a person is "heat giving."

27. The correct answer is choice d. This poem has a gloomy tone, and the poet uses gloomy words such as "dreary," "weak," and "weary" to set that gloomy tone at the beginning of the poem. Choice **a** is incorrect because "weak" and "weary" are not frightening adjectives. Choice **b** is incorrect because words such as "weak" and "weary" suggest a lack of energy, which is the opposite of the kinds of words needed to set an exciting, or thrilling, tone. Choice **c** is incorrect because although these words suggest a lack of energy, they are not necessarily boring, and the poet likely was not trying to bore the reader.

28. The correct answer is choice c. The narrator refers to Lenore as "lost," which means she is likely never coming back, and the raven makes the narrator unable to forget this by constantly repeating "nevermore." Choice **a** is incorrect because it is not clear whether the raven has any secrets, but it is clear that Lenore is gone. Choice **b** is incorrect because there is no evidence to support the idea that the raven will not return again. Choice **d** is incorrect because there is no evidence to support the idea that the narrator did not know Lenore.

29. The correct answer is choice d. The fact that Lenore is "lost" and the narrator spends so much time thinking about her suggests that she has died and he is mourning her. Choice **a** is incorrect because it is not clear whether the narrator lives alone. Choice **b** is incorrect because although the poem takes place in December, that is not why the narrator is miserable. Choice **c** is incorrect because although the narrator is trying to sleep, this is not a particularly important detail in the poem.

30. The correct answer is choice a. The purpose of this passage is to argue in favor of a new constitution to replace the Articles of Confederation. Choice **b** is incorrect because although the author clearly is not in favor of the Articles of Confederation, he spends more time explaining how a better constitution can be made than criticizing the previous one. Choice **c** is incorrect because the author mentions passions and prejudices in the second paragraph, but they are not the most important ideas in the passage. Choice **d** is incorrect because the author mentions patriotism in the second paragraph, but it is not the most important point of this passage.

31. The correct answer is choice c. The author makes this assumption in paragraph 3 of the passage. Choices **a** and **b** are incorrect because they are facts, not an assumptions. Choice **d** is incorrect because the author does not make this assumption in the passage.

32. The correct answer is choice d. The possible reactions the author describes in paragraph 3 are problematic reactions, and the author is preparing his audience for those problems that may arise if the United States adopts a new constitution. Choice **a** is incorrect because listing the problems that may arise is not a very effective way to build support for the thing that may cause those problems. Choice **b** is incorrect because the author clearly still supports a new constitution despite the fact that adopting it may cause problems. Choice **c** is incorrect because the author is not merely trying to prove what he understands; he has something more important in mind—namely, preparing his audience for the consequences of adopting a new constitution.

33. The correct answer is choice d. In paragraph 2, the author mentions that a new constitution would emphasize the importance of philanthropy. Choice **a** is incorrect because the author refers to human misfortune at the end of paragraph 1, but he does not suggest that a new constitution could end human misfortune. Choice **b** is incorrect because freedom of expression is not mentioned in this passage. Choice **c** is incorrect because paragraph 3 suggests that politicians may engage in untrustworthy behavior even if a new constitution is adopted.

34. The correct answer is choice d. The author refers to a "crisis" in the United States as an argumentative technique; if the country is in a state of crisis, then it requires a radical remedy immediately, and he is putting forth his idea for a new constitution as that remedy. Choice **a** is incorrect because the author has not lost faith in the United States; if he had, he would not propose adoption of a new constitution. Choice **b** is incorrect because stating that the country is in a state of crisis does not mean that adopting a new constitution will require a lot of work. Choice **c** is incorrect because stating that the country is in a state of crisis does not imply that everyone in the country will not agree to the adoption of a new constitution.

35. The correct answer is choice d. The author mentions that the passage takes place in South Australia, December, and the summer, so it is reasonable to conclude that South Australia experiences summer in December. Choice **a** is incorrect because the author does not suggest that there is anything unusual about summer in December in South Australia. Choice **b** is incorrect because if there were only one season in South Australia, there would be no point in specifying that this passage takes place during summer. Choice **c** is incorrect because the author does not suggest that there is anything unrealistic about summer in December in South Australia.

36. The correct answer is choice a. The author contrasts the description of the punishing heat in paragraph 2 with the more serene descriptions of trees and gardens in the paragraphs that follow. Choice **b** is incorrect because while there may be contrast in the descriptions of the punishing heat and the serenity of trees and gardens, their coexistence is not so strange that it should actually confuse the reader. Choice **c** is incorrect because the author is establishing setting throughout this passage; without the introduction of characters, there cannot be much plot. Choice **d** is incorrect because a setting can be extremely hot and serene at the same time.

37. The correct answer is choice c. After establishing that the setting is an extremely hot day, the author states that there are days that are even worse. Choice **a** is incorrect because the author is suggesting that things are not as bad as they may seem. Choice **b** is incorrect because the fact that people can endure extreme heat is not the main purpose of the author's discussion of days on which the temperature rises to 104° before noon. Choice **d** is incorrect because there is nothing about the author's discussion of hot days that implies a major change is about to occur.

38. The correct answer is choice b. In the first sentence of the paragraph, the author explains what the gardens in Adelaide were not; this sentence refines that information by explaining what those gardens are. Choice **a** is incorrect because this is the first line of the paragraph; there isn't anything earlier in the paragraph to refine. Choice **c** is incorrect because this line introduces new information; it does not refine information from earlier in the passage. Choice **d** is incorrect because this line introduces new information; it does not refine information from earlier in the passage.

39. The correct answer is choice a. This accounts for the most important ideas in paragraph 4. Choices **b**, **c**, and **d** are minor details in the paragraph.

40. The correct answer is choice c. In paragraph 2, "phenomenal" is used to explain days that are extremely hot that occur only a few times each season. Such days could be described as "highly unusual," so this choice is the best explanation for how "phenomenal" is used in this particular paragraph. Choice **a** is incorrect because the author hardly seems to believe that such unpleasantly hot days are "absolutely wonderful." Choice **b** is incorrect because although extremely hot days can be sensed, and this is a definition of "phenomenal," choice **c** is a more specific explanation for how the word is used in the context of paragraph 2. Choice **d** is incorrect because if extremely hot days occur a few times every summer in Adelaide, they cannot be "without precedent."

Language Arts—Writing Part 1

To calculate your HiSET® score on the Language Arts—Writing section, first take a look at the correct answer for each of the 50 questions of the exam. Count up your **correct answers** only, and give yourself 1 point for each. Then, add up all of your points. This is your **raw score**.

Find your raw score and your **scaled score** in the following table. Remember, for each test section, a passing score is 8. (For the essay, a passing score is 2.)

You need a scaled score of 45 to pass the complete HiSET® exam.

LANGUAGE ARTS—WRITING SCORING			
RAW	SCALED	RAW	SCALED
0	1	26	9
1	2	27	9
2	3	28	9
3	3	29	9
4	4	30	9
5	4	31	10
6	5	32	10
7	5	33	10
8	5	34	10
9	6	35	10
10	6	36	11
11	6	37	11
12	6	38	11
13	6	39	11
14	7	40	11
15	7	41	12
16	7	42	12
17	7	43	12
18	7	44	12
19	8	45	13
20	8	46	13
21	8	47	13
22	8	48	14
23	8	49	14
24	8	50	14
25	9		

1. **The correct answer is choice d.** All of the items in the list should be parallel, which means the verbs should all be in the same tense. In this choice, all of the verbs are in the past tense. Choices **a**, **b**, and **c** are incorrect because all of the items in the list should be parallel, which means the verbs should agree. These versions have mismatched verb tenses.

2. **The correct answer is choice b.** It combines the three sentences most effectively by turning the first sentence into an independent clause ("there were some very creative entries this year") and the next two into subordinate clauses. Choice **a** is incorrect because the original sentences were choppy and repetitive, but joining them with commas and a conjunction does not correct that issue. Choice **c** is incorrect because there's no predicate in this version of the sentence; there are only three subjects. Therefore, it is a fragment. Choice **d** is incorrect because it awkwardly introduces the examples of creative entries with "that were."

3. **The correct answer is choice d.** This is a double possessive: the recipe belongs to the grandmother, and the grandmother belongs to Jill. Both "Jill" and "grandmother" are singular, so both should end in 's. Choice **a** is incorrect because the possessive form of "grandmothers" is required here. Choice **b** is incorrect because neither noun should be in the plural form; they should both be in the possessive form, so they need apostrophes. Choice **c** is incorrect because an apostrophe after the "s" makes the noun a plural possessive. Written this way, the phrase implies that the recipe belongs to more than one of Jill's grandmothers.

4. **The correct answer is choice c.** This version turns part of the sentence into a dependent clause that works with the independent clause, so this is a good way to balance the sentence. Choice **a** is incorrect because as written, the sentence has two competing main clauses. Choice **b** is incorrect because this version takes a declarative statement ("There were so many great dishes on the tables") and unnecessarily turns it into a question. Choice **d** is incorrect because the two main clauses are spliced together with commas incorrectly.

5. **The correct answer is choice d.** "Fierce" is a standard *i-before-e* word and is spelled incorrectly in paragraph 3. Choice **a** is incorrect because there is an incorrectly spelled word. Choice **b** is incorrect because "assured" is spelled correctly. Choice **c** is incorrect because "deliberations" is spelled correctly.

6. **The correct answer is choice d.** "Ultimately" emphasizes a decision made after long and serious consideration. Choice **a** is incorrect because while "yet" makes grammatical sense in this sentence, it is not the appropriate word. It implies a contradiction of the previous idea. Choice **b** is incorrect because while "basically" makes grammatical sense in this sentence, it is not the appropriate word. The correct word should emphasize a decision made after long and serious consideration. Choice **c** is incorrect because "someday" suggests that the decision had not been made yet, but the sentence indicates that the winner was decided after long and serious consideration.

7. **The correct answer is choice c.** Sentence 3 sets up the idea that prizes were given to the winners, and the specifics of those prizes follow that setup logically. Choice **a** is incorrect because this would be an odd place to put the prize information since it would be right in the middle of two statements announcing the winners. Choice **b** is incorrect because this is not the best place to include the information about the prizes since another sentence in the paragraph sets up the idea that prizes were given to the winners. This additional information should be placed after that setup. Choice **d** is incorrect because sentence 4 provides a clear conclusion to the passage, so placing extra details after it does not make sense.

8. **The correct answer is choice c.** This sentence introduces a list of ingredients to make the chocolate chip cookies. A colon should be used to set off lists. Choice **a** is incorrect because using a comma creates a run-on sentence. Choice **b** is incorrect because the original sentence was a run-on sentence, and replacing the comma with a semicolon does not fix that error. Choice **d** is incorrect because using a period and separating the list into its own sentence creates a sentence fragment.

9. **The correct answer is choice b.** This part of the directions discusses an ongoing action (the oven is in the process of heating), so the present-continuous tense is needed. Choice **a** is incorrect because this part of the directions discusses an ongoing action (the oven is in the process of heating), so the present-continuous tense is needed. Choice **c** is incorrect because this part of the directions discusses an ongoing action (the oven is in the process of heating), so the present-continuous tense is needed. Choice **d** is incorrect because this part of the directions discusses an ongoing action (the oven is in the process of heating), so the present-continuous tense is needed.

10. **The correct answer is choice c.** The writer intends to use an idiomatic phrase meaning "gather" here, and "round up" is the only choice that conveys that meaning. Choice **a** is incorrect because the writer seems to intend to use an idiomatic phrase meaning "gather" here, but "circle up" is not a common idiom. Choice **b** is incorrect because the writer seems to intend to use an idiomatic phrase meaning "gather" here, but "gather through" is not a common idiom. Choice **d** is incorrect because the writer seems to intend to use an idiomatic phrase meaning "gather" here, but "bunch around" is not a common idiom.

11. The correct answer is choice d. It places the modifying phrase "one at a time" after "eggs." Choice **a** is incorrect because the issue in this sentence is a confusing modifier; putting "one at a time" before "eggs" is awkward. Choice **b** is incorrect because the butter and sugar are combined, not the eggs. Choice **c** is incorrect because it leaves out the important information that each egg is added one at a time and makes it seem as though the cook is only supposed to add a single egg.

12. The correct answer is choice d. The recipe is written in a very neutral, informational voice. There's no other point in the passage where the writer makes exclamatory statements, so this is the best answer choice. Choice **a** is incorrect because this recipe is written in an informative and impersonal tone, and the use of the exclamation "hey" and the exclamation mark is too informal for this context. Choice **b** is incorrect because this recipe is written in an informative and impersonal tone, so referring to the reader as "my friend" is inappropriately personal. Choice **c** is incorrect because it does not suit the impersonal and informative tone of the rest of the recipe.

13. The correct answer is choice c. The dough is formed after the dry ingredients and moist ingredients have been combined, so this is the best place for this extra information. Choice **a** is incorrect because no dough has been formed before the beginning of the paragraph, so this information would not make sense here. Choice **b** is incorrect because the dough has not been formed yet, so this information would not make sense here. Choice **d** is incorrect because it does not make sense to inform the reader that he or she has dough after providing directions to put that dough into the refrigerator.

14. The correct answer is choice b. The dough will get cool in the refrigerator, so "chills" makes the most sense here. Choice **a** is incorrect because while the dough will indeed get cold in the refrigerator, it will not freeze. Choice **c** is incorrect because while the dough will indeed get cold in the refrigerator, it does not make sense to say that something "colds." "Colds" is not a verb. Choice **d** is incorrect because while the dough will indeed get cold in the refrigerator, "ices" is not the best word to describe what is happening to it.

15. The correct answer is choice d. The writer intends to use an idiomatic phrase meaning a large space away from human habitation here, and "great outdoors" is a commonly used idiom conveying that meaning. Choices **a**, **b**, and **c** are incorrect because the writer seems to intend to use an idiomatic phrase meaning a large space away from human habitation, but "great outside," "huge outside," and "great out of doors" are not commonly used idioms.

16. The correct answer is choice b. It simplifies the list of degrees. Choice **a** is incorrect because the original sentences are not grammatically incorrect but they can be combined in a way that makes them more concise. This answer choice fails to make them more concise and introduces a punctuation error by joining them with a colon. Choice **c** is incorrect because "minimum" should not describe the bachelor's degree, and the list of degrees does not need to be set off by a colon. Choice **d** is incorrect because "minimum" shouldn't describe the applicants. The correct answer will not misplace the modifier.

17. The correct answer is choice a. Paragraph 2 is about applicant qualifications. This sentence is about healthcare qualifications, so it is the best fit. Choice **b** is incorrect because this sentence is about ranger duties, which is the topic of paragraph 3. Choices **c** and **d** are incorrect because these sentences are not really related to the ranger job or its duties, so they don't fit into paragraph 2.

18. The correct answer is choice c. The sentence is written in the present tense, so the verbs should be consistent with both that tense and each other. Choice **a** is incorrect because it has one noun ("protection") and one present-tense verb ("supervising") where two present-tense verbs are needed. Choice **b** is incorrect because "protection" and "supervision" are nouns, not the verbs that this sentence needs. Choice **d** is incorrect because both verbs are in the past tense when they should be in the present tense.

19. The correct answer is choice d. This version moves the modifier to clarify the fact that the program is for children between the ages of 4 and 12. Choice **a** is incorrect because as written, the numbers "4 to 12" are confusing. Are there 4 to 12 children, or are the children age 4 to 12? Choice **b** is incorrect because the modifier "aged" is misplaced before "children." Choice **c** is incorrect because it removes the crucial word "children."

20. The correct answer is choice c. The original sentence used a slang phrase that violated the otherwise businesslike tone of the passage. This answer choice corrects that error with friendly yet businesslike language. Choice **a** is incorrect because while the job description is friendly, the overall tone is businesslike. There is no slang elsewhere, so the phrase "hit us up" is inconsistent with the rest of the passage. Choice **b** is incorrect because the problem with the original sentence is that it uses slang ("hit us up") that fails to maintain the businesslike style of the passage. This answer choice merely replaces one slang phrase with another ("give us a shout"). Choice **d** is incorrect because the original sentence was incorrect because it used a slang phrase that violated the otherwise businesslike tone of the passage. However, this answer choice is an awkward substitute.

21. The correct answer is choice d. It balances the subordinate clause ("If you find yourself in North Carolina's Outer Banks this summer") with the main clause. A complete sentence needs both types of clauses if it starts with a subordinate clause. Choice **a** is incorrect because as written, this sentence has a number of small clauses that add up to a fragment. It needs to be rewritten so that the clauses are joined into a complete sentence. Choice **b** is incorrect because it has several dependent clauses and no independent clauses. Therefore, like the original sentence, it is a fragment. Choice **c** is incorrect because the first clause ("Finding yourself in North Carolina's Outer Banks this summer"), in which the unwritten subject is "you," and the second clause, which stands on its own with a different subject ("event"), are not parallel.

22. The correct answer is choice a. None of the words are misspelled. Choice **b** is incorrect because "weather" and "whether" are easily confused words. In this case, both are spelled correctly. Choice **c** is incorrect because "temperate" is spelled correctly. Choice **d** is incorrect because "weather" and "whether" are easily confused words. In this case, both are spelled correctly.

23. The correct answer is choice a. This opening sentence picks up an element from paragraph 1 (the "ghost" reference) and introduces the topic for paragraph 2: what ghost crabs are like. Choices **b**, **c**, and **d** are incorrect because these are supporting sentences that do nothing to set up the paragraph topic.

24. The correct answer is choice c. There's nothing wrong with the sentence grammatically, but it is repetitive and should be deleted. Choice **a** is incorrect because while it is true that this information is relevant to the passage, it had already been stated in the previous sentence. It is redundant. Choice **b** is incorrect because this sentence repeats information from the previous sentence; it does not introduce the topic of the next paragraph, which is about the time of day that ghost crabs come out of their homes. Choice **d** is incorrect because this sentence does not veer off the topic of ghost crabs, but it does provide redundant information.

25. The correct answer is choice d. "Only" is one of the trickiest adverbs to place. The best rule of thumb is to place it closest to the word or phrase it modifies. In this case, it's modifying "at sunset," so placing it right before that phrase is the best option.

26. The correct answer is choice b. This phrase helps connect the previous topic (ghost crabs) with other animals that visitors might want to see. Choice **a** is incorrect because this phrase would be too repetitious, as it includes "Outer Banks," which will be used again almost immediately after it. Choice **c** is incorrect because it makes little sense—how would a visitor see the North Carolina horses and dolphins before going to North Carolina? Choice **d** is incorrect because this phrase basically repeats the phrase "check out" that almost immediately follows it and adds nothing worthwhile to the sentence.

27. The correct answer is choice d. This answer choice corrects the original run-on sentence while also recognizing that the wild horses in Corolla and the clusters of dolphins are examples of Outer Banks wildlife. Choice **a** is incorrect because as written, it is a run-on sentence because its clauses are not separated correctly. Choice **b** is incorrect because the original sentence needs to be rewritten because it is a run-on sentence, but this answer choice is confusing. Choice **c** is incorrect because it fails to recognize that the wild horses in Corolla and the clusters of dolphins are examples of Outer Banks wildlife.

28. The correct answer is choice c. "Periodical" is the correct spelling of this word. Choice **a** is incorrect because there is a misspelled word in the sentence. Choice **b** is incorrect because "perusing" is spelled correctly. Choice **d** is incorrect because "forty" is spelled correctly.

29. The correct answer is choice b. This version specifies that the meeting, not the article's publishing, was on June 15. Choice **a** is incorrect because the placement of "June 15" is key in this sentence. It is unclear whether the article was published on June 15 or the meeting happened on June 15. Choice **c** is incorrect because the placement of "June 15" is key in this sentence. It is unclear whether the article was published on June 15 or the meeting happened on June 15. Choice **d** is incorrect because the placement of "June 15" is key in this sentence. It is unclear whether the article was published on June 15 or the meeting happened on June 15.

30. The correct answer is choice a. The writer uses the idiomatic expression "out of line," which means "inappropriate," correctly here. Choice **b** is incorrect because this expression does not make sense in this context. Choice **c** is incorrect because this idiomatic expression does not make sense in this context. Choice **d** is incorrect because this is not the best expression for this context. "Beyond the pale" means "outrageously intolerable," which is too extreme. A phrase meaning "inappropriate" is more appropriate in this context.

31. The correct answer is choice d. This version allows the sentences to flow together into a single sentence while avoiding repetitive phrasing. Choice **a** is incorrect because there is a less repetitious answer choice. Choice **b** is incorrect because there needs to be a semicolon or a conjunction between the two clauses. Choice **c** is incorrect because it removes an important detail from the original sentences.

32. The correct answer is choice d. In paragraph 2, the writer set up a series of points by using "First of all," so it makes sense to continue this pattern with paragraph 3. Choice **a** is incorrect because paragraph 3 supports the writer's main points; it doesn't compare any information. Choice **b** is incorrect because paragraph 3 supports the writer's main points; it doesn't contrast any information. Choice **c** is incorrect because "therefore" suggests a conclusion when the writer is introducing another supporting point.

33. The correct answer is choice d. This answer choice uses a colon to join the first clause with the explanatory information correctly. Choice **a** is incorrect because this answer choice combines the sentences into a run-on sentence; there needs to be a semicolon or a conjunction between the two clauses. Choice **b** is incorrect because it uses the wrong punctuation to join the two sentences. Choice **c** is incorrect because a colon is used correctly to join the two sentences, but the parentheses serve no purpose.

34. The correct answer is choice b. It eliminates the unnecessary extra "who," and transforms a fragment into a complete sentence. Choice **a** is incorrect because the extra "who" in the underlined text is confusing and prevents this fragment from being a complete sentence. Choice **c** is incorrect because the original sentence was a fragment, and this answer choice does not correct that issue and introduces a new grammatical mistake. Choice **d** is incorrect because the original sentence was a fragment and this answer choice not only fails to correct that issue but also deletes essential information.

35. The correct answer is choice c. Only this option is written in the present tense and works with the first-person pronoun "I." Choice **a** is incorrect because in the final paragraph, the writer is using the present tense, so this verb should be in the present tense. It should also agree with the pronoun "I." Choice **b** is incorrect because "expects" is in the present tense, matching the tense of the paragraph, but it doesn't work with the first-person pronoun "I." Choice **d** is incorrect because "will expect" is in the future tense, yet the rest of the paragraph is written in the present tense.

36. The correct answer is choice c. This answer choice corrects the run-on sentence by separating it into two sentences. Choice **a** is incorrect because as written, this is a run-on sentence. Choice **b** is incorrect because the colon isn't introducing an explanatory point or a list. Choice **d** is incorrect because removing the comma doesn't correct this run-on sentence.

37. The correct answer is choice d. This option places the adverb right after the verb it modifies and makes the meaning of the sentence clear. Choice **a** is incorrect because the adverb should be placed right after the verb it modifies to avoid confusion. Choices **b** and **c** are incorrect because the adverb placement is confusing.

38. The correct answer is choice c. It sets off the title of the book with commas, so the reader knows that the title is describing the novel. Choices **a** and **b** are incorrect because these sentences have two phrases that mean essentially the same thing: "her novel" and "*To Kill a Mockingbird.*" If you remove either one of them, the sentence can still stand on its own. That means that there needs to be a non-restrictive adjective clause with one of them so that it's clear one is describing the other. Choice **d** is incorrect because it places the book's title after "July 1960," which is confusing.

39. The correct answer is choice c. The author intends to use an idiom referring to the attention that comes with being famous here, and the "spotlight" is an accepted idiom that conveys that meaning. Choices **a**, **b**, and **d** are incorrect because the author seems to intend to use an idiom referring to the attention that comes with being famous here. However, "big lights," "stage lights," and "lights" are not accepted idioms that convey that meaning.

40. The correct answer is choice d. The previous sentence states that Lee once described her feelings about being a celebrity herself. The most appropriate source would follow up on that statement with a personal quote from Harper Lee.

41. The correct answer is choice c. This sentence transitions from the discussion of Lee's feelings about fame directly to her withdrawal from the literary world, which is the main topic of the final paragraph. Choice **a** is incorrect because while this is relevant information to include in a biography of Harper Lee, it does not belong here. The best opening sentence should transition from the discussion of Lee's feelings about fame to her withdrawal from the literary world. Choice **b** is incorrect because it offers new information that has little, if anything, to do with the topic of the paragraph. Choice **d** is incorrect because while this is relevant information to include in a biography of Harper Lee, it does not belong here. The best opening sentence should transition from the discussion of Lee's feelings about fame to her withdrawal from the literary world.

42. The correct answer is choice a. As originally written, the sentences were somewhat choppy and awkward. This answer choice combines them clearly and correctly. Choice **b** is incorrect because while the choppy original sentences needed to be combined, joining them without punctuation or a conjunction creates a run-on sentence. Choice **c** is incorrect because this answer choice is awkwardly worded and needs punctuation to separate the two clauses. Choice **d** is incorrect because removing the pronoun "we" makes it seem as though it was Lee who lost a truly unique voice, which changes the intended meaning of the original sentences.

43. The correct answer is choice b. The writer is describing Lee's life in the past tense, so the verb should reflect that here. Choice **a** is incorrect because the writer is describing Lee's life in the past tense, so the verb should reflect that here. As written, the verb is in the present tense. Choice **c** is incorrect because the writer is describing Lee's life in the past tense, so the verb should reflect that here. The verb here is in the future tense. Choice **d** is incorrect because the writer is describing Lee's life in the past tense, so the verb should reflect that here. The verb here is in the present progressive tense.

44. The correct answer is choice c. The compound sentence as originally written shifts from the second-person point of view ("you") to the first person ("I"). This answer choice maintains grammatical agreement. Choice **a** is incorrect because this compound sentence shifts from the second-person point of view ("you") to the first person ("I"). It needs to maintain grammatical agreement. Choice **b** is incorrect because the first sentence is very choppy. There is a better way to correct the sentences. Choice **d** is incorrect because it shifts the perspective entirely to the second person ("you") when the rest of the passage is written in the first person.

45. The correct answer is choice d. The underlined word needs to indicate that someone is speaking about running in a big marathon, which would probably be somewhat boastful. Choice **a** is incorrect because the underlined word needs to indicate that someone is speaking about running in a big marathon, which would probably be somewhat boastful. However, "babbling" refers to a confused and aimless way of speaking. Choice **b** is incorrect because the underlined word needs to indicate that someone is speaking about running in a big marathon, which would probably be somewhat boastful. However, "echoing" indicates that something is being repeated, not boasted. Choice **c** is incorrect because while the underlined word needs to indicate that someone was speaking, it is not proper to say that someone was "pronouncing" something.

46. The correct answer is choice c. This sentence does not add anything of value to the passage and addresses someone else. Choice **a** is incorrect because the writer maintains a lighthearted and friendly tone throughout the narrative, so it does not need any extra humor. Choice **b** is incorrect because this sentence does not add anything important to the passage. Choice **d** is incorrect because the sentence is not a fragment.

47. The correct answer is choice a. The sentence is fine as written. Choice **b** is incorrect because this version removes information about what the "hard" part was. Choice **c** is incorrect because it is awkward to include "the easy part" in parentheses when "the hard part" is not. The semicolon is also misused here. Choice **d** is incorrect because this answer choice is awkwardly phrased.

48. **The correct answer is choice c.** It creates more interesting clauses and joins them with a coordinating conjunction ("but"). Choice **a** is incorrect because dashes should not be used to separate the clauses in a compound sentence. Choice **b** is incorrect because joining the two sentences without any punctuation turns them into a run-on sentence. Choice **d** is incorrect because ellipses should not be used to separate the clauses in a compound sentence.

49. **The correct answer is choice a.** It calls back to the "couch potato" reference in the first paragraph and also suggests the writer's pride in his accomplishment. Choice **b** is incorrect because there's no suggestion anywhere in the essay that the author runs the marathon to get the better of his friend Jeff. Choice **c** is incorrect because it is repetitive—the previous sentence already said that he'd beaten his personal record time. Choice **d** is incorrect because this story is about the Memorial Day 5K. The writer hasn't given any indication before now that he plans to take part in the marathon.

50. **The correct answer is choice b.** This sentence indicates the beginning of the race, which takes place between the second and third sentences of the paragraph. Choice **a** is incorrect because this sentence indicates the beginning of the race, which takes place between the second and third sentences of the paragraph. Choice **c** is incorrect because this sentence indicates the beginning of the race, but the writer is already running in the race by sentence 3. Choice **d** is incorrect because this sentence indicates the beginning of the race, but the writer has already been running in the race for some time by sentence 4.

Language Arts—Writing Part 2

On test day, your essay will be scored by two graders. Each will read over your essay, and assign it a score from 1 to 6 using the following grading criteria. Using this table, assign your own essay a score from 1 to 6. Then, read the provided sample essays and explanations to get a sense of what an essay at every level looks like. You need a score of 2 to pass this portion of the exam.

SCORE	EXPLANATION
1	*Essays at this score point do not sufficiently support an argument. They do not take a stance on the given question and do not provide solid evidence or reasoning to back up any claims.* These essays: • do not offer a clear opinion, as requested by the given prompt. The topic at hand might be mentioned, but there is no context for the information and no main idea to tie any information together into a cohesive thought. • are not structured: There is no introduction, conclusion, or main thesis. They often are not separated into paragraphs, and if they are, they lack smooth transitions from one paragraph to the next. • feature very simple vocabulary and sentence structure throughout. There is often a misuse of grammar, along with frequent errors in capitalization, punctuation, and spelling.
2	*Essays at this score point might bring up points related to the given prompt, but they do not sufficiently support an argument with a well-thought-out stance, backed by evidence. Thoughts are often jumbled and unrelated, and there is not a firm grasp of language rules or sentence and paragraph structure.* These essays: • do not fully develop a clear stance on the given issue. Often, if an opinion is given, it is either not developed or expanded on with examples from the given texts or relies too heavily on pulling information from the given texts. • often do not feature an introduction, conclusion, or paragraphs—if they do, these elements are not cohesive and do not flow properly. • do not have a solid command of sentence structure—sentences are either short and choppy or long and run-on. Sentences do not flow into one another, and there is no cohesive tone throughout the piece. • have limited command of grammar, usage, spelling, capitalization, and punctuation rules.
3	*Essays at this score point take a solid stance on the given issue and show partial command of developing an argument using proper usage rules.* These essays: • take a definitive stance on the given issue but do not fully develop this point of view with sufficient evidence—from the given texts and from the writer's personal experiences. Several points are presented to clarify the author's point of view, but a cohesive and well-rounded argument is not presented. • might feature an introduction, supporting paragraphs, and a conclusion, although one or all of these may be underdeveloped. If present, transitions are simple and used inconsistently. • begin to feature a command of language, although word choice and sentence structure are often unvaried or repetitive. Sentences in score 3 essays also might be too long and uncontrolled. Essays often feature errors in capitalization, punctuation, and spelling.
4	*Essays at this score point adequately take a stance on the argument presented and back it up with some evidence and reasoning. Basic writing rules are followed, but mistakes are often presented and be too casual.* These essays: • begin to develop a point of view in response to the given topic. The writer has a clear stance on the issue. Essays bring in personal examples and examples from the given essays, along with some discussion of alternate claims and/or counterclaims. • usually contain a clear introduction and conclusion but often lack sufficient development of supporting paragraphs within. Transitions are used, although they may be simple, and organization of sentences within paragraphs is often jumbled and awkward. • feature an adequate command of grammar, usage, sentence structure, and punctuation. Word choice and sentence format are somewhat varied, and a cohesive tone is used throughout. Errors are often present, but they do not interfere with the essay's clarity in message.

5   *Essays at this score point take a definitive stance on the argument presented, backing it up with solid examples, reasoning, and presentation of counterarguments. While these essays may feature minor mistakes, they show a good command of language, usage, and variety of word choice and sentence structure.* These essays:

- solidly present and back up a central position or claim on the given prompt. These essays also include a balanced discussion of counterclaims. Several ideas to back up a point of view are provided and expanded on, along with evidence from real life and the provided texts.
- feature a clear introduction, conclusion, and supporting paragraphs. Transitions are used throughout to unify ideas and create a cohesive point of view.
- show a very solid command of grammar, usage, spelling, punctuation, and sentence structure. Words are used correctly and varied throughout, and sentences vary in length and complexity. Thee essay may contain some errors in usage and some deviations in tone, but nothing detracts from the overall stance and content of the essay.

6   *Essays at this score point present a strongly written and defended argument using sufficient evidence from varied sources, presentation of counterarguments, and a solid command of language and grammar conventions.* These essays:

- expertly present, develop, and defend a point of view on a given topic. They explore the topic from all sides and present arguments countering differing opinions. Writers have a clear point of view and defend it with many examples taken from real life and from the given texts in the prompt.
- feature a definitive and well-written introduction, conclusion, and set of supporting paragraphs to back up all claims made. Strong transitions are used to connect thoughts and link together all claims and evidence made.
- demonstrate extremely strong command of language and grammar. Vocabulary and sentence structure throughout are varied in length and complexity. These essays have very few, if any, errors in spelling, punctuation, and usage. Essays feature a cohesive tone throughout that is appropriate for the topic at hand.

Sample Score 1 Essay:

Drones are everywere. people use it for personal use. They use them for hobby flying. They use them for photography. Something that brings people so much plesure can only be good! So I think it is good for people to have Drones. Some people do not think its good to sell. And have Drones. I say they are wrong. How can you know about them and not want a Drone yourself?

About This Essay

This essay does talk about the given topic, but the response does not relate to the question posed by the prompt. The author does not take a point of view that answers the question. There is no defined introduction or conclusion, and there are no paragraphs to separate information points. The author also does not offer supporting details and evidence to back up any claims. Finally, this essay is filled with errors in grammar ("Drones are everywere. people use it for

personal use."), spelling ("Drones are *everywere*"), and capitalization ("And have *Drones*").

Sample Score 2 Essay:

The government thinks people should register if they have drones. That seems really nosy. Why does the government need to know if people have drones? Are they illegil? No. There is nothing bad about drones people can use them for all kinds of different reasons. They aren't automaticly going to do the things the government doesn't want. Like fly near stadiums. Or fly below 400 feet. I dont like the idea that I have to let the government know about everything I do. So if I had a drone, I would register it. That's the law!

About This Essay

While this essay does discuss the given topic and take a one-sided point of view, it does not develop this point of view with a proper introduction, a conclusion, or supporting paragraphs with transitions. It also does not back up the point of view with examples from the given texts accompanying the prompt or from real life. The tone is too casual ("That seems really nosy."), and the essay is filled with errors in spelling ("Are they *illegil?*"), grammar/usage ("There is nothing bad about drones people can use them for all kinds of different reasons."), and punctuation ("I *dont* like the idea").

Sample Score 3 Essay:

A lot of people have drones these days. They are kind of like model airplanes that fly on their own I guess. The thing is that these drones can cause problems. Like they are cameras. They can just take pictures of anyone! What kind of toy is that? I think that is really a problem. So the Government wants to know who has a drone. It's not like a soccer ball or anything. These toys can really be used for bad purpuses. So is it so wrong for the government to want to know?

No, it's not. Some people think the fines are too serious. Well I'll tell you what's serious. Having a drone take your picture in private! No one wants that. Think about it.

So I agree with the government on this one. Give people who have drones fines. When they pay $27,500 for having a drone, they will think twice about taking your picture with them!

About This Essay

This essay takes a stance on the given topic, but it is not a well-developed argument with concrete examples taken from the given texts. Although there is a definable introduction, supporting paragraph, and conclusion, the paragraphs are not focused and the content jumps from topic to topic. More supportive points need to be made within the body of the essay, along with a less casual tone, to make it a strong persuasive piece. Additionally, although they do not make the piece unreadable, there are various errors in spelling ("used for bad *purpuses*.") and grammar ("Like they are cameras.").

Sample Score 4 Essay:

The government feels it is necessary for people to register drones? I think it is completly unnecessary. These things are basically toys and would you ask a little kid to register a teddy bear? I would not.

The problem is that drones can be dangerous or they can be used to conduct illegal surveillance. OK, that could be a problem. But I think people are responsible enough to just stick to the guidelines the FAA released. If you own a drone, you will probably know the rules; don't fly more than 400 feet, keep the aircraft within visual line, remain well clear of objects, and so on. Those people probably spent a lot of money on there drones and do not want them to get destroyed. So they will automatically do the things the FAA wants. Charging them $27,500 for making a mistake is completly ridiculous. Its especially ridiculous when little children are being fined.

Drone owners need to make their voices heard. They need to protest new requirements that have penalties that do not match the crimes. If the government starts making you pay for having a drone today they could make you pay for having some other kind of silly toy in the future. It is a slipping slope.

About This Essay

This essay takes a definitive stance on the given topic, with a well-defined introduction, body paragraph with supporting details, and conclusion. The essay pulls in details from the given texts to help define the point of view. The tone, however, is casual ("OK, that could be a problem.") and could be better developed with more varied word choice and sentence structure. With better development of ideas in the introduction and a more careful attention to detail, this essay could receive a higher score. There are spelling and other usage errors throughout ("I think it is *completly* unnecessary.") that do not detract from understanding but weaken the final product.

Sample Score 5 Essay:

We have so many freedoms in America, and with freedom comes responsibility. People of all ages may fly unmanned aircraft systems any place those devices can travel. UAS, or drones, are small vehicles without pilots and they can be great fun to fly. I have flown drones myself, so I should know. Still they can be used in ways that are anything but fun. Drones can be used for surveillence. If flown improperly, they can crash into people causing injuries or worse. With all that in mind, I think it is totally reasonable for the FAA to ask people to register their drones.

Anyone who feels this is unfair is being unrealistic. If you can afford to buy a drone (and my friend says they cost more than two thousand dollars!) you can certainly spring for the five dollars necessary to register it. The fees that come with misusing your drone are pretty steep, but missusing your drone can have serious consequences, so I firmly believe those fees are justified. You might have to pay a fine if you break the drone-flying guidelines the FAA has announced, but those guidelines are just as reasonable as the small fee required to register the vehicle. After all, why would someone who has spent two thousand dollars on a drone not want to keep it clear of obstacles or manned aircraft that could damage it? Why would that person not want to keep it "within visual sight at all times" so that it does not get lost? Any responsible person would not want to hurt anyone else to, so they would want to keep clear of people and the places where people gather, like stadiums.

Ultimately, these registration requirements are not meant to hurt people who have drones. They are meant to protect the drones and protect the people who could get hurt by the drones. Remember that with freedom comes responsibility. We are free to have drones. We should be responsible with them too.

About This Essay

This essay takes a strong stance on the given issue. It opens with a comprehensive introduction that begins the author's point of view, moves on to a strong body paragraph with examples that serve to strengthen the stance, and closes with a conclusion to wrap up. The author would have been better served breaking up the large body paragraph into several paragraphs, each taking on one aspect of the argument in more focus, linked together with strong transition sentences. The essay's sentences vary in structure, and although there are some grammar and spelling errors throughout ("Any responsible person would not want to hurt anyone else *to*"), mistakes are minimal.

Sample Score 6 Essay:

It's hard to go to a park or a beach these days without seeing small drones flying overhead, and hearing that high-pitched noise that sounds like a very large bee buzzing overhead. People love the advantages that drones provide: they can take photographs from up high, or spend an afternoon enjoying the high-tech version of a kite on a sunny afternoon. However, as drones become more a part of our landscape, we need to make sure we're doing everything to make sure they're operated safely for everyone around. Because of this, our state should require that all drone owners register their devices.

Although the Federal Aviation Administration has released fairly strict safety guidelines, I believe they don't go far enough. These guidelines limit where people can fly their drones in public places, and let users know that if these tiny aircraft interfere with larger aircraft, there will be fines to pay. Still, I believe that registration is the logical next step here. The guidelines are a good baseline, but how do you enforce them if you don't catch someone violating them? Registering a drone would be like registering a car—if there's an accident or an incident, it makes it easier to track who owns what, and who's responsible.

This has real-world consequences, as well. Last year, there was a big news story where someone crashed a drone into the U.S. Open stadium because he was trying to take photos. Police had the drone in hand right away, but it took time to track down the drone's owner (who had violated the FAA regulation on flying drones near stadiums). If the drone were registered in a database, it would be easier to find out who's responsible for the actions.

Drones can also affect safety in everyday areas, like the aforementioned parks and beaches. If anything happens and someone gets hurt from a crashed drone, or if someone's privacy is invaded by a drone looking in their windows, there needs to be an extra level of accountability. If the affected person can recover the drone body, then registration would ideally mean that the person at fault could be tracked down.

The serious consequences of improper drone use justify the serious penalties that come with violating the FAA's guidelines or failing to register a device that also functions as a deadly weapon. A $27,500 fine or even prison time is not an outlandish penalty for endangering human life. Essentially, we have good regulations in place to guide the recreational use of drones, and we need to make sure that people are accountable for anything that happens when they're flying their drones. We have a duty to public safety to do everything we can to ensure that people are flying safely while they have fun.

About This Essay

This is a strong essay that directly addresses the given prompt. The author takes a clear stance on the issue presented and expands on it in a well-developed introduction, set of body paragraphs, and conclusion. Transitions are used expertly throughout ("This has real-world consequences, as well."), and the author brings in examples from real life and from the given texts to strengthen and support the point of view. Grammar, spelling, and usage in the essay are correct, and sentence structure and vocabulary are varied and interesting.

Mathematics

To calculate your HiSET® score on the Mathematics section, first take a look at the correct answer for each of the 50 questions of the exam. Count up your **correct answers** only, and give yourself 1 point for

each. Then, add up all of your points. This is your **raw score**.

Find your raw score and your **scaled score** in the following table. Remember, for each test section, a passing score is 8. (For the essay, a passing score is 2.)

You need a scaled score of 45 to pass the complete HiSET® exam.

MATHEMATICS SCORING			
RAW	SCALED	RAW	SCALED
0	1	26	12
1	1	27	12
2	2	28	12
3	2	29	13
4	3	30	13
5	3	31	13
6	4	32	13
7	5	33	14
8	6	34	14
9	7	35	14
10	8	36	14
11	8	37	15
12	8	38	15
13	9	39	15
14	9	40	15
15	9	41	16
16	10	42	16
17	10	43	16
18	10	44	17
19	10	45	17
20	10	46	18
21	11	47	18
22	11	48	19
23	11	49	20
24	11	50	20
25	12		

1. **The correct answer is choice d.** Subtract the two equations to eliminate the x terms to obtain the equation $-3y = -b^2$. So, $y = \frac{1}{3}b^2$. Plug this value of y back into one of the original equations of the system, say the first one, to solve for x:

$$bx - \frac{1}{3}b^2 = 2b^2$$
$$bx = \frac{7}{3}b^2$$
$$x = \frac{7}{3}b$$

So, the solution of the system is $x = \frac{7}{3}b$, $y = \frac{1}{3}b^2$. Choice **a** is incorrect because you added the equations of the system when you should have subtracted them to eliminate the x terms. Choice **b** is incorrect because this satisfies the first equation of the system but not the second. Choice **c** is incorrect because this satisfies the second equation of the system but not the first. Choice **e** is incorrect because while the x value is correct, the y value is not; you must have made an error when solving the linear equation for y obtained by substituting the value of x back into one of the original equations.

2. **The correct answer is choice c.** This is the only function that satisfies all three conditions. It has a factor of $(x + 4)^2$, which means $(x + 4)^2$ divides it evenly. Evaluating this function at $x = -4, 3, 0,$ and 1 yields 0, so the second condition is satisfied. And it has degree 6. Choices **a** and **b** are incorrect because these polynomials do not have degree 6. Choice **d** is incorrect because this polynomial has a zero of -3, which is not in the list of zeros, so the second condition is not satisfied. Choice **e** is incorrect because 0 is not an x-intercept of this polynomial, but it is included in the list of zeros in the second condition, so that the condition is not satisfied.

3. **The correct answer is choice e.** Note that the color and the type of bike seat do not factor into how the bike is chosen when asking for the probability that the bike chosen is a mountain bike. So, since there is an equal likelihood of choosing any of the three types of bikes, the probability of randomly choosing a mountain bike is $\frac{1}{3}$. Choice **a** is incorrect because this would insist on a specific structure, color, and type of bike seat. Choice **b** is incorrect because this would insist on a specific type of seat. Choice **c** is incorrect because this would insist on a specific color. Choice **d** is incorrect because this is the probability of selecting a bike of a specific color.

4. **The correct answer is choice d.** The radius of the given sphere must be 2 cm. So the radius of the desired sphere is $3(2\text{ cm}) = 6\text{ cm}$. So its volume is $\frac{4}{3}\pi(6\text{ cm})^3 = 288\pi$ cubic centimeters. Choice **a** is incorrect because you used the diameter instead of the radius when computing the volume. Choice **b** is incorrect because you used the diameter instead of the radius when computing the volume, and you forgot to include the $\frac{1}{3}$ in the volume formula for a sphere. Choice **c** is incorrect because you used the diameter instead of the radius and used the surface area formula instead of the volume formula. Choice **e** is incorrect because you forgot to include the $\frac{1}{3}$ in the volume formula for a sphere.

5. The correct answer is choice c. FOIL the binomials and combine like terms:

$$(2x^2 + 3)(2 - 4x^2) = (2x^2)(2) - (2x^2)(4x^2)$$
$$+ (3)(2) - (3)(4x^2)$$
$$= 4x^2 - 8x^4 + 6 - 12x^2$$
$$= -8x^4 - 8x^2 + 6$$

Choice **a** is incorrect because $(a + b)(c + d) \neq ac + bd$. Choice **b** is incorrect because you dropped the middle square term. Choice **d** is incorrect because this is the negative of the correct answer. Choice **e** is incorrect because you dropped the highest-power term.

6. The correct answer is choice a. The radius of the circle is $\frac{\sqrt{2}}{2}$ inches. Using the formula for the area of a sector yields the area to be

$$\frac{140°}{360°}\left[\pi \cdot \left(\frac{\sqrt{2}}{2} \text{ in.}\right)^2\right] = \frac{7}{36}\pi \text{ square inches.}$$

Choice **b** is incorrect because this is the area of the entire circle, not just the shaded portion. Choice **c** is incorrect because you used the diameter instead of the radius. Choice **d** is incorrect because this is the length of the arc opposite the 140° angle, not the area of that sector. Choice **e** is incorrect because this is the area of the unshaded sector.

7. The correct answer is choice b. Convert the radicals to rational exponents and apply the exponent rules:

$$\sqrt[3]{x^2} \cdot \sqrt{x^5} = x^{\frac{2}{3}} \cdot x^{\frac{5}{2}} = x^{\frac{2}{3} + \frac{5}{2}} = x^{\frac{19}{6}}$$

Choice **a** is incorrect because $x^a \cdot x^b = x^{a+b}$, not $x^{a \cdot b}$. Choice **c** is incorrect because $\sqrt[m]{x^n} = x^{\frac{n}{m}}$, not $x^{\frac{m}{n}}$. Choice **d** is incorrect because $x^a \cdot x^b = x^{a+b}$, not $x^{a \cdot b}$, and $\sqrt[m]{x^n} = x^{\frac{n}{m}}$, not $x^{\frac{m}{n}}$. Choice **e** is incorrect because $x^a \cdot x^b = x^{a+b}$, not x^{a-b}.

8. The correct answer is choice a. Let x be the original price. Then the price z of the markup is given by $z = x + \frac{q}{100}x$. Solve for x:

$$z = \left(1 + \frac{q}{100}\right)x$$
$$x = \frac{1}{1 + \frac{q}{100}}z$$
$$x = \frac{100}{100 + q}$$

Choice **b** is incorrect because you applied the $q\%$ markup to the sale price. Choice **c** is incorrect because $q\%$ is a percent of an amount, not a quantity to be added to a given dollar amount. Choice **d** is incorrect because the denominator is incorrect. Choice **e** is incorrect because you did not apply the definition of a percentage correctly.

9. The correct answer is choice b. Since more than 50% of those polled preferred this song, this is a reasonable conclusion. Choice **a** is incorrect because while this is true about the sample, it does not have to be true of the entire audience. Choice **c** is incorrect because while this is true about the sample, it does not have to be true of the entire audience. Choice **d** is incorrect because the song could be a very well-liked older song. Choice **e** is incorrect because while this is true about the sample, it does not have to be true of the entire audience.

10. The correct answer is choice e. Solve the equation as follows:

$$-2(x + 2) - 1 = 2(2 - x)$$
$$-2x - 4 - 1 = 4 - 2x$$
$$-2x - 5 = 4 - 2x$$
$$-5 = 4$$

Since the resulting statement is false, we conclude that the equation has no solution. Choices **a**, **b**, **c**, and **d** are incorrect because substituting these values for x does not yield a true mathematical statement.

11. The correct answer is choice e. Substitute the given information into the equation and solve for g:

$$56.1 = \frac{151.47}{g}$$
$$56.1g = 151.47$$
$$g = \frac{151.47}{56.1} = 2.7$$

Choice **a** is incorrect because you should divide 151.47 by 56.1, not subtract 56.1 from it. Choice **b** is incorrect because you divided in the wrong order. Choice **c** is incorrect because this is an arithmetic error—the decimal point is in the wrong location. Choice **d** is incorrect because you divided in the wrong order, and you have a place value error.

12. The correct answer is choice c. The given sequence is an arithmetic sequence in which consecutive terms differ by –8. Since the first term of the sequence is –7, we conclude that an expression for the nth term is $f(n) = -7 - 8n$, $n \geq 0$. Choice **a** is incorrect because while consecutive terms do differ by –8, this formula does not accurately capture the pattern. Choice **b** is incorrect because you are missing a negative sign in front of the term $8n$. Choice **d** is incorrect because the 7 should be replaced by –7. Choice **e** is incorrect because the placement of the –7 and –8 is wrong. When you plug $n = 0$ into this formula, you do not get the first term of the given sequence.

13. The correct answer is choice a. Since sine of an angle is the length of the side opposite the angle divided by the hypotenuse, this equation accurately relates the given angle θ to the given two sides. Choice **b** is incorrect because the tangent of an angle is the length of the side opposite the angle divided by the length of the side adjacent to the angle. You are not given the side length adjacent to the angle θ, and you therefore cannot use tangent. Choice **c** is incorrect because the cosine of an angle is the length of the side adjacent the angle divided by the hypotenuse. You are not given the side length adjacent to the angle θ, and you therefore cannot use cosine. Choice **d** is incorrect because the right side needs to be the reciprocal of what is given. The sine of an angle is the length of the side opposite the angle divided by the hypotenuse, not the other way around. Choice **e** is incorrect because the left side should be sin θ.

14. The correct answer is choice c. Reading the data values from left to right, the x-values are getting larger while the y-values are getting smaller. So the points fall from left to right, which means the best fit line would do the same. Therefore, the best fit line would have a negative slope. Choice **a** is incorrect because these points are not all collinear. Choice **b** is incorrect because reading the data values from left to right, the x-values are getting larger while the y-values are getting smaller. A horizontal best fit line would imply there is little or no change in the y-values. Choice **d** is incorrect because the best fit line would have a negative slope, not a positive slope. Choice **e** is incorrect because the best fit line always exists.

15. The correct answer is choice e. First, we need to determine the number of seconds in one day: 1 minute = 60 seconds, 1 hour = 60 minutes = 60(60) = 3,600 seconds, so 1 day = 24 hours = 24(3,600) seconds = 86,400 seconds. Therefore, light travels $(86,400) \times (3.2 \times 10^8) = 2.7648 \times 10^{13}$ meters. Choice **a** is incorrect because you multiplied by the number of hours in a day, but you did not multiply by the number of seconds in an hour. Choice **b** is incorrect because this is the distance traveled in 1 minute, not 1 day. Choice **c** is incorrect because this is the distance traveled in 1 week, not 1 day. Choice **d** is incorrect because this is the distance traveled in 1 hour, not 1 day.

16. The correct answer is choice c. Since you are reflecting the segment across a vertical line, the y-coordinates remain the same, but the x-coordinates change by the distance between $x = -6$ and the respective x-coordinates of A and B. So, the image A' of A is $(-8,5)$, and the image B' of B is $(-15,2)$. Choice **a** is incorrect because this is the reflection across the line $x = 6$, not $x = -6$. Choice **b** is incorrect because this is the reflection across the line $y = 6$, not $x = -6$. Choice **d** is incorrect because this is the reflection across the line $y = -6$, not $x = -6$. Choice **e** is incorrect because this is the reflection across the line $y = x$.

17. The correct answer is choice d. This expression is not equivalent to the others because when simplifying the original expression, this is obtained by inadvertently canceling $6x^2$ with $-3(-2x^2)$. Choice **a** is incorrect because this is equivalent to the original expression by the commutative property since the order of the terms being added has been changed. Choice **b** is incorrect because this is equivalent to the original expression, since $x - 1$ has been factored out and the order of the resulting terms rearranged. Choice **c** is incorrect because if you multiply the terms and simplify the original expression, you get $14x^2 - 3x - 12$. If you then factor out -3 from the last two terms, you get the expression here. Choice **e** is incorrect because if you distribute and simplify, you get $14x^2 - 3x - 12$, which is equivalent to the original expression expressed in simplest form.

18. The correct answer is choice a. Solve the equation as follows:

$$x^2 + 16 = 0$$
$$x^2 = -16$$
$$x = \pm\sqrt{-16} = \pm i\sqrt{16} = \pm 4i$$

So its solution set is $\{\pm 4i\}$. Choice **b** is incorrect because the solution set of this equation is $\{\pm 4\}$. Choice **c** is incorrect because the solution set of this equation is $\{0,16\}$. Choice **d** is incorrect because the solution set of this equation is $\{0,-16\}$. Choice **e** is incorrect because the solution set of this equation is $\{\pm\frac{1}{4}i\}$.

19. **The correct answer is choice b.** Note that $P(both) = 0.47(0.35) = 0.1645$. Now use the addition formula for computing the probability of a union of two events that have common outcomes to conclude that $P(EITHER\ scores\ the\ point\ OR\ has\ one\ fault) = 0.35 + 0.47 − 0.1645 = 0.6555$, or about 0.66. Choice **a** is incorrect because you did not subtract $P(both)$. Choice **c** is incorrect because you did not account for the probability of having one fault. Choice **d** is incorrect because you did not account for the probability of scoring the point. Choice **e** is incorrect because you identified the events incorrectly when using the addition formula.

20. **The correct answer is choice e.** The central angle for the shaded sector is 250°. So the length of the arc of the shaded sector is $6 \cdot (250°) \cdot \frac{\pi}{180°} = \frac{25}{3}\pi$ feet. The two radii contribute $2 \cdot 6$ ft. $= 12$ ft. to the total perimeter. So the perimeter of the shaded region is $(12 + \frac{25}{3}\pi)$ feet. Choice **a** is incorrect because you used the diameter instead of the radius when calculating the arc length of the sector. Choice **b** is incorrect because you did not include the lengths of the two radii segments in the perimeter. Choice **c** is incorrect because you did not convert the central angle to radians. Choice **d** is incorrect because you did not include the lengths of the two radii segments in the perimeter, and you did not convert the central angle to radians.

21. **The correct answer is choice a.** Since the only difference here is a change in grouping, the associative property is being illustrated. Choice **b** is incorrect because you are not adding zero to a real number and getting that same number back as a result in this equality. Choice **c** is incorrect because you did not change the order in which terms were added or multiplied in this equality. Choice **d** is incorrect because you are not adding the opposite of a real number and getting zero as a result in this equality. Choice **e** is incorrect because you are not multiplying a binomial by a real number by multiplying each term of the binomial by the number in this equality.

22. **The correct answer is choice a.** Questions about maximum profit for quadratic profit equations are best addressed using the vertex form. What is given here is the standard form for a quadratic expression. It reveals that the vertex is (4,8). The coefficient of the squared term is negative, so we know that a maximum occurs at the vertex and is 8. So the maximum profit is $800, obtained when selling a roll for $4. Choice **b** is incorrect because this would be most useful for determining when the profit will be zero. Choices **c** and **d** are incorrect because these choices are useful for determining the profit for a given price per roll, but you cannot immediately determine maximum profit. Choice **e** is incorrect because it is not as useful as choice **a**; the trinomial should be factored to reveal the vertex coordinates completely. Choice **a** takes this one step further and so is more useful for finding the maximum profit.

23. The correct answer is choice d. To get the graph of g from the graph of f, we must translate the graph of f left 3 units and then down 2 units. This entails subtracting 3 from all values of the domain of f to get the domain of g and subtracting 2 units from all values in the range of f to get the range of g. Doing so gives the domain and range listed here. Choice **a** is incorrect because the domain of g is not the same as the domain of f; rather, it should be shifted left 3 units. Choice **b** is incorrect because the domain of f should be translated left 3 units, not right 3 units, to get the domain of g. Choice **c** is incorrect because the range of f should be translated 2 units down, not 2 units up, to get the range of g. Choice **e** is incorrect because the domain of f should be translated left 3 units, not right 3 units, to get the domain of g, and the range of f should be translated 2 units down, not 2 units up, to get the range of g.

24. The correct answer is choice e. Let x be the cost of one plum and y be the cost of one peach. The first equation in this system describes the "cost for 5 plums and 6 peaches" and the second equation describes the "cost of 8 plums and 3 peaches." Choice **a** is incorrect because you should set up two cost equations, not combine the costs into one equation. Choice **b** is incorrect because the right sides of the two equations should be interchanged. Choice **c** is incorrect because the y-terms in the two equations should be interchanged. Choice **d** is incorrect because the x-terms in the two equations should be interchanged.

25. The correct answer is choice e. Convert the radicals to rational exponents and use the exponent rules to simplify:

$$\sqrt[3]{\sqrt{\tfrac{1}{5}}} = \left(\left(5^{-1}\right)^{\frac{1}{2}}\right)^{\frac{1}{3}} = 5^{(-1)\cdot\left(\frac{1}{2}\right)\cdot\left(\frac{1}{3}\right)} = 5^{-\frac{1}{6}}$$

Choice **a** is incorrect because the exponent has the wrong sign. $\frac{1}{5} = 5^{-1}$. Choice **b** is incorrect because you added the exponents instead of multiplying them. $(a^b)^c = a^{b\cdot c}$. Choice **c** is incorrect because $\sqrt[m]{a} = a^{\frac{1}{m}}$, not a^m. Choice **d** is incorrect because $\sqrt{\tfrac{1}{5}} = 5^{-\frac{1}{2}}$, not 5^{-2}.

26. The correct answer is choice a. The center of the circle is the midpoint of the shown segment with endpoints $(-1,-1)$ and $(4,3)$: $\left(\frac{-1+4}{2},\frac{-1+3}{2}\right)$ $= \left(\frac{3}{2},1\right)$. The radius is one-half the length of the shown segment since it passes through the center O, making it a diameter:

$$\tfrac{1}{2}\sqrt{[4-(-1)]^2 + [3-(-1)]^2} = \tfrac{1}{2}\sqrt{41}$$

So the equation of the circle is $(x-\frac{3}{2})^2 + (y-1)^2 = \frac{41}{4}$. Choice **b** is incorrect because you used the diameter instead of the radius on the right side of the equation. Choice **c** is incorrect because you should subtract the coordinates of the center, not add them, on the left side of the equation. Choice **d** is incorrect because you should square the radius on the right side of the equation. Choice **e** is incorrect because you used the diameter instead of the radius on the right side of the equation, and you should square the radius on the right side.

27. The correct answer is choice d. Add up the angles corresponding to all sectors that are either red or white, divide by 360 degrees (the total for the whole circle), and subtract from 1:

$$1 - \frac{20° + 45° + 70°}{360°} = \frac{5}{8} = 0.625$$

Choice **a** is incorrect because this is the probability of landing on a white or red sector. Choice **b** is incorrect because this probability includes the 45° red sector among the desired outcomes. Choice **c** is incorrect because this is the probability of not landing on white—you did not exclude the red sectors. Choice **e** is incorrect because not all of the wedges have the same size, so the probabilities of landing on different colored sectors are different.

28. The correct answer is choice d. Adding P_1 to both sides of the inequality $P_1 > P_2$ yields the inequality given here. Choice **a** is incorrect because since $P_1 + P_2$ is positive, dividing both sides of the inequality $P_1 > P_2$ by $P_1 + P_2$ preserves the direction of the inequality. The inequality sign should be reversed here. Choice **b** is incorrect because since $P_1 > P_2$, P_2 must be less than half of the combined turtle population. Choice **c** is incorrect because since $P_1 > P_2$, $\frac{P_1}{P_2}$ must be larger than $\frac{P_2}{P_1}$. Choice **e** is incorrect because the inequality sign should be reversed. Note that since $P_2 < P_1$, the left side is less than $\frac{1}{2}$ and the right side is > 1.

29. The correct answer is choice a. The slope of both lines of this system is 2. So the lines are parallel and they have different y-intercepts. Hence, they do not intersect and the system has no solution. Choice **b** is incorrect because these two lines have the same slope and y-intercept. So the system has infinitely many solutions. Choice **c** is incorrect because this system is composed of one vertical line and one horizontal line. So it has a unique solution given by $x = 4$, $y = -1$. Choice **d** is incorrect because these two equations are equivalent, so that the system has infinitely many solutions. Choice **e** is incorrect because these lines are perpendicular (since their slopes are negative reciprocals of each other), so the system has a unique solution.

30. The correct answer is choice e. Compute the average value as follows:

$$\frac{g(2) - g(-1)}{2 - (-1)} = \frac{[2^2 - 3(2)] - [(-1)^2 - 3(-1)]}{3} = \frac{-2 - 4}{3}$$
$$= \frac{-6}{3} = -2$$

Choice **a** is incorrect because this is the total change in the value of the function over the given interval. To find the average rate of change, divide this amount by the length of the interval, $2 - (-1)$. Choice **b** is incorrect because the average cannot be zero because $g(-1)$ does not equal $g(2)$. Choice **c** is incorrect because you subtracted incorrectly: $g(2) - g(-1) = 6$, not -2. Choice **d** is incorrect because $(-1)^2 = 1$, not -2.

31. The correct answer is choice c. The mode is the data value that occurs most frequently, which is 2. The median is the middle value when the data is arranged in increasing order, which is 7. The mean is $\frac{2+2+2+7+7+11+11}{7} = 6$. Choice **a** is incorrect because while this data set has mode 2 and median 7, the mean is not 6 (it is approximately 5.4). Choice **b** is incorrect because the median is 6 and mean is 6.8. Choice **d** is incorrect because the mode is 6, median is 6, and mean is 7. Choice **e** is incorrect because the data set is bimodal, with modes 2 and 7. The median is 6 and mean is 7.

32. The correct answer is choice e. Using similar triangles, we obtain the proportion $\frac{x}{a} = \frac{c}{b}$. Solving for x yields $bx = ac$ and so $x = \frac{a \cdot c}{b}$. Choice **a** is incorrect because this is the reciprocal of the correct value. Choice **b** is incorrect because when solving the proportion $\frac{x}{a} = \frac{c}{b}$ for x, cross multiply, don't cross add. Also, you have the reciprocal of one of the fractions in the proportion rather than the two listed. Choice **c** is incorrect because you must use similar triangles to obtain a proportion relating the sides; you don't simply add all sides to get the desired side. Choice **d** is incorrect because when solving the proportion $\frac{x}{a} = \frac{c}{b}$ for x, cross multiply, don't cross add.

33. The correct answer is choice d. First, convert 6 miles per hour to feet per minute:
$$\frac{6 \text{ mi.}}{1 \text{ hour}} \times \frac{5{,}280 \text{ ft.}}{1 \text{ mi.}} \times \frac{1 \text{ hour}}{60 \text{ min.}} = 528 \text{ feet per minute}$$
Let x be the number of minutes it takes to jog 5,000 feet. Solve the equation $528x = 5{,}000$ to get $x = \frac{5{,}000}{528} \approx 9.5$ minutes. Choice **a** is incorrect because you divided 5,000 by 6. You must first convert units appropriately. Choice **b** is incorrect because you mistakenly used 1,760 feet instead of 5,280 in the mile-to-feet conversion, and you looked for the number of seconds, not the number of minutes. Choice **c** is incorrect because you mistakenly used 1,760 feet instead of 5,280 in the mile-to-feet conversion. Choice **e** is incorrect because this is the number of seconds, not the number of minutes.

34. The correct answer is choice a. First, apply the 15% coupon to get $75.50 − $75.50(0.15) = $64.18. Now apply the 6% tax to this amount to get $64.18 + $64.18(0.06) = $68.03. Now apply the 20% tip to this amount to get the final bill: $68.03 + $68.03(0.20) = $81.64. Choice **b** is incorrect because you did not apply the tax. Choice **c** is incorrect because you did not include tax or tip in this amount. Choice **d** is incorrect because you did not include the tip in this amount. Choice **e** is incorrect because you did not apply the 15% coupon.

35. The correct answer is choice a. The portion of the findings in this scavenger hunt that is quarters is 12/40, and the portion that is silver dollars is 4/40. Adding these, you would expect that 16/40, or 40%, of the findings from a similar scavenger hunt would be composed of quarters and silver dollars. Choice **b** is incorrect because this is the portion of the findings that you would expect to be quarters. Choice **c** is incorrect because this is the portion of the findings that you would expect to be silver dollars. Choice **d** is incorrect because this is the portion of the findings that you would expect to be pennies. Choice **e** is incorrect because this is the portion of the findings that you expect to NOT be quarters or silver dollars.

36. The correct answer is choice e. Factor all expressions, convert the division problem to a multiplication problem, and cancel like factors in top and bottom:

$$\frac{5x^3 + x^2}{2x - 5} \div \frac{75x^3 + 30x^2 + 3x}{4x^2 - 8x - 5} = \frac{x^2(5x + 1)}{2x - 5}$$
$$\times \frac{(2x - 5)(2x + 1)}{3x(5x + 1)^2}$$
$$= \frac{x(2x + 1)}{3(5x + 1)} = \frac{2x^2 + x}{15x + 3}$$

Choice **a** is incorrect because you have an extra x in the numerator. Choice **b** is incorrect because you multiplied the given rational expressions instead of dividing them. Choice **c** is incorrect because you incorrectly factored both trinomials in the second rational expression. Choice **d** is incorrect because you cannot cancel terms in fractions like this:

$$\frac{x(2x + 1)}{3(5x + 1)} \neq \frac{x(2x + 1)}{3(5x + 1)}$$

37. The correct answer is choice d. First, multiply both sides of the equation by the least common denominator $x(1 - x)$ to clear the fractions: $x(x) + 2(1 - x) = -x(1 - x)$. Solving for x then yields

$$x^2 - 2x + 2 = x^2 - x$$
$$x = 2$$

Since this does not make the least common denominator equal to zero, it is a solution. Choice **a** is incorrect because you did not solve the linear equation obtained by clearing the fractions correctly. Choice **b** is incorrect because these are the values that make each denominator equal to zero. Choice **c** is incorrect because there is a real solution. Choice **e** is incorrect because you forgot to multiply the right side by the least common denominator when clearing the fractions.

38. The correct answer is choice b. Let x be the length and y be the width. Since the area is 88 square feet, we have $xy = 88$, which implies that $y = \frac{88}{x}$. Since the perimeter is 38 feet, we know that $2x + 2y = 38$, so that substituting in $y = \frac{88}{x}$ yields the equation $2x + 2(\frac{88}{x}) = 38$, which is equivalent to $2x + \frac{176}{x} = 38$. Choice **a** is incorrect because the two sides x and y are not related by $x + y = 88$; you misused the information regarding the area. Choice **c** is incorrect because you forgot to multiply the width and length by 2 in the perimeter formula. Choice **d** is incorrect because using the area formula, the two sides of the rectangle are x and $\frac{88}{x}$, not x and $\frac{x}{88}$. Choice **e** is incorrect because the right side should be 19 since the perimeter is 38 feet, not 88 feet.

39. The correct answer is choice b. Use the two labeled points $(1,9)$ and $(3,7)$ to get that the slope of the best fit line is -1. The equation of the best fit line is $y - 9 = -(x - 1)$, so that $y = -x + 10$. Thus, $y(4) = 6$. This means that you would expect to make 6 errors if you had 4 hours of sleep. Choice **a** is incorrect because this is the y-intercept of the best fit line and would represent the number of errors you would expect to make based on 0 hours of sleep. Choice **c** is incorrect because 1 is the slope, but is not the number of errors you would expect to make based on 4 hours of sleep. Choice **d** is incorrect because this is the number of errors based on 5 hours of sleep. Choice **e** is incorrect because this is the number of errors based on 2 hours of sleep.

40. The correct answer is choice e. The denominator is never equal to zero, so we do not need to exclude any real numbers from the domain. Choice **a** is incorrect because this makes the numerator equal to zero, which is allowed for a fraction. Choice **b** is incorrect because these values do not make the denominator equal to zero; you are confusing $x^2 + 16$ with $x^2 - 16$. Choice **c** is incorrect because this value does not make the denominator equal to zero; you are confusing $x^2 + 16$ with $x^2 - 16$. Choice **d** is incorrect because 0 makes the numerator equal to zero, which is allowed for a fraction, and -4 and 4 do not make the denominator equal to zero; you are confusing $x^2 + 16$ with $x^2 - 16$.

41. The correct answer is choice d. Note that $\sqrt{36} - \sqrt{20} \neq \sqrt{36 - 20}$. Even though $\sqrt{36} = 6$ is a rational number, $\sqrt{20}$ is irrational. Since the sum of a rational number and an irrational number is irrational, this must be irrational. Choice **a** is incorrect because $(\frac{3}{5})^{-4} = (\frac{5}{3})^4 = \frac{5^4}{3^4} = \frac{625}{81}$, which is rational. Choice **b** is incorrect because repeating decimals are rational numbers. Choice **c** is incorrect because $\sqrt[3]{2} \cdot \sqrt[3]{32} = \sqrt[3]{64} = 4$, which is rational. Choice **e** is incorrect because any nonzero real number raised to the power of zero is 1, which is rational.

42. The correct answer is choice c. Begin by drawing a diagram:

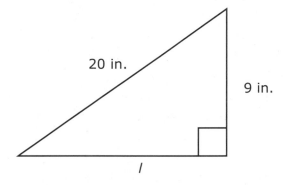

Using the Pythagorean theorem, we obtain $9^2 + l^2 = 20^2$. Solving for l then yields $l^2 = 20^2 - 9^2$, so that $l = \sqrt{20^2 - 9^2}$. Choice **a** is incorrect because you forgot the square root. Choice **b** is incorrect because 20 is the hypotenuse, not a leg, of the triangle. Choice **d** is incorrect because you forgot the square root, and 20 is the hypotenuse, not a leg, of the right triangle. Choice **e** is incorrect because $\sqrt{a^2 - b^2} \neq a - b$.

43. The correct answer is choice e. First find the slope of the line containing this line segment:

$$m = \frac{-3 - (-5)}{3 - (-2)} = \frac{2}{5}$$

To get other points on the line, you can add 2 to the y-coordinate and 5 to the x-coordinate of a point known to be on the line, or you can subtract 2 from the y-coordinate and subtract 5 from the x-coordinate of a point known to be on the line. Using the latter twice in succession gives the points $(-7,-7)$ and $(-12,-9)$. Choice **a** is incorrect because you seem to have eyeballed the y-intercept. You must use the slope of the line to accurately place points on it. Choice **b** is incorrect because you subtracted 2 from the x-coordinate and 5 from the y-coordinate of point A but should have done the reverse. Choice **c** is incorrect because you added 2 to the x-coordinate and 5 to the y-coordinate of point B but should have done the reverse. Choice **d** is incorrect because the y-coordinate is wrong. You must have computed the slope incorrectly.

44. The correct answer is choice a. Determine the average of the 40th and 41st ratings: $\frac{3 + 4}{2} = 3.5$ stars. Choice **b** is incorrect because this is the average of the 41st and 42nd ratings, but the median is the average of the 40th and 41st ratings. Choice **c** is incorrect because this is the average of the 39th and 40th ratings, but the median is the average of the 40th and 41st ratings. Choice **d** is incorrect because this is the mean rating, not the median. Choice **e** is incorrect because you computed the mean but divided the sum by 74 instead of 80; remember to include the number of "0" entries in the total number of points in the data set.

45. The correct answer is choice c. Since the left side is always nonnegative and the right side is less than zero, the solution set of this inequality is the set of all real numbers. Choice **a** is incorrect because the x-values strictly between -2 and 2 do not satisfy this inequality. Choice **b** is incorrect because positive x-values and x-values less than -5 do not satisfy this inequality. Choice **d** is incorrect because 3 does not satisfy this inequality. Choice **e** is incorrect because the solution set is empty for this inequality.

46. The correct answer is choice d. Solve the equation as follows:

$$x\sqrt{4x} - 1 = 0$$
$$x\sqrt{4x} = 1$$
$$\sqrt{4} \cdot x\sqrt{x} = 1$$
$$2x^{\frac{3}{2}} = 1$$
$$x^{\frac{3}{2}} = \frac{1}{2}$$
$$x = \left(\frac{1}{2}\right)^{\frac{2}{3}} = \frac{1}{2^{\frac{2}{3}}} = 2^{-\frac{2}{3}}$$

Choice **a** is incorrect because when computing a power, you do not multiply the base by the exponent. Choice **b** is incorrect because this value renders the left side equal to -1, not 0. Choice **c** is incorrect because when solving the equation $x^{\frac{m}{n}} = a$, you get $x = a^{\frac{n}{m}}$, not $a^{\frac{m}{n}}$. Choice **e** is incorrect because this is the reciprocal of the correct solution.

47. The correct answer is choice e. Let x = number of days and $r(x)$ = number of inches of rain in 7 days. Then the equation $r(x) = 7$ would be solved for x to answer the posed question. Choice **a** is incorrect because $r(7)$ = number of inches of rain after 7 days. Choice **b** is incorrect because this means that after 7 days, you would have 7 inches of rain. This need not be the case. Choice **c** is incorrect because the 7 should be on the right side, not multiplied by $r(x)$. Choice **d** is incorrect because this would be solved to determine the number of days needed to get 1 inch of rain.

48. The correct answer is choice d. This measurement is approximately 4 inches, so it is the most reasonable measurement listed. Choices **a** and **b** are incorrect because they are too small. Choice **c** is incorrect because this is about 1.5 feet, which is too large. Choice **e** is incorrect because since 1 foot = 12 inches, this is approximately 0.192 inches, which is too small.

49. The correct answer is choice e. If $x - 3$ is a factor of a polynomial $p(x)$, then $p(3)$ must equal 0. But the graph does not cross the x-axis when $x = 3$. So, $x - 3$ cannot be a factor of this polynomial. All other choices are incorrect because the graph crosses the x-axis at the corresponding zero of these factors.

50. The correct answer is choice e. The function is exponentially increasing, so the range is obtained by starting at the y-coordinate corresponding to $t = 1$ and ending at the y-coordinate corresponding to $t = 4$. Doing so yields the set here. Choice **a** is incorrect because this is the domain, not the range. Choice **b** is incorrect because this is the range of the function if you did not restrict the domain to the interval $[1,4]$. Choice **c** is incorrect because $f(t)$ cannot be negative for any value of t. So the range cannot be all real numbers. Choice **d** is incorrect because you evaluated the $f(4)$ incorrectly. $3 \cdot 2^4 = 3 \cdot 16 = 48$, not 24.

Science

To calculate your HiSET® score on the Science section, first take a look at the correct answer for each of the 50 questions of the exam. Count up your **correct answers** only, and give yourself 1 point for each. Then, add up all of your points. This is your **raw score**.

Find your raw score and your **scaled score** in the following table. Remember, for each test section, a passing score is 8. (For the essay, a passing score is 2.)

You need a scaled score of 45 to pass the complete HiSET® exam.

SCIENCE SCORING			
RAW	SCALED	RAW	SCALED
0	1	26	12
1	1	27	12
2	2	28	12
3	2	29	13
4	3	30	13
5	3	31	13
6	4	32	13
7	5	33	14
8	6	34	14
9	7	35	14
10	8	36	14
11	8	37	15
12	8	38	15
13	9	39	15
14	9	40	15
15	9	41	16
16	10	42	16
17	10	43	16
18	10	44	17
19	10	45	17
20	10	46	18
21	11	47	18
22	11	48	19
23	11	49	20
24	11	50	20
25	12		

1. **The correct answer is choice c.** Cations must be more basic to neutralize acidic soil. Choice **a** is incorrect because cations are charged and therefore hydrophilic. Choices **b** and **d** are incorrect because cations must be more basic to neutralize acidic soil.

2. **The correct answer is choice a.** Standard deviation indicates how far individual data points are away from the mean. A low standard deviation means that the numbers in a data set are not far from the mean, which indicates high precision. Choice **b** is incorrect because standard deviation indicates how far individual data points are away from the mean. A low standard deviation means that the numbers in a data set are not far from the mean, which indicates high precision. Choices **c** and **d** are incorrect because accuracy is not relevant here. There is no "true" value to use for comparison; accuracy describes the closeness of a measured value to a "true" value.

3. **The correct answer is choice d.** The A_{565} readings represent relative carbon biomass, the dependent variable in the experiment. Choice **a** is incorrect because the time points represent an independent variable. The dependent variable is the variable that is measured in an experiment. Choice **b** is incorrect because the presence or absence of liming is an independent variable. The dependent variable is the variable that is measured in an experiment. Choice **c** is incorrect because the concentration of magnesium ions is vaguely associated with the presence or absence of liming, an independent variable. The dependent variable is the variable that is measured in an experiment.

4. **The correct answer is choice d.** You can never say that data evidence proves or disproves a conclusion; you can only state that it supports or does not support a given hypothesis or prediction. In this case, the data do support the given statement because the location with soil liming exhibited a more dramatic decrease in sequestered carbon biomass over time. Choices **a** and **b** are incorrect because you can never say that data evidence proves or disproves a conclusion; you can only state that it supports or does not support a given hypothesis or prediction. Choice **c** is incorrect because in this case, the data do support the given statement because the location with soil liming exhibited a more dramatic decrease in sequestered carbon biomass over time.

5. **The correct answer is choice a.** Only this procedure would test for changes in bacterial population diversity. Choice **b** is incorrect because the liming additives must be in the soil itself, not added after the dilution of the sample, for a representative bacterial population collection. Choice **c** is incorrect because this experiment would measure soil aggregation. Choice **d** is incorrect because this experiment measures biomass rather than bacterial diversity.

6. **The correct answer is choice b.** Only this hypothesis links the two variables of interest, distance from the sun and surface temperature. Choice **a** is incorrect because this hypothesis does not link the two variables of interest, distance from the sun and surface temperature. Choice **c** is incorrect because this hypothesis does not link the two variables of interest, distance from the sun and surface temperature. Choice **d** is incorrect because the hypothesis incorrectly refers to the temperature as the upper-atmosphere temperature rather than the surface temperature.

7. **The correct answer is choice b.** With one exception each at the top and bottom of the list, the surface temperatures decrease as the distances increase. Choice **a** is incorrect because this conclusion correctly identifies the variables but states the trend in reverse. Choice **c** is incorrect because planet diameter is irrelevant to the scientific question. Choice **d** is incorrect because planet diameter is irrelevant to the scientific question.

8. **The correct answer is choice b.** The elliptical orbits of the planets, which are more dramatic for some planets than for others, result in huge differences between some planets' closest and farthest distances from the sun. Choices **a**, **c**, and **d** are incorrect because while they are true statements, they do not explain the wide array of planetary distances that lead to the determined average distance.

9. **The correct answer is choice d.** Atmospheric conditions certainly could cause surface temperature variations. Venus, for instance, is especially hot because it has a very thick atmosphere that, upon penetration of sunlight, traps heat at the surface of the planet. Choice **a** is incorrect because nearby stars are not located close enough to the solar system to drastically influence temperatures. The nearest first-magnitude stars include Alpha Centauri and Sirius. Choice **b** is incorrect because revolution times, or the times needed for planets to move around the sun, are not features that would influence outlier surface temperatures (although the shape of elliptical orbits might). Choice **c** is incorrect because planet diameters would not affect surface temperature variation.

10. **The correct answer is choice d.** With planetary distances on the *x*-axis and planetary surface temperatures on the *y*-axis, the curve generally forms a negative exponential function. Choice **a** is incorrect because the relationship between the two variables is clearly not positive. Choice **b** is incorrect because the relationship between the two variables is indeed negative, but the decline in temperature is not proportional to the increase in distance such that a line would form from the plotted data. Choice **c** is incorrect because the relationship between the two variables is clearly not positive.

11. **The correct answer is choice c.** Three different test objects were used, so test object identity was actually the independent variable. Choice **a** is incorrect because the positioned angle was the same for every trial. Choice **b** is incorrect because the temperature in the fog chamber was the same for every trial. Choice **d** is incorrect because the size of the fog chamber was the same for every trial.

12. **The correct answer is choice a.** After one hour, the grass collected, on average, approximately 10 μL. Choice **b** is incorrect because this is the volume collected by the beetles after one hour. Choice **c** is incorrect because this is the volume collected by the beetles after two hours. Choice **d** is incorrect because this is the volume collected by the grass after two hours.

13. **The correct answer is choice d.** The bars are marked as "not significant" because, given the error bar magnitudes, the bars could technically be the same size since the error bars overlap. Choice **a** is incorrect because there is no indication that anything went wrong during the experiment. Choice **b** is incorrect because closeness to a "true" value, or accuracy, is not applicable here since no known values are provided. Choice **c** is incorrect because there is no minimal number of trials that make a data set significant, although more trials are usually better when it comes to data reliability.

14. **The correct answer is choice d.** The most efficient water collector will collect the highest μL/mm² of water. Therefore, the objects should be ranked from largest bar to smallest bar.

15. **The correct answer is choice a.** Over the course of the two hours, the line for the grass ended at a higher number of volume than the beetle, so it collected more water than the beetle; however, the volume increase observed for the beetle was more steady, whereas the grass exhibited a large spike toward the end of the experiment. Choices **c** and **d** are incorrect because no wire was involved in the Figure 2 experiment.

16. **The correct answer is choice a.** If swabs are not kept sterile, bacteria that were not actually removed from the food samples may end up on the plates. Choice **b** is incorrect because growth medium removal wouldn't be productive in this experiment since it supplies nutrients for bacterial growth. Choice **c** is incorrect because the swab will not sterilize the plates; the swab only maintains sterility for the item that is introduced to the plate. Choice **d** is incorrect because this would be the function, generally, of antibiotics, which are not used in this experiment.

17. The correct answer is choice c. The food in the control trials did not come into contact with either the laboratory floor or the sidewalk, so these trials show how many bacterial colonies would grow from swabs from the unaffected food items of interest.

18. The correct answer is choice b. At either food item at any time point, the bars on the graph were higher for the sidewalk samples than for the laboratory floor samples. It can therefore be concluded that more bacteria were transferred to the food samples from the sidewalk surface than from the laboratory floor sample. Choice **d** is incorrect because the bars on the graph demonstrate that both surfaces conferred colonies to the food.

19. The correct answer is choice c. You can never say that data evidence proves or disproves a conclusion; you can only state that it supports or does not support a given hypothesis or prediction. In this case, the data conflict with the given statement because the food items exposed to either surface grew significantly more bacterial colonies than the control food items that were not exposed to either surface.

20. The correct answer is choice c. The number of bacterial colonies increases over time, so the graphs would be positive. The number of bacterial colonies does not increase by the same number per day, so the increase is not linear.

21. The correct answer is choice c. Invertebrates are sampled from both locations to gather data for water that would and would not be affected by pollution. Choice **a** is incorrect because the rate of water flow is not a relevant variable in this experiment. Choice **b** is incorrect because Location 2 does not include "water that is definitely polluted"; it covers water that should be clean and unpolluted. Choice **d** is incorrect because the indicators here are pollution specific, not pH specific.

22. The correct answer is choice a. The greatest relative abundance of pollution-tolerant organisms can be found on the data table by looking for the highest percentage value in a row labeled "Pollution-tolerant species." Choice **b** is incorrect because 5.0 < 5.2. Choice **c** is incorrect because this is where the lowest relative abundance of pollution-tolerant organisms was observed. Choice **d** is incorrect because this is where the greatest relative abundance of pollution-sensitive (rather than pollution-tolerant) organisms was observed.

23. The correct answer is choice a. The reading taken one month before the factory opening provides a negative control because it shows invertebrate relative abundances in both locations prior to the factory arriving, with the factory serving as a potential source of pollution. Therefore, these readings should be pollution free.

24. The correct answer is choice c. In this case, the data do not support the given statement. At Location 1, the relative abundance of pollution-tolerant organisms stays constant over time, while the relative abundance of pollution-sensitive organisms actually increases over time; the latter is the opposite of what would occur if significant pollution was being contributed to Location 1 by the factory. Thus, it seems that the data support the factory's claim that it is not polluting the river. In fact, the water quality has actually improved at Location 1, based on the invertebrate indicators. Choices **a** and **b** are incorrect because you can never say that data evidence proves or disproves a conclusion; you can only state that it supports or does not support a given hypothesis or prediction.

25. **The correct answer is choice b.** Based on the descriptions of the species in the passage, pollution-sensitive species can tolerate a narrow range of environmental conditions, while pollution-tolerant species can tolerate a wide range of environmental conditions. By definition, that would make pollution-sensitive species specialists and pollution-tolerant species generalists. Choice **c** is incorrect because these species types are completely unrelated to the types of foods they eat. Choice **d** is incorrect because these species types are completely unrelated to the types of foods they eat.

26. **The correct answer is choice d.** The independent variable is the salt concentration, and the dependent variables are the boiling point and boiling time.

27. **The correct answer is choice b.** This is the time obtained by using the line graph and the correct axis. Choice **a** is incorrect because this answer would be obtained if the bar graph was used rather than the line graph for 0 tablespoons of water. Choice **c** is incorrect because this answer would be obtained if the bar graph and wrong axis were used for 0 tablespoons of water. Choice **d** is incorrect because this answer would be obtained if one used the wrong axis for 0 tablespoons of water.

28. **The correct answer is choice b.** Five cups of water were used in each trial, so this was a constant among all trials. Choice **a** is incorrect because the number of tablespoons of salt was the independent variable. Choice **c** is incorrect because the boiling point of the water was a dependent variable. Choice **d** is incorrect because the time required by the water sample to reach its boiling point was a dependent variable.

29. **The correct answer is choice c.** Based on the graph, as the number of tablespoons of salt increases, the boiling point gets higher, but the time required to reach that boiling point actually decreases.

30. **The correct answer is choice b.** 0.5 tablespoons is between 0 and 1 tablespoon, so the boiling point should be between the boiling points for 0 and 1 tablespoons. These boiling points were 99.9°C and 101.1°C.

31. **The correct answer is choice a.** The independent variable is what the experimenter changes, while the dependent variable is what the experimenter measures. The mass of F_2 is the independent variable because the scientists change this variable per trial. Choices **b, c,** and **d** are incorrect because the initial mass of C is a tenet of the dependent variable.

32. **The correct answer is choice d.** F_2 is limiting, and the experiment is detecting the usage of C in this reaction. Choices **a** and **b** are incorrect because this experiment involves no measurement of mass of CCl_4. Choice **c** is incorrect because F_2 is the limiting reagent, not C.

33. **The correct answer is choice b.** The plot should be positive and linear. As demonstrated in the trials that use 10.00 and 20.00 g F_2, doubling the mass of F_2 entered into the reaction doubles the mass of C used up in the reaction.

34. **The correct answer is choice a.** For every 10.00 g increase in F_2 mass used, there is a 1.58 g increase in C mass used up in the reaction. Since the starting mass is 5.00 g C, and 4.74 + 1.58 is far more than 5.00 g (it is equal to 6.32 g), carbon will officially be the limiting reactant at this point and will be used up completely during the reaction, leaving behind 0.00 g.

35. **The correct answer is choice a.** CF_4 should appear as a product of the reaction. Choice **b** is incorrect because CF_4 is a product of the reaction and should appear, not disappear. Choices **c** and **d** are incorrect because tracking the appearance or disappearance of a chemical species as a function of time will provide rate data, not stoichiometric data.

36. **The correct answer is choice b.** The angle of bob release should be the same in every trial since Noah performed the experiment the same way every time. Choice **a** is incorrect because the mass of the bob is an independent variable in this experiment. Choice **c** is incorrect because the length of the pendulum rod is an independent variable in this experiment. Choice **d** is incorrect because the period length of the pendulum is the dependent variable in this experiment.

37. **The correct answer is choice a.** To find the most precise pair of trials, one must find the trial that has the two numbers that are closest to one another. Of all the trials in this experiment, the trial with the 100 g bob and 50 cm pendulum length is by far the most precise.

38. **The correct answer is choice a.** Based on the data, namely the last three test trials, bob mass does not affect pendulum period length, and a horizontal line accurately conveys this trend. Choices **b**, **c**, and **d** are incorrect because there is no increase or decrease in period length as bob mass increases, so these answers do not make sense.

39. **The correct answer is choice b.** According to the data, namely the first three test trials, increasing the length of the pendulum results in an increase in the period length.

40. **The correct answer is choice c.** The moon is smaller than the earth and has a lower gravitational acceleration. As such, the period would increase because it would take longer for the bob in any of the described scenarios to complete a full oscillatory cycle.

41. **The correct answer is choice c.** The dependent variable is the variable that is being measured, and here that variable is O_2 concentration, which the O_2 gas sensor is detecting. Choice **a** is incorrect because CO_2 concentration is not a variable in this experiment. Choice **b** is incorrect because time is an independent variable in this experiment. Choice **d** is incorrect because temperature is an independent variable in this experiment.

42. **The correct answer is choice b.** The brief wait allows for the respiration chamber and cricket to reach the same temperature as the water bath via heat exchange. Choice **a** is incorrect because there are no methods in place to control which physiological processes are or are not functioning in the crickets. Choice **c** is incorrect because the crickets are immobilized. Choice **d** is incorrect because in fact the opposite is true. The brief wait allows for the respiration chamber and cricket to reach the same temperature as the water bath via heat exchange.

43. **The correct answer is choice c.** The slope of the line becomes increasingly negative as temperature increases, indicating that oxygen is being used up more quickly in the respiration reaction. Choices **a** and **b** are incorrect because photosynthesis does not occur in animals because they do not have chloroplasts. Choice **d** is incorrect because the slope of the line becomes increasingly negative as temperature increases, indicating that oxygen is being used up more quickly in the respiration reaction.

44. **The correct answer is choice b.** Since energy is released during respiration, energy release could potentially be measured as an indicator of respiration. Choice **a** is incorrect because carbon dioxide is produced, not consumed, during respiration. Choice **c** is incorrect because there shouldn't be a fluorescence signal due to simple respiration in the cricket. Choice **d** is incorrect because even though respiration is the reverse of photosynthesis, there is no light output due to photosynthetic light input.

45. **The correct answer is choice a.** Because both respiration and photosynthesis occur in peas, only a net O_2 concentration change can be determined. Choice **b** is incorrect because peas do have mitochondria and do perform respiration. Choice **c** is incorrect because peas will perform cellular processes at 10°C. Choice **d** is incorrect because peas will respire even if they haven't germinated.

46. **The correct answer is choice a.** Multiple trials ensure replicability and allow for outlier identification. Choice **b** is incorrect because only *M. capitata* was used. Choice **c** is incorrect because there is no "known" value for accuracy determination. Choice **d** is incorrect because it describes the purpose of a control trial set, not trial repetition.

47. **The correct answer is choice c.** The light gray bar provides CFU/mL data for the general growth medium, on which all bacteria can grow. The dark gray bar provides CFU/mL data for the *Vibrio*-selective medium, on which only *Vibrio* can grow. Dividing the dark gray bar value by the light gray bar value gives the fraction of total bacteria that were *Vibrio*.

48. **The correct answer is choice b.** Between the pre-inoculation control and the seawater trial, the general bacterial CFU/mL count decreases, as does the *Vibrio* bacterial count. Choices **a** and **c** are incorrect because these choices describes the opposite trend. Choice **d** is incorrect because the decrease in bar size indicates that seawater does in fact have an effect on general bacterial growth.

49. **The correct answer is choice d.** The overall quantity of bacteria is lower in healthy coral mucus than in diseased coral mucus. Most of the bacteria in the diseased coral mucus were *Vibrio*, while very few of the bacteria in the healthy coral mucus were *Vibrio*. Choice **a** is incorrect because the overall quantity of bacteria is lower in healthy coral mucus than in diseased coral mucus, but the healthy coral mucus still contained some bacteria. Choice **b** is incorrect because most of the bacteria in the diseased coral mucus were *Vibrio*, while very few of the bacteria in the healthy coral mucus were *Vibrio*. Choice **c** is incorrect because the overall quantity of bacteria is lower in healthy coral mucus than in diseased coral mucus.

50. **The correct answer is choice d.** Smaller error bars indicate increased precision. Among all of the light gray bars, the smallest bar is observed for the diseased coral fragments exposed to OCN0002.

Social Studies

To calculate your HiSET® score on the Social Studies section, first take a look at the correct answer for each of the 50 questions of the exam. Count up your **correct answers** only, and give yourself 1 point for each. Then, add up all of your points. This is your **raw score**.

Find your raw score and your **scaled score** in the following table. Remember, for each test section, a passing score is 8. (For the essay, a passing score is 2.)

You need a scaled score of 45 to pass the complete HiSET® exam.

SOCIAL STUDIES SCORING			
RAW	SCALED	RAW	SCALED
0	1	26	12
1	1	27	12
2	2	28	12
3	2	29	13
4	3	30	13
5	3	31	13
6	4	32	13
7	5	33	14
8	6	34	14
9	7	35	14
10	8	36	14
11	8	37	15
12	8	38	15
13	9	39	15
14	9	40	15
15	9	41	16
16	10	42	16
17	10	43	16
18	10	44	17
19	10	45	17
20	10	46	18
21	11	47	18
22	11	48	19
23	11	49	20
24	11	50	20
25	12		

1. **The correct answer is choice c.** Both private enterprises and the government have influence in the agricultural industry, evidence of a mixed economy. Choice **a** is incorrect because private enterprises control much of Canada's agriculture industry. Choice **b** is incorrect; because the Canadian government plays a fairly large role in the industry, Canada does not have a market economy. Choice **d** is incorrect because the descriptions of Canada's agriculture industry do not match the definition of a traditional economy.

2. **The correct answer is choice a.** A command economy is one in which the government exerts great control over economic affairs, such as in North Korea. Choice **b** is incorrect because the market decisions in North Korea are not being made by individuals. Choice **c** is incorrect because a mixed economy would require some aspects of a market economy. Choice **d** is incorrect because there is not enough information in the description of North Korea to make the claim that it is a traditional economy. The evidence suggests that the best answer is a command economy.

3. **The correct answer is choice d.** Feudalism as practiced in China had a traditional economy in which people lacked social and wealth mobility. Choice **a** is incorrect because the Chinese feudal states were not dominated by a central government but rather by many less powerful rulers. Choice **b** is incorrect because the description of feudal China does not match that of a market economy. Choice **c** is incorrect because the feudal states did not have market or command economies.

4. The correct answer is choice a. The passage contains no information on Lucy's age relative to other possible human ancestors. Choice **b** is incorrect because information in the passage states that Lucy had similarities to both chimpanzees and humans. Choice **c** is incorrect because Lucy can be called a transitional fossil because she illustrates changes, or transitions, in the development of humans from early hominins to a more human-like species. Choice **d** is incorrect because the passage describes Lucy's physical size as roughly that of a modern human child.

5. The correct answer is choice b. Scientists studied Lucy's pelvis and knees, two important body parts that allow humans to walk upright, and discovered that they were similar to humans'. Choice **a** is incorrect because it is not supported by information in the passage. Choice **c** is incorrect because there is no discussion of how size might affect the ability to walk upright. Choice **d** is incorrect because information in the passage does not discuss how Lucy's belly impacted how she moved.

6. The correct answer is choice b. Lucy forced experts to reexamine how humans became bipedal. Choice **a** is incorrect because the passage clearly states that Lucy was a hominin, or member of the human lineage, and not a chimp. Choices **c** and **d** are incorrect because the location of Lucy's discovery is only mentioned once and is not crucial to the remainder of the passage.

7. The correct answer is choice c. It correctly states what scientists learned from studying Lucy and the implication of that knowledge. Choice **a** is incorrect because scientists can tell a great deal with few fossils. However, this statement does not reflect the main theme of this passage. Choice **b** is incorrect because there are no direct references to chimpanzee evolution in the passage. Choice **d** is incorrect because there is no evidence in the passage that scientists have reached this conclusion.

8. The correct answer is choice b. There were fewer voters from this age group in three successive elections. Choice **a** is incorrect because in 2008, participation for 18- to 29-year-olds increased. Choices **c** and **d** are incorrect because voter participation in these age groups increased in each election from 2004 to 2012.

9. The correct answer is choice c. This is the age group that accounts for the most voters. Choice **a** is incorrect because this age group produces the fewest voters. Choice **b** is incorrect because voters in the 30 to 44 age range have accounted for the second most voters. Choice **d** is incorrect because Americans in the 65 and older group have accounted for the third most voters.

10. The correct answer is choice d. The most plausible scenario is that fewer 30- to 44-year-old Americans will vote in 2016. This would continue the trend that began in the 2004 election. Choice **a** is incorrect because the number of 18- to 29-year-olds has gone up and down in no recognizable pattern. Choice **b** is incorrect because this statement runs counter to the trend in the previous three elections. If the trend holds, there will be more voters. Choice **c** is incorrect because voter turnout for Americans 65 and older has risen each election since 2004. There is no plausible reason to think that the turnout will be lower in 2016.

11. The correct answer is choice d. The small family-operated business would not have the resources to compete. Consequently, it would have been driven out of business. Choice **a** is incorrect because a large manufacturer would most likely have no financial reason to acquire a small family-run business. Choice **b** is incorrect because a small family business would most likely not have the resources to upgrade its facilities to a competitive level. Choice **c** is incorrect because reducing production capabilities would not benefit the family's business.

12. The correct answer is choice c. Traditional family structures were changed by the shifting employment structures. Choice **a** is incorrect because this example describes an economic effect. Choice **b** is incorrect because this example describes a political and economic effect. Choice **d** is incorrect because this example describes technological effects.

13. The correct answer is choice a. New technologies helped create new machines to increase production of more and more products using fewer workers in more efficient ways. Choice **b** is incorrect because the Industrial Revolution often led to hand tools being replaced. Choice **c** is incorrect because home-base industries were generally driven out of business by newer production methods. Choice **d** is incorrect because the passage does not provide information about factory labor laws.

14. The correct answer is choice b. Skilled workers have advanced knowledge of their specific job, usually learned after extensive training and experience, increasing the wages an employer would need to pay for their services. Choice **a** is incorrect because there is nothing to suggest that skill level has an effect on how many hours a worker can work. Choice **c** is incorrect because it is not necessarily true that unskilled workers can learn more. Choice **d** is incorrect because this claim is not supported by information in the passage.

15. The correct answer is choice c. Voting is a right and a civic responsibility but is not legally required. Choice **a** is incorrect because all citizens must obey local, state, and federal laws. Choice **b** is incorrect because all citizens are required to be prepared to serve on a jury even though they may eventually be excused. Choice **d** is incorrect because paying state and local taxes is a legal duty for American citizens.

16. The correct answer is choice a. Participating in a school board meeting is a civic responsibility. It is a voluntary action that demonstrates good citizenship. Choice **b** is incorrect because driving with a valid driver's license is a legal requirement. Choice **c** is incorrect because trespassing laws are legal requirements citizens must obey. Choice **d** is incorrect because with very few exceptions, children are required to receive a public, private, or homeschool education that has been approved by the state.

17. The correct answer is choice d. More revenue is brought in by intergovernmental revenues—28%—than the other means. Choice **a** is incorrect because licenses and fees account for only 19% of revenue. Choice **b** is incorrect because property taxes account for 24% of revenue. Choice **c** is incorrect because utility taxes account for only 14% of revenue.

18. **The correct answer is choice c.** According to the charts, the police department, at 33%, receives the most money from the city. Choice **a** is incorrect because the city spends 27% of its revenue on the fire department. Choice **b** is incorrect because the streets and sanitation department is allotted just 15% of the city's revenue. Choice **d** is incorrect because the city spends only 18% of revenue on general government.

19. **The correct answer is choice c.** The city is spending more money than it is receiving and therefore is running a deficit. Choice **a** is incorrect because the city is technically not bankrupt. The city is still generating revenue and has the ability to pay off its debts. Choice **b** is incorrect because the term "in the black" means that a person or organization is making a profit. Choice **d** is incorrect because a surplus means that the city is bringing in more money than it is spending.

20. **The correct answer is choice a.** The action city leaders would most likely take is to raise taxes. This would provide the city with more revenue and would reduce the deficit. Choice **b** is incorrect because hiring additional employees would cost the city more money, increasing the deficit. Choice **c** is incorrect because additional services would cost more money and would most likely not generate additional revenue. Choice **d** is incorrect because the streets and sanitation department performs vital services that benefit the city.

21. **The correct answer is choice b.** The city receives most of its revenue from intergovernmental revenues. If the state government has financial problems, it most likely will reduce payouts to other government levels, including cities. The city will not receive as much money from the state, decreasing revenues. Choice **a** is incorrect because city revenues would be reduced. Choice **c** is incorrect because the city already has a deficit. Reduced revenues would increase the deficit, not create a surplus. Choice **d** is incorrect because the city would have to reduce expenditures because of the decrease in revenues.

22. **The correct answer is choice c.** The cartoon shows Mayor Thompson pouring out city money to a line of workers, presumably as a reward for supporting him. Choice **a** is incorrect because if Thompson were seeking political revenge, handing out money wouldn't make sense. Choice **b** is incorrect because the cartoon was drawn in 1920, nine years before the Great Depression started. Choice **d** is incorrect because the image shows Thompson rewarding city workers, not trying to weaken them.

23. **The correct answer is choice a.** The cartoonist depicts Thompson almost as an adult among children. His size reflects the political influence he exerts over the city workers. Choice **b** is incorrect because it is not clear from the details that this is the case. Choice **c** is incorrect because as mayor, Thompson would obviously be in charge of the city's finances, as any city mayor would. Choice **d** is incorrect because the presence of the Tammany Hall tiger, which shares its stripes with Thompson, shows that Thompson is similarly corrupt but does not illustrate Thompson's power.

24. The correct answer is choice d. Thompson is using city money to line the pockets of the city workers, who will then continue to support him. Choice **a** is incorrect because the men in the line look happy and favorable toward Thompson. Choice **b** is incorrect because the cartoon shows only some city workers taking money from Thompson. The viewer cannot assume that all workers are corrupt. Choice **c** is incorrect because Thompson appears to be politically savvy and skilled to hold on to his power, although corrupt.

25. The correct answer is choice d. The Prime Meridian at 0 degrees longitude is the most important line. Choice **a** is incorrect because the Equator is a line of latitude. Choice **b** is incorrect because the North Pole is not a line of longitude; it is the northern end of the earth's axis of rotation. Choice **c** is incorrect because the South Pole is not a line of longitude; it is the southern end of the earth's axis of rotation.

26. The correct answer is choice c. This choice correctly identifies the number of longitude degrees represented on the globe. There are 180 degrees east of the Prime Meridian and 180 degrees west of the Prime Meridian. Choice **a** is incorrect because 180° of longitude reflects only one-half of the circumference of the globe. Choice **b** is incorrect because 90° represents only one-fourth of the circumference of the globe. Choice **d** is incorrect because 270° reflects three-fourths of the circumference of the globe.

27. The correct answer is choice c. The Equator is the imaginary line drawn around the earth equally distant from both poles, dividing the earth into northern and southern hemispheres. It constitutes the parallel of 0 degrees latitude. Choice **a** is incorrect because 90 degrees latitude would identify the North Pole. Choice **b** is incorrect because the Equator is a line of latitude. Choice **d** is incorrect because 0 degrees longitude is the Prime Meridian, not the Equator.

28. The correct answer is choice b. It was not until the late 18th century that a relatively accurate method using clocks, or marine chronometers, provided navigators with an effective way to determine longitude. Choice **a** is incorrect because the distance of a voyage does not affect a person's ability to determine his or her location. Choice **c** is incorrect because there is no difference in the accuracy of measurements east or west of the Prime Meridian. Choice **d** is incorrect because winds do not affect the accuracy of determining one's location.

29. The correct answer is choice c. Ten years is the maximum length of time that one can serve as president. If a person served as president for up to two years without being elected as president (if the president died in office, for example), that person can still serve two four-year terms as president. Choice **a** is incorrect because a person could possibly serve two years from a previous term if he or she assumed the office, as well as two additional four-year terms. Choice **b** is incorrect because a person can constitutionally serve eight years by election in addition to having served as president for up to two years without being elected as president (if the president died in office, for example). Choice **d** is incorrect because the Constitution provides that a person can be elected for up to two four-year terms, or eight years in addition to having served as president for up to two years without being elected as president (if the president died in office, for example).

30. The correct answer is choice b. The 22nd Amendment was added in 1951, only a few years following the four terms of President Franklin D. Roosevelt. Always cautious about granting too much power to one individual, political leaders wanted to limit this possibility. Choice **a** is incorrect because citizens are still bound to constitutional rules regarding how the president is elected. They do not have the right to choose presidents freely. Choice **c** is incorrect because there was never a clear opinion on the matter from the Framers. In fact, the Constitution initially placed no term limits on the office. Choice **d** is incorrect because there is no age limit requirement within the 22nd Amendment.

31. The correct answer is choice a. Some Americans would think that if a president has performed well in office, voters should have the right to choose whom they think is best. Choice **b** is incorrect because candidates seeking the presidency are usually politically experienced and have been vetted by the American people. Choice **c** is incorrect because gridlock is not necessarily an outcome of a long-serving president. Choice **d** is incorrect because the concept of separation of powers concerns the branches of government. It is highly unlikely that one individual could upset that balance.

32. The correct answer is choice d. Churchill uses powerful and descriptive language throughout the passage to illustrate how Europe has become divided. Choice **a** is incorrect because Churchill describes the tensions and anxieties nations are experiencing. Choices **b** and **c** are incorrect because Churchill makes it clear that Soviet Russia has spread its power throughout Eastern Europe and desires to spread it even more. He opens the passage by pointing out areas in the very far north all the way to the very south that have been affected.

33. The correct answer is choice b. Churchill meant that the Soviet Union had separated the Eastern European countries from the West, preventing all interaction between the two regions. Choice **a** is incorrect because Churchill wasn't talking about an actual wall—he was using a metaphor to describe the separation of Western Europe from Eastern Europe. Choice **c** is incorrect because Churchill referred to political ideologies, not social ideologies. Choice **d** is incorrect because Churchill's iron curtain described the separation between Eastern and Western Europe, not the ideas spread by Soviet Russia.

34. **The correct answer is choice c.** Churchill clearly states that he thinks Russia's goal is not war but "the fruits of war and the indefinite expansion of their power and doctrines." Choice **a** is incorrect because Churchill states that he thinks Soviet Russia does not want war. Choice **b** is incorrect because the Soviet Union had already gained control of these areas. Choice **d** is incorrect because this statement is not supported by any information in the passage.

35. **The correct answer is choice a.** Churchill is warning the West about what Soviet Russia is doing in hopes of more unity in Europe. Choice **b** is incorrect because this information is not mentioned by Churchill. Choice **c** is incorrect because Churchill advocates unity and pacification, not military intervention at this point. Choice **d** is incorrect because Churchill was not suggesting more division, but rather unity.

36. **The correct answer is choice a.** Montesquieu argues that if the branches of government are not separated, there can be no liberty because the government could do anything it desired and not be stopped. Choice **b** is incorrect because Montesquieu describes branches of government, not levels of government. Choice **c** is incorrect because Montesquieu advocated the separation of judiciary and legislative powers. Choice **d** is incorrect because Montesquieu refers to violence and oppression as possible actions by judges, not individual citizens.

37. **The correct answer is choice b.** Montesquieu states that if the legislative and executive powers are held by one body, there can be no liberty. Choice **a** is incorrect because Montesquieu implies that all three branches are necessary. Choice **c** is incorrect because Montesquieu's view of government requires that the three branches balance power. Choice **d** is incorrect because Montesquieu advocated separating judiciary and legislative powers.

38. **The correct answer is choice d.** In this excerpt, Montesquieu clearly describes the separation of powers between branches of government. The writers of the U.S. Constitution built this principle into one of the key features of American government. Choice **a** is incorrect because popular sovereignty is the idea that the power of government lies with the people, a principle Montesquieu does not describe in the passage. Choice **b** is incorrect because the rule of law, although a key democratic principle, is not the topic of the passage. Choice **c** is incorrect because limited judicial power is not a principle of American democracy but rather a result of separation of powers.

39. **The correct answer is choice b.** Montesquieu's ideas reflect Enlightenment concepts such as using human reason to solve social, political, and economic problems. Choice **a** is incorrect because the Protestant Reformation was a religious revolt against the Catholic Church, not political governance. Choice **c** is incorrect because Abolitionism was the movement that fought to end slavery in the United States. Choice **d** is incorrect because the First Great Awakening was a widespread resurgence of religious fervor in the 1730s and 1740s.

40. **The correct answer is choice c.** The statement describes the key issues of racial bigotry and the risks of nuclear weapons in the Cold War as the motivation to activism. Choice **a** is incorrect because the writer does not point to poverty or economic decline as prime reasons for activism but rather as a backdrop to the other reasons. Choice **b** is incorrect because slavery is not mentioned in the passage, and the term "social disorder" is vague. The passage gives a more specific rationale. Choice **d** is incorrect because these reasons are not supported by statements in the passage.

41. The correct answer is choice a. The *Statement* contains references to the "Bomb" and the possibility that all "might die at any time." These threats heightened the activists' sense of urgency. Choice **b** is incorrect because economic issues are not the main focus of the *Statement*. Choice **c** is incorrect because the racial tensions in the "Southern struggle," although of importance, were not as compelling as the destruction of millions of people around the world. Choice **d** is incorrect because U.S. military involvement in Vietnam was in its infancy in 1962. The writers of the *Statement* would not have been able to predict future situations.

42. The correct answer is choice d. Members of SDS thought that the democratic principles on which the country were founded and worked best had been corrupted and lost. The hope lay in finding new ways in which democracy could be structured to provide the best living conditions for all Americans. Choice **a** is incorrect because the *Statement* never mentions a "return" to traditional lifestyles or systems but rather a search for "alternatives" and experimenting with them. Choice **b** is incorrect because there is no evidence in the passage that SDS advocated this action. Choice **c** is incorrect because SDS's stance on the Cold War and the "Bomb" make it clear that the group would not favor a more powerful military or economic control.

43. The correct answer is choice c. SDS was advocating for social and political changes and for limiting the power of the military, all things that many liberal groups agree with more than conservative groups. Choice **a** is incorrect because conservatives tend to prefer slow or no political and social changes in the country. Choice **b** is incorrect because a high-ranking officer would more than likely support maintaining order and would not advocate great changes to the military capabilities. Choice **d** is incorrect because someone opposed to affirmative action and equal rights would not support SDS's stance on freedom and equality for all.

44. The correct answer is choice b. The purpose of lemon laws is to protect consumers. Choice **a** is incorrect because manufacturers are not protected; they are held to the warranties they attached to the vehicles they made. Choice **c** is incorrect because the dealers usually must fix the lemon vehicles, costing them time and money. Choice **d** is incorrect because although keeping lemon vehicles off the road does lead to safer driving, this statement does not describe the real purpose of lemon laws, which is to protect consumers.

45. The correct answer is choice d. The cars are described as "lemons" because of the sourness of the fruit. Choice **a** is incorrect because not all people like lemons, and there is no evidence to suggest that "everyone" will buy a lemon car. Choice **b** is incorrect because this definition contradicts the true definition of a lemon purchase, which is a bad purchase. Choice **c** is incorrect because the phrase would most likely not have been given by those who sell the cars. This would not be in their best interest as dealers.

46. The correct answer is choice b. The effects of the defect on the vehicle's use, safety, and value along with the number of times a vehicle's defect has been worked on are the main criteria. Choice **a** is incorrect because Brenda's car was new and the issues started as soon as she took the car. The warranty would still apply. Choice **c** is incorrect because the cost to fix the defect does not matter. Choice **d** is incorrect because Brenda must bring her vehicle in to have the defect worked on.

47. The correct answer is choice b. The American system for passing laws is a form of checks and balances, with each house and the president providing input to write the best laws possible. Choice **a** is incorrect because although passing some legislation might be difficult, it is not impossible. This is a result of the process, not the purpose of the process. Choice **c** is incorrect because Congress members and the president don't have to agree. The president can veto legislation, and Congress can override the veto. Choice **d** is incorrect because Congress and the president share powers, without one holding more power than the other.

48. The correct answer is choice c. Subsection 3 clearly states that the only exception is Congress's adjournment. Choices **a** and **b** are incorrect because these situations are not described as exceptions to the process. Choice **d** is incorrect because all laws must be presented to the president.

49. The correct answer is choice d. Issues of taxation have long been a key topic among the country's leaders. Standing for election every two years makes these members of Congress the most accountable to the American voters. Choice **a** is incorrect because there is nothing in the Constitution that prevents the Senate from discussing and voting on revenue bills. Choice **b** is incorrect because senators are allowed to and do work on a wide variety of issues important to the functioning of the country. Choice **c** is incorrect because the only requirements for House members is that they are at least 25 years of age, have lived in the United States for 7 years, and have been a resident of the state they represent.

50. The correct answer is choice a. The statistics demonstrate that Congress has been able to gather the two-thirds threshold very few times. Choice **b** is incorrect because Congress has, in fact, overridden a veto 110 times. Choice **c** is incorrect because this statement contradicts the statistics. Choice **d** is incorrect because the Constitution allows a process for Congress to override a veto; it makes the process difficult but not impossible.

4 ▶ HiSET®
PRACTICE TEST 3

This practice test is modeled on the format, content, and timing of the official HiSET® test.

You can choose either to take each test separately, or to take all five tests together. However you decide to use this practice test, try to take each part under the most test-like conditions you can.

Try to take your test in a quiet spot, as free from distraction as possible. At the beginning of each test section, you will find test information, including the actual time liimts you will be given on your exam day. If you want to work under testing conditions, set a timer and aim to complete each test section within the given time limit.

You should work carefully, but not spend too much time on any one question. And remember—be sure you answer every question! You *are not* penalized for incorrect answers; you are only rewarded for correct ones!

When you complete this entire practice exam, you will find complete answer explanations for cvcry question that explain not only why correct answers are right, but also why incorrect answers are wrong. You will also find sample essays at every level, and information on scoring your exam.

Good luck!

Language Arts—Reading

65 Minutes
40 Questions

This practice test is modeled on the content and timing of the official HiSET® Language Arts—Reading test and, like the official test, presents a series of questions that assess your ability to understand, interpret, and analyze a broad range of literary and informational texts. Refer to the passages as often as necessary when answering the questions.

Use the following information to answer questions 1–6.

A British teacher takes a job at a girls' school in France. In this excerpt from *Villette* by Charlotte Bronte, she learns that she will be meeting a new companion.

(1)

The next day, on my return from a long walk, I found, as I entered my bedroom, an unexpected change. In addition to my own French bed in its shady recess, appeared in a corner a small crib, draped with white; and in addition to my mahogany chest of drawers, I saw a tiny rosewood chest. I stood still, gazed, and considered.

(2)

"Of what are these things the signs and tokens?" I asked. The answer was obvious. "A second guest is coming: Mrs. Bretton expects other visitors."

(3)

On descending to dinner, explanations ensued. A little girl, I was told, would shortly be my companion: the daughter of a friend and distant relation of the late Dr. Bretton's. This little girl, it was added, had recently lost her mother. . . . That same evening at nine o'clock, a servant was dispatched to meet the coach by which our little visitor was expected. Mrs. Bretton and I sat alone in the drawing-room waiting her coming; John Graham Bretton being absent on a visit to one of his schoolfellows who lived in the country. My godmother read the evening paper while she waited; I sewed. It was a wet night; the rain lashed the panes, and the wind sounded angry and restless.

(4)

"Poor child!" said Mrs. Bretton from time to time. "What weather for her journey! I wish she were safe here."

(5)

A little before ten the door-bell announced Warren's return. No sooner was the door opened than I ran down into the hall; there lay a trunk and some band-boxes, beside them stood a person like a nurse-girl, and at the foot of the staircase was Warren with a shawled bundle in his arms.

(6)

"Is that the child?" I asked.

(7)

"Yes, miss."

(8)

I would have opened the shawl, and tried to get a peep at the face, but it was hastily turned from me to Warren's shoulder.

(9)

"Put me down, please," said a small voice when Warren opened the drawing-room door, "and take off this shawl," continued the speaker, extracting with its minute hand the pin, and with a sort of fastidious haste doffing the clumsy wrapping. The creature which now appeared made a deft attempt to fold the shawl; but the drapery was much too heavy and large to be sustained or wielded by those hands and arms. "Give it to Harriet, please," was then the direction, "and she can put it away." This said, it turned and fixed its eyes on Mrs. Bretton.

(10)

"Come here, little dear," said that lady. "Come and let me see if you are cold and damp: come and let me warm you at the fire."

(11)

The child advanced promptly. Relieved of her wrapping, she appeared exceedingly tiny; but was a neat, completely-fashioned little figure, light, slight, and straight. Seated on my godmother's ample lap, she looked a mere doll; her neck, delicate as wax, her head of silky curls, increased, I thought, the resemblance.

(12)

Mrs. Bretton talked in little fond phrases as she chafed the child's hands, arms, and feet; first she was considered with a wistful gaze, but soon a smile answered her. Mrs. Bretton was not generally a caressing woman: even with her deeply-cherished son, her manner was rarely sentimental, often the reverse; but when the small stranger smiled at her, she kissed it, asking, "What is my little one's name?"

(13)

"Missy."

(14)

"But besides Missy?"

(15)

"Polly, papa calls her."

(16)

"Will Polly be content to live with me?"

(17)

"Not *always*; but till papa comes home. Papa is gone away." She shook her head expressively.

(18)

"He will return to Polly, or send for her."

(19)

"Will he, ma'am? Do you know he will?"

(20)

"I think so."

(21)

"But Harriet thinks not: at least not for a long while."

1. Which of the following lines from paragraph 11 refines information from earlier in the paragraph?
   a. "The child advanced promptly."
   b. "Relieved of her wrapping, she appeared exceedingly tiny"
   c. "Seated on my godmother's ample lap, she looked a mere doll"
   d. "her neck, delicate as wax, her head of silky curls"

2. Based on the way Mrs. Bretton reacts to the rain, Mrs. Bretton is most likely
   a. conscious of how she is expected to react.
   b. aware of how much Polly dislikes rain.
   c. afraid there could be a flood.
   d. genuinely concerned about Polly.

3. In what way is Mrs. Bretton's treatment of Polly different from her treatment of her own son?
   a. Mrs. Bretton is more sentimental with her son.
   b. Mrs. Bretton is less comfortable with her son.
   c. Mrs. Bretton is more loving with her son.
   d. Mrs. Bretton is less affectionate with her son.

4. Mrs. Bretton and Polly will most likely
   a. have some problems in the future.
   b. enjoy a totally loving relationship.
   c. have trouble getting to know each other.
   d. be saddened when Polly's papa arrives.

5. When Warren carried Polly into the school, she was most likely
   a. uncomfortable around him.
   b. eager to get settled.
   c. excited to meet Mrs. Bretton.
   d. afraid to be put on the floor.

6. What does "dispatched" (paragraph 3) mean?
   a. volunteered
   b. hired
   c. designed
   d. sent

Use the following information to answer questions 7–12.

Napoleon Bonaparte was Emperor of France from 1804 to 1815. This excerpt from *The Story of Napoleon* by Harold F.B. Wheeler gives details of the future emperor's early life.

(1)

Whenever we hear the name of Napoleon mentioned, or see it printed in a book, it is usually in connection with a hard-fought victory on the battlefield. He certainly spent most of his life in the camp, and enjoyed the society of soldiers more than that of courtiers. . . .

(2)

We are apt to forget that this mighty conqueror, whom Carlyle calls "our last great man," had a childhood at all. He was born nearly a century and a half ago, on the 15th August 1769 to be exact, in the little town of Ajaccio, the capital of picturesque Corsica. This miniature island rises a bold tree-covered rock in the blue waters of the Mediterranean, fifty miles west of the coast of Italy. It had been sold to France by the Republic of Genoa the previous year, but the inhabitants had fought for their independence with praiseworthy determination. Then civil war broke out, and the struggle finally ended three months before the birth of the boy who was to become the ruler of the conquering nation. The Corsicans had their revenge in time, although in a way very different from what they could have expected.

(3)

Letizia Bonaparte, Napoleon's mother, was as beautiful as she was energetic, and her famous son never allowed anyone to speak ill of her. "My excellent mother," said he, not long before his death, "is a woman of courage and of great talent . . . she is capable of doing everything for me," and he added that the high position which he attained was due largely to the careful way in which she brought him up.

(4)

"It is to my mother, to her good precepts and upright example, that I owe my success and any great thing I have accomplished," he averred, while to a general he remarked, "My mother was a superb woman, a woman of ability and courage." A truly great man always speaks well of his mother. . . .

(5)

The house in which the Bonaparte family lived at Ajaccio is still standing, but has been patched up and repaired so frequently that probably little of the original fabric remains. It now belongs to the ex-Empress Eugénie, the consort of Napoleon's ill-fated nephew who is known to history as Napoleon III. You would not call it a mansion, and yet it contains a spacious ballroom, a large square drawing-room, Charles Bonaparte's study, a dining-room, a nursery, several bedrooms, and a dressing-room.

Some of the old furniture is left, namely the Chippendale sofa on which the future Emperor was born, his mother's spinet, and his father's desk. There is also a little etching of Napoleon on horseback by the late Prince Imperial, and one or two statuettes and portraits.

7. The author most likely suggests that we are prone to forget that Napoleon had a childhood at all because
   a. one rarely thinks about powerful adults being small children.
   b. details about his childhood are never included in biographies of Napoleon.
   c. Napoleon wanted to keep the details of his childhood a secret.
   d. the childhood of a conqueror is never particularly important.

8. In paragraphs 3 and 4, Napoleon draws the conclusion that his mother was
   a. an excellent mother.
   b. a woman of great talent.
   c. responsible for his success.
   d. a superb woman.

9. Based on details in paragraph 3, the reader can conclude that the author
   a. believes Napoleon deserved to become famous.
   b. thinks Napoleon was too dependent on Letizia Bonaparte.
   c. knows Napoleon's opinions of Letizia Bonaparte were not shared by others.
   d. shares Napoleon's feelings about Letizia Bonaparte.

10. What is the most likely reason that the author begins the passage by describing the image of Napoleon that most people have?
   a. to show that the image is actually very accurate
   b. to prove that the image is completely false
   c. to explain that Napoleon was uncomfortable with the image
   d. to suggest that there was more to Napoleon than that image

11. In paragraph 4, the author includes a quote from Napoleon to repeat the author's own observation that Letizia Bonaparte was
   a. a woman of courage.
   b. responsible for Napoleon's success.
   c. beautiful and energetic.
   d. a truly brilliant military leader.

12. This passage would be of the most use to someone who is
   a. analyzing how Napoleon became so powerful.
   b. writing an essay about the geography of Corsica.
   c. planning to visit the Bonaparte family house in Ajaccio.
   d. researching Napoleon's relationship with his soldiers.

Use the following information to answer questions 13–18.

Adventurer Phileas Fogg proposes that he can travel around the entire world in just 80 days in a time before airplanes made such trips easy. This excerpt from *Around the World in Eighty Days* by Jules Verne shows how Fogg decided to take this incredible voyage.

(1)

It was Phileas Fogg, whose head now emerged from behind his newspapers, who made this remark. He bowed to his friends, and entered into the conversation. The affair which formed its subject, and which was town talk, had occurred three days before at the Bank of England. A package of banknotes, to the value of fifty-five thousand pounds, had been taken from the principal cashier's table, that functionary being at the moment engaged in registering the receipt of three shillings and sixpence. . . .

(2)

There were real grounds for supposing, as the *Daily Telegraph* said, that the thief did not belong to a professional band. On the day of the robbery a well-dressed gentleman of polished manners, and with a well-to-do air, had been observed going to and fro in the paying room where the crime was committed. A description of him was easily procured and sent to the detectives; and some hopeful spirits, of whom Ralph was one, did not despair of his apprehension. The papers and clubs were full of the affair, and everywhere people were discussing the probabilities of a successful pursuit; and the Reform Club was especially agitated, several of its members being Bank officials.

(3)

Ralph would not concede that the work of the detectives was likely to be in vain, for he thought that the prize offered would greatly stimulate their zeal and activity. But Stuart was far from sharing this confidence; and, as they placed themselves at the whist-table, they continued to argue the matter. Stuart and Flanagan played together, while Phileas Fogg had Fallentin for his partner. As the game proceeded the conversation ceased, excepting between the rubbers, when it revived again.

(4)

"I maintain," said Stuart, "that the chances are in favour of the thief, who must be a shrewd fellow."

(5)

"Well, but where can he fly to?" asked Ralph. "No country is safe for him."

(6)

"Pshaw!"

(7)

"Where could he go, then?"

(8)

"Oh, I don't know that. The world is big enough."

(9)

"It was once," said Phileas Fogg, in a low tone. "Cut, sir," he added, handing the cards to Thomas Flanagan.

(10)

The discussion fell during the rubber, after which Stuart took up its thread.

(11)

"What do you mean by 'once'? Has the world grown smaller?"

(12)

"Certainly," returned Ralph. "I agree with Mr. Fogg. The world has grown smaller, since a man can now go round it ten times more quickly than a hundred years ago. And that is why the search for this thief will be more likely to succeed."

(13)

"And also why the thief can get away more easily."

(14)

"Be so good as to play, Mr. Stuart," said Phileas Fogg.

(15)

But the incredulous Stuart was not convinced, and when the hand was finished, said eagerly: "You have a strange way, Ralph, of proving that the world has grown smaller. So, because you can go round it in three months—"

(16)

"In eighty days," interrupted Phileas Fogg.

13. Stuart most likely said "Pshaw!" (paragraph 6) because Stuart
   a. wants to make Ralph angry.
   b. is very angry with Ralph.
   c. thinks Ralph's suggestion is ridiculous.
   d. is not sure of how he feels about Ralph.

14. In paragraph 12, the phrase "The world has grown smaller" means that the world
   a. has literally shrunk.
   b. has become easier to travel.
   c. seems smaller as one grows older.
   d. seems less interesting as people get more educated.

15. Stuart and Ralph both
   a. believe that the thief is a very shrewd fellow.
   b. express interest in the story about the thief.
   c. agree with Phileas Fogg's observations.
   d. are extremely argumentative people.

16. Phileas Fogg has most likely
   a. been uninterested in the argument between Stuart and Ralph.
   b. already taken several trips around the world.
   c. thought a lot about how long it takes to travel around the world.
   d. developed the desire to lie to his friends.

17. What is the most likely reason the author included the argument about the robbery in this story?
   a. to set up the fact that Fogg, Stuart, Ralph, and Flanagan are going to commit a crime
   b. to prove that someone is capable of traveling around the world in 80 days
   c. to give an example of why Stuart and Ralph dislike each other so much
   d. to lead into Fogg's suggestion that one could travel the world in 80 days

18. Which of the following meanings associated with the word "grounds" seems most intended in paragraph 2?
   a. surfaces
   b. reasons
   c. areas
   d. subjects

Use the following information to answer questions 19–23.

The Pennsylvania Dutch are descendants of early German-speaking immigrants to Pennsylvania. This excerpt from *Pennsylvania Dutch Cooking* explains why they are famous for their cooking.

(1)

The Pennsylvania Dutch are a hard working people and as they say, "Them that works hard, eats hearty." The blending of recipes from their many home lands and the ingredients available in their new land produced tasty dishes that have been handed down from mother to daughter for generations. Their cooking was truly a folk art requiring much intuitive knowledge, for recipes contained measurements such as "flour to stiffen," "butter the size of a walnut," and "large as an apple." Many of the recipes have been made more exact and standardized providing us with a regional cookery we can all enjoy.

(2)

Soups are a traditional part of Pennsylvania Dutch cooking and the Dutch housewife can apparently make soup out of anything. If she has only milk and flour she can still make rivel soup. However, most of their soups are sturdier dishes, hearty enough to serve as the major portion of the evening meal. One of the favorite summer soups in the Pennsylvania Dutch country is Chicken Corn Soup. Few Sunday School picnic suppers would be considered complete without gallons of this hearty soup.

(3)

Many of the Pennsylvania Dutch foods are a part of their folklore. No Shrove Tuesday would be complete without raised doughnuts called "fastnachts." One of the many folk tales traces this custom back to the burnt offerings made by their old country ancestors to the goddess of spring. With the coming of Christianity the custom became associated with the Easter season and "fastnachts" are eaten on Shrove Tuesday to insure living to next Shrove Tuesday. Young dandelion greens are eaten on Maundy Thursday in order to remain well throughout the year. . . .

(4)

Regardless of the time of the year or the time of the day there are pies. The Pennsylvania Dutch eat pies for breakfast. They eat pies for lunch. They eat pies for dinner and they eat pies for midnight snacks. Pies are made with a great variety of ingredients from the apple pie we all know to the rivel pie which is made from flour, sugar, and butter. The Dutch housewife is as generous with her pies as she is with all her cooking, baking six or eight at a time not one and two.

(5)

The apple is an important Pennsylvania Dutch food. Dried apples form the basis for many typical dishes. Each fall barrels of apples are converted into cider. Apple butter is one of the Pennsylvania Dutch foods which has found national acceptance. The making of apple butter is an all-day affair and has the air of a holiday to it. Early in the morning the neighbors gather and begin to peel huge piles of apples that will be needed. Soon the great copper apple butter kettle is brought out and set up over a wood fire. Apple butter requires constant stirring to prevent burning. However, stirring can be light work for a boy and a girl when they're young and the day is bright and the world is full of promise. By dusk the apple butter is made, neighborhood news is brought up to date and hunger has been driven that much further away for the coming winter.

(6)

Food is abundant and appetites are hearty in the Pennsylvania Dutch country. The traditional dishes are relatively simple and unlike most regional cookery the ingredients are readily available. Best of all, no matter who makes them the results are "wonderful good."

19. Which of the following states the primary purpose of this passage?
   a. to explain the role food plays in Pennsylvania Dutch culture
   b. to provide recipes for several Pennsylvania Dutch dishes
   c. to describe all the foods that the Pennsylvania Dutch eat
   d. to praise the work ethic of the Pennsylvania Dutch

20. The author contributes to the passage's tone by describing Pennsylvania Dutch cooking as
   a. "wonderful good."
   b. "hearty."
   c. "a folk art."
   d. "standardized."

21. In paragraph 1, the author expresses the opinion that Pennsylvania Dutch recipes
   a. are handed down from mother to daughter.
   b. require intuitive knowledge.
   c. produce tasty dishes.
   d. are used to make regional cookery.

22. Read the following paragraph.

   Travelling from door to door to shout "Trick or Treat!" has long been one of the most integral Halloween customs. Costumed children hold out their bags to collect fruit, candy, or other edible treats. While this custom is well known, its background is harder to pinpoint, although a popular theory is that it evolved from a European practice of impersonating the spirits of the dead and asking for gifts on the behalf of those who could no longer eat and enjoy them.

   Both this paragraph and the passage are concerned with
   a. the European origins of American customs.
   b. how fruit is often eaten as a snack or treat.
   c. the role that food plays in folklore.
   d. how ancient customs change over time.

23. The making of apple butter is
   a. hard work.
   b. time consuming.
   c. a special skill.
   d. childish.

Use the following information to answer questions 24–29.

An area in the English countryside known as Sussex Downs is the setting of the poem "On Sussex Downs" by Eugene Parker Chase.

(1) A boy stood on the windy Sussex downs,
  Resting a moment in his lonely walk
  To gaze at the fresh fields, and their neighbour
    towns
  Sunk in the valleys watered by thin streams
  And sheltered by the pallid hills of chalk.

(2) It seemed a land for slow and leisured dreams,
  For fantasy, vague and cool as the mist.
  The church there in the field, with yew-trees round
  Should send across the air a silver sound
  Of holy bells. The loud rooks should desist
  A moment from their cawing; the dim sun
  Brighten his face, the rounded meadows glisten,
  And all the windswept grassy hillsides listen
  And then take up the sound the bells begun.

(3) Slowly, at length, rounding the hill, a white,
  Long, slender, floating airship flies.
  It, of this quiet landscape, is the sight
  Most peaceful—white splash on the blue spring
    skies.
  It passes over the church-crowned slope, it blends
  Its whiteness for a moment with the cloud,
  And finally, with nose a little bowed,
  Off towards the distant sea its course it bends.

(4) The watching boy beheld no other change
  In all the placid, comfortable scene,
  And yet he deeply realized what mean
  The airships and the other things that are strange,
  But form a living part of England now;
  And when he left the place where he had been,
  He seemed to have become a man somehow.

24. This poem is mainly about how
  a. observing change causes a boy to mature.
  b. a boy enjoys walking across Sussex downs.
  c. resting seems to make a boy grow into a man.
  d. the sight of an aircraft frightens a young boy.

25. What does "pallid" (stanza 1) mean?
  a. pale
  b. poor
  c. paltry
  d. pleasing

26. The poet describes Sussex downs in stanza 2 to
  a. suggest the boy will still find pleasure after he becomes a man.
  b. illustrate the less modern world the aircraft is replacing.
  c. prove the boy has keen skills of observation.
  d. indicate that the boy needs to move away from such a simple place.

27. The poet most likely describes the aircraft as a "white splash" (stanza 3) in order to
  a. suggest that it is a fabulous piece of machinery.
  b. show how its color is out of place in the environment.
  c. add some excitement to an otherwise peaceful poem.
  d. illustrate how it is intruding on the scene.

28. The boy most likely found the sight of the aircraft
  a. confusing.
  b. angering.
  c. disturbing.
  d. delightful.

29. In stanza 2, the phrase "the windswept grassy hillsides listen and then take up the sound the bells begun" means that the hillsides are
   a. as quiet as someone who is listening.
   b. echoing the sounds of the church bells.
   c. creating the sound of blowing wind.
   d. fantastical and have human abilities.

Use the following information to answer questions 30–34.

On January 1, 1863, President Abraham Lincoln issued an executive order of tremendous historical importance. This order is known as the Emancipation Proclamation.

(1)

That on the first day of January, in the year . . . one thousand eight hundred and sixty-three, all persons held as slaves within any State, or designated part of a State, the people whereof shall then be in rebellion against the United States, shall be then, thenceforward, and for ever free; and the Executive Government of the United States, including the military and naval authority thereof, will recognize and maintain the freedom of such persons, and will do no act or acts to repress such persons, or any of them, in any efforts they may make for their actual freedom.

(2)

That the Executive will, on the first day of January aforesaid, by proclamation, designate the States and parts of States, if any, in which the people thereof respectively shall then be in rebellion against the United States; and the fact that any State, or the people thereof, shall on that day be in good faith represented in the Congress of the United States by members chosen thereto at elections wherein a majority of the qualified voters of such State shall have participated, shall in the absence of strong countervailing testimony be deemed conclusive evidence that such State and the people thereof are not then in rebellion against the United States.

(3)

Now, therefore, I, Abraham Lincoln, President of the United States, by virtue of the power in me vested as commander-in-chief of the army and navy of the United States, in time of actual armed rebellion against the authority and government of the United States, and as a fit and necessary war measure for suppressing said rebellion, do, on this first day of January, in the year . . . one thousand eight hundred and sixty-three, and in accordance with my purpose so to do, publicly proclaimed for the full period of one hundred days from the day first above mentioned, order and designate as the States and parts of States wherein the people thereof, respectively, are this day in rebellion against the United States, the following, to wit:

(4)

Arkansas, Texas, Louisiana (except the parishes of St. Bernard, Plaquemines, Jefferson, St. John, St. Charles, St. James, Ascension, Assumption, Terrebonne, Lafourche, St. Mary, St. Martin, and Orleans, including the city of New Orleans), Mississippi, Alabama, Florida, Georgia, South Carolina, North Carolina, and Virginia (except the forty-eight counties designated as West Virginia, and also the counties of Berkeley, Accomac, Northampton, Elizabeth City, York, Princess Anne, and Norfolk, including the cities of Norfolk and Portsmouth), and which excepted parts are for the present left precisely as if this proclamation were not issued.

(5)

And by virtue of the power and for the purpose aforesaid, I do order and declare that all persons held as slaves within said designated States and parts of States are, and henceforward shall be, free; and that the Executive Government of the United States, including the military and naval authorities thereof, will recognize and maintain the freedom of said persons.

(6)

And I hereby enjoin upon the people so declared to be free to abstain from all violence, unless in necessary self-defence; and I recommend to them that, in all cases when allowed, they labour faithfully for reasonable wages.

(7)

And I further declare and make known that such persons of suitable condition will be received into the armed service of the United States to garrison forts, positions, stations, and other places, and to man vessels of all sorts in said service. . . .

(8)

In witness whereof, I have hereunto set my hand, and caused the seal of the United States to be affixed.

(9)

Done at the city of Washington, this first day of January, in the year . . . one thousand eight hundred and sixty-three, and of the independence of the United States of America the eighty-seventh.

30. Which of the following states the primary purpose of this passage?
a. to declare there is a rebellion against the United States
b. to outlaw slavery in states in rebellion against the United States
c. to free enslaved people in Texas, Louisiana, and Mississippi
d. to allow previously enslaved people to join the armed service

31. Information in this passage would be most useful for someone who is
a. writing a book about the history of slavery in the United States.
b. arguing that President Lincoln was the United States' greatest president.
c. researching rural life in the United States during the 1800s.
d. considering joining the United States army or navy.

32. Read the following paragraph.

The Emancipation Proclamation not only changed the designation of previously enslaved people to free people, but it also served as a war measure in the conflict between the Union and Confederate territories. However, it only applied to enslaved people in the states the president officially declared in rebellion against the United States. That means it initially only declared that three million of the four million people who were enslaved in the United States at the time were free.

What might one learn from this paragraph that cannot be learned in the main passage?
a. that the Emancipation Proclamation was a war measure
b. the number of people to whom the Emancipation Proclamation applied
c. the number of territories that were in rebellion against the United States
d. the fact that the Emancipation Proclamation declared enslaved people to be free

33. Which of the following was most likely an area the anti-slavery Union controlled before President Lincoln issued the Emancipation Proclamation?
a. Alabama
b. New Orleans
c. North Carolina
d. Florida

34. Which of the following meanings associated with the word "recognize" seems most intended in paragraph 5?
a. identify
b. cherish
c. know
d. acknowledge

Use the following information to answer questions 35–40.

A spaceship is leaving Mars for another planet called Terra. In this excerpt from *The Crystal Crypt* by Philip K. Dick, it is announced that the spaceship is being forced to land prematurely.

(1)

"Attention, Inner-Flight ship! Attention! You are ordered to land at the Control Station on Deimos for inspection. Attention! You are to land at once!"

(2)

The metallic rasp of the speaker echoed through the corridors of the great ship. The passengers glanced at each other uneasily, murmuring and peering out the port windows at the small speck below, the dot of rock that was the Martian checkpoint, Deimos.

(3)

"What's up?" an anxious passenger asked one of the pilots, hurrying through the ship to check the escape lock.

(4)

"We have to land. Keep seated." The pilot went on.

(5)

"Land? But why?" They all looked at each other. Hovering above the bulging Inner-Flight ship were three slender Martian pursuit craft, poised and alert for any emergency. As the Inner-Flight ship prepared to land the pursuit ships dropped lower, carefully maintaining themselves a short distance away.

(6)

"There's something going on," a woman passenger said nervously. "Lord, I thought we were finally through with those Martians. Now what?"

(7)

"I don't blame them for giving us one last going over," a heavy-set business man said to his companion. "After all, we're the last ship leaving Mars for Terra. . . ."

(8)

"You think there really will be war?" A young man said to the girl sitting in the seat next to him. "Those Martians won't dare fight, not with our weapons and ability to produce. We could take care of Mars in a month. It's all talk."

(9)

The girl glanced at him. "Don't be so sure. Mars is desperate. They'll fight tooth and nail. I've been on Mars three years." She shuddered. "Thank goodness I'm getting away. If—"

(10)

"Prepare to land!" the pilot's voice came. The ship began to settle slowly, dropping down toward the tiny emergency field on the seldom visited moon. Down, down the ship dropped. There was a grinding sound, a sickening jolt. Then silence.

(11)

"We've landed," the heavy-set business man said. "They better not do anything to us! Terra will rip them apart if they violate one Space Article."

(12)

"Please keep your seats," the pilot's voice came. "No one is to leave the ship, according to the Martian authorities. We are to remain here."

(13)

A restless stir filled the ship. Some of the passengers began to read uneasily, others stared out at the deserted field, nervous and on edge, watching the three Martian pursuit ships land and disgorge groups of armed men.

(14)

The Martian soldiers were crossing the field quickly, moving toward them, running double time. This Inner-Flight spaceship was the last passenger vessel to leave Mars for Terra. All other ships had long since left, returning to safety before the outbreak of hostilities. The passengers were the very last to go, the final group of Terrans to leave the grim red planet, business men, expatriates, tourists, any and all Terrans who had not already gone home.

(15)

"What do you suppose they want?" the young man said to the girl. "It's hard to figure Martians out, isn't it? First they give the ship clearance, let us take off, and now they radio us to set down again. By the way, my name's Thacher, Bob Thacher. Since we're going to be here awhile—"

35. When the girl says "Thank goodness I'm getting away" in paragraph 9, she most likely means that she
   a. wants to see her family again.
   b. was being kept prisoner on Mars.
   c. had bad experiences on Mars.
   d. is not being serious about leaving Mars.

36. One of this passage's themes is
   a. anxiety of the unknown.
   b. the horrors of war.
   c. the thrill of meeting people.
   d. the strangeness of new places.

37. As the passage continues, Bob Thacher will most likely
   a. go to war against the Martians.
   b. find out the Martians mean no harm.
   c. have to pilot the Inner-Flight ship.
   d. continue talking with the girl.

38. The businessman differs from Bob Thacher because the businessman is more
   a. misinformed.
   b. frightened.
   c. powerful.
   d. confident.

39. The announcement from the Martian ship is most likely described as a "metallic rasp" to
   a. suggest the speaker on the ship is broken.
   b. prove that the Martians do intend to harm the passengers.
   c. present the Martians as inhuman and threatening.
   d. establish the story's humorous and absurd tone.

40. Based on information in paragraph 11, a "Space Article" is most likely a
   a. story.
   b. entryway.
   c. law.
   d. battle.

Language Arts—Writing

Part 1: Multiple Choice

50 Questions

75 Minutes

This practice test is modeled on the content and timing of the official HiSET® Language Arts—Writing test and, like the official test, presents a series of questions that assess your ability to recognize and produce effective standard American written English. Like the official test, this practice is broken up into two parts: Part 1 consists of multiple-choice questions; Part 2 consists of an essay.

Part 1 is a test of skills involved in revising written materials that contain grammatical and stylistic errors. In this section, you will find the types of passages you come across in everyday life—letters, memos, articles, and so on.

You will find each passage presented twice: first in a box without any marks so you can read it uninterrupted, and then in a spread-out format with certain parts underlined and numbered.

For each numbered portion of the passage, you will be asked to choose the alternative that fixes the writing to make it correct, clear, organized, and free of grammatical errors. If you think the original underlined version is best, choose "No change."

Read through the draft advertisement. Then proceed to the suggestions for revision that follow.

Spring has sprung, and so has the Springfield Farmer's Market! Starting May 1, the farmer's market will be open Saturdays. Returning this year will be a number of your favorite fruit, vegetable, and farm vendors, a few new faces we're sure you'll love.

We're also adding a play space for kids to keep it busy while you pick out your kale farm-fresh eggs and organic apples. On the third Saturday of each month, Marvelous Max the magician will be performing at 12:00 noon in the afternoon. Mark your calendars, and prepare to be amazed!

Among our new vendors this year is the Best Buds Animal Shelter, which will be offering human coffee and dog treats, as well as the chance to mingle with adoptable dogs and cats. Another newbie this year is CupCaked, a Springfield bakery that specializes in gourmet you guessed it cupcakes.

Lots of great vendors and events we have lined up for your visit! There are also some new features for your visit. For the first time, we'll be accepting credit and debit cards as payment. Just look for the red tents for more information. All that's left is for you to come on down!

---

(1)

Spring has sprung, and so has the Springfield Farmer's Market! Starting May 1, the farmer's market will be open Saturdays. Returning this year will be a number of your favorite fruit, vegetable, and farm vendors, a few new faces we're sure you'll love. [1]

(2)

We're also adding a play space for kids to keep it busy [2] while you pick out your kale farm-fresh eggs and organic apples. [3] On the third Saturday of each month, Marvelous Max the magician will be performing at 12:00 noon in the afternoon. [4] Mark your calendars, and prepare to be amazed!

(3)

Among our new vendors this year is the Best Buds Animal Shelter, which will be offering human coffee and dog treats, as well as the chance to mingle with adoptable dogs and cats. Another newbie this year is CupCaked, <u>a Springfield bakery that specializes in gourmet you guessed it cupcakes.</u> [5]

(4)

<u>Lots of great vendors and events we have lined up for your visit! There are also some new features for your visit.</u> [6] For the first time, we'll be accepting credit and debit cards as payment. Just look for the red tents for more information. [7] All that's left is for you to come on down! [8]

1. **a.** *(No change)*
   b. vendors, who we're sure you'll love.
   c. vendors and also a few new faces we're sure you'll love.
   d. vendors which we're sure you'll love.

2. **a.** *(No change)*
   b. to keep their busy
   c. to keep us busy
   d. to keep them busy

3. **a.** *(No change)*
   b. your kale/farm-fresh eggs/and organic apples
   c. your kale; farm-fresh eggs; and organic apples
   d. your kale, farm-fresh eggs, and organic apples

4. **a.** *(No change)*
   b. Marvelous Max the magician will be performing at noon.
   c. Marvelous Max the magician will be performing at noon in the afternoon.
   d. Marvelous Max the magician will be performing at 12:00 p.m. noon.

5. **a.** *(No change)*
   b. a Springfield bakery that specializes in gourmet—you guessed it—cupcakes.
   c. a Springfield bakery that specializes in gourmet you guessed it cupcakes.
   d. you guessed it—a Springfield bakery that specializes in gourmet cupcakes.

6. **a.** *(No change)*
   b. There are also some new features for your visit. Lots of great vendors and events we have lined up for your visit!
   c. Lots of great vendors and events we have lined up for your visit, and there are also some new features for your visit.
   d. In addition to all the great vendors and events we have lined up for your visit, there are also some new features at the market.

7. Which of the following sentences should the writer insert as a transition to the closing sentence of the paragraph?
   a. Don't forget, parents are responsible for supervising children at the play place.
   b. With something for everyone, the Springfield's Farmer's Market has your Saturdays covered.
   c. If you adopt a pet from Best Buds at the market, you'll receive a free microchip for your new pet.
   d. Starting May 1!

8. What order should the writer use for the article?
   a. paragraph 1, paragraph 3, paragraph 2, paragraph 4
   b. paragraph 1, paragraph 2, paragraph 3, paragraph 4
   c. paragraph 1, paragraph 4, paragraph 3, paragraph 2
   d. paragraph 2, paragraph 1, paragraph 3, paragraph 4

Read through the draft article. Then proceed to the suggestions for revision that follow.

The do-it-yourself trend is about to hit a new level with the explosion of 3D printing. Once something you might see only in a lab, 3D printing has put creation in the hands of anyone what can buy a special printer and create a design.

3D printing, known more formerly as "additive manufacturing," was created as a way to create three-dimensional objects out of basic materials. The printer functions as kind of a robot, I guess. It was taking a computer design and transmits it to a small machine that layers material in the shape set by the computer's blueprint. However, the potential for this technology has spread beyond the walls of the laboratory.

Moreover, some also believe that 3D printers also have great potential for research. If 3D printers can produce medical devices or artificial body parts on demand, that could revolutionize the way doctors treat injuries. The printers could also be used to create technological devices, which would be extremely helpful in develloping countries that have fewer tech resources.

Although 3D printers started as a way to improve manufacturing processes in factories and laboratories, it has taken on a life of its own as a way for individuals to design and create objects in the privacy of home. We're still a long way off from there being a 3D printer in every household, but given that the price of a consumer-level 3D printer has dropped from $20,000 to less than $1,000, we are facing that time very soon.

(1)

The do-it-yourself trend is about to hit a new level with the explosion of 3D printing. Once something you might see only in a lab, 3D printing has put creation in the hands of anyone what can buy a special printer and create a design. [9]

(2)

3D printing, known more formerly [10] as "additive manufacturing," was created as a way to create three-dimensional objects out of basic materials. The printer functions as kind of a robot, I guess. It was taking a computer design [11] and transmits it to a small machine that layers material in the shape set by the computer's blueprint. However, the potential for this technology has spread beyond the walls of the laboratory. [12]

(3)

Moreover, some also believe that 3D printers also have great potential for research. [13] If 3D printers can produce medical devices or artificial body parts on demand, that could revolutionize the way doctors treat injuries. The printers could also be used to create technological devices, which would be extremely helpful in develloping [14] countries that have fewer tech resources.

(4) Although 3D printers started as a way to improve manufacturing processes in factories and laboratories, it has taken on a life of its own [15] as a way for individuals to design and create objects in the privacy of home. We're still a long way off from there [16] being a 3D printer in every household, but given that the price of a consumer-level 3D printer has dropped from $20,000 to less than $1,000, we are facing that time very soon.

9. a. *(No change)*
   b. anyone which can buy a special printer and create a design.
   c. anyone can buy a special printer and create a design.
   d. anyone who can buy a special printer and create a design.

10. a. *(No change)*
   b. formally
   c. formatively
   d. friendly

11. a. *(No change)*
   b. It will take a computer design
   c. It takes a computer design
   d. It took a computer design

12. Which sentence in paragraph 2 doesn't match the style and tone of the rest of the passage?
   a. *(No change)*
   b. 3D printing, known more formerly as "additive manufacturing," was created as a way to create three-dimensional objects out of basic materials.
   c. The printer functions as kind of a robot, I guess.
   d. However, the potential for this technology has spread beyond the walls of the laboratory.

13. Which of these sentences would be the best introductory sentence for paragraph 3?
   a. *(No change)*
   b. In comparison, some also believe that 3D printers also have great potential for research.
   c. Second, some also believe that 3D printers also have great potential for research.
   d. Anyway, some also believe that 3D printers also have great potential for research.

14. Which word is spelled incorrectly?
   a. artificial
   b. technological
   c. develloping
   d. *(None)*

15. a. *(No change)*
   b. it has taken on a life of their own own
   c. they have taken on a life of its own
   d. they have taken on a life of their own

16. a. *(No change)*
   b. their
   c. they're
   d. they are

Read through the draft memo. Then proceed to the suggestions for revision that follow.

To all employees,

As we approach summer, a friendly reminder that our company has an employee dress code that must be followed. Please note that the dress code guidelines must be adhered to whenever you are in the office:

We expect that employees will project a professional image at all times and use sound judgment as to what counts as appropriate dress. Your attire should not be distracting to you or your colleagues and should never prevent anyone from doing their job.

Our official dress code is "business casual attire," which means that suits, skirts, and pants they aren't jeans are always acceptable. Unacceptable clothing includes jeans, shorts, sweatshirts, flip-flops, most sneakers, and T-shirts with logos on them. We also ask that employees not wear anything too revealing (short skirts or low-cut shirts, for example).

If you have any questions about what constitutions appropriate business wear, please contact your Human Resources representative. If you're found to be in violation of the dress code, you could be reprimanded. As such, we're looking forward to a happy, productive summer.

(1)

To all employees,

As we approach summer, a friendly reminder that our company has an employee dress code that must be followed. [17] Please note that the dress code guidelines must be adhered to whenever you are in the office: [18]

(2)

We expect that employees will project a professional image at all times and use sound judgment [19] as to what counts as appropriate dress. Your attire should not be distracting to you or your colleagues and should never prevent anyone from doing their job. [20]

(3)

Our official dress code is "business casual attire," which means that suits, skirts, and pants they aren't jeans [21] are always acceptable. Unacceptable clothing includes jeans, shorts, sweatshirts, flip-flops, most sneakers, and T-shirts with logos on them. We also ask that employees not wear anything too revealing (short skirts or low-cut shirts, for example).

(4)

If you have any questions about what constitutions [22] appropriate business wear, please contact your Human Resources representative. If you're found to be in violation of the dress code, you could be reprimanded. [23] As such, we're looking forward to a happy, productive summer.

17. **a.** *(No change)*
    b. As we approach summer, we'd like to send a friendly reminder that our company has an employee dress code that must be followed.
    c. Our company has a dress code we'd like to follow as we approach summer.
    d. A dress code reminder that must be followed as we approach summer.

18. **a.** *(No change)*
    b. Please note that the dress code guidelines must be adhered to whenever you are in the office. . . .
    c. Please note that the dress code guidelines must be adhered to whenever you are in the office.
    d. Please note that the dress code guidelines must be adhered to whenever you are in the office?

19. **a.** *(No change)*
    b. sounded judgment
    c. Sound Judgment
    d. sounding judgment

20. **a.** *(No change)*
    b. doing his or her jobs
    c. doing his or her job
    d. doing my job

21. **a.** *(No change)*
    b. they're aren't jeans
    c. that aren't jeans
    d. which aren't jeans

22. **a.** *(No change)*
    b. constitutes
    c. constituents
    d. constants

23. Which of the following sentences could be inserted here as a transition to the closing sentence?
    a. If you violate the dress code, seriously don't even bother to coming to work.
    b. Keep your style "don'ts" at home in the closet.
    c. Flip-flops are not allowed in the office.
    d. We hope that everyone is as committed as we are to having a relaxed, comfortable office that is appropriate for all.

Read through the draft article. Then proceed to the suggestions for revision that follow.

There may be a lot going on in the world, but last night the hottest topic in town was whether to allow dogs at outdoor restaurants and bars. By a 5 to 4 margin, the Waterburg town council voted to allow people to bring to restaurants that have outdoor seating areas their furry friends.

This has been a contentious topic for years. Traditionally, animals have been banned from any restaurant setting indoor and outdoor due to cleanliness and health concerns. Any restaurant that was found to have evidence of animals would be fined. And fined severely. This included pets as well as common vermin like mice and bugs. The law made no special distinction between domestic animals and pests.

However, in 2004, that began to change. Marty Winklebaum, owner of the Waterburg Grill and Bar, started a petition to allow pet owners to bring their pets to restaurants as long as the seating was outside. "I didn't see the harm of letting someone bring a well-behaved dog to dinner," Winklebaum recalled, his petition picked up steam and then died in the town council vote that year, where he lost 7 to 2.

He kept fighting for his dog-loving customers, however, and started gaining the support of the local community online. Eventually the issue was brought back to the town council and added to last night's agenda. The argument was intense, as not everyone shared Winklebaum's view. "It just seems so unclean," Waterburg resident June Hawthorne argued. And what about people with allergies or who just don't want to eat with animals running around?

Ultimately, the debate in council chambers lasted more than two hours, by the end of it, Winklebaum's original vision was victorious. Starting June 1, restaurants may choose to allow pets in outdoor seating areas. There will be no more fines for bringing man's best friend out for dinner on the patio, as long as everyone's on their best behavior. Human or canine!

(1)

There may be a lot going on in the world, but last night the hottest topic in town was whether to allow dogs at outdoor restaurants and bars. By a 5 to 4 margin, the Waterburg town council voted to allow people <u>to bring to restaurants that have outdoor seating areas their furry friends.</u> [24]

(2)

This has been a contentious topic for years. Traditionally, animals have been banned from any restaurant setting <u>indoor and outdoor</u> [25] due to cleanliness and health concerns. <u>Any restaurant that was found to have evidence of animals would be</u> fined. And fined severely. This included pets as well as common vermin like mice and bugs. [26] The law made no special distinction between domestic animals and pests.

(3)

However, in 2004, that began to change. Marty Winklebaum, owner of the Waterburg Grill and Bar, started a petition to allow pet owners to bring their pets to restaurants as long as the seating was outside. <u>"I didn't see the harm of letting someone bring a well-behaved dog to dinner," Winklebaum recalled,</u> [27] his petition picked up steam and then died in the town council vote that year, where he lost 7 to 2.

(4)

He kept fighting for his dog-loving customers, however, and started gaining the support of the local community online. Eventually the issue was brought back to the town council and added to last night's agenda. The argument was intense, as not everyone shared Winklebaum's view. "It just seems so unclean," Waterburg resident June Hawthorne argued. And what about people with allergies or who just don't want to eat with animals running around? [28] [29]

(5)

Ultimately, the debate in council chambers lasted more than two hours, by the end of it, Winklebaum's original vision was victorious. [30] Starting June 1, restaurants may choose to allow pets in outdoor seating areas. There will be no more fines or bringing man's best friend out for dinner on the patio, as long as everyone's on their best behavior. Human or canine! [31]

24. **a.** *(No change)*
  b. to bring their furry friends.
  c. to bring to outdoor seating areas their furry friends (restaurants).
  d. to bring their furry friends to restaurants that have outdoor seating areas.

25. **a.** *(No change)*
  b. (indoor and outdoor)
  c. indoor and outdoor;
  d. indoor, or outdoor

26. **a.** *(No change)*
  b. Any restaurant that was found to have evidence of animals, from pets to common vermin like mice and bugs, would be fined severely.
  c. Any evidence of animals, including pets and common vermin like mice and bugs, would be fined severely.
  d. Restaurant fines include evidence of animals, which includes pets as well as common vermin like mice and bugs.

27. **a.** *(No change)*
  b. Winklebaum recalled, "I didn't see the harm of letting someone bring a well-behaved dog to dinner,"
  c. "I didn't see the harm of letting someone bring a well-behaved dog to dinner,"
  d. "I didn't see the harm of letting someone bring a well-behaved dog to dinner," Winklebaum recalled.

28. **a.** *(No change)*
  b. And what about people with allergies or who just don't want to eat with animals running around? She continued.
  c. "And what about people with allergies or who just don't want to eat with animals running around?" she continued.
  d. "And what about people with allergies or who just don't want to eat with animals running around" she continued.

29. Which of these sentences could the writer add to paragraph 4 as support?

a. By this year, Winklebaum's FriendBook group supporting the measure had 585 members.

b. June Hawthorne is planning to run for mayor next year.

c. June Hawthorne and Marty Winklebaum have a history of butting heads on local issues.

d. Paulie's Pizza is adding outdoor seating this summer.

30. a. *(No change)*

b. The debate in council chambers lasted more than two hours, but in contrast, by the end of it, Winklebaum's original vision was victorious.

c. The ultimate debate in council chambers lasted more than two hours, by the end of it, Winklebaum's original vision was victorious.

d. Ultimately, the debate in council chambers lasted more than two hours, but by the end of it, Winklebaum's original vision was victorious.

31. a. *(No change)*

b. Fines no more for bringing man's best friend out for dinner on the patio, as long as all humans and canines are on their best behavior!

c. There will be no more fines for bringing man's best friend out for dinner on the patio, as long as all humans and canines are on their best behavior.

d. There will be no more fines for bringing man's best friend out for dinner on the patio, as long as everyone's on their best behavior, human or canine!

Read through the draft personal narrative. Then proceed to the suggestions for revision that follow.

Last night I went to my first cooking class, and let me tell you. It. Was. A. Disaster. I've never thought I was a great chef or anything, but after last night I'm tempted to order takeout for the rest of my life.

Although I let my friend Karen talk me into signing up for the class together, I was skeptical. My signature dish consists of boxed macaroni and cheese and chunks of chicken sausage cooked on the stove. She wanted to do it. So I agreed. We signed up. What she neglected to tell me was that she had gotten us signed up for Advanced Pasta Cooking. I was pretty sure my mac-and-cheese experience didn't qualify me for advanced pasta *anything*.

Sadly, my instincts proved me right. When we got there, I realized there was no "pasta" at all. Just some ingredients lying around. Some eggs. A little salt. A big pile of flour. Karen didn't seem to mind. She was already making conversation with the lady next to us, who had previously taken three (three!) pasta-making courses with Chef Marco.

Once the class got underway, it was clear that Karen and I were in under our heads. There were instructions that made no sense, and the chef was saying things like you already know how to do this, so just breeze through it and let me know when you're on the next step. I tried to keep up, but I ended up with a gooey ball of flour while everyone around me had lovely strings of fresh linguine ready to be boiled. Even Karen's pasta didn't look half bad. She'd been copying everything her neighbor did.

By the end, I was exhausted and covered in flour. Hungry most of all, after watching everyone else eat all the pasta they'd made from scratch. I may not have learned much about advanced cooking, but I learned that I don't want to make pasta again anytime soon!

(1)

Last night I went to my first cooking class, and let me tell you. It. Was. A. Disaster. [32] I've never thought I was a great chef or anything, but after last night I'm tempted to order takeout for the rest of my life.

(2)

Although I let my friend Karen talk me into signing up for the class together, I was skeptical. [33] My signature dish consists of boxed macaroni and cheese and chunks of chicken sausage cooked on the stove. She wanted to do it. So I agreed. We signed up. What she neglected to tell me was that she had gotten us signed up for Advanced Pasta Cooking. I was pretty sure my mac-and-cheese experience didn't qualify me for advanced pasta *anything*.

(3)

Sadly, my instincts proved me right. When we got there, I realized there was no "pasta" at all. Just some ingredients lying around. Some eggs. A little salt. A big pile of flour. [34] Karen didn't seem to mind. She was already making conversation with the lady next to us, who had previously taken three (three!) pasta-making courses with Chef Marco. [35]

(4)

Once the class got underway, it was clear that Karen and I were in under our heads. [36] There were instructions that made no sense, and the chef was saying things like you already know how to do this, so just breeze through it and let me know when you're on the next step. [37] I tried to keep up, but I ended up with a gooey ball of flour while everyone around me had lovely strings of fresh linguine ready to be boiled. Even Karen's pasta didn't look half bad. She'd been copying everything her neighbor did. [38]

(5)

By the end, I was exhausted and covered in flour. Hungry most of all, after watching everyone else eat all the pasta they'd made from scratch. [39] I may not have learned much about advanced cooking, but I learned that I don't want to make pasta again anytime soon!

32. a. *(No change)*
   b. Last night I went to my first cooking class, and it was a disaster, let me tell you.
   c. Last night I went to my first cooking class— and let me tell you, it was a disaster.
   d. Last night I went to my first cooking class and let me tell you it was a disaster.

33. a. *(No change)*
   b. Yet I let my friend Karen talk me into signing up for the class together, I was skeptical.
   c. Because I let my friend Karen talk me into signing up for the class together, I was skeptical.
   d. Therefore, I let my friend Karen talk me into signing up for the class together, I was skeptical.

34. a. *(No change)*
   b. There were just some ingredients lying around: some eggs, a little salt, and a big pile of flour.
   c. There were some eggs lying around; a little salt and a big pile of flour.
   d. Some eggs lying around, and some other ingredients: a little salt and a big pile of flour.

35. What relevant detail could the writer add to paragraph 3?
   a. where the class took place
   b. who Chef Marco is and how he's related to the class
   c. how many people were in the class
   d. the writer's favorite kind of pasta

36. a. *(No change)*
   b. on our heads
   c. in our heads
   d. over our heads

37. a. *(No change)*
   b. the chef was saying things like: you already know how to do this, so just breeze through it and let me know when you're on the next step.
   c. the chef was saying things like You Already Know How To Do This, So Just Breeze Through It And Let Me Know When You're On The Next Step.
   d. the chef was saying things like, "You already know how to do this, so just breeze through it and let me know when you're on the next step."

38. Which potential concluding sentence for paragraph 4 matches the writer's style and tone?
   a. Way to cheat off someone else's paper, Karen.
   b. If only I'd thought of that!
   c. I expected better from Karen and from this class.
   d. Hmmmm.

39. **a.** *(No change)*

   b. Hungry most of all by the end but also I was exhausted and covered in flour after watching everyone else eat all the pasta they'd made from scratch.

   c. By the end, I was exhausted and covered in flour, hungry most of all, after watching everyone else eat all the pasta they'd made from scratch.

   d. By the end, I was exhausted, covered in flour, and—most of all—hungry after watching everyone else eat all the pasta they'd made from scratch.

Read through the draft article. Then proceed to the suggestions for revision that follow.

Given that water covers 70% of the planet, it may be hard to believe that much of the world is suffering from drowt conditions. However, the water we use in our everyday lives (drinking, bathing, water for crops, and etc.) is fresh water, whereas most of the water in the world is salt water from the oceans. With the world population passing 7 billion and showing no signs of slowing anytime soon, the global fresh water crisis needs attention right now.

Per statistics, only about 3% of the world's water is fresh water, and 2% of that is frozen in glaciers and various forms of ice. That leaves 1% of the world's water for us. Recent studies show that more than a billion people have little or no access to fresh water. Lack of water = no bathing. No sanitation = diseases. Lack of water = dehydration too. Combined with the millions of people who have only slightly more access to water, this means that much of the world is suffering already.

As if that extra strain weren't bad enough, the fresh water sources that some of us are lucky enough to have might not be around forever. Rivers and lakes are drying up from overuse in heavily populated areas and extreme weather problems, and more than half of the world's wetlands have disappeared in the past century. Don't even get me started on all of the water used for growing crops and raising agricultural animals around the world, plus good old-fashioned water waste.

What can we do about all of this? Groups like the United Nations are pushing to have water access identified as a human right and working toward finding sustainable resources. That doesn't mean we can't start this important fight at home, though, if we work to conserve water in our own homes, it's an important first step toward acknowledging and fighting this alarming water crisis.

(1)

Given that water covers 70% of the planet, it may be hard to believe that much of the world is suffering from <u>drowt</u> [40] conditions. However, the water we use in our everyday lives (<u>drinking, bathing, water for crops, and etc.</u>) [41] is fresh water, whereas most of the water in the world is salt water from the oceans. With the world population passing 7 billion and showing no signs of slowing anytime soon, the global fresh water crisis needs attention right now.

(2)

Per statistics, only about 3% of the world's water is fresh water, and 2% of that is frozen in glaciers and various forms of ice. [42] That leaves 1% of the world's water for us. Recent studies show that more than a billion people have little or no access to fresh water. Lack of water = no bathing. No sanitation = diseases. Lack of water = dehydration too. [43] Combined with the millions of people who have only slightly more access to water, this means that much of the world is suffering already.

(3)

As if that extra strain weren't bad enough, the fresh water sources that some of us are lucky enough to have might not be around forever. Rivers and lakes are drying up from overuse in heavily populated areas and extreme weather problems, and more than half of the world's wetlands have disappeared in the past century. Don't even get me started on all of the water used for growing crops and raising agricultural animals around the world, plus good old-fashioned water waste. [44]

(4)

What can we do about all of this? Groups like the United Nations are pushing to have water access identified as a human right and working toward finding sustainable resources. That doesn't mean we can't start this important fight at home, though, if we work to conserve water in our own homes, it's an important first step toward acknowledging and fighting this alarming water crisis. [45]

40. a. *(No change)*
   b. draught
   c. draft
   d. drought

41. a. *(No change)*
   b. drinking, bathing, watering crops, etc.
   c. drinks, bathing, water for crops, etc.
   d. drinking, bathing, watering crops, and etc.

42. How could the writer improve the information in this sentence?
   a. Note where the statistics come from.
   b. Add more percentages.
   c. Delete the sentence altogether.
   d. Do nothing; the sentence is fine as it is.

43. a. *(No change)*
   b. Lack of water . . . no bathing . . . No sanitation . . . diseases . . . Lack of water . . . dehydration too.
   c. Lack of water and proper sanitation can lead to serious health issues like dehydration and disease.
   d. Lack of water leads to no bathing. No bathing leads to diseases. Lack of water leads to dehydration too.

44. Which of these sentences in paragraph 3 does not fit with the overall passage?
   a. *(No change)*
   b. Rivers and lakes are drying up from overuse in heavily populated areas and extreme weather problems, and more than half of the world's wetlands have disappeared in the past century.
   c. As if that extra strain weren't bad enough, the fresh water sources that some of us are lucky enough to have might not be around forever.
   d. Don't even get me started on all of the water used for growing crops and raising agricultural animals around the world, plus good old-fashioned water waste.

45. a. *(No change)*

    b. However, that doesn't mean we can't start this important fight at home. Working to conserve water in our own homes is an important first step toward acknowledging and fighting this alarming water crisis.

    c. That doesn't mean we can't start this important fight at home, if we work to conserve water in our own homes, it's an important first step toward acknowledging and fighting this alarming water crisis.

    d. That doesn't mean we can't start this important fight at home. Though if we work to conserve water in our own homes. It's an important first step toward acknowledging and fighting this alarming water crisis.

Read through the draft review. Then proceed to the suggestions for revision that follow.

A tour of City Museum's recent exhibits show that the museum has an ambitious and wide-ranging approach to sharing art with the community.

    Of the new exhibits, "African Skies" is the most magnetic. This put-together collection by photographer Marcus Ammendola, includes photographs from 10 years' worth of expeditions in Africa's rural areas. More often than not, Ammendola handed his camera over to children he encountered in various African villages. The result is a fascinating glimpse into the daily lives of young people in some of the most remote places in the world.

    Not to be outdone by the newer and fleshier exhibits, the museum's permanent exhibits have gotten a makeover as well. The ancient museum's collection of Early Christian art now lives in its own wing, and the Elizabethan clothing collection can be found in a marble hall worthy of Henry VIII himself.

    To celebrate its half-centennial, City Museum will be hosting Open House Fridays, where members of the community can explore the museum for half off the admission price.

---

(1)

A tour of City Museum's recent exhibits show that the museum has an ambitious and wide-ranging approach to sharing art with the community. [46]

(2)

Of the new exhibits, "African Skies" is the most magnetic. This put-together collection by photographer Marcus Ammendola, includes photographs from 10 years' worth of expeditions in Africa's rural areas. [47] More often than not, Ammendola handed his camera over to children he encountered in various African villages. The result is a fascinating glimpse into the daily lives of young people in some of the most remote places in the world.

(3)

Not to be outdone by the newer and fleshier [48] exhibits, the museum's permanent exhibits have gotten a makeover as well. The ancient museum's collection of Early Christian art [49] now lives in its own wing, and the Elizabethan clothing collection can be found in a marble hall worthy of Henry VIII himself.

(4)

To celebrate its half-centennial, City Museum will be hosting Open House Fridays, where members of the community can explore the museum for half off the admission price. [50]

46. Which of these sentences would make an appropriate opening sentence for this passage?
   a. City Museum is located on Eastern Avenue.
   b. Of all the museums around here, City Museum is my favorite.
   c. Now in its 50th year, the City Museum is working hard to make this its best year yet.
   d. Marcus Ammendola's photography is truly something special.

47. a. (No change)
   b. Put together by photographer Marcus Ammendola, this collection includes photographs from 10 years' worth of expeditions in Africa's rural areas.
   c. This collection by photographer Marcus Ammendola put together, includes photographs from 10 years' worth of expeditions in Africa's rural areas.
   d. Photographs from 10 years' worth of expeditions in Africa's rural areas, put together by photographer Marcus Ammendola.

48. a. (No change)
   b. flightier
   c. flashier
   d. fairer

49. a. (No change)
   b. The museum's collection of Early ancient Christian art
   c. The museum's collection of Early Christian ancient art
   d. The museum's ancient collection of Early Christian art

50. If the writer needed to remove a paragraph for space, which one could be removed most easily?
   a. paragraph 1
   b. paragraph 2
   c. paragraph 3
   d. paragraph 4

Part 2: Essay Question
45 Minutes

This part of the practice test will assess your writing skills. On the official exam, you will have a 45-minute limit to plan and write your essay. Your essay will be scored on how well you

- develop a main idea and support it with strong reasons, examples, and details
- clearly organize your ideas, including the use of an introduction and conclusion, logical paragraphs, and effective transitions
- use language, including varied word choice and sentence constructions and appropriate voice
- clearly and correctly use writing conventions

Each passage offers a different perspective on the same important issue. Read both passages carefully, taking note of the strengths and weaknesses of each author's discussion. Then write an essay that explains your own opinion on the important issue discussed in both passages.

Read the following quotations about U.S. foreign policy.

> "Speak softly and carry a big stick; you will go far."
>
> —President Teddy Roosevelt

> "If everyone loves you, maybe you don't need so many tanks."
>
> —Author Craig Nelson

Write an essay in which you explain your own position on the issue of the U.S. approach to foreign policy in terms of how President Roosevelt and Craig Nelson summarize it. Think carefully about what reasons will help others understand your perspective, as well as what examples and details you can use to support your argument.

Be sure to use evidence from the text provided, as well as specific reasons and examples from your own experience and knowledge to support your position. Remember that every position exists within the context of a larger discussion of the issue, so your essay should, at minimum, acknowledge alternate and/or opposing ideas. When you have finished your essay, review your writing to check for correct spelling, punctuation, and grammar.

Mathematics

90 Minutes
50 Questions

This practice test is modeled on the content and timing of the official HiSET® Mathematics test and, like the official test, presents a series of questions that assess your ability to solve quantitative problems using fundamental concepts and reasoning skills.

1. The concentration of pollution in the air over a 24-hour period is described by the following graph:

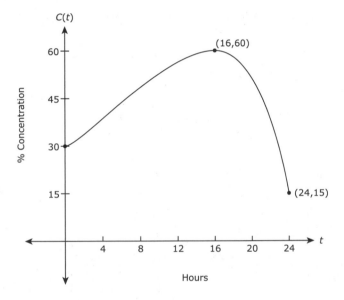

What is the range of $C(t)$?
a. the number 45
b. the number 30
c. all real numbers between 30 and 60, inclusive
d. all real numbers between 15 and 60, inclusive
e. all real numbers between 0 and 24, inclusive

2. Concert tickets for a famous cellist go on sale on March 15. The price of a ticket t days after March 15 is given by a function $P(t)$. Which of the following represents the difference in cost of tickets between March 19 and March 21?
a. $P(5) - P(3)$
b. $P(6) - P(4)$
c. $\frac{P(4) + P(6)}{2}$
d. $\frac{P(19) + P(21)}{2}$
e. $P(21) - P(19)$

3. What is the solution set of the equation $\frac{3}{4x + 1} - \frac{2}{(4x + 1)^2} = 0$?
a. $\{-\frac{1}{12}\}$
b. $\{\frac{1}{12}\}$
c. $\{-\frac{1}{4}\}$
d. $\{-12\}$
e. $\varnothing$

4. The final scores on a 60-second run of a video game played by seven friends are 168, 121, 210, 96, 215, 118, 320. It was determined later that the score recorded as 320 should have been 350. Which of the following statements is true?
a. Both the mean and median of the modified data set will increase.
b. The mean and median of the modified data set will remain unchanged.
c. The median of the modified data set will decrease, but the mean will increase.
d. The median of the modified data set remains unchanged, but the mean increases.
e. The modified data set will now have a mode.

5. A homeowner designed a deck on which he will place a hot tub. The hot tub is to be enclosed by a 12′ × 12′ cabana. If the homeowner wants two feet of deck surrounding the cabana, what is the distance from point *A* to point *B* in the diagram?

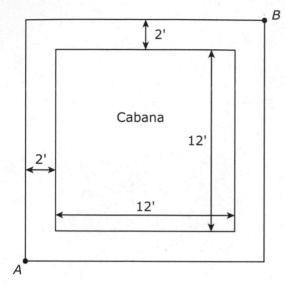

a. $\sqrt{14^2 + 14^2}$
b. $\sqrt{14^2 + 16^2}$
c. $14^2 + 14^2$
d. $\sqrt{16^2 + 16^2}$
e. $16^2 + 16^2$

6. What property of the real numbers is illustrated by the following mathematical sentence? Assume *a*, *b*, and *c* are nonzero real numbers.

$$(a + b) + (c + d) = (c + d) + (a + b)$$

a. additive identity
b. distributive property
c. additive inverse
d. associative property
e. commutative property

7. The number of cell phones in the United States in 2014 was 327,577,529. If 46% of these cell phones are owned by males, how many cell phones were owned by males? Round your answer to the nearest hundred thousand.
a. 150,000,000
b. 150,690,000
c. 150,680,000
d. 150,600,000
e. 150,700,000

8. A popsicle is taken out of the freezer and placed on the counter. Its temperature, *T* (measured in degrees Fahrenheit) at time *t* minutes after taking it out of the freezer is given by $T(t) = 60 - 40(\frac{3}{2})^{-t}$. Which of the following statements is true?
   I. The temperature after two minutes is 40 degrees.
   II. $T(t)$ never exceeds 60 degrees.
   III. The temperature of a popsicle the moment it is taken out of the freezer is 20 degrees.

a. II only
b. III only
c. II and III only
d. I and III only
e. I, II, and III

9. The following line graph shows the monthly electric bills for a customer over the course of a year.

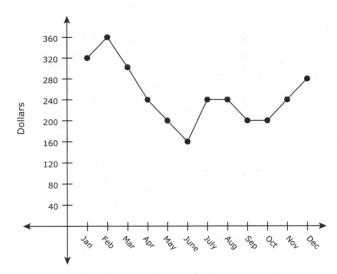

Which two consecutive months show the largest difference in cost?

a. January to February
b. September to October
c. October to November
d. June to July
e. May to June

10. Assume a is a nonzero real number. Solve the following system:

$$\begin{cases} 2x + y = a \\ x - y = 2a \end{cases}$$

a. $x = 0, y = a$
b. $x = -a, y = a$
c. $x = a, y = -a$
d. $x = a, y = 3a$
e. $x = 2a, y = 0$

11. What is the solution set of the inequality $3x - 2(4 - x) < -3x$?

a.

b.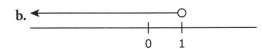

c.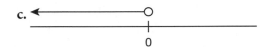

d.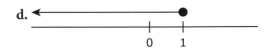

e.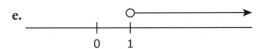

12. Consider the following graph of $p(x)$:

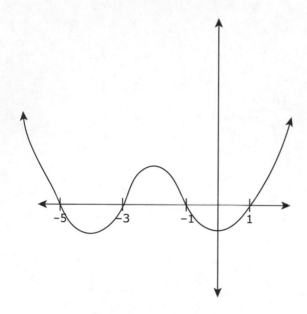

Which of the following does NOT divide evenly into $p(x)$?

a. $(x + 5)$
b. $(x^2 - 1)$
c. $(x + 1)$
d. $(x^2 - 9)$
e. $(x^2 + 8x + 15)$

13. Jacob asked all members of the yearbook staff, who are all juniors, to indicate their favorite subject this year. Here are the results:

SUBJECT	NUMBER FOR WHOM THIS IS THE FAVORITE
English	8
History	3
Math	2
Art	4

Based on these results, Jacob concluded that the favorite subject among all his classmates in the junior class is English. Which of the following offers the best explanation as to why his conclusion may be invalid?

a. Jacob should have included more subjects in the list.
b. The sample is not representative of the entire junior class.
c. Jacob should have also asked juniors from other schools this question.
d. Jacob should have surveyed only students NOT on the yearbook staff.
e. There are more English courses offered than there are math or history.

14. Members of a trading card game group compare their card collections at a weekly meeting. Each member counted the number of rare cards in his or her collection this week. The following are the results:

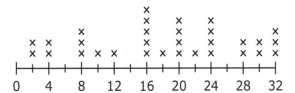

What is the mode number of rare cards in this group?

a. 32

b. 20

c. 16

d. 30

e. 18

15. Consider a sector of a circle with diameter D corresponding to a central angle θ. If the diameter is tripled and the central angle is divided in half, by what number would you multiply the arc length of the original circle to get the arc length of the new sector?

a. $\frac{3}{4}$

b. $\frac{3}{2}$

c. 3

d. $\frac{1}{2}$

e. $\frac{1}{6}$

16. Fill in the box with the appropriate exponent:

$$\frac{\sqrt{x}}{x\sqrt[3]{x}} = x^{\square}$$

a. $\frac{11}{6}$

b. $-\frac{5}{6}$

c. -2

d. $\frac{3}{8}$

e. $\frac{1}{6}$

17. Which of the following is equivalent to $\frac{2^3 \times 7^3}{14^{-2}}$?

a. 14^{-5}

b. 14^1

c. 14^8

d. 14^5

e. 14^{-6}

18. The table shows age and average number of text messages sent daily for eight randomly selected mall goers.

AGE	NUMBER OF TEXT MESSAGES
16	120
20	135
28	100
33	83
35	52
41	40
68	18
70	5

The scatter plot with best fit line is shown here:

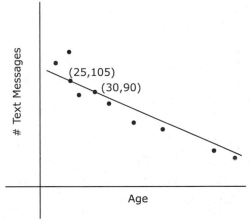

Based on this data, if a person is 50 years old, approximately how many text messages would you expect him or her to send daily?

a. 60

b. 90

c. 30

d. 135

e. 180

19. Which of the following expressions is equivalent to $-3x^2(1 - 4x - 2x^2)$?

a. $-6x^2 - 12x^3 + 3x^2$

b. $-5x^2 - 4x$

c. $-3x^2 - 7x^3 - 5x^4$

d. $6x^4 - 4x + 1$

e. $6x^4 + 12x^3 - 3x^2$

20. A shopper buys a mixture of CDs and vinyl albums online. The cost per CD is $11.50 and the cost per vinyl album is $15.75. She buys three fewer CDs than two times the number of vinyl albums and spends $275.50 on the entire purchase before tax. Which equation can be used to determine the number of CDs and number of vinyl albums that she purchases?

a. $11.50x + 15.75y = 275.50$

b. $1,150(2x + 3) + 1,575x = 27,550$

c. $15.75x + 11.50(2x - 3) = 275.50$

d. $27.25[x + (2x + 3)] = 275.50$

e. $15.75(2x - 3) + 11.50x = 275.50$

21. What is the domain of the function $h(x) = \sqrt{3 - x} + 4$?

a. $\{x \mid x \geq 3\}$

b. $\{x \mid x < 3\}$

c. $\{x \mid x \leq 3\}$

d. $\{x \mid x \geq 4\}$

e. $\{x \mid x > 3\}$

22. For which of the following functions is the average rate of change constant over all intervals of the form $[0,a]$, where a is any given positive real number?

a. $f(x) = x^2$

b. $g(x) = \sqrt{x}$

c. $h(x) = \frac{1}{x}$

d. $j(x) = 5x + 1$

e. $k(x) = x^3$

23. A dog's litter contained 9 puppies. There were 3 black males, 3 spotted males, 2 brown females, and 1 spotted female. What is the probability that a customer randomly selects a puppy from this litter that is either male or spotted?

a. $\frac{1}{9}$

b. $\frac{1}{3}$

c. $\frac{4}{9}$

d. $\frac{7}{9}$

e. $\frac{2}{3}$

24. The surface area of a cube is 150 square centimeters. What is its volume (in cubic centimeters)?

a. 750

b. 125

c. 5

d. 25

e. 15

25. Assume the two circles shown in the diagram are concentric:

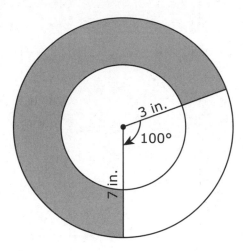

What is the area of the shaded region (in square inches)?

a. $\frac{500}{9}\pi$

b. 40π

c. $\frac{50}{9}\pi$

d. $\frac{250}{9}\pi$

e. $\frac{110}{9}\pi$

26. If the mass of 5 identical containers of soup is 3.2 kilograms, what would be the mass of 8 such identical containers of soup?

a. 12.5 kilograms

b. 5.12 grams

c. 6.4 kilograms

d. 12,500 grams

e. 5,120 grams

27. The point $P(a,b)$ is translated to the right 3 units and down 2 units and then reflected across the y-axis. What are the coordinates of the image P' of P under this sequence of transformations?

a. $(-a-3, 2-b)$

b. $(-a-3, b-2)$

c. $(b-2, a+3)$

d. $(a+3, b-2)$

e. $(3-a, b+2)$

28. A playground slide has length L feet. The ladder attached to it is 10 feet high and makes an angle of 50° with the slide, as shown:

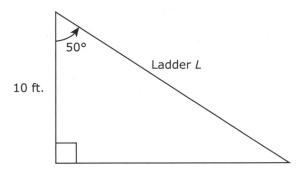

What is the length, L, of the ladder (in feet)?

a. $10 \cos 50°$

b. $10 \sin 50°$

c. $\frac{10}{\cos 50°}$

d. $\frac{\sin 50°}{10}$

e. $10 \tan 50°$

29. The following scatter plot shows the average number of steps walked daily by participants in a "Walk for Life" program at a local gym versus the percent success rate with losing weight experienced by others who have averaged a similar number of steps daily:

Which of the following best depicts the best fit line for this data?

a.

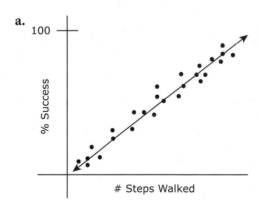

b.

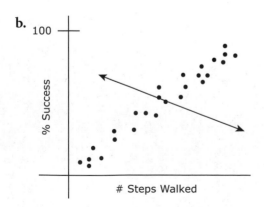

c.

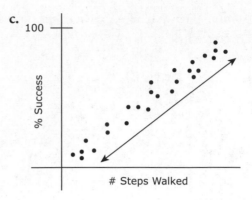

d.

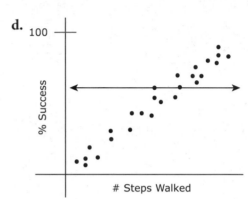

e.

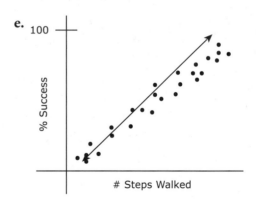

30. Consider the equation $Z = \frac{a}{\frac{1}{x}+\frac{1}{y}}$, where a, x, and y are positive real numbers. Which of the following statements is true?

   a. As x and y increase and a remains the same, Z increases.

   b. If a and x increase and y remains the same, then Z decreases.

   c. If x and y decrease and a remains the same, then Z increases.

   d. If $\frac{1}{x}$ and $\frac{1}{y}$ increase and a remains the same, then Z increases.

   e. If y increases and both a and x remain the same, then Z increases.

31. Which of the following expressions is equivalent to $\frac{4x^3 - 2x^2 - 2x}{4x^2 - 4x + 1} \cdot \frac{2x^2 - x}{x^2 - 1}$?

   a. $\frac{4x^3 + 2x^2}{2x^2 + x - 1}$

   b. $\frac{2x^2}{x + 1}$

   c. $\frac{4x^3}{x - 1}$

   d. $\frac{2(x-1)^2(x+1)}{(2x-1)}$

   e. $\frac{2x^2 + x - 1}{4x^3 + 2x^2}$

32. Which of the following systems has infinitely many solutions?

   a. $\begin{cases} y = 3x + 1 \\ y = 3x - 1 \end{cases}$

   b. $\begin{cases} x = -4y \\ y = 4x \end{cases}$

   c. $\begin{cases} 2x - y = 5 \\ -x + y = -1 \end{cases}$

   d. $\begin{cases} 2x - 3y = -1 \\ -4x + 6y = 2 \end{cases}$

   e. $\begin{cases} x = 3 \\ y = -2 \end{cases}$

33. For which of the following values of a does the quadratic equation $ax^2 + 40x + 25 = 0$ have a repeated real solution?

   a. 4

   b. 16

   c. 8

   d. −16

   e. −4

34. \$4,200 is deposited into an account that accrues interest continuously at an annual rate of 3%. Which of the following functions gives the amount in the account after t years?

   a. $f(t) = 4{,}200(0.97)^t$

   b. $f(t) = 4{,}200(1.03)^t$

   c. $f(t) = 4{,}200(1.03t)$

   d. $f(t) = 1.03(4{,}200)^t$

   e. $f(t) = 4{,}200(t^{1.03})$

35. A four-sided red die (with faces 1, 2, 3, 4) and an eight-sided blue die (with faces 1, 2, 3, 4, 5, 6, 7, 8) are rolled. The result is recorded in the form of a two-digit number, $\boxed{\text{Red Die}}\,\boxed{\text{Blue Die}}$. Assuming all rolls are equally likely, what is the probability that the number is greater than 25?

   a. $\frac{5}{8}$

   b. $\frac{19}{40}$

   c. $\frac{19}{32}$

   d. $\frac{13}{32}$

   e. $\frac{3}{4}$

36. Which of the following statements is false?

    a. The sum of two rational numbers is a rational number.

    b. The product of a positive rational number and an irrational number is an irrational number.

    c. The product of two irrational numbers is an irrational number.

    d. The quotient of two positive rational numbers is a positive rational number.

    e. The sum of two negative irrational numbers is a negative irrational number.

37. An amateur bowler must bowl five games for a ninepin tournament. Her first four scores are 191, 218, 210, and 171. Within what range must her fifth game fall to ensure that her five-game average is between 200 and 215?

    a. 200 to 215

    b. 10 to 70

    c. 210 to 285

    d. 171 to 218

    e. 70 to 199

38. Which of the following lines is neither parallel nor perpendicular to the line whose equation is given by $2y + ax = -a$, where a is a positive real number?

    a. $y = ax - \frac{a}{2}$

    b. $ay = 2x$

    c. $ax + 2y = -1$

    d. $\frac{a}{2}y = x - a$

    e. $2ay - 4x = a$

39. The following lettered tiles (with the number of each indicated beneath each letter) are placed in a bag:

E	P	U	R	B	C
4	2	1	3	2	2

If a single tile is selected at random from the bag, which of the following statements is false?

    a. It is equally likely to choose a vowel and a consonant.

    b. There is a 50% chance of selecting a tile that has an R, B, or C on it.

    c. It is equally likely to choose a tile with a P or B on it.

    d. It is twice as likely to choose an E as it is to choose a C.

    e. There is approximately a 7% chance of selecting a U.

40. Which of the following expressions is equivalent to $6x(1 - 3x) - 2x^2(9 - x^2)$?

    a. $6x - 36x^2 - 2x^4$

    b. $2x^4 - 36x^2 + 6x$

    c. $2x^4 - 18x^2 + 6x$

    d. $3x - 19x^2$

    e. $6x + 2x^4$

41. Solve for x: $4(3 - 2x) - 2(1 - 3x) = -2$.

    a. $\frac{12}{5}$

    b. $\frac{1}{6}$

    c. -4

    d. 6

    e. $\frac{6}{7}$

42. The volume V of a right circular cone with base radius r and height h is given by $V = \frac{1}{3}\pi r^2 h$. What is the formula for the radius r in terms of V and h?

    a. $r = \sqrt{3V\pi h}$

    b. $r = 6\pi h V$

    c. $r = \frac{6V}{\pi h}$

    d. $r = \sqrt{\frac{3V}{\pi h}}$

    e. $r = \frac{V}{3\pi h}$

43. The area of a rectangle is 96 square inches, and its perimeter is 40 inches. Which of the following systems can be used to determine the dimensions of the rectangle?

    a. $\begin{cases} 2x + 2y = 96 \\ xy = 40 \end{cases}$

    b. $\begin{cases} x + y = 20 \\ \frac{1}{2}xy = 96 \end{cases}$

    c. $\begin{cases} 2x + 2y = 40 \\ \frac{1}{2}xy = 96 \end{cases}$

    d. $\begin{cases} x + y = 20 \\ xy = 96 \end{cases}$

    e. $\begin{cases} x + y = 40 \\ xy = 96 \end{cases}$

44. What is the equation of a circle whose diameter has endpoints (7,0) and (0,9)?

    a. $(x - \frac{7}{2})^2 + (y - \frac{9}{2})^2 = \frac{1}{2}\sqrt{130}$

    b. $(x + \frac{7}{2})^2 + (y + \frac{9}{2})^2 = 130$

    c. $(x - \frac{7}{2})^2 + (y - \frac{9}{2})^2 = \frac{65}{2}$

    d. $(x - \frac{7}{2})^2 - (y - \frac{9}{2})^2 = \frac{65}{2}$

    e. $(x - \frac{7}{2})^2 - (y - \frac{9}{2})^2 = \frac{1}{2}\sqrt{130}$

45. A new computer can perform 2.9×10^9 calculations per second, whereas last year's model could only perform 3.2×10^8 calculations per second. How many more calculations can this year's model perform as compared to last year's model?

    a. 0.3×10^1

    b. 2.58×10^9

    c. 0.3×10^9

    d. 3.22×10^9

    e. 3.0×10^8

46. Which of the following polynomials has no real zeros?

    a. $p(x) = [x(x + 1)(x + 2)]^2$

    b. $q(x) = (x^2 + 5)(x^2 + 2)$

    c. $r(x) = (x^4 + 1)$

    d. $s(x) = (x^2 + 5x + 6)(x^2 + 2x + 1)$

    e. $t(x) = x^4 - 1$

47. What is the range of the function $g(x) = -5(x + 2)^2 - 6$?

    a. $y \le -6$

    b. $y \ge -6$

    c. $y \ge -2$

    d. $y \le 6$

    e. all real numbers

48. Two power walkers start at noon at opposite ends of a bike path that is 28 miles long. One walks at a rate of a miles per hour and the other walks at a rate of b miles per hour. After how many hours will they meet?

    a. $\frac{28}{a + b}$

    b. $28(a + b)$

    c. $\frac{14}{a}$

    d. $\frac{a + b}{28}$

    e. $\frac{28}{a - b}$

49. What is the solution set of the equation $\sqrt[3]{x^2 + 1} = 2$?

  a. $\left\{ -\sqrt{5}, \sqrt{5} \right\}$

  b. $\left\{ -\sqrt{7}, \sqrt{7} \right\}$

  c. $\{1,1\}$

  d. $\left\{ \sqrt{7} \right\}$

  e. $\left\{ \sqrt{5} \right\}$

50. A surveyor wants to determine the distance across a creek. She identifies four points, W, X, Y, and Z, and makes the measurements shown:

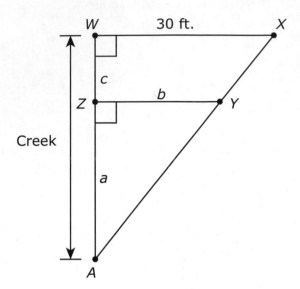

Which of the following expressions gives the distance from A to W? Assume that a, b, and c are positive real numbers (expressed in feet).

  a. $30 + b$

  b. $30(a + b)$

  c. $\frac{30a}{b}$

  d. $\frac{30a}{b} - a$

  e. $\frac{30}{b} - a$

Science

80 Minutes
50 Questions

This practice test is modeled on the content and timing of the official HiSET® Science test and, like the official test, presents a series of questions that assess your ability to use science content knowledge, apply principles of scientific inquiry, and interpret and evaluate scientific information.

Questions 1–4 are based on the following information.

Vultures are large birds of prey that feed on the carcasses of dead animals. In the 1820s, John James Audubon wanted to understand how black vultures found the carcasses to eat and ran a series of experiments to test different ways the vultures could find food. All of the experiments, described next, were conducted in an area where black vultures were common. The results are summarized in the table.

Experiment 1: Audubon took a clean deerskin, painted eyes on its head, and stuffed the skin with hay in the shape of a deer. He then left the dummy in an open field.
Result: A vulture quickly found the dummy and ripped it open.

Experiment 2: Audubon concealed a rotting pig carcass in an open field, hiding it under a pile of grass.
Result: Many vultures flew overhead but none approached the pig. Local dogs did find the pig.

Experiment 3: A very realistic painting of a carcass was placed face up in an open field.
Result: Many black vultures landed on the painting and tried to eat it.

Experiment 4: The painting was placed 15 feet from a pile of rotting meat under a tarp.
Result: Black vultures landed on the painting but ignored the nearby meat.

Summary of results:

EXPERIMENT	METHOD	RESULT
1	Dummy deer	Vultures found the dummy quickly
2	Hidden pig carcass	Vultures did not find the pig
3	Realistic painting of a carcass	Vultures quickly landed on the painting
4	Realistic painting next to hidden real meat	Vultures quickly landed on the painting, ignored the hidden meat

1. Which hypothesis is being tested in experiments 1 and 3?
   a. Black vultures find their prey through a systematic search.
   b. Black vultures find their prey visually.
   c. Black vultures find their prey through smell.
   d. Black vultures find their prey in multiple ways.

2. Based on the results of the experiments, which conclusion is valid?
   a. Black vultures use eyesight to find their prey.
   b. Black vultures use scent to find their prey.
   c. Black vultures first use eyesight to find their prey and then use scent to determine its exact location.
   d. Black vultures are not intelligent.

3. Based on the results of these experiments, if you wanted to test if vultures find food faster by looking for other vultures, what would be the best method?

   a. Play recorded sounds of vultures near a fake carcass and time how fast any vultures respond.

   b. Place vulture decoys on the ground near a fake carcass and record the vultures' response times.

   c. Place vulture decoys on tall poles high above a fake carcass and record the vultures' response times.

   d. Place a fake carcass in a field, wait for a live vulture to find it, and then time how long it takes for additional vultures to arrive.

4. Experiments 2 and 4 are repeated with a different species of vulture, the turkey vulture. This time, the turkey vultures did find the hidden pig carcass and ignored the painting while hunting for the hidden meat. Which conclusion is supported by the results of all the experiments with black vultures and turkey vultures?

   a. Each species of vulture uses multiple ways to find food.

   b. All vultures find food the same way.

   c. Sometimes different species of vulture use different senses to find food.

   d. Every species of vulture uses a different way to find food.

Questions 5–9 are based on the following information.

Mangrove trees grow at the edge of the ocean in tropical areas. Mangrove roots grow underwater, branching out in many directions and creating a dense, sheltered habitat for fish and other underwater life. Many organisms, called epibiotas or epibionts, live on the roots of the trees. Some examples of epibiotas are corals, sea anemones, sponges, and oysters. A biologist wanted to see if more fish lived among roots that had more epibiotas living on them and if the epibiotas were responsible for any increased numbers of fish. To test this hypothesis, he did two studies.

The first study was called the Experimental Removal Study. In this study, the biologist counted the fish in six sections of mangrove shoreline, each 10 m in length. Afterward, in three of those sections, he cleared all the epibiotas by walking the length of the section and scrubbing each root with a wire brush. He left the epibiotas on the roots in the other three sections. He waited two weeks after the removal was complete and then counted the fish in all six sections again. The results are shown in Figure 1.

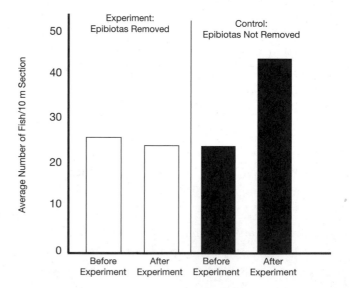

Figure 1

The second study was called the Survey Study. The biologist looked at many different sections of mangrove roots in sites across many square miles and in each section counted all the fish and measured the total area of each root in the section that was covered with epibiotas. The results are shown in Figure 2. Each circle represents a different site.

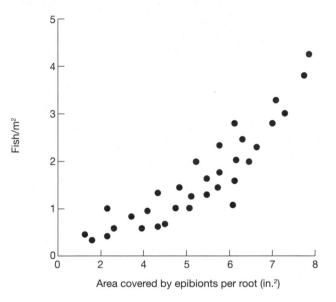

Figure 2

5. Which is the best reason for conducting the Survey Study?

   a. to confirm that the Experimental Removal Study was done properly

   b. to locate the best site for future studies

   c. to improve upon the Experimental Removal Study

   d. to confirm that the results of the first study are possible in real-life conditions

6. Based on Figure 2, what is the best description of the relationship between epibiotas and fish in the study area?

   a. As the total area of epibiotas increases, the number of fish decreases.

   b. As the total area of epibiotas increases, the number of fish increases.

   c. As the total area of epibiotas increases, the number of fish stays the same.

   d. As the total number of individual epibiotas increases, the number of fish increases.

7. In Figure 2, approximately what average density of fish would you expect to see at a site where each root averaged 7 square inches of epibiotas?

   a. 2

   b. 2.75

   c. 4

   d. 5.5

8. Which is the best description of the results of the Experimental Removal Study?

   a. Removal of epibiotas had no effect on fish numbers.

   b. Fish moved in where epibiotas were removed.

   c. Fish moved from where the epibiotas were removed to where they weren't.

   d. Fish moved in where epibiotas were not removed.

9. Which possible result for the Experimental Removal Study would demonstrate the strongest support for the hypothesis that epibiotas are a very important part of making mangrove roots into a good habitat for fish?

   a. the actual result shown in Figure 2
   b. The number of fish decreases a lot in the experimental sections and stays the same in the controls.
   c. The number of fish increases in the experimental sections and decreases in the controls.
   d. The number of fish decreases in both experimental sections and controls.

10. Yolande thinks that the chocolate explosion candy tastes more like chocolate than the chocolate blast candy. She analyzes a sample of each candy to see if chocolate explosion actually has more chocolate. Which of the following represents the hypothesis of her experiment?

    a. Chocolate explosion contains more chocolate than chocolate blast.
    b. Testing 20 of each candy reveals that the chocolate explosion averages 45% chocolate and the chocolate blast averages 50% chocolate.
    c. Chocolate explosion must contain more chocolate because it tastes like it does.
    d. Based on the results, chocolate explosion has 10% less chocolate than chocolate blast.

11. Christie believes that a loaded wagon will travel faster down a ramp than a standard wagon if the wagon has narrower wheels. A standard wagon has 3-inch-wide wheels. She makes special 2-inch-wide wheels, puts them on the wagon, and then times how long it takes the wagon to travel down a 45-degree ramp that is 100 feet long. What would be a good control for this experiment?

    a. Time an identical wagon with 3-inch wheels across a 100-foot horizontal surface.
    b. Time an identical wagon with 3-inch wheels down a 45-degree, 100-foot-long ramp.
    c. Time an identical wagon with 2-inch wheels down a 45-degree, 100-foot-long ramp.
    d. Time an identical wagon with 2-inch wheels across a 100-foot-long horizontal surface.

Questions 12–14 are based on the following information.

Lactose is a sugar found in dairy products (milk, cheese, etc.). Most children can easily digest lactose, but the majority of adults cannot. Adults who cannot digest lactose suffer from indigestion if they consume it, a condition known as lactose intolerance. People typically lose the ability to digest lactose in their late teens or early 20s.

However, a minority of humans are lactose tolerant and can continue to consume lactose into adulthood. Figures 3A and 3B are maps of Europe. The shaded area in Figure 3A shows the approximate area where almost all adults are lactose tolerant. (People whose ancestors originated in these areas, even if they no longer live there, are generally also lactose tolerant.) Lactose tolerance arose in the last 10,000 years, while lactose intolerance has existed since the very earliest humans.

Figure 3B shows the approximate area where approximately 6,500 years ago herding dairy animals was very common and the economy was heavily dependent on dairy products.

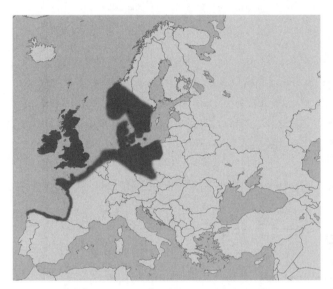

Figure 3A

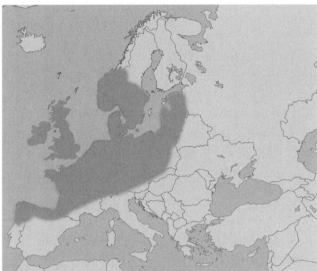

Figure 3B

12. Looking at the two maps, which statement is true?

   a. Lactose tolerance is highest in areas that had a prehistoric dairy economy.
   b. A prehistoric dairy economy developed because of lactose tolerance.
   c. Lactose tolerance is advantageous to lactose intolerance.
   d. Lactose tolerance started farther south and spread north.

13. Early humans were nomadic, always moving from place to place in search of food, and early humans were all lactose intolerant as adults. Lactose tolerance is the result of a mutation in one gene. What is the most likely explanation for the development of lactose tolerance?

   a. Early nomads were always moving and could not domesticate dairy animals, so they would have no access to milk.
   b. It was pure chance; there is no explanation.
   c. Babies need to be lactose tolerant so they can nurse.
   d. When animals were domesticated, milk was available past weaning, so it was an advantage to be able to consume it.

14. If you wanted to determine whether lactose tolerance made the economy based on dairy products possible, which information would be most useful?

   a. the year when the dairy economy began
   b. the first place where lactose tolerance developed
   c. the age of the lactose tolerance gene and the age of the dairy economy
   d. the average size of a family's dairy herd

15. There is a possibility that there is a ninth planet orbiting the sun at a great distance beyond Neptune, but it has never been observed. Which of the following offers the best support for the planet's existence?

   a. Astronomers have been looking for Planet 9 for nearly 100 years.
   b. Astronomers have observed motion of other objects that can be explained by Planet 9.
   c. At least 15% of astronomers believe that Planet 9 exists.
   d. Astronomers think they know where to look for Planet 9.

Questions 16–18 are based on the following information.

Flower color in snapdragon plants is controlled by one gene. The plant has red, white, or pink flowers. There are two different forms of the gene for flower color, or alleles, called *R* and *W*. *R* is associated with red flowers, and *W* is associated with white flowers. All red-flowered plants result from mating red-flowered plants with red-flowered plants for multiple generations, and all white-flowered plants result from mating white-flowered plants with white-flowered plants for multiple generations.

Six sets of matings between different snapdragon plants are carried out, and the results are shown in the following chart.

FLOWER COLOR OF PARENT 1	FLOWER COLOR OF PARENT 2	NUMBER OF RED-FLOWERED OFFSPRING	NUMBER OF WHITE-FLOWERED OFFSPRING	NUMBER OF PINK-FLOWERED OFFSPRING
Red	Pink	12	0	11
Red	Pink	7	0	9
Red	Pink	13	0	12
Pink	Pink	5	5	10
Pink	Pink	7	8	15
Pink	Pink	12	11	23

16. You hypothesize that the genotype, or genetic makeup, of pink-flowered plants is *RW*. What would be the best way to test that hypothesis?

   a. Cross a red-flowered plant with a white-flowered plant.
   b. Cross a red-flowered plant with a pink-flowered plant.
   c. Cross a red-flowered plant with a red-flowered plant.
   d. Cross a white-flowered plant with a white-flowered plant.

17. Looking at the chart, which of the following is true?

    a. Pink-flowered plants produce more red-flowered offspring than pink-flowered offspring when crossed with red-flowered plants.

    b. Pink-flowered plants produce more white-flowered offspring than red-flowered offspring when crossed with pink-flowered plants.

    c. Pink-flowered plants produce equal numbers of red-flowered and pink-flowered offspring when crossed with red-flowered plants.

    d. Pink-flowered plants will eventually produce three-quarters white flowers and one-quarter red flowers when crossed with pink-flowered plants.

18. From the results in the chart, what is the genotype of pink-flowered plants?

    a. *RR*

    b. *WW*

    c. *RW*

    d. It cannot be determined from the results of these matings.

Questions 19–23 are based on the following information.

Photosynthesis is the process in which plants use sunlight to convert carbon dioxide (CO_2) and water (H_2O) into glucose in their bodies. Oxygen is a by-product of the process. The effects of temperature and light intensity on photosynthesis were studied in two experiments.

Experiment 1

Persicaria perfoliata is a rapidly growing weed. Eight *Persicaria perfoliata* plants, each weighing 5 grams, were placed into eight separate small greenhouses. Each plant was given an identical, constant supply of CO_2 and water, but the temperature was different in each enclosure. The light intensity in each enclosure was 100 lux. At the end of two days, each plant was weighed again, and the results are shown in the table.

ENCLOSURE TEMPERATURE (°C)	MASS INCREASE AFTER 2 DAYS (g)
0	0.1
10	0.4
15	4.5
20	8
25	6
30	5
40	0
45	0

Experiment 2

An additional eight *Persicaria perfoliata* plants were placed into eight separate enclosures. Each of the enclosures was kept at 20°C with an identical, constant supply of CO_2 and water. The intensity of the light shining on each enclosure was different, and at the end of two days, each plant was weighed again. The results are shown in the table.

LIGHT INTENSITY (lux)	MASS INCREASE AFTER 2 DAYS (g)
0	0
4	0.2
10	0.7
15	1.2
50	5
75	7
100	9
120	10.5

19. If growth is a good measure of the rate of photosynthesis, what is the best conclusion that can be drawn about the effect of temperature on the rate of photosynthesis?

a. The rate of photosynthesis increases constantly with temperature.

b. The rate of photosynthesis peaks around 20°C and then gradually declines until 45°C.

c. The rate of photosynthesis increases rapidly above 0°C and then shuts down above 25°C.

d. The rate of photosynthesis peaks around 20°C and stops completely above 40°C.

20. In experiments 1 and 2, why is it necessary to keep the CO_2 concentration constant?

a. Too much CO_2 might suffocate the plants.

b. CO_2 is also a factor in photosynthesis, so the effect of temperature would be hard to tell from the effect of CO_2.

c. There needs to be enough CO_2 for the plants to grow enough to be measured.

d. CO_2 was kept constant for convenience; the exact concentration does not matter.

21. Which of the following graphs best illustrates the relationship between the rate of photosynthesis and light intensity shown in experiment 2?

a.

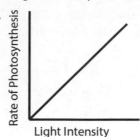

b.

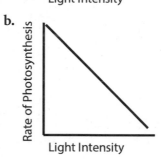

c.

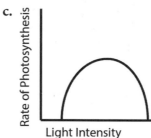

d.

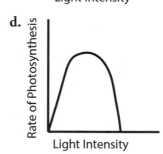

22. What hypothesis is being tested in experiment 2?
  a. Photosynthetic rate increases with light intensity up to 120 lux.
  b. Photosynthetic rate increases with light intensity.
  c. Photosynthetic rate is unconnected to light intensity.
  d. Many factors affect the rate of photosynthesis.

23. If experiment 1 were conducted at light levels of 1,000 lux, what would happen to the rate of photosynthesis at 20°C?
  a. The rate of photosynthesis would increase.
  b. The rate of photosynthesis would decrease.
  c. The rate of photosynthesis would remain the same.
  d. There is no way to tell from the information provided.

Questions 24 and 25 are based on the following information.

The graph shows different mammals and their average heart rates.

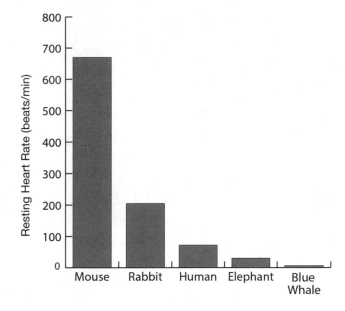

24. Judging from the graph, what can you conclude about mammal heart rates?
  a. Larger animals have smaller hearts.
  b. Smaller animals have larger hearts.
  c. Smaller hearts beat faster.
  d. Whales have the fastest heart rates.

25. From the information available, what would you estimate is the resting heart rate of a wolverine (adult wolverines weigh about 35 pounds)?
  a. 50 bpm
  b. 80 bpm
  c. 130 bpm
  d. 400 bpm

26. You are exploring a rain forest when you observe what you think is a new species of bird. Which piece of information would be most useful in confirming your claim?
   a. a photograph of the bird
   b. additional sightings of the bird
   c. recording the sounds of the bird
   d. a living specimen of the bird

Questions 27–30 are based on the following information.

Sea level, or the height of the ocean above the bottom of its basin, has been increasing since measurements were first made in the late 1800s. Sea level is measured either by satellites that can measure sea surface elevation or with tide gauges (a tide gauge is a device that measures the water level at high tide). The graph shows observed sea level rise over the level in 1900, averaged from different locations across the world (GMSL). The black line represents data recorded from tide gauges; the jagged gray line represents measurements taken by satellite.

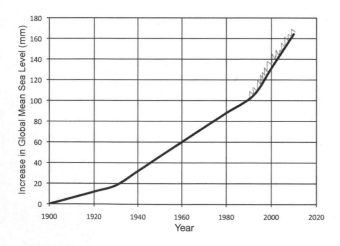

27. According to the tide gauges, during what time period did GMSL increase the most per year?
   a. 1900–1930
   b. 1930–1960
   c. 1960–1990
   d. 1990 to present day

28. What was the recorded sea level in the year 1900?
   a. <0 m
   b. 0 m
   c. >0 m
   d. 100 m

29. Which statement is true regarding the satellite data and the tide gauge data?
   a. The satellite data supports the basic trend of the recent tide gauge data.
   b. The satellite data and the tide gauge data are not connected at all.
   c. The satellite data is less valid than the tide gauge data.
   d. The satellite data undermines the tide gauge data since it is not identical.

30. Which question is best answered by this data set?
   a. Why is sea level rise increasing?
   b. Is satellite data more accurate than tide gauge data?
   c. How has the rate of sea level rise changed over time?
   d. How high will the sea level rise in 2030?

Questions 31–35 are based on the following information.

A geological fault is a crack in the earth where the land on one side of the crack moves relative to the land on the other side of the fault due to geological forces. The place where plates—the giant slabs of rock that the continents and oceans rest on—meet is called a plate boundary. Entire plates can also move relative to one another, acting like enormous faults. Faults may not move for years, but when they do, the movement is often sudden. Sudden, rapid movement of a fault results in an earthquake. Three of the most common types of faults are pictured. One type of plate boundary, a spreading zone, is also pictured.

The arrows indicate the direction of movement on either side of the fault or boundary.

Reverse Fault   Normal Fault   Strike Slip Fault

Spreading Zone

31. Which type of fault demonstrates mostly horizontal movement of land on each side of the fault?
  a. reverse fault
  b. normal fault
  c. strike slip fault
  d. spreading zone

32. If you discovered a new fault or boundary and had unlimited time, what would be an experiment that could be used to determine what type it is?
  a. Make a permanent marking across the fault.
  b. Place elevation meters on each side of the fault.
  c. Measure the width of the fault at regular intervals.
  d. Take rock samples from either side of the fault.

33. If older rock layers are typically below younger layers, at which type of fault or boundary is it possible to find older rock layers to be above the youngest layer?
  a. reverse fault
  b. normal fault
  c. strike slip fault
  d. spreading zone

34. If magma (molten rock) is circulating in the mantle beneath harder rocky layers, at which type of fault or boundary would you expect magma to rise up to the surface?
  a. reverse fault
  b. normal fault
  c. strike slip fault
  d. spreading zone

35. Considering only the faults, not spreading zones, which question can NOT be answered based solely on the information about fault movement in the diagram?
  a. An earthquake would cause the most damage at which kind of fault?
  b. Which kind of fault is most likely to see a drop in elevation on one side?
  c. Which type of fault is most likely to result in one side moving east while the other side moves west?
  d. What type of force will be applied to the land on each side of the fault?

36. Globally, the amount of CO_2 in the atmosphere decreases during the summer and rises during the winter. What is the best explanation for this pattern?

a. Cold winter air forces CO_2 out of the atmosphere.

b. In winter, plants are dormant and perform less photosynthesis.

c. There is more CO_2 released during the winter.

d. CO_2 stays the same, but measurement is less reliable during the winter.

37. A geologist is studying the distribution of phosphate deposits around the world. The geologist looks at marine deposits all over the planet and estimates the percentage of phosphate. Separately, she also measures phosphate in rock deposits that are completely terrestrial, not marine at all. Which of the following is a possible hypothesis for this study?

a. Phosphate is released from rocks by weathering.

b. Phosphate is more abundant in marine deposits than in terrestrial deposits.

c. Phosphate is very common in rock.

d. Phosphate can boost plant growth.

38. Mirabelle is conducting research on why chameleons change color. She hypothesizes that chameleons change color to camouflage themselves in their environment. She takes ten green chameleons and places them one at a time in an aquarium that is completely brown. After 30 minutes, she checks what color each chameleon is. Her results show that nine out of ten have remained green in color; the tenth turned brown. What statement best describes how the results apply to her hypothesis?

a. Her hypothesis was supported by the experiment.

b. Her hypothesis was not supported by the experiment.

c. She needs to run the experiment with another ten chameleons to fully test her hypothesis.

d. Chameleons change color due to temperature, not camouflage.

39. Obadiah notices that a spoon feels hotter to the touch after he leaves it in a cup of tea for a few minutes. This statement is an example of

a. a hypothesis.

b. a theory.

c. evidence.

d. an observation.

Questions 40–42 are based on the following information.

All materials have inherent characteristics, such as mass or streak color. The chart lists two properties, density (kg/m³) and hardness, for 12 different materials. Density is the mass of a material per a set amount of that material. Hardness is measured with the Mohs hardness scale, which ranges from 1 to 10 based on how difficult it is for a material to be scratched. For example, a material with a Mohs hardness of 1 can be scratched by a fingernail; a material with a Mohs hardness of 6 can be scratched with a metal nail.

MATERIAL	DENSITY (kg/m³)	MOHS HARDNESS
Lithium	534	0.6
Sodium	971	0.5
Calcium	1,540	1.5
Aluminum	2,712	3.0
Titanium	4,500	6.0
Iron	7,850	4.0
Steel	7,850	6.5
Bismuth	9,750	2.5
Mercury	13,593	0
Gold	19,320	2.5
Platinum	21,400	3.5
Osmium	22,610	7

40. Assume that all materials listed in the chart are in equally sized pieces. If the density of mineral oil is 870 kg/m³, which of the following materials will float in the oil?

   a. lithium

   b. sodium

   c. titanium

   d. platinum

41. You have a 1-ounce piece of each material. Each piece must be sent to a university in a different state. The shipping cost is based on the size of the package, not the weight or the distance. Under these conditions, which material will be cheapest to ship?

   a. aluminum

   b. iron

   c. gold

   d. osmium

42. What is the relationship between hardness and density?

   a. Hardness increases as density increases.

   b. Hardness decreases as density increases.

   c. Hardness stays flat as density decreases.

   d. There is no consistent relationship between hardness and density.

43. Diamonds are the hardest known naturally occurring material on Earth. With a Mohs hardness of 10, diamonds define the top of the scale. An engineer decides to test if diamonds really are harder than anything else. The engineer performs the test by trying to scratch a diamond with corundum, Mohs hardness 9. Why did the engineer use corundum?

   a. Corundum is known to be able to scratch diamonds.

   b. If a diamond can't be scratched by Mohs hardness 9, it can't be scratched by anything less hard.

   c. If the corundum can't scratch a diamond, then nothing can.

   d. The Mohs scale is faulty.

Questions 44 and 45 are based on the following information.

The rate of acceleration (the rate at which speed increases as an object moves) for an object, regardless of mass, falling freely toward the ground is 9.8 m/s.

44. Assuming no air resistance, if a 6-ounce aluminum cube and a 3-ounce aluminum cube are dropped from equal heights, which cube will hit the ground first?
 a. The 3-ounce cube will land first.
 b. The 6-ounce cube will land first.
 c. The cubes will hit the ground at the same time.
 d. It is impossible to tell from the information given.

45. The experiment is repeated, but this time, assume that air resistance is present. The 3-ounce cube has been replaced with a 3-ounce cylinder. If the objects were dropped from a height of 20 feet on a calm day, what would happen?
 a. The 3-ounce cylinder would clearly land first.
 b. The 6-ounce cube would clearly land first.
 c. It would depend on the wind speed.
 d. It would be difficult to tell.

Questions 46–50 are based on the following information.

Hydrogen peroxide is a common household disinfectant that can be used to clean surfaces or to clean minor wounds before bandaging. The chemical formula for hydrogen peroxide is $2H_2O_2$. Given time, hydrogen peroxide will degrade into water and oxygen through the following reaction:

$$2H_2O_2 \rightarrow 2H_2O + O_2$$

H_2O_2 is the reactant, and $H_2O + O_2$ are the reaction's products.

A catalyst is defined as a substance that speeds up the rate of a chemical reaction without itself being changed or used by the reaction. The catalyst must be in direct contact with the reagents to speed up the reaction. Hydrogen peroxide decomposes at a much faster rate in the presence of different catalysts than it does by itself. A chemist tested the rate of hydrogen peroxide decomposition in the presence of various catalysts. The following table lists the results of the experiment. Starting concentrations of hydrogen peroxide are kept constant.

H_2O_2 AMOUNT	PRODUCTS	CATALYST	TIME TO COMPLETION
75 cm³	$H_2O + O_2$	None	400 minutes
75 cm³	$H_2O + O_2$	0.5 g powdered platinum	10 seconds
75 cm³	$H_2O + O_2$	1.0 g powdered platinum	5 seconds
75 cm³	$H_2O + O_2$	1.0 g solid platinum	200 minutes
75 cm³	$H_2O + O_2$	0.5 g powdered lead oxide	6 seconds
75 cm³	$H_2O + O_2$	0.5 g powdered manganese oxide	6.5 seconds
75 cm³	$H_2O + O_2$	0.5 cm³ blood (contains catalase enzyme)	0.5 seconds

All reactions require some amount of energy to start, called the activation energy. Sometimes the required activation energy is very low, and often the reaction releases more energy afterward. The graph shows the general progression of a chemical reaction with and without a catalyst.

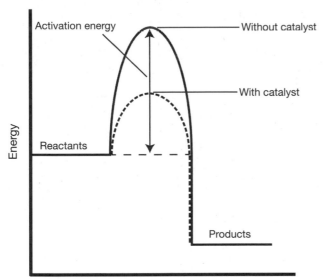

Progress of Reaction (Stage of Reaction)

46. If 0.25 g of powdered platinum is used as a catalyst, how much platinum will be left over at the end of the experiment?

a. 0 g

b. 0.125 g

c. 0.25 g

d. 0.5 g

47. Based on the information presented in the graph and the table, how does a catalyst speed up a chemical reaction?

a. Catalysts lower a reaction's activation energy.

b. Catalysts increase the concentration of reactants.

c. Catalysts increase the energy available to the reaction.

d. Catalysts decrease the amount of products from the reaction.

48. Which of the following is a potential hypothesis for this experiment?

a. Blood is the most effective catalyst.

b. Increasing the amount of platinum increases the reaction rate.

c. Catalysts speed up all reactions.

d. Different catalysts have different impacts on the rate of H_2O_2 decomposition.

49. The chemist believes that powdered platinum is a more effective catalyst because there is more surface area of catalyst to contact the reactants when the platinum is in powdered form. Which procedure would be the best way to test that hypothesis?

a. Include coarser powder, multiple small pieces of platinum, and highly polished platinum in the tests.

b. Test solid forms of the other catalysts in addition to the powdered forms.

c. Complete additional tests using 0.25 g, 0.75 g, 1.25 g, and 1.5 g of powdered platinum.

d. Complete the test again using powdered and solid platinum together.

50. Without additional information, what can you conclude from this experiment about catalase enzyme as a catalyst for H_2O_2 decomposition?

a. Catalase is the most effective catalyst there is for this reaction.

b. Catalase is a more effective catalyst than onlyplatinum.

c. Catalase is a much more effective catalyst than any of the metals tested.

d. A larger volume of blood would increase the reaction even more.

Social Studies

70 Minutes
50 Questions

This practice test is modeled on the content and timing of the official HiSET® Social Studies test and, like the official test, presents a series of questions that assess your ability to use social studies content knowledge and analyze and evaluate various kinds of social studies information.

Questions 1–3 are based on the following information.

Alaska's Arctic National Wildlife Refuge (ANWR) is a sizable nature preserve with an abundance of wildlife. It may also contain large deposits of crude oil. Some people want to drill for this oil, while others believe oil drilling would ruin the pristine wilderness.

Two points of view from the debate are presented below.

> There are some very good reasons to permit drilling in the ANWR. It could be done without damaging the environment. Presently, only 2,000 acres of the 19-million-acre ANWR refuge would be open to drilling. Most importantly, the economic benefits are potentially tremendous. Perhaps as many as 250,000 to 735,000 jobs nationwide would be created from the work. In addition, in these precarious times, drilling in an environmentally sensitive and prudent way is vital insurance against future energy shocks.

> First of all, we must point out that drilling in ANWR is not a path to energy independence. Nor will it lead to lower prices at the gas station. The United States Geological Survey estimates that ANWR has less than one year's supply of oil that would not reach the market

for at least ten years. Of vital concern, it must be said, is that the harm to wildlife and to the nation's greatest wildlife refuge would be irreparable. The area within ANWR targeted for drilling is vital to the entire region's ecosystem. We have seen oil spills in other locations that have caused massive devastation to the environment.

1. In the first source, which of the following is the main argument in support of drilling?
   a. the environmentally friendly drilling methods
   b. the loss of potential energy sources
   c. the economic benefits
   d. the protection of threatened wildlife

2. Which of the following is of most concern to the source that opposes drilling in the ANWR?
   a. finding better areas within ANWR to drill
   b. protecting ANWR wildlife and environment
   c. decreasing the amount of time from drilling to pump
   d. protecting the nation's sources of energy

3. Based on information presented in the two arguments, which of the following might best explain why balancing environmental protection with economic development can be very difficult?
   a. Reputable groups on both sides of an issue present contradictory claims, which confuses the debate.
   b. One side of the debate is not open to factual evidence.
   c. It is impossible to balance environmental protection with economic development.
   d. Environmental organizations are against all types of economic development.

4. The views expressed by the excerpt supporting drilling are probably most similar to those of

   a. a fishing boat captain who works the waters off ANWR.

   b. a member of an Alaskan Native American group that lives within ANWR.

   c. a lobbyist for an energy industry.

   d. an official with an environmental defense organization.

Questions 5–8 are based on the following information.

Within his annual address to Congress on December 2, 1823, President James Monroe outlined a U.S. policy on the new political order developing in North, South, and Latin America and the role of Europe in the Western Hemisphere. These statements, now known as the Monroe Doctrine, have become a cornerstone of U.S. foreign policy.

> [T]he occasion has been judged proper for asserting, as a principle in which the rights and interests of the United States are involved, that the American continents, by the free and independent condition which they have assumed and maintain, are henceforth not to be considered as subjects for future colonization by any European powers. . . . In the wars of the European powers in matters relating to themselves we have never taken any part, nor does it comport with our policy to do so. With the movements in this hemisphere we are of necessity more immediately connected. . . . We owe it, therefore, to candor and to the amicable relations existing between the United States and those powers to declare that we should consider any attempt on their part to extend their system to any portion of this hemisphere as dangerous to our peace and safety. With the existing colonies or dependencies of any European power we have not interfered and shall not interfere.

>   —from President Monroe's message to Congress, December 2, 1823

5. Which of the following outlines the central theme of the Monroe Doctrine?

   a. The United States has the right and duty to intervene in affairs among powers in Europe.

   b. The United States would consider existing European colonies in North America to be illegal.

   c. The United States would work with European powers to colonize remaining regions of North America.

   d. The Western Hemisphere was closed to future colonization by European powers.

6. Which of the following statements best justifies Monroe's position that European powers should respect the U.S. position of a closed Western Hemisphere?

   a. The United States agreed to not interfere in the affairs or wars between European powers.

   b. The United States was a growing military power.

   c. There were no more unsettled lands in the Americas to colonize.

   d. The European powers were incapable of creating sustainable colonies in the Americas.

7. In 1904, President Theodore Roosevelt announced an extension of the Monroe Doctrine that became known as the Roosevelt Corollary. The Roosevelt Corollary expanded the Monroe Doctrine and was used as a justification for U.S. intervention in Latin American affairs. Which of the following best explains how the Roosevelt Corollary changed the Monroe Doctrine?

a. The Monroe Doctrine concerned only European colonies in North America; the Roosevelt Corollary expanded that to include Latin America.

b. The Monroe Doctrine expressed United States' intention to promote further colonization; the Roosevelt Corollary declared that the United States would prohibit further colonization in Latin America.

c. The Monroe Doctrine expressed the United States' interest in colonizing South America; the Roosevelt Corollary expanded this interest to include Latin America.

d. The Monroe Doctrine expressed the United States' intention to not interfere with existing European colonies in the Americas; the Roosevelt Corollary stated that the United States would interfere if necessary.

8. According to the Monroe Doctrine, what was the U.S. position on existing colonies?

a. The United States will seek to disband any existing European colonies.

b. The United States will allow existing colonies to remain for a maximum of 50 years.

c. The United States has not and shall not interfere with the existing colonies or dependencies of any European power.

d. The United States is only concerned about existing North American colonies and has no interest in Latin or South America.

Questions 9–11 are based on the following information.

Inflation can produce many effects in the U.S. economy. The most obvious effect is that the dollar buys less. Because the purchasing power of the dollar falls as prices rise, a dollar loses value over time. A second effect is that inflation can change people's spending habits, disrupting the economy. In the early 1980s, for example, when prices went up, interest rates—the price of borrowed money—also went up. This caused spending on durable goods—goods that are not consumed immediately and that can be used for longer than three years—especially housing and cars, to fall significantly.

9. Which of the following is the most likely effect inflation has on lenders and borrowers?

a. Lenders will lower interest rates; borrowers will borrow more money.

b. Inflation causes lenders to raise interest rates; borrowers borrow less money.

c. Inflation will force lenders to raise interest rates; borrowers will borrow more money.

d. Inflation will cause lenders to keep interest rates stable; borrowers will borrow more money.

10. Which of the following would be the most likely effect on spending habits during a period of inflation for a retired person on a fixed income?

a. The person would spend more on durable goods that last for several years.

b. The person would cut back on all purchases.

c. The person would borrow more money to make up for the drop in purchasing power.

d. The person would cut back on durable goods purchases but increase other purchases.

11. Based on information in the passage, which of the following businesses would be affected most by a sharp increase in inflation?
   a. a home construction company
   b. an auto repair shop
   c. a discount department store
   d. a fast food restaurant

Questions 12–15 are based on the following information.

Criminal law concerns offenses, called *crimes*, committed against the public interest as defined by a government. In criminal law, the government charges someone with a crime and is always the prosecutor. The person accused of the crime is the defendant. Crimes are punishable by fines, imprisonment, or both. Civil law, on the other hand, concerns disputes or offenses, called torts, between two or more individuals or between individuals and the government. In general, a civil case is a private complaint that accuses a person or organization, including government bodies, of failing to uphold a legal obligation or exercising more authority than existing law allows. If successful, the party initiating the lawsuit, called the plaintiff, may be awarded money by the court or may obtain a court order requiring the defendant to do something or to stop doing something.

12. Which of the following is an example of a criminal case?
   a. After surgery, a patient sues her doctor for malpractice because of ongoing health issues.
   b. A wife sues her husband for divorce.
   c. One brother sues his younger brother concerning the distribution of an inheritance.
   d. The state attorney general prosecutes a voter for casting multiple votes in an election.

13. Which of the following is an example of a civil case?
   a. A corporate executive is charged with bribing a federal judge.
   b. A young woman is arrested for breaking into a friend's apartment.
   c. A homeowner sues the development association for not allowing satellite television dish installation.
   d. A person is charged with driving without a valid driver's license.

14. Which of the following conclusions can be drawn from the information in the passage?
   a. Villages, towns, and states cannot initiate civil law cases.
   b. Being denied one's constitutional rights is a civil law case.
   c. Governments can be the defendant in a criminal case.
   d. Civil case defendants who lose can be imprisoned or fined.

15. Which of the following actions would the federal government most likely take if it discovered a hospital overbilling Medicare and Medicaid patients?
   a. Initiate a civil lawsuit.
   b. Support the patients who were overcharged in their civil suits against the hospital.
   c. Criminally charge the hospital with fraud.
   d. Sentence the hospital administrators to prison.

Questions 16–19 are based on the following information.

From around 1300 to 1600, an explosion of creativity and artistic flowering swept through Europe. Historians call this period the Renaissance, a term that means rebirth. This era was a rebirth of art and learning. European scholars rediscovered the works of ancient Greek and Roman poets, philosophers, geographers, and mathematicians. Although it started as renewed interest in the past, the Renaissance quickly led to a renewed commitment to reason, eventually triggering a scientific revolution.

Renaissance scholars studied not only ancient Greek and Roman texts but also Arab texts. From the Arabs they acquired the knowledge of key navigational instruments such as the astrolabe and the compass, which the Arabs acquired from the Chinese. The most important development, however, was that European shipbuilders, most notably the Portuguese, were learning to build faster and more reliable ships capable of long-distance voyages. New sail shapes and rudder designs adopted from Arab traders greatly increased maneuverability and sailing speeds. First the Renaissance, then a scientific revolution, and finally Christopher Columbus's voyage to the New World—a chain of events that changed the course of history.

16. Which of the following is the most accurate title for this passage?
  a. Advances in Portuguese Shipbuilding
  b. Chinese Inventions and Their Influence
  c. Rediscovering the Ancient Greek and Roman Greats
  d. How the Renaissance Led to a New Era of Exploration

17. Which of the following statements is supported by information in the passage?
  a. Renaissance scholars must have known about ancient Chinese technologies.
  b. Without the Arabs, the Renaissance would never have begun.
  c. Early Arab navigational technologies far surpassed European technologies prior to the Renaissance.
  d. The Chinese were influential navigators and explorers.

18. Which of the following technologies most likely contributed to successful Portuguese explorations?
  a. the astrolabe
  b. faster and more reliable ships
  c. navigation charts of distant lands
  d. the compass

19. What does the passage imply about the Renaissance and Columbus's voyage?
  a. Columbus's voyage was the greatest achievement of the Renaissance.
  b. Columbus's voyage, although important, was less an achievement than Portuguese sailing innovations.
  c. Without the Renaissance, Columbus's voyage would not have been possible.
  d. The Renaissance ended with Columbus's voyage.

Questions 20–22 are based on the following information.

The gross domestic product (GDP) is a measure of the economy's output. GDP is the dollar value of all final goods and services produced in a country in a year.

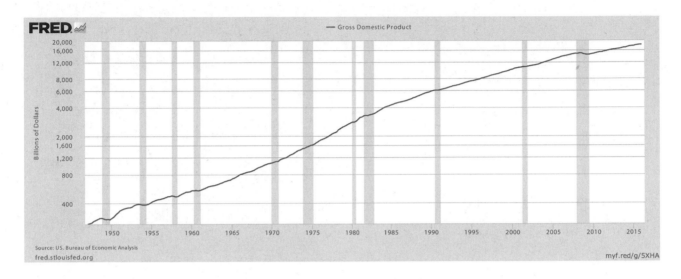

20. Which of the following is the most likely purpose of the gray vertical bars?
   a. The bars mark off every five years.
   b. The gray bars indicate periods in which the United States was at war.
   c. The gray areas show a spike upward in GDP.
   d. The bars identify periods where the GDP dropped.

21. Which of the following conclusions is supported by the graph?
   a. The period from 1950 to 2015 was one of steady increase in GDP.
   b. The early years of the 1950s showed an upward spike in GDP.
   c. The 1970s showed lower than average GDP gains.
   d. GDP increased nearly three times from 1950 to 2015.

22. According to the economic principle called Okun's Law, there is a direct correlation between economic growth and the unemployment rate. As an economy grows, unemployment drops. Which of the following is a valid conclusion using Okun's Law and the graph?
   a. The entire 1960s would have experienced high levels of unemployment.
   b. The unemployment rate during 1981–1983 would have risen.
   c. The period 2008–2010 saw a sharp drop in the unemployment totals.
   d. The end of the 1940s would have been marked by steady gains in employment numbers.

Questions 23–25 are based on the following information.

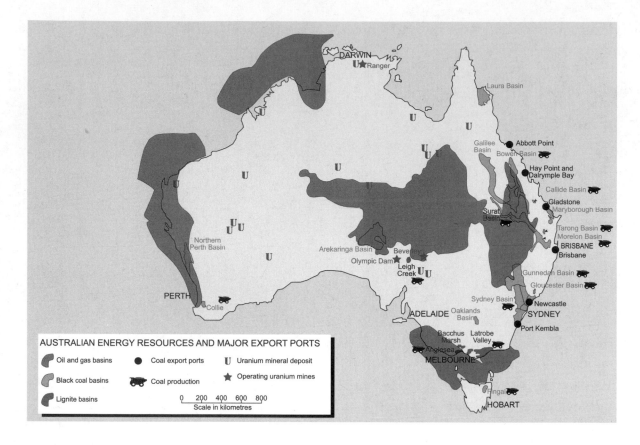

AUSTRALIAN ENERGY RESOURCES AND MAJOR EXPORT PORTS

- Oil and gas basins
- Black coal basins
- Lignite basins
- Coal export ports
- Coal production
- U Uranium mineral deposit
- ★ Operating uranium mines

Scale in kilometres
0 200 400 600 800

23. Which of the following is the dominate natural resource near Sydney, on the southeast coast?

a. coal

b. oil and gas

c. lignite

d. uranium

24. Which of the following assumptions can be based on information from the map?

a. The lignite industry must be one of the larger employers in Australia.

b. The entire west coast of Australia must be poorly developed.

c. The most industrialized area of Australia is the east coast.

d. The coal production capabilities of the region around Darwin have been consumed.

25. Based on the map, which of the following is a valid conclusion?

a. Australia does not have a significant shipping industry.

b. The west coast of Australia is the center of Australia's coal export industry.

c. Oil and gas do not contribute much to the Australian GDP.

d. The majority of Australia's uranium deposits have yet to be developed.

Questions 26–29 are based on the following information.

In the landmark Supreme Court case of *Marbury* v. *Madison* (1803), the Court ruled that an act of Congress in conflict with the Constitution was void and that it is the function of the Court to determine whether such a conflict exists. The decision marked the first time the Supreme Court asserted the power of judicial review—the power to decide whether laws passed by Congress were constitutional and to strike down those that were not.

In his opinion, Marshall wrote:

> It is emphatically the province and duty of the of the judicial department to say what the law is. Those who apply the rule to particular cases must of necessity expound and interpret that rule. If two laws conflict with each other, the courts must decide on the operation of each.

26. What was the implication of *Marbury* v. *Madison*?
   a. The judicial branch could write legislation.
   b. The Constitution was no longer valid.
   c. Congress was essentially placed under the power of the judicial branch.
   d. The Supreme Court was defined as the final authority on interpreting the Constitution.

27. Which of the following best summarizes the main duty of the judiciary according to Chief Justice John Marshall?
   a. Rewrite laws that are ruled unconstitutional.
   b. Interpret the meaning of the law—the Constitution.
   c. Provide checks and balances against Congress.
   d. Revise the Constitution to align it with congressional objectives.

28. Thomas Jefferson, who was president when *Marbury* v. *Madison* was decided, disagreed with Marshall's support of judicial review. Jefferson later wrote: "My construction of the Constitution . . . is that each department is truly independent of the others, and has an equal right to decide for itself what is the meaning of the Constitution in the cases submitted to its action. . . ."

What do Jefferson's words suggest he thinks?
   a. The executive department and the president should hold final constitutional authority.
   b. Constitutional meaning is arbitrary and therefore irrelevant and unnecessary to governing the nation.
   c. Judicial review violates the principles of separation of powers.
   d. The Constitution needs to be amended.

29. Which of the following best describes why the principle of judicial review has been a controversial subject?
   a. The Constitution does not give the Supreme Court the power of judicial review.
   b. The Supreme Court has prevented any action to eliminate or weaken judicial review.
   c. Judicial review had been proven time and time again to be ineffective.
   d. The Constitution prevents Congress or the executive branch from ignoring judicial review.

Questions 30–34 are based on the following information.

Mikhail Gorbachev became the Soviet Union's new secretary general in 1985. By the late 1980s the Soviet economy was suffering from years of inefficient central planning and huge expenditures on the arms race. A life-long Marxist and Soviet bureaucrat, Gorbachev introduced a policy of economic reform, known as *perestroika*, or "restructuring." This new policy allowed some limited free-market mechanisms into the Soviet economy and made modest attempts to democratize the Soviet political system. Gorbachev also introduced *glasnost*, or "openness." Under *glasnost*, the freedoms of speech, the press, and access and dissemination of information were significantly expanded. Gorbachev's new policies spread quickly and were embraced by citizens in Soviet-bloc countries, often leading to civil unrest.

30. Which of the following best explains why foreign observers might have been taken by surprise by Gorbachev's introduction of *glasnost* and *perestroika*?
   a. Secretary generals of the Soviet Union had very little power to make such sweeping changes.
   b. These policies had been tried before but had failed.
   c. Gorbachev was a Marxist, and he introduced policies that were contrary to the Soviet system.
   d. Gorbachev was known to have opposed any progressive policies.

31. Which of the following statements is best supported by information in the passage?
   a. The Soviet Union was losing ground in the Cold War.
   b. Gorbachev was a minor political figure in the twentieth century.
   c. Gorbachev was an extremely popular leader of the Soviet Union.
   d. Gorbachev completely renounced his Marxist ideology.

32. Which of the following is an inference that can be made about the spread of *glasnost*?
   a. Freedom of speech always leads to unrest.
   b. Citizens in western countries opposed *glasnost* because of its negative effects.
   c. *Glasnost* allowed people to criticize governments and demand more and more freedoms.
   d. The Soviet government would eventually repeal the policy of *glasnost*.

33. During Gorbachev's leadership of the Soviet Union, U.S. President Ronald Reagan continued an aggressive foreign policy approach against Soviet-style communism, while keeping the lines of communication open. Reagan also began a massive military buildup to deter possible Soviet nuclear attacks. What do Reagan's actions suggest?
   a. He feared the spread of *glasnost* throughout Eastern Europe.
   b. Reagan did not trust that the Soviet Union would adopt Gorbachev's new policies.
   c. He opposed introducing free-market concepts into the Soviet economy.
   d. Reagan wanted to isolate the Soviet Union and all its satellite nations.

34. Which of the following would least likely be a consequence of *perestroika*?
   a. elections with multiple candidates
   b. government takeover of key industries
   c. private ownership of businesses
   d. option to use a secret ballot when voting

Questions 35–38 are based on the following information.

The mayor-council form of city government follows the traditional principle of separation of powers. Executive power belongs to a mayor, and legislative power to a council. Voters elect a mayor and the members of a city council. Two main types of mayor-council government exist, depending on the power given to the mayor. These two types are the strong-mayor system and the weak-mayor system

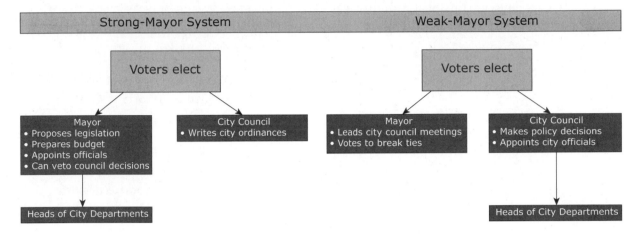

35. Which of the following statements best describes the "weak-mayor system?"
   a. Mayors are excluded from council meetings.
   b. Mayors only get a half-vote when appointing city department heads.
   c. Mayors are not allowed to vote on policy matters.
   d. Mayors do not have the authority to make policy or appoint department heads.

36. Which of the following statements reflects a weak-mayor system of government?
   a. The mayor vetoes the council's decision to loosen sign restrictions in the downtown district.
   b. The mayor hires a relative to replace the retiring manager of the streets and sanitation department.
   c. The mayor decides to increase revenue by raising the local sales tax against the advice of the council.
   d. The city council overwhelmingly passes a new city ordinance against the opinion of the mayor.

37. Which of the following is supported by the information in the paragraph and charts?

    a. Department heads report to the mayor in a strong-mayor system.

    b. A weak-mayor system allows a mayor to prepare the town budget.

    c. Council decisions are final in a strong-mayor system.

    d. A strong-mayor system requires a mayor to be willing to follow city council authority rather than lead.

38. Hank Johnson, the head of his city's water department, has had six individual meetings with the members of the city council, which controls the city's departments. Each council member has ordered him to accomplish different tasks and meet conflicting goals. Consequently, Hank has not been able to successfully implement any of the orders because he is unsure which task is most important.

Which of the following statements best explains why it is important who controls the heads of city departments?

    a. Having one strong boss operating without oversight will allow jobs to be completed much quicker and more efficiently.

    b. Department heads cannot do their jobs if they must listen to those who do not have hiring authority.

    c. Having too many bosses with conflicting ideas can lead to mismanagement and duplication of efforts.

    d. Department heads would spend too much money if they had to implement every idea a city council presents.

Questions 39–41 are based on the following information.

Between 1865—the year the the Civil War ended—and 1914—the year World War I began—nearly 25 million Europeans immigrated to the United States. By the late 1890s, more than half of all immigrants in the United States were from eastern and southern Europe. This pattern of immigration held until about 1960, when the numbers and origins of immigrants began to shift. According to the U.S. Census Bureau, 67% of the foreign-born population in 2010 lived in states in the West and South, including large numbers in Texas, California, and Florida.

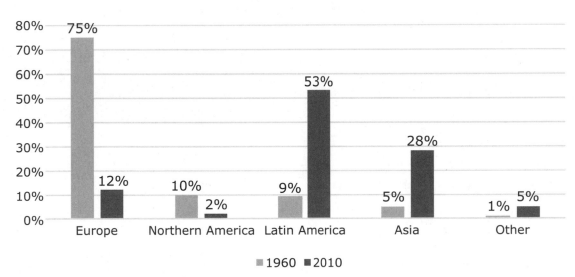

Change in Foreign-Born Population by Region of Birth
1960–2010

39. The region that has experienced the greatest decrease in the number of immigrants to the United States is
a. Latin America.
b. Europe.
c. Asia.
d. Northern America.

40. Which statement best describes the shift in the foreign-born population since 1960?
a. Asian immigrants account for the most foreign-born residents in the United States as of 2010.
b. More immigrants now come from Europe and Asia than the other regions combined.
c. Europe continues to provide the most immigrants to the United States.
d. Latin America provides more than twice as many immigrants than the other regions combined.

41. Based on the information in the paragraph and graph, which of the following is the most valid statement?

a. Texas, California, and Florida probably have large numbers of immigrants from Latin America.

b. The Midwest and Northeast must have many immigrants from Asia.

c. The West and South probably have large numbers of immigrants from Northern America.

d. Texas, Florida, and California have more new immigrants than the other 47 states combined.

Questions 42–44 are based on the following information.

PRINCIPLES OF AMERICAN DEMOCRACY
Rule of Law
All people, including those who govern, are bound by the law.
Limited Government
Government is not all-powerful—it may do only those things that the people have given it the power to do.
Consent of the Governed
American citizens are the source of all governmental power.
Individual Rights
In the American democracy, individual rights are protected by government.
Representative Government
People elect leaders to make the laws and govern on their behalf.

42. Which principle of American democracy prevents a president from serving more terms than allowed in the Twenty-Second Amendment of the Constitution?

a. limited government

b. individual rights

c. representative government

d. rule of law

43. Which of the following practices best reflects the principle of representative government?

a. working for an organization that polls public opinions

b. submitting a "letter to the editor" in a local newspaper

c. voting for a state senator

d. fulfilling obligatory jury duty

44. According to the principles of American democracy, who is the source of power in the representative democracy?

a. the Constitution

b. american citizens

c. the representatives the American people elect

d. the president

Questions 45–47 are based on the following information.

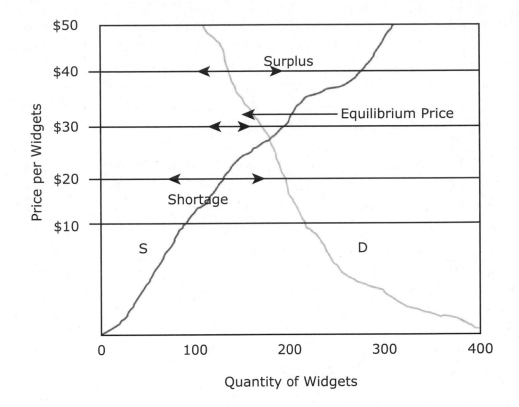

45. The price adjustment graph shows that at a price of more than $30
   a. consumer demand would remain stable.
   b. consumer demand would increase.
   c. supply would increase and cause a surplus.
   d. supply would decrease, causing a shortage.

46. The graph illustrates that at the equilibrium price of widgets,
   a. there may be a shortage of gains.
   b. consumers will demand more than 400 units.
   c. demand will fall.
   d. producers will supply nearly 200 units.

47. What is the most likely action for the producer if consumer demand drops sharply?
   a. The producer will decrease supplies.
   b. The producer will raise the price.
   c. The producer will keep supplies stable.
   d. The producer will increase supplies and lower the price.

Questions 48–50 are based on the following information.

By 1871, Jay Gould had become the most powerful railroad man in New York. He never formally learned how to run a railroad, but he understood how the stock market worked. A decade later he controlled the largest rail network in the nation and had amassed a great fortune. Gould's story illustrates the remarkable mixture of politics and business in the Gilded Age, a term invented by Mark Twain, to describe 1870–1900 America. *Gilded* means "covered with a thin layer of gold." The Gilded Age was one of great industrialization, poverty, crime, and disparities in wealth between the rich and the poor.

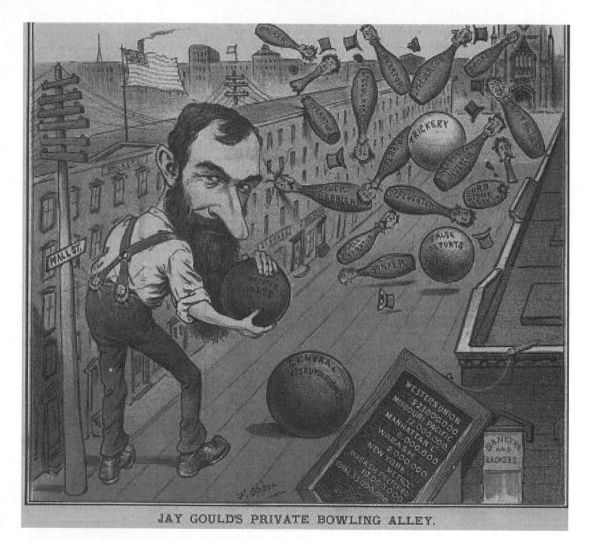

JAY GOULD'S PRIVATE BOWLING ALLEY.

48. What is the subject of the cartoon?
   a. the inexperience of railroad tycoons when dealing with Wall Street bankers
   b. the dishonesty and corruptness of Jay Gould
   c. the rise of the Wall Street banks.
   d. the rise of bowling in post-Reconstruction America

49. According to the cartoon, how did Jay Gould amass his fortune?
   a. by chance and good luck
   b. through dishonest means, such as trickery and false reports
   c. by working with other businesses and partners on Wall Street
   d. through hard work and determination

50. Which of the following statements best describes how Jay Gould reflects the Gilded Age?
   a. Gould's financial decisions were as valuable as gold.
   b. Gould helped Americans to aspire to overcome unimpressive backgrounds.
   c. Gould's wealth and persona covered up his dishonesty and corruption.
   d. Gould's corruptness covered up and overshadowed the noble work of many Americans in the era.

Practice Test 3
Answers and Explanations

Language Arts—Reading

To calculate your HiSET® score on the Language Arts—Reading section, first take a look at the correct answer for each of the 40 questions of the exam. Count up your **correct answers** only, and give yourself 1 point for each. Then, add up all of your points. This is your **raw score**.

Find your raw score and your **scaled score** in the following table. Remember, for each test section, a passing score is 8. (For the essay, a passing score is 2.)

You need a scaled score of 45 to pass the complete HiSET® exam.

LANGUAGE ARTS—READING SCORING			
RAW	SCALED	RAW	SCALED
0	1	21	12
1	2	22	12
2	3	23	13
3	4	24	13
4	5	25	13
5	6	26	14
6	7	27	14
7	7	28	14
8	8	29	15
9	8	30	15
10	9	31	15
11	9	32	15
12	9	33	16
13	10	34	17
14	10	35	17
15	10	36	18
16	11	37	18
17	11	38	19
18	11	39	20
19	11	40	20
20	12		

1. **The correct answer is choice c.** Earlier in the paragraph, the narrator noted that Polly is "tiny," and this line refines that information with a more descriptive image. Choice **a** is incorrect because this is the first line of the paragraph, and it cannot refine information from earlier in the paragraph because there is no information in the paragraph before this opening line. Choice **b** is incorrect because the information in this line is new to the paragraph, and it is this information that the correct answer refines. Choice **d** is incorrect because it merely describes additional details that make Polly look like a doll; it does not repeat information already stated in more refined language.

2. **The correct answer is choice d.** Mrs. Bretton's behavior throughout this passage seems genuine, and she expresses true concern about Polly both when Polly is travelling in the rain and when Polly arrives and might be cold and wet. Choice **a** is incorrect because the genuineness of Mrs. Bretton's behavior overall contradicts the idea that she may only be reacting with concern because she is expected to react with concern. Choice **b** is incorrect because there is no evidence in the passage that Polly has a particular opinion about rain. Choice **c** is incorrect because Mrs. Bretton only reacts to the rain in terms of how it might affect Polly and not whether it might cause a flood.

3. **The correct answer is choice d.** In paragraph 12, the narrator indicates that Mrs. Bretton was "not generally a caressing woman: even with her deeply-cherished son," but she expresses affection toward Polly by kissing the girl. Choice **a** is incorrect because the narrator specifies that Mrs. Bretton is not sentimental with her son. Choice **b** is incorrect because affection and comfort are not the same thing: There is not evidence to support the idea that Mrs. Bretton is more comfortable with Polly than with her own son. Choice **c** is incorrect because the narrator states that Mrs. Bretton cherishes her son, and affection is not the only way one might express loving feelings.

4. **The correct answer is choice a.** Polly states that she will not always be content to live with Mrs. Bretton, which suggests that they may have problems in the future. Choice **b** is incorrect because Polly's statement about her contentment indicates that her relationship with Mrs. Bretton will not always be loving. Choice **c** is incorrect because there is no evidence that the two characters will have trouble getting to know each other. Choice **d** is incorrect because perhaps Mrs. Bretton and Polly will be so fond of each other that they will be saddened when Polly's papa arrives to take her away, but there is not enough evidence to make such a prediction at this point in the passage.

5. The correct answer is choice b. As soon as Warren brings Polly into the school, she wants to be put down on the floor and to get out of her shawl, which indicates that she wanted to get settled in her new environment. Choice **a** is incorrect because it assumes that Polly wanted to be put on the floor because Warren made her uncomfortable, and there is not enough evidence to reach such a conclusion about her feelings. Choice **c** is incorrect because Polly does not seem to express excitement in this passage. Choice **d** is incorrect because Polly never seems particularly afraid in this passage.

6. The correct answer is choice d. The word "sent" makes the most sense if used in place of "dispatched" in the sentence. Choice **a** is incorrect because it is more likely that a servant would be sent to do something than that the servant would be allowed to volunteer to perform a task. Choice **b** is incorrect because it is not likely that servant was specifically hired to perform this one task. Choice **c** is incorrect because it does not make sense to say that a servant was "designed" to do a particular task.

7. The correct answer is choice a. The author is implying that one rarely thinks about powerful adults being small children in this statement. Choice **b** is incorrect because a conclusion like this requires some specific evidence, and there is no such evidence in this passage. Choice **c** is incorrect because a conclusion like this requires some specific evidence, and there is no such evidence in this passage. Choice **d** is incorrect because the author would not likely have spent so much time discussing Napoleon's childhood if he felt that it was not important.

8. The correct answer is choice c. In these paragraphs, Napoleon expresses quite a few opinions about his mother, but the idea that she was responsible for his success is a conclusion that he draws. Choices **a**, **b**, and **d** are incorrect because they are opinions, not conclusions.

9. The correct answer is choice d. In paragraph 3, the author expresses his own opinion that Letizia Bonaparte was "beautiful" and "energetic" and then quotes Napoleon's own very positive opinions about his mother. Therefore, it is clear that both the author and Napoleon thought highly of Letizia Bonaparte. Choice **a** is incorrect because the author refers to the fact that Napoleon was famous without expressing any opinion about whether Napoleon deserved to become so famous. Choice **b** is incorrect because although Napoleon seemed very dependent on his mother, the author only speaks positively of Letizia Bonaparte and never suggests that Napoleon was *too* dependent on her. Choice **c** is incorrect because the author clearly shares Napoleon's feelings about Letizia Bonaparte.

10. The correct answer is choice d. In paragraph 1, the author briefly describes the common image of Napoleon as a warrior but then goes on to show that there was more to Napoleon than his warlike nature by showing how much Napoleon loved his own mother. Choice **a** is incorrect because the fact that the author provides details that show a different side to Napoleon than that image suggests that the author was not describing the image to show its accuracy. Choice **b** is incorrect because even though there was more to Napoleon than his warlike image, he was still warlike, so that image could not be described as completely false. Choice **c** is incorrect because there is no indication in the passage that Napoleon was uncomfortable with his warlike image.

11. **The correct answer is choice b.** In paragraph 3, the author writes that "the high position which [Napoleon] attained was due largely to the careful way in which she brought him up," and includes a quote from Napoleon stating, "It is to my mother . . . that I owe my success and any great thing I have accomplished." Choice **a** is incorrect because only Napoleon refers to his mother's courage in the passage; the author does not make a similar observation about her. Choice **c** is incorrect because only the author describes Letizia Bonaparte as beautiful and energetic, and these opinions are not repeated in the passage. Choice **d** is incorrect because there is no indication that Letizia Bonaparte was a military leader like her son would become.

12. **The correct answer is choice a.** Much of this passage discusses Napoleon's relationship with his mother, which he believed had a great influence on his success as a powerful military leader and ruler, so an analysis of how Napoleon became so powerful should begin with the information in this passage. Choice **b** is incorrect because although there is a little description of the Corsican landscape in paragraph 2, there is hardly enough to be useful in a complete essay about the island's geography. Choice **c** is incorrect because although paragraph 5 discusses the Bonaparte house, that description would not be of much use to a tourist who might be planning to visit the house. Choice **d** is incorrect because Napoleon's relationship with his soldiers is only briefly mentioned in paragraph 1; there is not enough information on that topic for this passage to be an adequate resource for someone researching it.

13. **The correct answer is choice c.** After Ralph suggests that no country is safe for the thief, Stuart exclaims "Pshaw!" Ralph reacts as if Stuart had said he did not believe Ralph's suggestion, and the fact that Stuart's "Pshaw!" is an exclamation implies an extreme feeling about the suggestion. Choice **a** is incorrect because Stuart's exclamation seems more designed to express something about his own feelings than to make Ralph feel angry. Choice **b** is incorrect because although Stuart disagrees with Ralph, there is no evidence that he is angry with Ralph. Choice **d** is incorrect because Stuart's exclamation seems to express a very strong feeling about Ralph's comment.

14. **The correct answer is choice b.** Ralph immediately follows his nonliteral comment by observing that "a man can now go round [the world] ten times more quickly than a hundred years ago." Choice **a** is incorrect because the phrase is not meant to be taken literally. Choice **c** is incorrect because there is no discussion of how perceptions change as one gets older. Choice **d** is incorrect because there is no discussion of how perceptions change as one becomes more educated.

15. **The correct answer is choice b.** Although there are four men playing the game in this passage, only Stuart and Ralph get into a deep discussion about the thief, which indicates that they share interest in the story. Choice **a** is incorrect because only Stuart expresses the opinion that the thief is very shrewd. Choice **c** is incorrect because only Ralph agrees with Phileas Fogg. Choice **d** is incorrect because although Stuart and Ralph are having an argument in this passage, one argument is not enough evidence to conclude that two characters are extremely argumentative in general.

16. The correct answer is choice c. Fogg's statement that a person could travel around the world in 80 days is so specific that it is likely he has already thought a lot about how long such a trip would take. Choice **a** is incorrect because Fogg had clearly been interested in the argument; otherwise he probably would not have gotten involved in it. Choice **b** is incorrect because more evidence is needed to reach such a specific conclusion. Choice **d** is incorrect because there is no evidence in the passage to suggest that Fogg was lying about how long it would take to travel around the world.

17. The correct answer is choice d. As the discussion of the robbery in this excerpt from a book called *Around the World in 80 Days* becomes a discussion about how one could travel the world in 80 days, it is likely that such a trip will be more important than the robbery as this story continues. Choice **a** is incorrect because there is no evidence that the four men will commit a crime of their own just because they are discussing a crime. Choice **b** is incorrect because simply discussing the robbery does not prove that one could travel around the world in 80 days in itself. Choice **c** is incorrect because the simple fact that Stuart and Ralph are having an argument is not enough to indicate that the two characters dislike each other.

18. The correct answer is choice b. "Reasons" is the only answer choice that would make sense if used in place of "grounds" in paragraph 2.

19. The correct answer is choice a. Overall, the passage explains the role food plays in Pennsylvania Dutch culture. Choice **b** is incorrect because even though the author mentions several Pennsylvania Dutch dishes, and even mentions a few ingredients in some of those dishes, this passage does not actually contain any full recipes. Choice **c** is incorrect because it is not likely that the few dishes mentioned in this passage are all the foods the Pennsylvania Dutch eat. Choice **d** is incorrect because although the passage begins by mentioning that "The Pennsylvania Dutch are a hard working people," the details that follow are more focused on their food than their work ethic.

20. The correct answer is choice a. The overall tone of this passage is lighthearted, and using the warm and informal phrase "wonderful good" to describe Pennsylvania Dutch cooking contributes to that lighthearted tone. Choice **b** is incorrect because simply using the word "hearty" has no effect on the tone. Choice **c** is incorrect because the term "folk art" has much less effect on the lighthearted tone than the cheerier "wonderful good" does. Choice **d** is incorrect because a word such as "standardized" would more likely contribute to a formal or scientific tone, and that is not the kind of tone this passage has.

21. The correct answer is choice c. Not everyone may agree that the dishes Pennsylvania Dutch recipes produce are tasty. Choice **a** is incorrect because it is a fact, not an opinion. Choice **b** is incorrect because it is an observation, not an opinion. Choice **d** is incorrect because it is a fact that cannot be argued.

22. **The correct answer is choice c.** The passage discusses the role food plays in Pennsylvania Dutch folklore in paragraph 3, and this paragraph discusses the folkloric origins of trick or treating—or asking for food from door to door. Choice **a** is incorrect because the passage does not discuss the European origins of Pennsylvania Dutch customs. Choice **b** is incorrect because the passage and the paragraph mention in passing the fact that fruit is sometimes eaten as a snack or treat; this is not a central concern of either piece. Choice **d** is incorrect because only the paragraph refers to a custom that has changed over time.

23. **The correct answer is choice b.** The author explains that the making of apple butter "is an all-day affair," so it is clearly time consuming. Choice **a** is incorrect because although the author indicates that it is time consuming, he or she also describes it as "light work" and an affair that "has the air of a holiday to it," which is not how one would describe a hard chore. Choice **c** is incorrect because something that children can do as "light work" probably does not require special skills. Choice **d** is incorrect because something is not childish simply because children are capable of doing it.

24. **The correct answer is choice a.** The poem is about how a boy observes an aircraft, which is something he must get used to seeing now, and how observing and accepting that change causes him to grow into a man. Choice **b** is incorrect because it does not account for all of the information in the poem. Choice **c** is incorrect because it is not his resting that causes the boy to grow into a man; it is his observation and acceptance of change. Choice **d** is incorrect because the boy does not actually seem frightened of the aircraft.

25. **The correct answer is choice a.** The poet uses "pallid" to describe chalk, which is usually white, so "pale" is the most likely definition of the word. Choices **b**, **c**, and **d** are incorrect because "poor," "paltry," and "pleasing" are not words one would use to describe chalk and would make less sense than "pallid" if used in place of it in stanza 1.

26. **The correct answer is choice b.** Stanza 2 describes the simple, dreamy, and old-fashioned environment that the appearance of a modern aircraft disrupts. Choice **a** is incorrect because although the boy probably finds pleasure in the environment described in stanza 2, the appearance of the aircraft shatters the peacefulness of that environment. Choice **c** is incorrect because the description is not meant to make any statement about the boy's observational skills; it plays a more important role in the overall theme of the poem. Choice **d** is incorrect because the positive way the environment is described in stanza 2 does not support the idea that the environment is one the boy should leave.

27. **The correct answer is choice d.** The aircraft is intruding on a scene that was peaceful, and the use of "splash," which suggests sudden movement, illustrates that fact. Choice **a** is incorrect because it implies a more positive attitude toward the aircraft than the poet seems to have. Choice **b** is incorrect because there already is a lot of white in the scene the poem describes. Choice **c** is incorrect because the "splash" is meant to be more intrusive than exciting, which implies the aircraft has a more positive effect than the poet intends it to have.

28. The correct answer is choice c. The fact that the sight of the aircraft struck the boy as "strange" and seemed to make him undergo a significant change supports the conclusion that it disturbed him. Choice **a** is incorrect because even though the boy thought the aircraft was strange, he seemed to understand what it was, so he probably was not confused by it. Choice **b** is incorrect because it suggests an extreme reaction that is not indicated in the poem. Choice **d** is incorrect because the boy's reaction seemed considerably less positive than delighted.

29. The correct answer is choice b. In these lines, the poet is using nonliteral language to suggest that the hillsides are echoing the sound of the ringing church bells. Choice **a** is incorrect because something that is producing an echo is not quiet. Choice **c** is incorrect because the fact that the hillsides are "windswept" is not related to taking up "the sound the bells begun." Choice **d** is incorrect because the phrase is not meant to be taken literally.

30. The correct answer is choice b. By declaring that states that continue to allow slavery to exist are in rebellion, and declaring that all enslaved people are free, President Lincoln is outlawing slavery. Choice **a** is incorrect because even though it was true that several states were in rebellion against the United States, according to the Emancipation Proclamation, this declaration is not the main purpose of the order. Choice **c** is incorrect because the Emancipation Proclamation freed enslaved people in more than the three states mentioned in this answer choice, and the proclamation declared that a number of Louisiana territories were not in rebellion. Choice **d** is incorrect because President Lincoln refers to joining the armed service only in paragraph 7; it is not the main purpose of the passage as a whole.

31. The correct answer is choice a. This passage would be of most use to someone who is writing a book about the history of slavery in the United States since the Emancipation Proclamation was such an important event in that history. Choice **b** is incorrect because even though ordering the Emancipation Proclamation is widely considered to be a great achievement of President Lincoln, this passage would be even more useful to someone who is writing a book about the history of slavery in the United States. Choice **c** is incorrect because the passage does not reference rural life in the 1800s specifically, even though slavery did exist in rural areas; the passage has a more useful purpose than this. Choice **d** is incorrect because the simple fact that the passage refers to the United States army and navy does not mean it would be of much use to someone who is considering joining one of these military branches.

32. The correct answer is choice b. The main passage only gives the number of states to which the Emancipation Proclamation applied; it does not give the number of individuals to whom it applied. Choice **a** is incorrect because it describes information that could be learned in both the main passage and the paragraph. Choice **c** is incorrect because it describes information that can only be learned in the main passage. Choice **d** is incorrect because it describes information that could be learned in both the main passage and the paragraph.

33. The correct answer is choice b. According to the Emancipation Proclamation, President Lincoln declared that the Louisiana parish of New Orleans was not in rebellion against the United States, which means that it is the area most likely to have been controlled by the anti-slavery Union before Lincoln issued his order. Choice **a** is incorrect because Alabama is a state that the Emancipation Proclamation declared to be in rebellion against the United States without exception. Choice **c** is incorrect because North Carolina is a state that the Emancipation Proclamation declared to be in rebellion against the United States without exception. Choice **d** is incorrect because Florida is a state that the Emancipation Proclamation declared to be in rebellion against the United States without exception.

34. The correct answer is choice d. The word "acknowledge" makes the most sense if used in place of "recognize" in paragraph 5. Choice **a** is incorrect because simply identifying that someone is free is not enough; according to the Emancipation Proclamation, it is important that the Executive Government of the United States completely acknowledges that formerly enslaved people are free. Choice **b** is incorrect because whether or not the Executive Government cherishes that freedom is less important than the government's duty to acknowledge and honor that freedom. Choice **c** is incorrect because simply knowing that someone is free is not enough; according to the Emancipation Proclamation, it is important that the Executive Government of the United States completely acknowledges that formerly enslaved people are free.

35. The correct answer is choice c. In paragraph 9, the girl explains that she'd been on Mars for three years before shuddering, which suggests that she likely had bad experiences there. Choice **a** is incorrect because there is no evidence in the passage that the girl has family on another planet. Choice **b** is incorrect because a person can be happy she is leaving a place without actually having been kept prisoner in that place. Choice **d** is incorrect because the girl's comments seem genuine; there is no reason to believe she is making them ironically or sarcastically.

36. The correct answer is choice a. The crew members and passengers are anxious because they do not know what the Martians want, which is an example of anxiety of the unknown. Choice **b** is incorrect because even though there is some discussion of war in the passage, the characters are discussing only the possibility of war, which represents the theme of anxiety of the unknown better than the horrors of war. Choice **c** is incorrect because even though some of the characters are meeting new people, the passage is less concerned with the thrill of such first meetings than with the anxiety of the unknown. Choice **d** is incorrect because there is not much discussion of the strangeness of Mars in the passage.

37. The correct answer is choice d. The passage ends with Bob Thacher introducing himself to the girl, so it is likely they will continue talking as the story continues. Choices **a**, **b**, and **c** are incorrect because they are too specific and the passage lacks any strong evidence suggesting they are likely to happen.

38. **The correct answer is choice d.** While Bob Thacher is concerned about what the Martians will do, the businessman is convinced that they will be no threat in a conflict against Terra. The businessman does not seem concerned at all. Choice **a** is incorrect because there is only a possibility that the businessman is misinformed about Terra's power; there is no reason to reach that conclusion based on the details in this particular passage. Choice **b** is incorrect because Bob Thacher is more frightened than the businessman. Choice **c** is incorrect because the businessman is confident about Terra's powers; there is no reason to conclude he is particularly powerful himself.

39. **The correct answer is choice c.** The author most likely used this harsh and ominous description to establish the idea that the Martians are inhuman and threatening. Choice **a** is incorrect because a speaker can sound metallic and raspy without being broken. Choice **b** is incorrect because it reaches too firm a conclusion from the merely suggestive information given. Choice **d** is incorrect because even though the idea of Martians forcing a spaceship to land is unrealistic, stories that are not realistic are not always intended to be absurd, which implies a tale much sillier and more confusing than this one. This story is not particularly humorous, either.

40. **The correct answer is choice c.** Based on the way the businessman uses the term "Space Article" in paragraph 11, the reader can infer that it is a sort of law and that the Martians could violate it as a criminal might violate a law. Choice **a** is incorrect because even though "article" and "story" can share the same meaning, it does not make sense that the businessman would suggest that the Martians might violate a story. Choice **b** is incorrect because it is already known that the Martians plan to board the Inner-Flight ship for inspection, most likely through some sort of entryway. So it does not make sense that the businessman would expect Terra to "rip apart" the Martians for doing something they are already expected to do. Choice **d** is incorrect because the businessman is suggesting that a battle between Mars and Terra could take place; it does not make sense for him to suggest that Mars might violate a battle that is not actually taking place at the moment.

Language Arts—Writing Part 1

To calculate your HiSET® score on the Language Arts—Writing section, first take a look at the correct answer for each of the 50 questions of the exam. Count up your **correct answers** only, and give yourself 1 point for each. Then, add up all of your points. This is your **raw score**.

Find your raw score and your **scaled score** in the following table. Remember, for each test section, a passing score is 8. (For the essay, a passing score is 2.)

You need a scaled score of 45 to pass the complete HiSET® exam.

LANGUAGE ARTS—WRITING SCORING			
RAW	SCALED	RAW	SCALED
0	1	26	9
1	2	27	9
2	3	28	9
3	3	29	9
4	4	30	9
5	4	31	10
6	5	32	10
7	5	33	10
8	5	34	10
9	6	35	10
10	6	36	11
11	6	37	11
12	6	38	11
13	6	39	11
14	7	40	11
15	7	41	12
16	7	42	12
17	7	43	12
18	7	44	12
19	8	45	13
20	8	46	13
21	8	47	13
22	8	48	14
23	8	49	14
24	8	50	14
25	9		

1. **The correct answer is choice c.** The first part of the sentence tells you that the vendors will be returning, so they can't be the "new" faces promised. This version correctly separates the two by adding the coordinating conjunction "and" to clarify. Choice **a** is incorrect because the first part of the sentence tells you that the vendors will be returning, so they can't be the "new" faces promised. It is unclear that there is a difference between the vendors and the new faces. Choices **b** and **d** are incorrect because they leave out reference to the "new" faces promised. This version suggests that the vendors *are* the new faces.

2. **The correct answer is choice d.** The plural pronoun "them" matches "kids." Choice **a** is incorrect because the underlined phrase contains a pronoun that should refer to the "kids" in the subject of the sentence. "Kids" is plural. "It" is not. Choice **b** is incorrect because this version replaces the pronoun with a possessive. Choice **c** is incorrect because it the wrong plural pronoun; the writer is talking about the children, not himself or herself plus the children.

3. **The correct answer is choice d.** This is a simple list and doesn't require any punctuation more complicated than commas. Choice **a** is incorrect because it has no punctuation, which makes the list difficult to read and understand. Choice **b** is incorrect because slash marks are not an appropriate punctuation mark for a list. Choice **c** is incorrect because it uses semicolons when they're not necessary. The list is short and has short items in it, so there's no need for semicolons.

4. The correct answer is choice b. This version eliminates the extra modifiers ("12:00" and "in the afternoon"). Choice **a** is incorrect because the sentence tells the reader the show time three different ways; having all three is redundant. The word "noon" on its own tells the reader that the show is happening at 12:00 P.M.—no additional context is needed. Choices **c** and **d** are incorrect because they both have two redundant time modifiers.

5. The correct answer is choice b. Choices **a** and **c** are incorrect because the phrase "you guessed it" is an aside to the reader and should be set off as a modifying phrase that describes "cupcakes," as is done in choice **b**. Choice **d** is incorrect because placing the phrase right after "Cup-Caked" is confusing.

6. The correct answer is choice d. It turns the first part of the sentence into a subordinate clause and doesn't repeat the word "feature." It also adds the transitional phrase "in addition," which acts as a transition from the previous paragraph. Choices **a** and **b** are incorrect because the first underlined sentence is a fragment. The best solution is to find a way to combine it with the second sentence. Switching the order of the sentences doesn't solve the problem. Choice **c** is incorrect because the first part of the sentence is missing a noun and verb, so it's incomplete.

7. The correct answer is choice b. The writer needs to move from giving information about the market and its related events to closing out the paragraph (and the advertisement). The best way to do this is not to insert new information that supports points in previous paragraphs but rather to summarize the main point of the entire passage. Choice **d** repeats information from the first sentence without adding anything. It's also a fragment.

8. The correct answer is choice a. Look at the opening sentences of paragraphs 2 and 3. The opener for paragraph 3 seems more closely related to the end of paragraph 1, and the opener for paragraph 2 says "We're also" when there's nothing to add to (yet). It would make sense to swap these two paragraphs so that the overall piece flows best. Choice **d** is incorrect because paragraph 1 is clearly an introductory paragraph, so it should stay where it is.

9. The correct answer is choice d. The pronoun in the sentence refers to "anyone," so it should be a singular relative pronoun. "Who" is the relative pronoun that refers to a person. Choice **a** is incorrect because the pronoun in the sentence refers to "anyone," so it should be a singular relative pronoun. Choice **b** is incorrect because the pronoun in the sentence refers to "anyone," so it should be a singular relative pronoun. Although "which" is a relative pronoun, it refers to a thing, not a person. Choice **c** is incorrect because it removes the pronoun altogether, and while the underlined portion of the sentence makes sense on its own, when it's combined with the non-underlined part, it creates a fragment.

10. The correct answer is choice b. The phrase in quotation marks tells you that the writer is referring to a specific name for the 3D printer, so the underlined word needs to match that context. Of the options, "formally" is the best one. Choice **a** is incorrect because "formerly" doesn't work; there's no indication that 3D printing has a new name. Choice **c** is incorrect because "formatively" doesn't work; it means "at creation," and there's no context that tells you when 3D printing was known as "additive manufacturing." Choice **d** is incorrect because the meaning of the word "friendly" does not match the correct context.

11. The correct answer is choice c. The rest of the sentence is present tense, describing how the printer works. This version has the present tense of the verb "take." Choice **a** is incorrect because the underlined text is in the past tense. Choice **b** is incorrect because this version is in the future tense. Choice **d** is incorrect because this version is in the past tense.

12. The correct answer is choice c. The passage is very informational, with a neutral writer. The second sentence of paragraph 2 inserts a statement directly from the author that seems out of place. Choices **b** and **d** are incorrect because these sentences are in line with the informational style of the rest of the article.

13. The correct answer is choice a. "Moreover" can mean "additionally," so it is the best transition word out of the choices. Choice **b** is incorrect because there's no comparison between the statement at the end of paragraph 1 and the one at the beginning of paragraph 2. The writer is giving supporting details, not contrasting ones. Choice **c** is incorrect because there's no numerical structure to the essay. Choice **d** is incorrect because it's both too informal and not informative enough. In writing, a transition word or phrase should tie to the information before and after it in a way that makes sense.

14. The correct answer is choice c. There is only one "l" in "developing." Choice **a** is incorrect because "artificial" is spelled correctly. Choice **b** is incorrect because "technological" is spelled correctly. Choice **d** is incorrect because there is only one "l" in "developing."

15. The correct answer is choice d. The pronouns refer to "printers," so they should both be plural. Only this version has the consistently plural pronouns.

16. The correct answer is choice a. "There" fits with the placement in the sentence. Choice **b** is incorrect because "their" is a possessive pronoun, which doesn't work in the underlined spot. Choice **c** is incorrect because "they're" is a contraction of "they are." "They are" is inappropriate because it inserts a full noun and verb phrase, which creates an incomplete sentence. Choice **d** is incorrect because "they are" is inappropriate because it inserts a full noun and verb phrase, which creates an incomplete sentence.

17. The correct answer is choice b. Neither clause in this sentence is capable of standing on its own, so the sentence is incomplete as written. This version inserts a subject and verb that create an independent clause. Choice **c** is incorrect because it suggests that the writer wants to follow the code, when this letter is directed at the employees. Choice **d** is incorrect because it is a fragment.

18. The correct answer is choice c. This version ends the sentence with a period. Choice **a** is incorrect because the sentence should not end on a colon. Choice **b** is incorrect because a sentence should not end with an ellipsis unless some of the text has been removed. Choice **d** is incorrect because the sentence is not a question, so it should not end with a question mark.

19. The correct answer is choice a. "Sound judgment" is a common idiom, and it's correct as written. Choice **b** is incorrect because it misuses "sound," turning it into a verb instead of an adjective. Choice **c** is incorrect because this phrase is not a proper noun. There's no need to capitalize it. Choice **d** is incorrect because it misuses "sound," turning it into a verb instead of an adjective.

20. The correct answer is choice c. The indefinite pronoun "anyone" is singular, and the pronouns and the object are singular. Choice **a** is incorrect because the indefinite pronoun "anyone" is singular, but "their" is a plural possessive. Choice **b** is incorrect because this version pluralizes "jobs." Choice **d** is incorrect because it's a shift in perspective; the writer is addressing employees, not speaking for himself or herself.

21. The correct answer is choice c. "That" is used to set off an essential clause. Choice **a** is incorrect because the personal pronoun "they" creates a sentence fragment. Choice **b** is incorrect because "they're" is a contraction meaning "they are," which does not make sense in this context. Choice **d** is incorrect because "that," not "which," is used to set off an essential clause.

22. The correct answer is choice b. "Constitutes" is a verb, and it means "to consist of," so it fits in with the context of the sentence. Choice **a** is incorrect because "constitutions" is a noun, not a verb, so it doesn't fit. Choice **c** is incorrect because "constituents" is a noun, not a verb, so it doesn't fit. Choice **d** is incorrect because "constants" is a noun, not a verb, so it doesn't fit.

23. The correct answer is choice d. This sentence starts to turn the paragraph toward summarizing and concluding, so it works as a transition. Choices **a** and **b** are incorrect because they throw off the tone of the passage. Both sentences are too casual. Choice **c** is incorrect because paragraph 3 already talked about what people aren't allowed to wear.

24. The correct answer is choice d. In the underlined text, there are too many modifiers crowding in before "furry friends," so it's difficult to tell what or whom people are bringing to restaurants. This version corrects that problem. Choice **a** is incorrect because in the underlined text, there are too many modifiers crowding in before "furry friends," so it's difficult to tell what or whom people are bringing to restaurants. Choice **b** is incorrect because it cuts too much out of the sentence. How will the reader know where people want to bring their dogs? Choice **c** is incorrect because in the underlined text, there are too many modifiers crowding in before "furry friends," so it's difficult to tell what or whom people are bringing to restaurants. This version has the same issue of putting the modifying phrase ("to outdoor seating areas") before "furry friends." It also has a clarifying comment about restaurants in parentheses, but it is unclear what this has to do with the rest of the sentence.

25. The correct answer is choice b. In this case, "indoor or outdoor" is a nonessential phrase— the sentence already indicates that pets are not allowed in any restaurant. Since it's nonessential, it should be set off with appropriate punctuation. This version sets off the phrase with parentheses. Choice **a** is incorrect because in this case, "indoor and outdoor" is a nonessential phrase— the sentence already indicates that pets are not allowed in any restaurant. Since it's nonessential, it should be set off with appropriate punctuation. Choice **c** is incorrect because it adds an unnecessary semicolon. Choice **d** is incorrect because it adds an unnecessary comma.

26. The correct answer is choice b. This version condenses the sentences into a single, clearer sentence. Choice **a** is incorrect because as written, the sentences could be condensed to form a single, clearer sentence. Choice **c** is incorrect because it suggests that the evidence, not the restaurant, would be fined. Choice **d** is incorrect because the fine itself does not contain evidence of animals; the restaurant does.

27. The correct answer is choice d. The original sentence is a run on. The easiest way to fix this is to break up the quote with a period before starting the second part of the quotation. Choice **a** is incorrect because as written, the sentence is a run-on sentence. Choice **b** is incorrect because this version is a run-on sentence, even though it moved the subject and predicate to the beginning of the sentence. Choice **c** is incorrect because it removes the part where the speaker is identified and is a run-on sentence.

28. The correct answer is choice c. This is the second part of June Hawthorne's quote, so it should be set off in quotation marks. Because "she continued" is part of the same sentence, it does not need to be capitalized. Choice **a** is incorrect because this is the second part of June Hawthorne's quote, so it should be set off in quotation marks. Choice **b** is incorrect because it leaves out the necessary quotation marks and creates a fragment out of "she continued." Choice **d** is incorrect because it takes out the question mark at the end of the quotation.

29. The correct answer is choice a. This sentence supports the main topic of the paragraph (the support and opposition from community members). Choice **b** is incorrect because this sentence is irrelevant because June Hawthorne isn't a subject of the article outside of the one quote. Choice **c** is incorrect because it's not clear what Hawthorne and Winklebaum's history has to do with the issue at hand. Choice **d** is incorrect because the information about the pizza restaurant does not relate to the issue of allowing dogs in outdoor seating areas.

30. The correct answer is choice d. The original sentence is a run-on sentence. This version solves this problem by adding the conjunction "but." Choice **a** is incorrect because as written, the sentence is a run-on sentence. Choice **b** is incorrect because this version tries to coordinate the two halves of the sentence by using the phrase "in contrast," but the writer isn't setting up a comparison. Choice **c** is incorrect because it is a run-on sentence even though it removes the opening adverb "ultimately."

31. The correct answer is choice c. It eliminates the wordiness and is a complete sentence. Choice **a** is incorrect because the sentences need to be combined. Choice **b** is incorrect because although the placement of the "human or canine" modifier makes sense, the sentence is incomplete. Choice **d** is incorrect because it is a run-on sentence.

32. The correct answer is choice c. It is a complete sentence that joins two related statements with an em dash. Choice **a** is incorrect because the sentences are incomplete. Choice **b** is incorrect because it is a run-on sentence. Choice **d** is incorrect because it joins two independent clauses without punctuation.

33. The correct answer is choice a. The sentence uses the conjunction "although" to create a subordinate clause that complements the independent clause "I was skeptical." Choice **b** is incorrect because "yet" makes less sense than "although" in the context of the sentence. Choice **c** is incorrect because "because" makes less sense than "although" in the context of the sentence. Choice **d** is incorrect because "therefore" makes less sense than "although" in the context of the sentence.

34. The correct answer is choice b. This version creates a clear and parallel list of ingredients set off by a colon. Choice **a** is incorrect because the underlined sentences need to be combined. Choice **c** is incorrect because the semicolon breaks the sentence in half, but not at a point that makes sense. Eggs, salt, and flour should be grouped together. Choice **d** is incorrect because the colon breaks the sentence in half, but not at a point that makes sense.

35. The correct answer is choice b. The writer mentions the name Chef Marco without giving much context. He's taught three classes, but is he teaching this one? Is he a famous chef? This is information that would flesh out the story. Choice **a** is incorrect because the location of the class is not directly related to the paragraph and its topic. Choice **c** is incorrect because the number of students is not directly related to the paragraph and its topic. Choice **d** is incorrect because the writer's own pasta preferences are not directly related to the paragraph and its topic.

36. The correct answer is choice d. "In over our heads" is the proper idiom.

37. The correct answer is choice d. The writer is trying to reproduce what the chef said, so it needs to be punctuated as a quote. Choice **a** is incorrect because the sentence has no punctuation, so the reader can't tell where the writer's voice ends and the chef's voice begins. Choice **b** is incorrect because the writer is trying to reproduce what the chef said, so it needs to be punctuated as a quote. Choice **c** is incorrect because it has incorrect capitalization and no quotation marks.

38. The correct answer is choice b. The writer is comparing his own results to others' (especially Karen's), so the sentence makes sense in context. Choices **a** and **c** are incorrect because they do not match the tone of the rest of the passage. Choice **d** is incorrect because it doesn't give enough information to add anything to the paragraph.

39. The correct answer is choice d. The key to combining these sentences is making sure the adjectives line up. This version does this by making them a basic list and setting off "most of all" as a clear nonessential clause. Choice **a** is incorrect because these sentences need to be combined. Choice **b** is incorrect because it is a run-on sentence. Choice **c** is incorrect because it incorrectly uses commas.

40. The correct answer is choice d. The writer is using a noun that means "a lack of water." The correct spelling is "drought."

41. The correct answer is choice b. This version aligns the verbs and removes the unnecessary "and." Choice **a** is incorrect because there are two issues with the underlined text: the verbs in the list should all match, and using both "and" and "etc." is redundant. Choice **c** is incorrect because the words in the list should match. Choice **d** is incorrect because using both "and" and "etc." is redundant.

42. **The correct answer is choice a.** When offering specific information like percentages and statistics, it's best to be as clear as possible about where the information comes from. This sentence could benefit most from having the writer say what the source of the statistics was. Choice **b** is incorrect because adding more percentages wouldn't necessarily help and could distract from what the writer is trying to say.

43. **The correct answer is choice c.** This version arranges the information in a way that makes sense. Choice **a** is incorrect because as written, the information is choppy. Choice **b** is incorrect because it improperly uses ellipses to join the information. Choice **d** is incorrect because another choice arranges the information in a way that makes better sense.

44. **The correct answer is choice d.** This report is informational. The sentence "Don't even get me started" doesn't fit with how the writer has presented the rest of the passage.

45. **The correct answer is choice b.** The original sentence is a run-on sentence. This version fixes this by breaking it into separate sentences. Choice **a** is incorrect because it is a run-on sentence. Choice **c** is incorrect because the it is a run-on sentence. Choice **d** is incorrect because it creates a sentence fragment.

46. **The correct answer is choice c.** This sentence gives the most information about the topic of the piece. From paragraph 4, the word "half-centennial" tells you that the museum is celebrating 50 years, so it makes sense to mention that anniversary earlier on as well. Choice **a** is incorrect because the location would be more appropriate as a supporting detail. Choice **b** is incorrect because the writer stays neutral throughout the review, so using "my favorite" at the very beginning doesn't match the rest of the passage. Choice **d** is incorrect because the writer goes on to talk about Marcus Ammendola in paragraph 2, but this information is not central enough to open the passage.

47. **The correct answer is choice b.** It separates the confusing information into an introductory clause and lets "the collection includes . . ." stand as an independent clause. Choice **a** is incorrect because the modifier "by photographer Marcus Ammendola" is in an odd place, and it makes the sentence difficult to read. Choice **c** is incorrect because the modifier "by photographer Marcus Ammendola" is in an odd place, and it makes the sentence difficult to read. Choice **d** is incorrect because it is a fragment.

48. **The correct answer is choice c.** "Flashier" is a common way to say "more exciting," which fits with the sentence (as indicated by "newer"). Choice **a** is incorrect because "fleshier" means fatter, which doesn't fit with the sentence. Choice **b** is incorrect because "flightier" means "more fickle," which doesn't fit with the sentence. Choice **d** is incorrect because "fairer" doesn't fit with the sentence because it's not clear what the exhibit would be fairer than.

49. **The correct answer is choice d.** In the underlined text, the placement of "ancient" is confusing. This version specifies that the collection is ancient. Choice **a** is incorrect because in the underlined text, the placement of "ancient" is confusing. Choice **b** is incorrect because "ancient" breaks up the proper noun "Early Christian." Choice **c** is incorrect because it breaks up the noun "Early Christian art."

50. **The correct answer is choice d.** Paragraph 4 only gives a few small details about the museum itself, so it is least important to the main topic of the passage. Choice **a** is incorrect because paragraph 1 is the introduction and is essential to the rest of the passage. Choice **b** is incorrect because paragraph 2 provides important supporting information on the new exhibit. Choice **c** is incorrect because paragraph 3 provides important supporting information about the existing exhibits.

Language Arts—Writing Part 2

On test day, your essay will be scored by two graders. Each will read over your essay, and assign it a score from 1 to 6 using the following grading criteria. Using this table, assign your own essay a score from 1 to 6. Then, read the provided sample essays and explanations to get a sense of what an essay at every level looks like. You need a score of 2 to pass this portion of the exam.

SCORE	EXPLANATION
1	*Essays at this score point do not sufficiently support an argument. They do not take a stance on the given question and do not provide solid evidence or reasoning to back up any claims.* These essays: • do not offer a clear opinion, as requested by the given prompt. The topic at hand might be mentioned, but there is no context for the information and no main idea to tie any information together into a cohesive thought. • are not structured: There is no introduction, conclusion, or main thesis. They often are not separated into paragraphs, and if they are, they lack smooth transitions from one paragraph to the next. • feature very simple vocabulary and sentence structure throughout. There is often a misuse of grammar, along with frequent errors in capitalization, punctuation, and spelling.
2	*Essays at this score point might bring up points related to the given prompt, but they do not sufficiently support an argument with a well-thought-out stance, backed by evidence. Thoughts are often jumbled and unrelated, and there is not a firm grasp of language rules or sentence and paragraph structure.* These essays: • do not fully develop a clear stance on the given issue. Often, if an opinion is given, either it is not developed or expanded on with examples from the given texts or it relies too heavily on pulling information from the given texts. • often do not feature an introduction, conclusion, or paragraphs—if they do, these elements are not cohesive and do not flow properly. • do not have a solid command of sentence structure—sentences are either short and choppy or long and run-on. Sentences do not flow into one another, and there is no cohesive tone throughout the piece. • have limited command of grammar, usage, spelling, capitalization, and punctuation rules.
3	*Essays at this score point take a solid stance on the given issue and show partial command of developing an argument using proper usage rules.* These essays: • take a definitive stance on the given issue but do not fully develop this point of view with sufficient evidence—from the given texts and from the writer's personal experiences. Several points are presented to clarify the author's point of view, but a cohesive and well-rounded argument is not presented. • might feature an introduction, supporting paragraphs, and a conclusion, although one or all of these may be underdeveloped. If present, transitions are simple and used inconsistently. • begin to feature a command of language, although word choice and sentence structure are often unvaried or repetitive. Sentences in score 3 essays also might be too long and uncontrolled. Essays often feature errors in capitalization, punctuation, and spelling.
4	*Essays at this score point adequately take a stance on the argument presented and back it up with some evidence and reasoning. Basic writing rules are followed, but mistakes are often presented and tone can be too casual.* These essays: • begin to develop a point of view in response to the given topic. The writer has a clear stance on the issue. Essays bring in personal examples and examples from the given essays, along with some discussion of alternate claims and/or counterclaims. • usually contain a clear introduction and conclusion but often lack sufficient development of supporting paragraphs within. Transitions are used, although they may be simple, and organization of sentences within paragraphs is often jumbled and awkward. • feature an adequate command of grammar, usage, sentence structure, and punctuation. Word choice and sentence format are somewhat varied, and a cohesive tone is used throughout. Errors are often present, but they do not interfere with the essay's clarity in message.

5   *Essays at this score point take a definitive stance on the argument presented, backing it up with solid examples, reasoning, and presentation of counterarguments. While these essays may feature minor mistakes, they show a good command of language, usage, and variety of word choice and sentence structure. These essays:*

- solidly present and back up a central position or claim on the given prompt. These essays also include a balanced discussion of counterclaims. Several ideas to back up a point of view are provided and expanded on, along with evidence from real life and the provided texts.
- feature a clear introduction, conclusion, and supporting paragraphs. Transitions are used throughout to unify ideas and create a cohesive point of view.
- show a very solid command of grammar, usage, spelling, punctuation, and sentence structure. Words are used correctly and varied throughout, and sentences vary in length and complexity. Thee essay may contain some errors in usage and some deviations in tone, but nothing detracts from the overall stance and content of the essay.

6   *Essays at this score point present a strongly written and defended argument using sufficient evidence from varied sources, presentation of counterarguments, and a solid command of language and grammar conventions. These essays:*

- expertly present, develop, and defend a point of view on a given topic. They explore the topic from all sides and present arguments countering differing opinions. Writers have a clear point of view and defend it with many examples taken from real life and from the given texts in the prompt.
- feature a definitive and well-written introduction, conclusion, and set of supporting paragraphs to back up all claims made. Strong transitions are used to connect thoughts and link together all claims and evidence made.
- demonstrate extremely strong command of language and grammar. Vocabulary and sentence structure throughout are varied in length and complexity. These essays have very few, if any, errors in spelling, punctuation, and usage. Essays feature a cohesive tone throughout that is appropriate for the topic at hand.

Sample Score 1 Essay:

Teddy Roosevelt was the president. So hes really famus! I've heard of him. I have never heard of Craig Nelson. He is not so famus. Maybe some people know who he is but I do not at all. So I'm sure Teddy is right! I think I have even heard the thing he said here so it must be really really famus!

About This Essay

This essay does mention the two provided quotes, but otherwise it does not address the given prompt. The author writes a few sentences on the identity of the men but does not discuss their points of view on the issue at hand. No stance is taken. There is no structure to the essay, and there are punctuation errors (*hes*) and spelling errors (*famus*) throughout.

Sample Score 2 Essay:

Teddy Roosevelt once said "carry a big stick." It is a very famous line. He was talking about foriegn policy. I think he was probably right even though I'm not really sure what he was saying. Was he saying that we need to scare other countries with weapons like sticks? Probably, but I never totaly understood what he ment. I think thts a good way. Craig Nelson says people do not love tanks. Some probably do but I don't. So that's a good way too. It all depends on your point of view!

About This Essay

While the writer of this essay starts to present a point of view and explore his or her thoughts on the given topic, they are not developed or explored in any meaningful way. The essay does not feature any clear organization—there is no distinct introduction, body, or conclusion. Sentence structure is weak throughout (*I think thts a good way.*), and the essay has a number of spelling errors (*totaly*, *ment*).

Sample Score 3 Essay:

Two people have opinions about foreign policy. One person was the president of the United States. One person was some author named Craig Nelson. Have you read his book? I have not. But a president is president for a reason, so I agree with him.

The president knows a lot about running the country. Its his job! So if he says we need to carry a big stick, which is like a weapon, than that is what we must do. I like that he says we need to speak softly to. That means before we use our weapons we should try to talk for piece. But when that goes wrong, its weapons time! Some guy named Craig Nelson says no one will love America if we have tanks. I say who cares? We do not need love. We need to protect.

So, we need to do what makes America great, that's how I feel. I like that. You like it too even if you think you don't.

About This Essay

This essay takes a stance on the topic (coming out in favor of Roosevelt's thoughts on foreign policy) and sticks with it throughout. However, the author's arguments are not strong—he or she does not give solid examples to back up his or her opinions. The author goes back to the given quote to back up the essay's main thesis (*The president knows a lot about running the country. Its his job! So if he says we need to carry a big stick, which is like a weapon, than that is what we must do.*), which is not the mark of a strong essay.

Although the essay does feature a clear introduction, body, and conclusion, there are not strong transitions between thoughts or paragraphs.

The author also makes errors throughout in punctuation (*Its* his job!), grammar ("I like that he says we need to speak softly *to.*"), and spelling ("That means before we use our weapons we should try to talk for *piece.*").

Sample Score 4 Essay:

President Teddy Roosevelt has a very famous quote about foreign policy: "Speak softly and carry a big stick; you will go far." I think he means that even though you may talk nicely to people in other countries, you should always be ready to use force. I cannot believe that quote is so famous! It makes a really scary image of America. Is this country we really want to be?

I much prefer author Craig Nelsons quote about foreign policy. He says that "If everyone loves you, maybe you don't need so many tanks." What a beautiful sentiment! What he is saying is that we should eliminate our weapons to win the love of other countries. Clearly war is a horrible, horrible thing. We do not become a better country by threatening other countries with our guns, tanks, and bombs. We do not improve human life by going to war. Get rid of the weapons of war and you get rid of war.

So I am on the side of Nelson. "If everyone loves you, maybe you don't need so many tanks." That's what I believe too.

About This Essay

This essay has a defined introduction, body, and conclusion and takes a firm stance on the given topic. However, the writing and argument are somewhat simplistic and underdeveloped. To strengthen this essay, the author should back up his or her opinion, which is clear throughout, with solid examples from real life that help to illustrate his or her point. The essay repeats the point of view throughout without evidence to help strengthen it.

The essay's sentence structure is solid, and while there are a few errors in spelling (*threatening*) and punctuation ("I much prefer author Craig *Nelsons* quote about foreign policy."), they do not interfere with the essay's message.

Sample Score 5 Essay:

"Speak softly and carry a big stick; you will go far." President Teddy Roosevelt's quote about foreign policy is one of the most famous quotes in American history. It may be somewhat humorous sounding (the idea of America holding a stick against its enemies) but it packs a very serious message. When peaceful negotiations fail, it is time to use military strength.

My problem with this quote is that it makes foreign policy seem to simple. It gives politicians who are eager to rush to war a handy quote for justifying military moves.

The thing is, author Craig Nelson's less well-known quote about foreign policy is too simple too. Nelson said, "If everyone loves you, maybe you don't need so many tanks." This creates the idea that without any military tools, there will be a sort of heaven on earth. Now, I would honestly love to believe such a thing could be true. Who wouldn't? But it simply is not realistic. I doubt the terrorist groups that are currently causing trouble throughout the world will love America if we got rid of all of our tanks.

Foreign policy is an extremely complicated issue. You can not boil it down with a quote even if that quote comes from someone on Mount Rushmore. Peace should always be an option. Tanks may be necesary when peaceful talks do not work out. It is a difficult world we live in and sound bites will not solve our problems. No matter who says them.

About This Essay

This essay takes a solid stance on the argument presented and features a clear introduction, body, and conclusion. The author's point of view is explored throughout, and different points of view are also considered (*Now, I would honestly love to believe such a thing could be true. Who wouldn't? But it simply is not realistic.*), making for a strong argumentative essay. The author uses transitions well, and there is a variety in sentence length and word choice. There are a few errors in usage and grammar (*Tanks may be necesary when peaceful talks do not work out.*) but none that detract from the essay's message. What could improve this essay's score are a few more concrete examples to back up its point of view and make a more sophisticated argument.

Sample Score 6 Essay:

The United States has always been a nation of action. You need only look at our Revolution against England to see that great things have been achieved by our men and women who take charge and push loudly for freedoms. However, when President Teddy Roosevelt suggested that we would be successful if we "speak softly and carry a big stick," I agree with it because it shows that we have grown and evolved as a country.

To me, "speak softly" means that we can accomplish things around the world without shouting or bullying to get what we want. In my experience, people listen closely to people who keep their voices down and stay calm. The people who yell and carry on are just tuned out in the end. This applies to all aspects of life. In my classes and at work, the ones who are calm and firm are the ones who get the most work done. Personally, I would rather lead by example than by screaming or fear, and as a result, I'd like to see my country lead by example as well.

Similarly, the "big stick" is a necessary part of life, as well. Some people just don't respond well no matter how rationally you talk to them (for example, England when we were still colonies). We still see this around the world with nations who threaten war and destruction at every turn, especially with the conflicts in the Middle East right now. There need to be consequences—in the world as in my previous workplace example. People need to know that if they disregard rational discussion and decision making, there will be consequences. The "big stick" is an essential part of American policy, because without it we would run the risk of being ignored by bullying factions. Consequently, author Craig Nelson clearly means well by suggesting that America should win the love of other nations to eliminate its reliance on weapons of war, but that suggestion is too simplistic and unrealistic.

Together, the diplomacy of "speaking softly" and the "big stick" of potential military consequences make a balanced foreign policy. Because the United States has grown to be a world leader in so many things, I believe we have a responsibility to grow into that role with politeness and dignity. Yet it's important that the bullies of the world know that if we're pushed out beyond our limits, we will always push back.

About This Essay

This is a strong essay that takes a definitive stance on the given topic, backs it up with examples throughout (*In my experience, people listen closely to people who keep their voices down and stay calm. The people who yell and carry on are just tuned out in the end.*), features a strong introduction and conclusion, and shows a good command of language, word choice, grammar, spelling, and punctuation. The author makes his or her point of view clear from paragraph 1 and then goes on in the body of the essay to expand on this point of view, with definitive transitions (*Similarly, the "big stick" is a necessary part of life, as well.*) and varied sentence structure. Finally, the author acknowledges the other point of view and discusses why he or she disagrees (*Consequently, author Craig Nelson clearly means well by suggesting that America should win the love of other nations to eliminate its reliance on weapons of war, but that suggestion is too simplistic and unrealistic.*).

Mathematics

To calculate your HiSET® score on the Mathematics section, first take a look at the correct answer for each of the 50 questions of the exam. Count up your **correct answers** only, and give yourself 1 point for each. Then, add up all of your points. This is your **raw score.**

Find your raw score and your **scaled score** in the following table. Remember, for each test section, a passing score is 8. (For the essay, a passing score is 2.)

You need a scaled score of 45 to pass the complete HiSET® exam.

MATHEMATICS SCORING			
RAW	SCALED	RAW	SCALED
0	1	26	12
1	1	27	12
2	2	28	12
3	2	29	13
4	3	30	13
5	3	31	13
6	4	32	13
7	5	33	14
8	6	34	14
9	7	35	14
10	8	36	14
11	8	37	15
12	8	38	15
13	9	39	15
14	9	40	15
15	9	41	16
16	10	42	16
17	10	43	16
18	10	44	17
19	10	45	17
20	10	46	18
21	11	47	18
22	11	48	19
23	11	49	20
24	11	50	20
25	12		

1. **The correct answer is choice d.** The range of a function is the set of outputs, or *y*-values of all points on the graph. In this case, the range is [15,60]. Choice **a** is incorrect because this is the difference between the maximum and minimum *y*-values; the word *range* when applied to a data set would mean this, but it means something different for a function. Choice **b** is incorrect because this is the *y*-intercept of the function, which belongs in the range but does not constitute the entire range. Choice **c** is incorrect because you forgot to include the portion of the graph to the right of *t* = 16. Choice **e** is incorrect because this is the domain.

2. **The correct answer is choice b.** Here, *t* = 4 corresponds to March 19 and *t* = 6 corresponds to March 21. The difference in the corresponding functional values, namely $P(6) - P(4)$, is the difference in price between these two dates. Choice **a** is incorrect because each input is off by 1; here, *t* = 4 (not *t* = 3) corresponds to March 19 and *t* = 6 (not *t* = 5) corresponds to March 21. Choice **c** is incorrect because this is the average price of a ticket for these two dates. Choice **d** is incorrect because this is an average price of a ticket, but not for the dates shown—you must convert the actual date to the correct *t*-value. Choice **e** is incorrect because you must convert the actual date to the correct *t*-value. Here, *t* = 4 corresponds to March 19 and *t* = 6 corresponds to March 21.

3. **The correct answer is choice a.** Multiply the first rational expression by $\frac{4x+1}{4x+1}$ and then solve for *x*:

$$\frac{3}{4x+1} - \frac{2}{(4x+1)^2} = 0$$
$$3(4x+1) - 2 = 0$$
$$12x + 3 - 2 = 0$$
$$12x + 1 = 0$$
$$x = -\frac{1}{12}$$

Since this value does not make either denominator equal to 0, it is a solution of the original equation. So the solution set is $\{-\frac{1}{12}\}$. Choice **b** is incorrect because once you multiplied both sides by the least common denominator, you did not distribute the 3 to both terms of the binomial $(4x+1)$. Choice **c** is incorrect because this is an *x*-value that makes the least common denominator (as well as the numerator) equal to 0, not a solution of the equation. Choice **d** is incorrect because when solving a linear equation of the form $ax = b$ for *x*, the solution is $x = \frac{b}{a}$, not $\frac{a}{b}$. Choice **e** is incorrect because there is a solution to this equation. Once you multiply both sides of the equation by the least common denominator and then solve the resulting linear equation, the value you get satisfies the original equation.

4. The correct answer is choice d. First arrange the data in increasing order. The median of the original data set is 168, and replacing 320 by 350 does not change this value since 168 remains the middle value in the data set. The mean, however, will increase since the sum of the data has increased. Choice **a** is incorrect because the median remains unchanged since it is concerned with position within the data set, and replacing 320 by 350 does not change this. Choice **b** is incorrect because the mean will increase since it is obtained by summing the values and dividing by the same number, 7. Choice **c** is incorrect because the median remains unchanged since it is concerned with position within the data set, and replacing 320 by 350 does not change this. Choice **e** is incorrect because each outcome in this data set occurs exactly once even if 320 is replaced by 350.

5. The correct answer is choice d. The length of the deck is $12 + 2 + 2 = 16$, and the width is the same. Using the Pythagorean theorem, the distance from point A to point B is $\sqrt{16^2 + 16^2}$. Choice **a** is incorrect because you added 2 feet of walkway to the width and to the length of the cabana, but the walkway goes all the way around the cabana; you should have added 4 feet to the width and length of the cabana. Choice **b** is incorrect because you added 2 feet of walkway to one of sides, but the walkway goes all the way around the cabana; 4 feet should have been added to both the width and the length of the cabana. Choice **c** is incorrect because you added 2 feet of walkway to the width and to the length of the cabana, but the walkway goes all the way around the cabana; you should have added 4 feet to the width and length of the cabana. And, when applying the Pythagorean theorem, you forgot to include the square root. Choice **e** is incorrect because you forgot the square root.

6. The correct answer is choice e. Only the order in which terms are being added is changed, which illustrates the commutative property. Choice **a** is incorrect because you are not adding zero to a quantity and getting that same quantity back as a result. Choice **b** is incorrect because you are not multiplying a quantity by a real number and doing so by multiplying each term of the quantity by this real number and summing the results. Choice **c** is incorrect because you are not adding the negative of a real number to itself and getting zero. Choice **d** is incorrect because even though there are parentheses in the equality, terms are not being regrouped in this sentence.

7. The correct answer is choice e. 46% of 327,577,529 is approximately 150,685,663.3. So rounding to the hundred thousands place gives 150,700,000. Choice **a** is incorrect because you rounded to the ten millions place. Choice **b** is incorrect because you rounded to the ten thousands place. Choice **c** is incorrect because you rounded (incorrectly) to the ten thousands place. Choice **d** is incorrect because you should have rounded the digit in the hundred thousands place up since the digit to its immediate right is 5 or greater.

8. The correct answer is choice c. Since the term $40(\frac{3}{2})^{-t}$ is positive for all values of t, and it is being subtracted from 60, it follows that $T(t)$ must always be less than 60. So II is true. III is also true because when you evaluate $T(0)$, you get $60 - 40 = 20$. Choice **a** is incorrect because III is also true because when you evaluate $T(0)$, you get $60 - 40 = 20$. Choice **b** is incorrect because II is also true. Since the term $40(\frac{3}{2})^{-t}$ is positive for all values of t, and it is being subtracted from 60, it follows that $T(t)$ must always be less than 60. Choice **d** is incorrect because I is false because when you evaluate $T(2)$, you do not get 40. Also, II is true. Since the term $40(\frac{3}{2})^{-t}$ is positive for all values of t, and it is being subtracted from 60, it follows that $T(t)$ must always be less than 60. Choice **e** is incorrect because I is false because when you evaluate $T(2)$, you do not get 40.

9. The correct answer is choice d. The difference in the bill for these two months is $\$240 - \$160 = \$80$, which is the largest of the differences between any two consecutive months. Choice **a** is incorrect because the difference in the bills for these two months is $40, and other choices produce a larger difference. Choice **b** is incorrect because there is no difference between the bills for these two months, and other choices do produce a difference. Choice **c** is incorrect because the difference in the bills for these two months is $40, and other choices produce a larger difference. Choice **e** is incorrect because the difference in the bills for these two months is $40, and other choices produce a larger difference.

10. The correct answer is choice c. Add the equations to eliminate the y terms, resulting in the equation $3x = 3a$. So $x = a$. Plug this into one of the equations in the original system to find y. Using the second equation yields $a - y = 2a$, so that $y = -a$. Choice **a** is incorrect because this satisfies the first equation but not the second. Choice **b** is incorrect because you switched the values of x and y. Choice **d** is incorrect because when substituting the x-value $x = a$ (which is correct) back into an equation of the original system to find y, you solved that linear equation incorrectly. Choice **e** is incorrect because this satisfies the second equation but not the first.

11. The correct answer is choice b. Solve the inequality as follows:

$$3x - 2(4 - x) < -3x$$
$$5x - 8 < -3x$$
$$8x < 8$$
$$8x < 1$$

This is precisely the set illustrated in this choice. Choice **a** is incorrect because the endpoint should be open, and the ray should extend to the left, not to the right. Choice **c** is incorrect because when solving the final inequality $8x < 8$, you seem to have subtracted 8 from both sides instead of dividing. The endpoint of the ray should be 1, not 0. Choice **d** is incorrect because you should not include the endpoint of the ray, 1, since this is strict inequality. Choice **e** is incorrect because the ray should extend to the left, not to the right.

12. **The correct answer is choice d.** Observe that $x^2 - 9 = (x - 3)(x + 3)$. While $(x + 3)$ divides evenly into $p(x)$ since -3 is a zero, $(x - 3)$ does not because 3 is not a zero of $p(x)$. Therefore, the expression $x^2 - 9$ does not divide $p(x)$. Choice **a** is incorrect because -5 is a zero of the function, so $x + 5$ divides $p(x)$. Choice **b** is incorrect because both -1 and 1 are zeros of the function, so $(x + 1)(x - 1) = x^2 - 1$ divides $p(x)$. Choice **c** is incorrect because -1 is a zero of the function, so $x + 1$ divides $p(x)$. Choice **e** is incorrect because both -5 and -3 are zeros of the function, so $(x + 5)$ and $(x + 3)$ divide $p(x)$. Therefore, $(x + 5)(x + 3) = x^2 + 8x + 15$ also divides $p(x)$.

13. **The correct answer is choice b.** Since only members of the yearbook staff were asked the question, and such a group might naturally tend to like more writing-focused courses, the sample is not representative of the entire junior class. Choice **a** is incorrect because the choices themselves are not as relevant as those being asked to select one of them. Choice **c** is incorrect because he is trying to draw a conclusion about juniors at his school. Choice **d** is incorrect because you do want to get as inclusive a sample as possible, which would include those on the yearbook staff. The point, though, is that you do not want to include just people on the yearbook staff in the sample. Choice **e** is incorrect because this is not discernible from the given description.

14. **The correct answer is choice c.** The mode of a data set is the most frequently occurring data value, which is 16. Choice **a** is incorrect because this is the maximum value, not the mode. Choice **b** is incorrect because this is the median, not the mode. Choice **d** is incorrect because this is the range (maximum value – minimum value), not the mode. Choice **e** is incorrect because this is approximately the mean, not the mode.

15. **The correct answer is choice b.** The arc length S of the original sector is $S = \frac{D}{2} \cdot \theta$. The arc length S' of the new sector is $S' = \frac{3D}{2} \cdot \left(\frac{1}{2}\theta\right) = \frac{3}{2}\left[\frac{D}{2} \cdot \theta\right] = \frac{3}{2}S$. So multiply S by $\frac{3}{2}$ to find the new arc length. Choice **a** is incorrect because you incorporated an extra factor of $\frac{1}{2}$. Choice **c** is incorrect because you tripled the diameter but did not take $\frac{1}{2}$ of the central angle. Choice **d** is incorrect because you took $\frac{1}{2}$ of the central angle but did not triple the diameter. Choice **e** is incorrect because you divided the diameter by 3 instead of tripling it.

16. **The correct answer is choice b.** Convert the radicals to fractional exponents and apply the exponent rules:
$$\frac{\sqrt{x}}{x \cdot \sqrt[3]{x}} = \frac{x^{\frac{1}{2}}}{x \cdot x^{\frac{1}{3}}} = \frac{x^{\frac{1}{2}}}{x^{\frac{4}{3}}} = x^{\frac{1}{2} - \frac{4}{3}} = x^{-\frac{5}{6}}$$
Choice **a** is incorrect because $\frac{x^a}{x^b} = x^{a-b}$, not x^{a+b}. Choice **c** is incorrect because $\sqrt[m]{x^n} = x^{\frac{n}{m}}$ not $x^{\frac{m}{n}}$. Choice **d** is incorrect because $\frac{x^a}{x^b} = x^{a-b}$, not $x^{\frac{a}{b}}$. Choice **e** is incorrect because $x^a \cdot x^b = x^{a+b}$, not $x^{a \cdot b}$.

17. **The correct answer is choice d.** Apply the exponent rules, as follows:
$$\frac{2^3 \times 7^3}{14^{-2}} = \frac{(2 \times 7)^3}{14^{-2}} = \frac{14^3}{14^{-2}} = 14^3 \cdot 14^2 = 14^5$$
Choice **a** is incorrect because the sign of the exponent is incorrect. Choice **b** is incorrect because $\frac{x^b}{x^c} = x^{b-c}$, not x^{b+c}. Choice **c** is incorrect because $x^b \cdot y^b = (x \cdot y)^b$, not $(x \cdot y)^{b+b}$. Choice **e** is incorrect because $\frac{x^b}{x^c} = x^{b-c}$, not $x^{b \cdot c}$.

18. **The correct answer is choice c.** Use the two points labeled on the line to find the slope of the line: $m = \frac{105 - 90}{25 - 30} = -3$. So the equation of the line is $y - 105 = -3(x - 25)$, which is equivalent to $y = -3x + 180$. So $y(50) = 30$. Choice **a** is incorrect because this is the average number of text messages for a 40-year-old. Choice **b** is incorrect because this is the average number of text messages for a 30-year-old. Choice **d** is incorrect because this is the average number of text messages for a 15-year-old. Choice **e** is incorrect because this is the y-intercept of the best fit line.

19. **The correct answer is choice e.** Distribute the $-3x^2$ through all terms of the trinomial:
$$-3x^2(1 - 4x - 2x^2) = (-3x^2)(1) - (-3x^2)(4x) - $$
$$(-3x^2)(2x^2)$$
$$= -3x^2 + 12x^3 + 6x^4$$
$$= 6x^4 + 12x^3 - 3x^2$$

Choice **a** is incorrect because you ignored the negative sign in front of the $3x^2$ term. Choice **b** is incorrect because you only multiplied the first term of the trinomial by $-3x^2$. Choice **c** is incorrect because when applying the distributive property, multiply the coefficient of each term by the expression outside the parentheses. Choice **d** is incorrect because you only multiplied the highest degree term of the trinomial by $-3x^2$.

20. **The correct answer is choice c.** Let x be the number of vinyl albums. Then the number of CDs is $2x - 3$. Multiply each quantity by the cost per unit and add the resulting expressions to get the total cost \$275.50. Doing so results in the equation in choice **c**. Choice **a** is incorrect because you cannot use two different variables and just one equation if you hope to determine the values of both variables. Choice **b** is incorrect because the number of CDs is $2x - 3$, not $2x + 3$, where x is the number of vinyl albums. Choice **d** is incorrect. Let x be the number of vinyl albums. You must multiply the number of CDs by the cost of one CD and the number of vinyl albums by the cost of one vinyl album, rather than combining them into a single term. Also, the number of CDs is $2x - 3$, not $2x + 3$. Choice **e** is incorrect because you interchanged the costs of one CD and one vinyl album in the equation.

21. **The correct answer is choice c.** The radicand must be nonnegative for the function to be defined. This means $3 - x \geq 0$, so $x \leq 3$. Choice **a** is incorrect because the inequality should be reversed. Choice **b** is incorrect because 3 should be included in the domain, since $\sqrt{0} = 0$. Choice **d** is incorrect because this is the range, not the domain. Choice **e** is incorrect because the inequality should be reversed, and 3 should be included in the domain, since $\sqrt{0} = 0$.

22. **The correct answer is choice d.** The average rate of change of this function on the interval $[0,a]$, for any value a, is
$$\frac{j(a) - j(0)}{a - 0} = \frac{(5a + 1) - (5 \cdot 0 + 1)}{a - 0} = \frac{5a}{a} = 5$$
Choices **a**, **b**, **c**, and **e** are incorrect because these functions are nonlinear and so cannot have a constant rate of change. For instance, the average rate of change is different on $[0,1]$ than it is on $[0,2]$ or $[0,4]$.

23. **The correct answer is choice d.** Use the addition formula because the events share common outcomes:

$$P(\text{male or spotted}) = P(\text{male}) + P(\text{spotted})$$
$$- P(\text{male and spotted})$$
$$= \frac{6}{9} + \frac{4}{9} - \frac{3}{9}$$
$$= \frac{7}{9}$$

Choice **a** is incorrect because this is the probability that the puppy selected is a spotted female. Choice **b** is incorrect because this is the probability that the puppy selected is a spotted male. Choice **c** is incorrect because this is the probability that the puppy selected is spotted. Choice **e** is incorrect because this is the probability that the puppy selected is male.

24. **The correct answer is choice b.** Let e be the edge length of the cube. The surface area formula is $6e^2 = 150$, so that $e^2 = 25$ and $e = 5$. Thus, the volume of the cube is $e^3 = 5^3 = 125$ cubic centimeters. Choice **a** is incorrect because you used $6e^3$ for the volume formula instead of e^3, where e is an edge of the cube. Choice **c** is incorrect because this is the length of an edge of the cube, not its volume. Choice **d** is incorrect because this is the area of a face of the cube, not its volume. Choice **e** is incorrect because 5^3 does not equal 15.

25. **The correct answer is choice d.** The area of the larger circular sector is $\frac{250°}{360°}(\pi \cdot 7^2) = \frac{25}{36}(49\pi)$ in.^{2}. The area of the smaller circular sector is $\frac{250°}{360°} = (\pi \cdot 3^2) = \frac{25}{36}(9\pi)$ in.^{2}. So the area of the shaded region is the difference between these two areas, namely $[\frac{25}{36}(49\pi) - \frac{25}{36}(9\pi)]$ in.$^2 = \frac{25}{36}(40\pi)$ in.$^2 = \frac{250}{9}\pi$ in.^{2}.

Choice **a** is incorrect because you used $\frac{\theta}{180°}$ instead of $\frac{\theta}{360°}$ in the area formula. Choice **b** is incorrect because this uses a central angle of 360° (which corresponds to the entire circle) instead of 250°. Choice **c** is incorrect because this is the difference in the lengths of the circular arcs formed using the two concentric circles for the given sectorial region. Choice **e** is incorrect because this is the area of such a region corresponding to a central angle of 110°.

26. **The correct answer is choice e.** Let x be the desired mass. Set up a proportion and solve for x:

$$\frac{5 \text{ containers}}{3.2 \text{ kg}} = \frac{8 \text{ containers}}{x \text{ kg}}$$
$$5x = 8(3.2) = 25.6$$
$$x = 5.12 \text{ kg} = 5{,}120 \text{ g}$$

Choice **a** is incorrect because you set up the proportion incorrectly by inverting one of the fractions. Choice **b** is incorrect because you used the wrong units; this should be 5.12 kg, not 5.12 g. Choice **c** is incorrect because this would correspond to 10 containers, not 8. Choice **d** is incorrect because you set up the proportion incorrectly by inverting one of the fractions.

27. **The correct answer is choice b.** The steps of the transformation are as follows:

(a,b) moves to the right 3 units to arrive at $(a + 3,b)$

$(a + 3,b)$ moves down 2 units to arrive at $(a + 3, b - 2)$

$(a + 3, b - 2)$ is reflected over the y-axis to arrive at $(-a - 3, b - 2)$

So the final coordinates are $(-a - 3, b - 2)$. Choice **a** is incorrect because while you implemented the translations to the right 3 units and down 2 units correctly, you reflected the resulting point over the origin, not the y-axis. Choice **c** is incorrect because while you implemented the translations to the right 3 units and down 2 units correctly, you reflected the resulting point over the line $y = x$, not the y-axis. Choice **d** is incorrect because you did not reflect the correctly translated point over the y-axis. Choice **e** is incorrect because you translated the original point left 3 units and up 2 units, which is incorrect, but then correctly reflected that resulting point over the y-axis.

28. **The correct answer is choice c.** Since you are given the side adjacent to the angle 50° and the hypotenuse L, you want to use cosine. Since cosine of an angle is the length of the side adjacent to the angle divided by the hypotenuse, we get $\cos 50° = \frac{10}{L}$. Solving for L yields $L = \frac{10}{\cos 50°}$. Choice **a** is incorrect because 10 should be divided by $\cos 50°$, not multiplied by it. Choice **b** is incorrect because you cannot use sine since you do not have the side opposite the given angle. Choice **d** is incorrect because you cannot use sine since you do not have the side opposite the given angle. Choice **e** is incorrect because you cannot use tangent since you do not have the side opposite the given angle.

29. **The correct answer is choice a.** Of all of the scatter plots with best fit lines shown, this particular one correctly illustrates the rising from left to right pattern of the data points and minimizes the vertical distance between the points and the line itself. Choice **b** is incorrect because this line does not accurately illustrate the rising from left to right trend evident in the data points. Choice **c** is incorrect because while this correctly illustrates the rising from left to right trend in the data points, it lies beneath all the points and therefore does not minimize the vertical distance between the points and the line. Choice **d** is incorrect because this line does not accurately illustrate the rising from left to right trend evident in the data points. Choice **e** is incorrect because while this correctly illustrates the rising from left to right trend in the data points, the vast majority of the points are below the line and therefore do not minimize the vertical distance between the points and the line itself.

30. **The correct answer is choice e.** As y increases, its reciprocal $\frac{1}{y}$ decreases. Therefore, you would be dividing by less in the expression for Z, which makes its value increase. Choice **a** is incorrect because you are dividing by less, which means the value of Z would increase. Choice **b** is incorrect because you are dividing by less, which means the value of Z would increase. Choice **c** is incorrect because as x and y decrease, their reciprocals increase. So you are dividing by more, which means the value of Z would decrease. Choice **d** is incorrect because you are dividing by more, which means the value of Z would decrease.

31. **The correct answer is choice a.** Factor all expressions and then cancel like factors in the numerator and denominator:

$$\frac{4x^3 - 2x^2 - 2x}{4x^2 - 4x + 1} \cdot \frac{2x^2 - x}{x^2 - 1} = \frac{2x(x-1)(2x+1)}{(2x-1)(2x-1)} \cdot \frac{x(2x-1)}{(x-1)(x+1)}$$

$$= \frac{2x(x-1)(2x+1)}{(2x-1)(2x-1)} \cdot \frac{x(2x-1)}{(x-1)(x+1)}$$

$$= \frac{2x^2(2x+1)}{(2x-1)(2x+1)}$$

$$= \frac{4x^3 + 2x^2}{2x^2 + x - 1}$$

Choice **b** is incorrect because you mistakenly canceled $2x + 1$ in the top with $2x - 1$ in the bottom; these are not like factors. Choice **c** is incorrect because you cannot cancel terms like this in a fraction:

$$\frac{4x^3 - 2x^2 - 2x}{4x^2 + x - 1} \neq \frac{4x^3 + 2x^2}{2x^2 + x - 1}$$

Choice **d** is incorrect because you divided the two rational expressions instead of multiplying them. Choice **e** is incorrect because this is the reciprocal of the correct answer.

32. **The correct answer is choice d.** Multiply the first equation by -2, and you get the second one. Therefore, these equations are equivalent; every point on the line satisfies both equations in the system, so the system has infinitely many solutions. Choice **a** is incorrect because this system has no solution. The lines are parallel since they have the same slope 3 and different y-intercepts. Choice **b** is incorrect because these lines are perpendicular, so the system has a unique solution. Choice **c** is incorrect because this system has a unique solution since the lines have different slopes. Choice **e** is incorrect because this system has a unique solution since it is composed of a horizontal line and a vertical line.

33. **The correct answer is choice b.** For a quadratic equation to have a repeated real solution, the expression must be a perfect trinomial square. If $a = 16$, the trinomial factors as $(4x + 5)^2$, and so the resulting quadratic equation has one solution, namely $x = -\frac{5}{4}$. Alternatively, if you use the fact that the discriminant equals 0, meaning $b^2 - 4ac = 0$, with $b = 40$ and $c = 25$, you can solve for a to get 16. Choice **a** is incorrect because this would be the coefficient of the x term obtained when factoring the correct trinomial as a binomial squared. This is not, however, the value of a. Choice **c** is incorrect because when you multiply $4x$ times $4x$, you get $16x^2$, not $8x^2$. So, $a = 16$, not 8. Choice **d** is incorrect because this would require the middle term of the trinomial to be $-40x$, not $40x$, for it to factor as a perfect square trinomial. Choice **e** is incorrect because this would be the coefficient of the x term obtained when factoring the correct trinomial as a binomial squared, assuming the middle term of the trinomial were $-40x$.

34. **The correct answer is choice b.** The correct formula to use is $P_0(1 + 4)^t$, where P_0 is the amount invested and r is the interest rate. Using $P_0 = \$4{,}200$ and $r = 0.03$ yields the formula in choice **b**. Choice **a** is incorrect because this would mean the value went down 3% each year, not up. Choice **c** is incorrect because the term $1.03t$ should be $(1.03)^t$. Choice **d** is incorrect because the 4,200 and 1.03 must be interchanged. Choice **e** is incorrect because the term $t^{1.03}$ should be $(1.03)^t$.

35. **The correct answer is choice c.** There are 32 possible outcomes:

11	12	13	14	15	16	17	18
21	22	23	24	25	26	27	28
31	32	33	34	35	36	37	38
41	42	43	44	45	46	47	48

Of these, 19 satisfy the condition. So the probability is $\frac{19}{32}$. Choice **a** is incorrect because this probability includes the number 25 as one of the desired outcomes, but the event specifies greater than 25, not greater than or equal to 25. Choice **b** is incorrect because since the red die is four-sided and the blue die is eight-sided, there is a total of $8 \times 4 = 32$ possible outcomes. Choice **d** is incorrect because this is the probability of the complement of the event. Choice **e** is incorrect because this may have resulted from reversing the order of the red and blue dice when recording the outcomes.

36. **The correct answer is choice c.** The product of two irrational numbers can be irrational or rational. For instance, $\sqrt{2} \cdot \sqrt{2} = 2$, which is rational. So this statement is not true. Choice **a** is incorrect because this is a property of rational numbers. Choice **b** is incorrect because this is a property of rational and irrational numbers. Choice **d** is incorrect because this is a property of rational numbers. Choice **e** is incorrect because this is a property of irrational numbers.

37. **The correct answer is choice c.** Let x be the score in the fifth game. We need the range of x for which the following inequality is satisfied:
$$200 \leq \frac{191 + 218 + 210 + 171 + x}{5} \leq 215$$
Solving this inequality yields
$$200 \leq \frac{790 + x}{5} \leq 215$$
$$1,000 \leq 790 + x \leq 1,075$$
$$210 \leq x \leq 285$$

So, the necessary range is 210 to 285. Choice **a** is incorrect because this cannot work because the average of the first four games is 197.5. Choice **b** is incorrect because you divided by 4, not 5. Choice **d** is incorrect because this is the range that describes her first four games. Choice **e** is incorrect because this range is too low.

38. **The correct answer is choice a.** First solve the given equation for y: $y = -\frac{a}{2}x - \frac{a}{2}$. Its slope is $-\frac{a}{2}$. So any line whose slope is neither $-\frac{a}{2}$ (parallel) nor $\frac{2}{a}$ (perpendicular) is a viable answer. Since the slope of the line in choice **a** is a, it is the correct answer. Choice **b** is incorrect because the slope of this line is $\frac{2}{a}$, which makes it perpendicular to the given line. Choice **c** is incorrect because the slope of this line is $-\frac{a}{2}$, which makes it parallel to the given line. Choice **d** is incorrect because the slope of this line is $\frac{2}{a}$, which makes it perpendicular to the given line. Choice **e** is incorrect because the slope of this line is $\frac{2}{a}$, which makes it perpendicular to the given line.

39. The correct answer is choice a. There are 5 vowels and 9 consonants in the bag, so it is not equally like to choose a vowel and a consonant. The statement is false. Choice **b** is incorrect because 7 of the 14 tiles (50%) in the bag satisfy this condition, so this statement is true. Choice **c** is incorrect because there are 2 P tiles and 2 B tiles, so this statement is true. Choice **d** is incorrect because there are 4 E tiles and 2 C tiles, so the statement is true. Choice **e** is incorrect because $\frac{1}{14}$ is approximately 0.071, which is approximatcly 7%. This statement is true.

40. The correct answer is choice b. Use the distributive property and then combine like terms:

$$6x(1-3x)-2x^2(9-x^2)=6x-18x^2-18x^2+2x^4$$
$$=2x^4-36x^2+6x$$

Choice **a** is incorrect because the coefficient of the x^4 term should be positive. Choice **c** is incorrect because the middle term should be doubled. Choice **d** is incorrect because you did not apply the distributive property correctly when initially multiplying the terms outside each set of parentheses by those enclosed within them. Choice **e** is incorrect because you likely made a sign error because you canceled the x^2 terms, which have the same sign.

41. The correct answer is choice d. Solve for x as follows:

$$4(3-2x)-2(1-3x)=-2$$
$$12-8x-2+6x=-2$$
$$10-2x=-2$$
$$-2x=-12$$
$$x=6$$

Choice **a** is incorrect because you did not apply the distributive property correctly. You must multiply both terms of the binomial by the term outside the parentheses. Choice **b** is incorrect because the solution of a linear equation of the form $ax=b$ is $x=\frac{b}{a}$, not $\frac{a}{b}$. Choice **c** is incorrect because when solving a linear equation of the form $a+bx=c$, subtract a from both sides; do not add it to both sides. Choice **e** is incorrect because you did not multiply $-3x$ in the second binomial by -1.

42. The correct answer is choice d. Solve for r, as follows:

$$V=\frac{1}{3}\pi r^2 h$$
$$3V=\pi r^2 h$$
$$\frac{3V}{\pi h}=r^2$$
$$\sqrt{\frac{3V}{\pi h}}=r$$
$$\text{So } r=\sqrt{\frac{3V}{\pi h}}.$$

Choice **a** is incorrect because you should be dividing by πh inside the radicand, not multiplying by it. Choice **b** is incorrect because you should be dividing by πh, not multiplying by it, and you mishandled the square root. Choice **c** is incorrect because you did not apply the square root correctly. When solving for r, take the square root of both sides instead of multiplying both sides by 2. Choice **e** is incorrect because you should have multiplied both sides by 3 instead of dividing by it and then taken the square root.

43. The correct answer is choice d. Let x denote the width of the rectangle and y the length. The perimeter equation is $2x + 2y = 40$, which is equivalent to $x + y = 20$ (where we have divided both sides by 2), and the area equation is $xy = 96$. So the system in choice **d** is correct. Choice **a** is incorrect because the right sides of the equations should be interchanged. Choice **b** is incorrect because the area equation is incorrect. You used the area formula for a triangle. Choice **c** is incorrect because the area equation is incorrect. You used the area formula for a triangle. Choice **e** is incorrect because the perimeter equation is incorrect. You should double both the length and the width to get the perimeter of a rectangle.

44. The correct answer is choice c. The center of the circle is the midpoint of the diameter: $(\frac{7+0}{2}, \frac{0+9}{2}) = (\frac{7}{2}, \frac{9}{2})$. The radius is one-half the length of the diameter: $\frac{1}{2}\sqrt{7^2 + 9^2} = \frac{1}{2}\sqrt{130}$. So the equation of the circle in standard form is $(x - \frac{7}{2})^2 + (y - \frac{9}{2})^2 = \frac{65}{2}$ (where the right side is the square of the radius). Choice **a** is incorrect because the right side should be the square of the radius, not the radius itself. Choice **b** is incorrect because you used the diameter instead of the radius on the right side, and you should subtract the coordinates of the center when using the standard form of the circle, not add them. Choice **d** is incorrect because the squared terms on the left side of the equation should be added, not subtracted. Choice **e** is incorrect because the right side should be the radius squared, and the squared terms on the left side of the equation should be added, not subtracted.

45. The correct answer is choice b. Subtract the two quantities:

$$(2.9 \times 10^9) - (3.2 \times 10^8) = (29 \times 10^8) - (3.2 \times 10^8)$$
$$= (29 - 3.2) \times 10^8$$
$$= 25.8 \times 10^8$$
$$= 2.58 \times 10^9$$

Choice **a** is incorrect because you subtracted incorrectly. You must first convert the quantities to those that involve the same power of 10; then you can subtract the decimal parts. Choice **c** is incorrect because you cannot subtract $3.2 - 2.9$ and keep 10^9 as the power of 10 like this. Convert (2.9×10^9) to (29×10^8) and then subtract the decimal parts. Choice **d** is incorrect because you added instead of subtracting the quantities. Choice **e** is incorrect because this is equivalent to the expression in choice **c** and is incorrect. You cannot subtract $3.2 - 2.9$ and keep 10^9 as the power of 10 like this. Convert (2.9×10^9) to (29×10^8) and then subtract the decimal parts.

46. The correct answer is choice b. Neither $x^2 + 5 = 0$ nor $x^2 + 2 = 0$ has real solutions. And since both factors are positive, this graph would always be above the x-axis, which means it has no x-intercepts and, hence, no real zeros. Choice **a** is incorrect because $0, -1,$ and -2 are real zeros for this polynomial. Choice **c** is incorrect because 0 is a real zero for this polynomial. Choice **d** is incorrect because the expression factors as $(x + 3)(x + 2)(x + 1)^2$ and has real zeros of $-3, -2,$ and -1. Choice **e** is incorrect because the expression factors as $(x - 1)(x + 1)(x^2 + 1)$ and has real zeros of -1 and 1.

47. The correct answer is choice a. The graph of $g(x)$ has vertex at $(-2,-6)$. Since it is opening downward (because the coefficient of the squared term is negative), the range includes all y-values starting at -6 and going down. That is, the range is $\{y|y \leq -6\}$. Choice **b** is incorrect because the graph of $g(x)$ opens downward, not upward. Choice **c** is incorrect because you are using the x-coordinate of the vertex to guide your decision about the range, but should be using the y-coordinate. Choice **d** is incorrect because 6 should be replaced by -6 since the vertex is $(-2,-6)$, not $(-2,6)$. Choice **e** is incorrect because this is the domain, not the range.

48. The correct answer is choice a. Organize the information in a table as follows:

	RATE	TIME	DISTANCE
Walker 1	b	t	$28 - D$
Walker 2	a	t	D

Using distance = rate × time, we see that

$$28 - D = bt$$
$$D = at$$

Adding these two equations yields $28 = (a + b)t$, so that $t = \frac{28}{a+b}$. Choice **b** is incorrect because you should be dividing by $a + b$, not multiplying by it. Choice **c** is incorrect because the walkers are not necessarily walking at the same speed, so a need not equal b. Choice **d** is incorrect because this should be the reciprocal of what is listed. When solving for t, divide both sides of the equation by its coefficient, not by the right side. Choice **e** is incorrect because you should be adding the speeds in the denomination, not subtracting them.

49. The correct answer is choice b. Solve for x as follows:

$$\sqrt[3]{x^2 + 1} = 2$$
$$x^2 + 1 = 2^3$$
$$x^2 + 1 = 8$$
$$x^2 = 7$$
$$x = \pm\sqrt{7}$$

Both of these values satisfy the original equation. So the solution set is $\{-\sqrt{7}, \sqrt{7}\}$. Choice **a** is incorrect because $2^3 = 8$, not 6. Choice **c** is incorrect because you neglected the cube root entirely. Choice **d** is incorrect because you forgot to include $-\sqrt{7}$. Remember that when solving an equation of the form $x^2 = a$, there are two solutions, $x = \pm\sqrt{a}$. Choice **e** is incorrect because $2^3 = 8$, not 6, and when solving an equation of the form $x^2 = a$, there are two solutions, $x = \pm\sqrt{a}$.

50. The correct answer is choice c. First, triangles AWX and AZY are similar by the angle-angle property. So the following proportion relating the sides holds: $\frac{a+c}{a} = \frac{30}{b}$. Observe that the distance from A to W is $a + c$. Using this proportion and multiplying both sides by a, we see that $a + c = \frac{30a}{b}$. Choice **a** is incorrect because this expression is the sum of the base lengths but not the distance from one side of the creek to the other. Choice **b** is incorrect because you did not set up the proportion relating the sides correctly; specifically, you inverted one of the fractions. Choice **d** is incorrect because this is the value of c; you must add a to this to get the distance across the creek. Choice **e** is incorrect because you did not set up the proportion relating the sides correctly; specifically, you inverted one of the fractions.

Science

To calculate your HiSET® score on the Science section, first take a look at the correct answer for each of the 50 questions of the exam. Count up your **correct answers** only, and give yourself 1 point for each. Then, add up all of your points. This is your **raw score**.

Find your raw score and your **scaled score** in the following table. Remember, for each test section, a passing score is 8. (For the essay, a passing score is 2.)

You need a scaled score of 45 to pass the complete HiSET® exam.

SCIENCE SCORING			
RAW	SCALED	RAW	SCALED
0	1	26	12
1	1	27	12
2	2	28	12
3	2	29	13
4	3	30	13
5	3	31	13
6	4	32	13
7	5	33	14
8	6	34	14
9	7	35	14
10	8	36	14
11	8	37	15
12	8	38	15
13	9	39	15
14	9	40	15
15	9	41	16
16	10	42	16
17	10	43	16
18	10	44	17
19	10	45	17
20	10	46	18
21	11	47	18
22	11	48	19
23	11	49	20
24	11	50	20
25	12		

1. **The correct answer is choice b.** Experiments 1 and 3 both use purely visual means to alert the vultures to a potential meal—experiment 1 uses a fake carcass and experiment 3 uses a painting of a carcass, but neither one uses real meat or anything else with a scent. Choice **a** is incorrect because this hypothesis is not ruled out by the results, but the experiment does not examine the searching process, only whether the vultures find a meal. Choice **c** is incorrect because no scented objects were used in experiments 1 or 3, so these experiments could not have been testing the sense of smell. Choice **d** is incorrect because experiments 1 and 3 each have only one variable. They are testing only sight.

2. **The correct answer is choice a.** The vultures were quickly attracted to images of food but were unable to locate real, smelly food that was hidden from view. Those results clearly suggest that the vultures are looking for food rather than smelling it. Choice **b** is incorrect because this conclusion can be drawn only if the results of the experiment are reversed. Choice **c** is incorrect because this conclusion was considered by Audubon, but the results of experiment 4 suggest that even when a smelly meal is nearby the vultures ignore the smell in favor of the painting of the carcass. That suggests that the vultures do not use smell to find food at all, even when it is nearby. Choice **d** is incorrect because the vultures being attracted to a realistic image of a carcass does not suggest that they are intelligent or unintelligent, only that they use eyesight to locate food.

3. **The correct answer is choice c.** Vultures approach the carcass from the air, and vultures looking for vultures would first see them flying above the carcass. Choice **a** is incorrect because this method would be a good test of whether vultures might find prey by listening for other vultures, but the question asks how to test if vultures look for other vultures. Choice **b** is incorrect because this method places the decoys too close to the real carcass; by the time a vulture can see the decoys, it can see the carcass, too. By then there is no way to tell if the sight of vulture decoys helped real vultures find the carcass. Choice **d** is incorrect because this method confuses the results in a few ways. One, if using living vultures, there is no way to tell if the additional vultures homed in on the sight of the new vultures or the sounds they make. The other problem is that the experiment times later vultures instead of the first to arrive, making it very difficult to standardize the vultures' response times.

4. **The correct answer is choice c.** The test has been performed on two different species of vultures, one of which used visual cues to find the food and one of which (the turkey vulture) seems to have used its sense of smell instead of its eyesight. The statement is true, at least for these two species. Choice **a** is incorrect because this conclusion is suggesting that each species has more than one way to find food, but that statement is not supported by any of the experiments. Both the black and the turkey vultures used only one method to look for a carcass; black vultures used their eyesight and turkey vultures used their sense of smell. Choice **b** is incorrect because this conclusion is disproved by the opposite results of the same experiment for each species of vulture. Choice **d** is incorrect because this is too broad a conclusion to draw from the available evidence. In all of the experiments combined, only two species of vulture were tested. It is impossible to generalize from only two species that every single type of vulture finds food differently.

5. **The correct answer is choice d.** The Experimental Removal Study tests the idea that more fish are attracted to roots that have more epibiotas. Looking at this relationship in a wide variety of different areas confirms that the relationship actually exists in the world, not just under the conditions of the experiment. Choice **a** is incorrect because even if the results of the experiment are confirmed in different sites, that information does not prove that the experimental methods were sound. Choice **b** is incorrect because this could be the reason, but there is no mention of what future studies might be or why examining the relationship between fish and epibiotas in different sites would help with additional studies. Choice **c** is incorrect because both studies are examining the relationship between fish and epibiotas in different ways, but there is no indication that one study is better than the other.

6. **The correct answer is choice b.** The horizontal axis of the graph shows the total area of each root that is covered with epibiotas, and the vertical axis shows the density of fish per square meter in each site. As the area of epibiotas increases, the density of fish increases as well. Choice **a** is incorrect because as the epibiota area increases, the fish density increases, not decreases. The line of circles would start high and slant downward if it were a negative relationship. Choice **c** is incorrect because the line of circles trends upward, whereas if the fish were not increasing the circles would be in a flat row. Choice **d** is incorrect because the x-axis of the graph says that it represents the total area of epibiotas. The graph does not specify how many individual organisms are present.

7. **The correct answer is choice b.** Since the graph is not a straight line, it is necessary to look at 7 on the horizontal axis and estimate where in the cluster of points you would find a corresponding value for the y-axis. All of the points with an x-axis value near 7 have y-axis values between 2.5 and 3; 2.75 is roughly in between all of them. Choice **a** is incorrect because it is too low. Most of the points that have 2 fish per m^2 are closer to 5 than to 7. Choice **c** is incorrect because it is too high; a density of 4 fish per m^2 does not occur until there are nearly 8 in^2 epibiotas per root. Choice **d** is incorrect because it is much too high; the highest density of fish on the entire graph is fewer than 5 fish per m^2.

8. **The correct answer is choice d.** Before the Experimental Removal Study, there were about 22 fish per section in the areas where epibiotas were not removed. Afterward, there were nearly 45 fish per section, so at some point between counts more fish must have moved into the untouched areas. Choice **a** is incorrect because fish numbers declined slightly where epibiotas were removed. Choice **b** is incorrect because the number of fish increased where the epibiotas were not removed. Choice **c** is incorrect because this description is not supported by the numbers; the increase in fish where the epibiotas were untouched is greater than the decline where they were removed.

9. **The correct answer is choice b.** If the hypothesis is that epibiotas are very important for the quality of the fish habitat, than removal of the epibiotas in the experimental sections should cause the fish to leave, while the fish should still remain in the untouched control sections. Choice **a** is incorrect because the result does support the hypothesis, but not as strongly as it might. Since most fish did not leave when the epibiotas were removed, there are clearly other factors aside from the epibiotas that attract fish to the roots. Choice **c** is incorrect because this would probably lead the biologist to reject the hypothesis, for if more fish entered the areas where the epibiotas were removed and simultaneously left the areas with epibiotas, the implication would be that epibiotas are not important to fish habitat quality. Choice **d** is incorrect because this would likely lead to rejection of the hypothesis, as if the fish also leave the control sections then the biologist cannot conclude that the removal of the epibiotas caused the fish to leave the experimental sections.

10. **The correct answer is choice a.** Yolande decided based on the taste of chocolate explosion to test whether it contained chocolate. This hypothesis is a testable statement based on her impression. Choice **b** is incorrect because it is actual data based on her experiments, not a testable statement. Choice **c** is incorrect because it is an assumption that more chocolate taste reflects a higher chocolate content. Choice **d** is incorrect because it is the conclusion of the experiment based on the data; her hypothesis is incorrect since chocolate blast actually had more chocolate.

11. **The correct answer is choice b.** A control is a benchmark set to make sure that the experimental change is actually responsible for the observed result. In this case, the only way to be certain if the wagon with narrow wheels is faster is test a wagon with standard wheels under identical circumstances and compare times. Choice **a** is incorrect because the two different types of wheels are being compared, but the test conditions are not identical, so this is not a good control. Choice **c** is incorrect because this procedure repeats the experiment again using the same narrow wheels. Most experiments need to be repeated to make sure the results are accurate, but repetition is not the same as a control. Choice **d** is incorrect because this procedure uses the same wheels under different conditions, so the effect being tested is the ramp compared to a flat surface. The two different types of wheels are not being compared.

12. **The correct answer is choice a.** The two maps are shaded in very similar areas, so there is overlap between modern-day lactose tolerance and areas where herding dairy animals was important to the economy. Choice **b** is incorrect because this statement might be true, but all the map says for sure is that there is geographic overlap between dairy herds and lactose tolerance. It cannot tell you which came first. Choice **c** is incorrect because this statement might be true in that lactose tolerance makes a whole new source of calories available where dairy animals are domesticated, but there is no way to make that claim based only on the maps. Choice **d** is incorrect because this statement might be true, but the map only shows the areas where lactose tolerance is common now; it does not provide any information about how or if lactose tolerance spread through Europe.

13. The correct answer is choice d. When humans had access to a steady supply of milk, the ability to digest milk as an adult gave them access to a whole new source of calories. Choice **a** is incorrect because this statement is true, but it explains why early humans were lactose intolerant, not why lactose tolerance became an advantage. Choice **b** is incorrect because the overlapping maps make this assertion unlikely; since tolerance arose in the same areas where dairy herding was common, a relationship between the herding and lactose tolerance can be inferred. Choice **c** is incorrect because this statement is true, but it does not explain why lactose tolerance in adults arose in the same locations where dairy herding was important.

14. The correct answer is choice c. It is highly possible that once lactose tolerance became widespread, dairy production became more economically important since more people could make use of dairy products and dairy animals. The only way to know which came first is to know exactly when the gene originated relative to the dairy economy. Choice **a** is incorrect; this information would be necessary, but without knowing if the lactose intolerance gene is older or younger than the dairy economy, there is no way to guess what the influence of lactose tolerance might have been. Choice **b** is incorrect because this information might help explain the spread of lactose tolerance, but without knowing how long ago the gene appeared, there is no way to know its impact on a dairy economy. Choice **d** is incorrect because this information would be useful in understanding more about how the prehistoric dairy economy functioned but would not help to explain the influence of the lactose tolerance gene.

15. The correct answer is choice b. It represents actual observed evidence of Planet 9. Even if Planet 9 is ultimately not found, observed evidence of its influence is a very credible reason to believe that it is there. Choice **a** is incorrect because, although it shows that there is long-standing interest in Planet 9, there is nothing in long-term interest by itself that provides reliable reason to believe that Planet 9 is real. Choice **c** is incorrect because, although it lends support to Planet 9, 15% is not a large number. In any event, the astronomers need to have a reliable reason to believe Planet 9 is real. Choice **d** is incorrect because it does not provide a good reason why Planet 9 might exist, only that some astronomers have enough confidence in its existence to actually spend their time searching.

16. The correct answer is choice a. It is probable from the information given that red flowers are *RR* and white flowers are *WW* because they are said to be the result of generations of breeding between same-colored plants. This suggests that red flowers are homozygous for a certain allele and that white flowers are homozygous for the other allele. As stated in the question, *R* is for red and *W* is for white. If you cross a red-flowered and a white-flowered plant, chances are that all the offspring will be genotype *RW*. You can then check the offspring's appearance to confirm that *RW* is indeed pink. Choice **b** is incorrect because this is not a good test because if you are not sure what the pink flower genotype is, you cannot be certain that the offspring will be *RW*. Choice **c** is incorrect because this test will not help because all the offspring of a *RR* × *RR* mating must be *RR*, not *RW*. Choice **d** is incorrect since all the offspring of an *WW* × *WW* mating will be *WW*, not *RW*.

17. The correct answer is choice c. Although the number of offspring is not exactly the same each time pink- and red-flowered plants are mated, the number of red- and pink-flowered offspring is roughly the same for each of these matings. Choices **a** and **b** are incorrect because they are not supported by the chart, which shows roughly equal numbers of red- and pink-flowered offspring for these crossings. Choice **d** is incorrect because while the individual numbers may vary, the ratio of offspring in a pink-pink cross will remain roughly one-quarter red, one-quarter white, and half pink. Performing multiple crosses will not radically alter those proportions.

18. The correct answer is choice c. You know that red flowers are genotype RR, but only 50% of the offspring of red- and pink-flowered plant matings have red flowers. Therefore, only 50% of the offspring are genotype RR. Since there are no white flowers, no offspring are WW. That leaves RW as the only possible genotype for pink flowers. A cross of RR plants with RW plants can produce only RR or RW flowers in equal proportions, which explains the lack of white offspring. As confirmation, white-flowered offspring do result from a pink (RW) × pink (RW) cross, proving that the W allele is present in the pink-flowered genotype. Choice **a** is incorrect; if pink-flowered plants were RR, then when two pink-flowered plants were crossed it would be $RR \times RR$ and all the offspring would be red, not one-quarter red, one-quarter white, and half pink. Choice **b** is incorrect since that would mean a cross of pink-flowered plants would be $WW \times WW$ and all the offspring would have white flowers. Choice **d** is incorrect since only a cross of $RW \times RW$ can produce offspring of all three types.

19. The correct answer is choice d. The highest increase in mass occurs at 20°C, while at 40°C the rate has returned to 0. Choice **a** is incorrect because it is not shown in the chart; the rate begins to drop after 20°C. Choice **b** is incorrect because although it has the correct peak in the rate, the temperature declines rapidly, not gradually, before shutting off entirely at 40°C. Choice **c** is incorrect because it misidentifies when the rate starts increasing; the rate increases very slowly from 0°C to 10°C but increases rapidly after that until about 20°C. It does not shut down until around 40°C.

20. The correct answer is choice b. If the experiment is trying to determine the rate of photosynthesis at different temperatures, then any other factor that might affect the rate of photosynthesis must be kept the same in all the greenhouses. Otherwise it will not be possible to tell if the results are due to temperature or light, or to CO_2 concentration. Choice **a** is incorrect because it only means that the CO_2 concentration must be kept at a level the plants can tolerate; it does not explain why the CO_2 must be identical in every greenhouse. Choice **c** is incorrect because it is true that without enough CO_2 the plants will not grow, but this choice means only that each plant must have enough CO_2. It does not explain why the CO_2 must all be equal above the minimum level. Choice **d** is incorrect because if all factors other than the one being tested, temperature or light, are not kept constant, then it will be impossible to tell if the differences in growth are the result of the factor being tested.

21. The correct answer is choice a. The plant growth increases steadily as the intensity of light increases, resulting in a straight-line, positive graph. Choice **b** is incorrect because it has the relationship reversed; in this graph the rate of photosynthesis is decreasing as light activity increases. Choice **c** is incorrect because this graph depicts a relationship where the rate of photosynthesis increases to a point and then decreases again. Choice **d** is incorrect because this graph depicts a relationship closer to the results of experiment 1, where the rate increases steadily before beginning to decline and then dropping to zero almost instantly.

22. The correct answer is choice a. The light intensity is increased across the different greenhouses, while other factors are constant, so the effects of increasing light intensity are being tested. There is a maximum light intensity in the experiment, so the effects of even higher light intensities are not being tested. Choice **b** is incorrect because this hypothesis would be correct if there were many more greenhouses up to the maximum possible light intensity. Choice **c** is incorrect because this hypothesis would be better tested by keeping all the greenhouses at the same light level. If light intensity truly didn't matter, then growth would vary from plant to plant anyway. Choice **d** is incorrect because if the object is to test multiple factors, then more factors need to be varied in each experiment. Testing this hypothesis would require many more greenhouses.

23. The correct answer is choice d. A level of 1,000 lux is much higher than any light intensity tested in experiment 2; there is simply no way to determine what would happen under such radically different conditions without more information. Choice **a** is incorrect because the rate of photosynthesis might increase at 150 lux or another number similar to the quantities tested in experiment 2, but 1,000 lux is much higher than any light intensity tested and there is no way to determine what would happen under such radically different conditions without more information. Choice **b** is incorrect because given that experiment 2 suggests that increased light intensity increases photosynthesis, even if you could tell what would happen, there is no reason to assume that the rate would decrease. Choice **c** is incorrect because it is unlikely that the results in experiment 1 would not change since you are changing a variable that is shown in experiment 2 to affect the rate of photosynthesis.

24. The correct answer is choice c. As the size of the animal increases, the resting heart rate gets slower. You can understand from the amount of space available in a body that the smaller the animal, the smaller heart, so the only logical conclusion is that at least in mammals smaller hearts beat faster. Choice **a** is incorrect because this is not a conclusion that can be drawn from the graph, as nothing in the chart suggests that heart size is inverse to animal size. Choice **b** is incorrect because it cannot be inferred from the information in the chart. Choice **d** is incorrect because it is backwards; whales have the slowest heart rates of any of the animals mentioned.

25. **The correct answer is choice c.** The question is asking you to estimate a value based on other information in the chart. The rabbit has an average resting heart rate of 205 bpm, and a human's is 72 bpm. A 35-pound animal is a size in between rabbit and human, so without any other information, 130 bpm is the best estimate. Choice **a** is incorrect because 50 bpm is too slow; from the chart, that would be the rate for an animal larger than a human, and adult humans weigh more than 35 pounds. Choice **b** is incorrect because 80 bpm is right around the normal range for an adult human, but humans are much larger than 35 pounds. Choice **d** is incorrect because 400 bpm is too rapid; from the chart, one would expect a heart rate of 400 bpm from an animal smaller than a rabbit.

26. **The correct answer is choice d.** Examining a living specimen of the bird will allow you to make a thorough comparison to similar birds to confirm that it is different. With a living bird in hand, measurements of the body can be taken, DNA samples collected, and so on. Choice **a** is incorrect because a photograph of the bird would be helpful but does not provide the same level of detail that can be obtained from closely examining a living bird. Choice **b** is incorrect because additional sightings of the bird will help you learn more about the bird and help confirm your belief that it is a new species, but only detailed comparison of the bird to similar birds can truly determine whether it is a new species. Many animals look similar from a distance. Choice **c** is incorrect because recording the sounds of the bird may be helpful, especially if the bird makes a unique sound, but you cannot be certain that it is not an existing species of bird making a different sound that nobody has heard before.

27. **The correct answer is choice d.** The slope of the tide gauge line gets much steeper around 1990, indicating that the sea level is rising more rapidly. So long as the total change over the given time period is larger than the others, the average change per year is also larger. Choice **a** is incorrect because the slope between 1900 and 1930 is much shallower than the slope between 1990 and the present day. Choice **b** is incorrect because there's a more rapid rise during 1930 to 1960 than during 1900 to 1930, but the slope of the line suggests that the increase during this period is more gradual than since 1990. Choice **c** is incorrect because between 1960 and 1990, sea level rise is similar or identical to the average rise between 1930 and 1960.

28. **The correct answer is choice c.** It is impossible to tell from the graph exactly what the sea level was in 1900 since the graph is measuring change in sea level relative to the 1900 level. It had to be higher than zero, even if you don't know the exact number. Choice **a** is incorrect because a sea level less than zero is not possible. The ocean cannot be below the level of its basin. Choice **b** is incorrect because the graph is measuring change in sea level, not absolute sea level. Be careful to double-check the axis of the graph. Choice **d** is incorrect because there is no information provided that indicates an exact measurement of the 1900 sea level.

29. The correct answer is choice a. The increased sea level readings taken by the satellite are slightly more variable than the smooth trend line of the tide gauge average, but they follow the same basic trajectory of a steep increase since the satellite data begins in the 1990s. Choice **b** is incorrect because while they are independent sources of data, they are measuring the same phenomenon and show very similar results. Choice **c** is incorrect because there are only 20 years of satellite data compared to nearly 120 years of tide gauge data, but the reduced time period does not invalidate the satellite results. Choice **d** is incorrect because it is common to measure the same phenomenon using multiple different instruments, and two completely different systems are not likely to give exactly the same results. For a study like this analyzing a long-term trend, the similar results between the satellites and the tide gauges make the overall data stronger.

30. The correct answer is choice c. Data is provided only on how high the sea level has risen over the past 115 years, so only questions about the sea level itself can be answered. Choice **a** is incorrect because there is no information provided that might explain why sea level is increasing, only on what is happening to the sea level. Choice **b** is incorrect because data from both sources is presented but there is no indication about which method of measuring sea level is more reliable. Choice **d** is incorrect because the rate of sea level rise has not been constant over time, so the best prediction that could be made for future sea levels is a rough guess.

31. The correct answer is choice c. From the diagram, it is clear that only strike slip faults have sides that are moving sideways relative to one another rather than up or down. Choice **a** is incorrect because in reverse faults, one side of the fault rises relative to the other side, a vertical movement. Choice **b** is incorrect because in normal faults, one side of the fault moves down relative to the other side, a vertical movement. Choice **d** is incorrect because spreading zones were defined as plate boundaries, not faults, and the movement is also away from one another, not next to each other.

32. The correct answer is choice a. With a marking that crosses both sides of the fault, if one or both side moves, you will be able to tell from how the line is broken which way the fault moved. Choice **b** is incorrect because elevation meters would be very helpful in determining whether it is a reverse or normal fault but would not help if there is no change in elevation, as in a strike slip fault. Choice **c** is incorrect because measuring the width of the fault could be used to determine the rate of spread in a spreading zone, but most faults do not necessarily open when they move. Choice **d** is incorrect because taking rock samples can be helpful, as attributes of the rock such as age might be related to the type of fault, but in many cases the rocks on each side will be similar.

33. **The correct answer is choice a.** Reverse faults raise the rocks on one side of a fault relative to the rocks on the opposite side. This process can carry older rocks on the rising side above younger rocks on the other side and all the way above the youngest layer (the surface). Choice **b** is incorrect because normal faults lower the land on one side relative to the opposite side. The older layers will always be below the very youngest layers at the surface. Note that if one side of the fault drops far enough, older layers on the stationary side may wind up above younger layers on the dropping side. However, the surface will always be at the top. Choice **c** is incorrect because strike slip faults don't move up and down relative to one another so will not displace rocks of different ages relative to one another. Choice **d** is incorrect because spreading zones don't move up and down relative to one another so will not displace rocks of different ages relative to one another.

34. **The correct answer is choice d.** When magma is pooled underneath a layer of harder rock, if it is to escape, it needs an opening, just like any liquid. In a spreading zone, the rock pulls apart, leaving a slit through which magma can, and often does, pour out. Choice **a** is incorrect because a reverse fault might raise the level of magma underneath the rock if magma is present but will not present it with an opportunity to escape. Choice **b** is incorrect because a normal fault will press an existing magma deeper but not let it out. Choice **c** is incorrect because a strike slip fault moves sideways and will not affect any buried magma.

35. **The correct answer is choice a.** The diagram explains which way the land will move if the fault moves in an earthquake, but damage will depend on many factors, such as what kind of infrastructure is built near the fault and the severity of the quake. There is no way to estimate damage solely by the type of fault. Choice **b** is incorrect because the answer to this question can be determined from the diagram; in a normal fault, the land one side will sink, resulting in a drop in elevation. Choice **c** is incorrect because the answer to this question can be determined, as only strike slip faults, which move horizontally, will move in an east-west direction. Choice **d** is incorrect because the answer to this question can be determined based on the diagram, as the nature of the fault movement will determine the forces placed on the land. It is not necessary to know the different kinds of forces that are possible to know that this information can be determined by the direction of movement.

36. **The correct answer is choice b.** Remember that plants pull CO_2 from the atmosphere to use in photosynthesis. As many plants drop their leaves and go dormant for winter, the amount of photosynthesis decreases and less CO_2 is pulled from the atmosphere. Choice **a** is incorrect because colder temperatures will cause solids that are dissolved in liquids to settle out, but the same is not true for mixtures of gases. Choice **c** is incorrect because sources of CO_2 released into the atmosphere, for example forest fires or industrial output, increase during the summer. Choice **d** is incorrect because no evidence supporting this statement is provided.

37. The correct answer is choice b. A hypothesis must be testable, and if the researcher is measuring the phosphate in marine and terrestrial rocks, she can test the idea that marine rocks hold more phosphate. Choice **a** is incorrect because this is a true fact about phosphate, but there is no mention in this study of how the phosphate leaves the rocks. Choice **c** is incorrect because this might be a true statement about phosphate, but if the geologist wanted to test that hypothesis she should look in all kinds of rocks, not just two kinds. Choice **d** is incorrect because this is a true statement about phosphate, but the study as described makes no mention of impacts on plant growth.

38. The correct answer is choice b. Her hypothesis was that chameleons change color in order to blend in to their environment. If only one out of ten chameleons changed into the background color, then the hypothesis that chameleons change color for camouflage is not supported. Choice **a** is incorrect because this statement would be true if most of the chameleons turned brown, but only one of them did. Choice **c** is incorrect because repeat trials are not necessary given the strong results. If five of the chameleons changed, then it would be difficult to draw conclusions. Choice **d** is incorrect because this is a good alternative hypothesis for this experiment but does not say anything about the stated hypothesis.

39. The correct answer is choice d. This is an example of an observation; Obadiah notices that the spoon feels warmer to the touch after being in the tea, not why or how the warming occurred. Choice **a** is incorrect because this is not a testable statement; it is an observation of a physical phenomenon. Choice **b** is incorrect because a theory is an idea that is not 100% confirmed but has been tested repeatedly over time and is mostly accepted as correct. Obadiah is not looking at this issue as a theory; he is simply noticing what happens to the spoon. Choice **c** is incorrect because this is a general observation, not evidence proving or disproving that heat conduction occurs.

40. The correct answer is choice a. A substance can float in another substance if its density is less than the substance it is floating in. In this case, the only material with a lower density than the mineral oil is lithium. Choice **b** is incorrect because a substance can float in another substance if its density is less than the substance it is floating in. Sodium has a density of 971 kg/m^3, greater than the mineral oil density of 870 kg/m^3, and will sink. Choice **c** is incorrect because a substance can float in another substance if its density is less than the substance it is floating in. Titanium has a density of 4,500 kg/m^3, greater than the mineral oil density of 870 kg/m^3, and will sink. Choice **d** is incorrect because a substance can float in another substance if its density is less than the substance it is floating in. Platinum is much denser than mineral oil.

41. The correct answer is choice d. Since osmium has a higher density than the other materials, a piece of osmium of equal weight will be smaller than any of the other materials. Choice **a** is incorrect because aluminum is much less dense than osmium, so 1 ounce of aluminum will take up more space than 1 ounce of osmium will. Choice **b** is incorrect because iron is not as dense as osmium and will still take up more space than 1 ounce of osmium. Choice **c** is incorrect because gold is very dense but not as dense as osmium. It will require more room than osmium.

42. The correct answer is choice d. There are denser materials that are harder than less dense materials and less dense materials that are harder. Iron and steel, for example, are the same density, but steel is harder. The chart does not indicate a consistent relationship between the two properties. Choice **a** is incorrect because this statement is true at the extremes, as the least dense materials in the chart are the softest and the densest is the hardest, but in the middle ranges of the chart there is no detectable pattern. Choice **b** is incorrect because since there is no consistent change in hardness as density changes, there is no sign that hardness decreases as density increases. Choice **c** is incorrect because even if there is no consistent link between how density and hardness vary, there is considerable variation in hardness; it does not stay the same as density changes.

43. The correct answer is choice b. The question states that diamonds are at the top of the scale, Mohs hardness 10. If the object is to prove that diamond really is the hardest material, there is no point in using anything softer than Mohs hardness 9, unless the diamond fails the test and is scratched by the corundum. Choice **a** is incorrect because it is not suggested by any of the information provided. Choice **c** is incorrect because it is not necessarily true. A diamond can be scratched by another diamond. Choice **d** is incorrect because this conclusion has no evidence to support it, but even if it were true, using corundum would still be the easiest way to proceed with this test.

44. The correct answer is choice c. The question states that objects will accelerate in free fall at 9.8 m/s regardless of mass. Both objects have the same starting speed, and over the same distance in the absence of air resistance, acceleration will work completely equally on both objects, so they will land at the same time. Choice **a** is incorrect because the 3-ounce cube will be affected equally by acceleration as the 6-ounce cube. Choice **b** is incorrect because many people assume that the heavier object will fall faster. However, acceleration of a free-falling object is exactly the same regardless of the mass of the falling object. Choice **d** is incorrect because this would be true if pertinent information were not included, for example if wind resistance were not discussed, but all the relevant information is provided. Acceleration will act equally on both cubes.

45. The correct answer is choice d. The acceleration is the same for both objects, whether air resistance is present or not, but in the presence of air resistance, the shape of the falling object becomes important. A cylinder would probably draw greater resistance than the compact cube, but over such a short distance it would be hard to tell. Choice **a** is incorrect because given the difference in shape, the cylinder will be subject to more resistance than the cube and fall slightly more slowly. Choice **b** is incorrect because the more compact cube will fall faster, but there needs to be a greater distance for enough air resistance to build up for the difference to be obvious. Choice **c** is incorrect because wind speed might be an issue if there is very strong wind and a greater drop distance; a very strong gust might redirect the cylinder more than a cube. However, on a calm day wind is not a factor.

46. The correct answer is choice c. Remember that part of the definition of a catalyst is that it does not become a part of the reaction; the amount of catalyst is the same at the end of a reaction as at the beginning. Choice **a** is incorrect because catalysts are not used up during a reaction; they only speed the rate of the reaction. Choice **b** is incorrect because catalysts are not used up during a reaction; they only speed the rate of the reaction. Choice **d** is incorrect because for there to be more catalyst after the reaction, the catalyst would have to be a product of the reaction.

47. The correct answer is choice a. Looking at the graph, far less energy is required to reach the stage where the reactants start actually forming products. Less energy will always take less time to occur. Choice **b** is incorrect because catalysts position reactants so they may more easily react, but they do not create extra reactants. Choice **c** is incorrect because catalysts facilitate the reaction but do not serve as an energy source. Lower activation energy is required with a reaction than without one. Choice **d** is incorrect because catalysts sometimes can increase the yield of products from a reaction, but the amount of products is not connected to how a catalyst speeds up a reaction.

48. The correct answer is choice d. With such a wide range of catalysts tested in this particular reaction, this is the most logical question being answered by the experiment. Choice **a** is incorrect because this is really an observation, not a true hypothesis. Choice **b** is incorrect because this might be true and would be a good hypothesis for a different experiment, but the best way to test this hypothesis would be to use varying amounts of platinum, not several different catalysts. Choice **c** is incorrect because it is too general. Only the decomposition of hydrogen peroxide has been examined. It would be necessary to test a wide variety of different reactions to test such a general hypothesis about catalysts.

49. The correct answer is choice a. If surface area is the variable being tested, keep the type of catalyst consistent and vary the available surface area of platinum in the test. Using different-sized pieces is a good way to vary the available surface area of catalyst. Choice **b** is incorrect because this procedure will support the surface area hypothesis, but it adds additional variables—other catalysts—and it compares only two different levels of available surface area rather than a range. Choice **c** is incorrect because this procedure will test the amount of catalyst, not the available surface area. Choice **d** is incorrect because this procedure will not provide much information, as it will not be possible to tell which catalyst is acting on the reactants.

50. The correct answer is choice c. Catalase is the only non-metallic catalyst being tested, and it makes the reaction proceed much more quickly. You can witness its effectiveness at home—if you put hydrogen peroxide on a cut, it immediately bubbles. The bubbles are the products of the reaction. Choice **a** is incorrect because it is too broad. You can only draw conclusions based on the catalysts that you have tested. There may be others. Choice **b** is incorrect because catalase is shown to be a better catalyst than all of the other catalysts tested, not just platinum. Choice **d** is incorrect because this conclusion is likely to be true but was not tested in this experiment.

Social Studies

To calculate your HiSET® score on the Social Studies section, first take a look at the correct answer for each of the 50 questions of the exam. Count up your **correct answers** only, and give yourself 1 point for each. Then, add up all of your points. This is your **raw score**.

Find your raw score and your **scaled score** in the following table. Remember, for each test section, a passing score is 8. (For the essay, a passing score is 2.)

You need a scaled score of 45 to pass the complete HiSET® exam.

SOCIAL STUDIES SCORING			
RAW	SCALED	RAW	SCALED
0	1	26	12
1	1	27	12
2	2	28	12
3	2	29	13
4	3	30	13
5	3	31	13
6	4	32	13
7	5	33	14
8	6	34	14
9	7	35	14
10	8	36	14
11	8	37	15
12	8	38	15
13	9	39	15
14	9	40	15
15	9	41	16
16	10	42	16
17	10	43	16
18	10	44	17
19	10	45	17
20	10	46	18
21	11	47	18
22	11	48	19
23	11	49	20
24	11	50	20
25	12		

1. **The correct answer is choice c.** The main argument in support of drilling focuses on the economic benefits it might bring, including jobs and energy security. Choice **a** is incorrect because the source only mentions this topic in one sentence without providing details. Choice **b** is incorrect because this statement is part of the source's general perspective, which is that drilling could provide large economic benefits. Choice **d** is incorrect because the source does not focus on wildlife.

2. **The correct answer is choice b.** The main opposition to drilling is the potential harm that it might have on wildlife and the environment, noted by the phrase "of vital concern." This source's greatest concern is protecting ANWR's environment. Choice **a** is incorrect because this source appears to oppose all drilling in ANWR, not just in one location. Choice **c** is incorrect because the source does not elaborate on this point or make it a key argument in the debate. Choice **d** is incorrect because the source does not appear to be arguing from an energy viewpoint but rather from an environmental position.

3. **The correct answer is choice a.** Both sides of the debate cite economic and environmental evidence that is contradictory, leading to confusion and uncertainty about what the facts actually are. Choice **b** is incorrect because there is no way to determine from the arguments which side is presenting the actual facts. Choice **c** is incorrect because one can confidently assume that some issues like these have been balanced at least a few times. Choice **d** is incorrect because one cannot assume all environmental groups are opposed to economic development.

4. **The correct answer is choice c.** An energy industry official would be in favor of expanding the market and seeking new opportunities. Choice **a** is incorrect because the person making a living from fishing would want to protect the water as much as possible. Drilling for oil carries the potential for oil spills, which can have devastating consequences to marine life. Choice **b** is incorrect because most people who live near oil-drilling sites face potential problems. Choice **d** is incorrect because an environmental defense organization would be against any drilling in a wildlife refuge.

5. **The correct answer is choice d.** According to Monroe, any new colonization or interfering in the affairs of nations in the Americas would be seen as a hostile act against the United States. Consequently, the Monroe Doctrine outlines the U.S. intentions to prevent that from happening. Choice **a** is incorrect because Monroe explicitly states that the United States has not and would not get involved in European affairs or wars. Choice **b** is incorrect because Monroe states at the end of this passage that the United States would not interfere with existing colonies. Choice **c** is incorrect because Monroe expressed that the United States would not allow European powers to form new colonies in the Americas.

6. The correct answer is choice a. Monroe supported his argument by illustrating that the United States had not interfered in European affairs and had no desire to do so. Monroe thought that the European powers should act similarly and not interfere in the affairs of nations in the Americas. Choice **b** is incorrect because Monroe appealed to diplomatic reason and knew that the U.S. could not militarily stop the European powers at this time. Choice **c** is incorrect because at this time, much of Western North America had not yet been fully colonized. Choice **d** is incorrect because the United States is an example of one colony that did survive. Canada and Spanish colonies in Latin and South America also proved sustainable.

7. The correct answer is choice d. The United States promised in the Monroe Doctrine to stay out of the affairs of European colonies in the Americas, while the Roosevelt Corollary broke this promise. Choice **a** is incorrect because the Monroe Doctrine covered all nations in the Americas. Choice **b** is incorrect because the Monroe Doctrine did not express the idea that the United States intended to promote additional colonies in the Americas. Choice **c** is incorrect because the Monroe Doctrine did not mention establishing American colonies in South America.

8. The correct answer is choice c. The final sentence of the passage expresses the U.S. position that *it has not and shall not* interfere with the existing colonies in the Americas. Choice **a** is incorrect because it contradicts what Monroe stated. Choice **b** is incorrect because Monroe does not outline this idea in the passage. Choice **d** is incorrect because Monroe refers to the American continents and the hemisphere, which include Latin and South America.

9. The correct answer is choice b. In a period of inflation, the cost of borrowing money goes up, forcing lenders to raise interest rates and causing borrowers to hold off on borrowing. Choice **a** is incorrect because inflation forces lenders to raise, not lower, interest rates. Choice **c** is incorrect because the cost to borrow money during periods of inflation increases, and borrowers borrow less money, not more. Choice **d** is incorrect because inflation forces lenders to raise, not lower, interest rates.

10. The correct answer is choice b. A person on a fixed income would experience a drop in purchasing power for all items bought. Consequently, purchases for all items would decrease. Choice **a** is incorrect because durable goods are usually higher-priced items. A person on a fixed income would hold off on these purchases until inflation eases. Choice **c** is incorrect because the price of borrowing during a period of inflation increases, costing more money. Choice **d** is incorrect because the loss of purchasing power will affect nearly everything the person buys, even smaller items. This means the person will not be able to buy as much and will have to cut back on all purchases.

11. The correct answer is choice a. The sale of durable goods, such as homes, decreases in periods of inflation. A home construction business would most likely see a sharp drop in business. Choice **b** is incorrect because a car repair business would likely see an increase in business, since new-car sales drop during periods of inflation and drivers try to keep their present cars running. Choice **c** is incorrect because discount department stores do not rely on durable goods sales. Small-item purchases are not affected as much as durable goods. Choice **d** is incorrect because fast food restaurants do not rely on durable goods sales. Small-item purchases are not affected as much as durable goods.

12. The correct answer is choice d. Voter fraud is a federal crime. Choices **a** and **b** are incorrect because they describe civil cases. Choice **c** is incorrect because inheritance issues are also civil cases.

13. The correct answer is choice c. This is a private complaint, which is a civil lawsuit. Choice **a** is incorrect because bribing a federal judge is a crime. Choice **b** is incorrect because this describes a criminal case. Choice **d** is incorrect because driving without a valid driver's license is breaking the law, a criminal offense.

14. The correct answer is choice b. A citizen suing the government for denial of constitutional rights is accusing the government of failing to uphold a legal obligation. This is a civil law case. Choice **a** is incorrect because these forms of government bodies can initiate civil lawsuits. Choice **c** is incorrect because governments cannot be defendants. Government officials can be charged with crimes, but the government will prosecute the case. Choice **d** is incorrect because civil case defendants are not accused of breaking the law and therefore cannot be imprisoned.

15. The correct answer is choice a. Medicare and Medicaid are government-run healthcare systems. In this case, the government would have been losing money and would most likely sue the hospital in a civil lawsuit. Choice **b** is incorrect because the government would most likely take the lead in any action against the hospital. Choice **c** is incorrect because the hospital was not guilty of fraud. Choice **d** is incorrect because the government cannot sentence the administrators without first charging them of a crime and then convicting them in a trial.

16. The correct answer is choice d. This title takes in both the Renaissance, the focus of the first paragraph, and the technological advances that triggered a new era of exploration, the focus of the second paragraph. Choice **a** is incorrect because this title would omit any reference to the Renaissance, which is the main topic of the first paragraph. Choice **b** is incorrect because the Chinese are referenced once in the passage and are not the main focus. Choice **c** is incorrect because this title would omit any reference to the Arabs or Portuguese, the focus of paragraph two.

17. The correct answer is choice c. Information in the second paragraph describes ways in which Arab navigational technologies were adopted by Europeans. Choice **a** is incorrect because there is not enough information in the passage to make this assumption. Choice **b** is incorrect because the European scholars who helped usher in the Renaissance were also focused on ancient Greek and Roman studies. Knowledge of the Arab world was a part of the Renaissance but not the cause. Choice **d** is incorrect because there is not enough information in the passage to confidently make this statement.

18. The correct answer is choice b. The passage states that although navigation technologies were important, the key factor was the development of faster and more reliable ships that could make long-distance voyages. Choice **a** is incorrect because the astrolabe is a navigational tool that helped explorers, but not as much as newer sailing vessels. Choice **c** is incorrect because navigation charts were only useful if one were sailing on reliable vessels. Choice **d** is incorrect because the compass is a navigational tool and not as vital as better sailing vessels.

19. **The correct answer is choice c.** The final sentence describes the connection between important events. The implication is that without the Renaissance, Columbus's voyage would probably not have happened. Choice **a** is incorrect because the passage only refers once to Columbus's voyage and does not compare it to other events. Choice **b** is incorrect because the passage does not compare Columbus's voyage to other events. Choice **d** is incorrect because the beginning of the passage states that the Renaissance lasted to roughly the year 1600. Columbus's voyage was in 1492, so the Renaissance would not have ended with the voyage.

20. **The correct answer is choice d.** The gray bars show a drop in GDP. Choice **a** is incorrect because the gray bars are not evenly spaced at 5-year increments. Choice **b** is incorrect because the gray bars are placed at times when the United States was not at war. Choice **c** is incorrect because the GDP line does not go up when it intersects the gray bars.

21. **The correct answer is choice a.** The U.S. economy showed steady and consistent growth between 1950 and 2015, increasing nearly five times the size by 2015. Choice **b** is incorrect because the first years of the 1950s were marked by a downturn in GDP. Choice **c** is incorrect because the 1970s showed tremendous growth in GDP. Choice **d** is incorrect because the GDP grew nearly five times the size between 1950 and 2015.

22. **The correct answer is choice b.** If GDP and unemployment are directly linked, 1981–1983 is a period when the unemployment rate would have gone up. Choice **a** is incorrect because the 1960s saw steady economic growth and therefore would not have had high levels of unemployment. Choice **c** is incorrect because the economy between 2008 and 2010 saw a near collapse, as illustrated by the falling GDP. Consequently, the unemployment rate would rise. Choice **d** is incorrect because the end of the 1940s saw a drop in GDP and would have also seen a rise in the unemployment rate.

23. **The correct answer is choice a.** Coal, in the form of black coal basins, production, and export ports, is the dominate resource industry in the Sydney region. Choice **b** is incorrect because the Sydney area does not have oil and gas basins or a significant industry presence. Choice **c** is incorrect because the Sydney area does not have lignite basins. Choice **d** is incorrect because the Uranium industry operates farther west and not in the Sydney area.

24. **The correct answer is choice c.** Based on information from the map, the east coast contains the most export ports and production facilities, suggesting that region is heavily industrialized. Choice **a** is incorrect because the map shows very few areas in which lignite is found, suggesting that this industry is not as fully developed as others and therefore requires fewer workers. Choice **b** is incorrect because there is not enough relevant information to make this claim. Choice **d** is incorrect because there is not enough information to make this statement.

25. The correct answer is choice d. Based on the number of uranium mineral deposits on the map, and the small number of operating uranium mines, it can be concluded that the industry has not fully developed yet. Choice **a** is incorrect because the east coast contains numerous ports through which coal products move. Choice **b** is incorrect because there are far fewer coal-related sites in western Australia than in the east. Choice **c** is incorrect because the map shows extensive areas in which oil and gas are located, suggesting that it is a fairly robust industry.

26. The correct answer is choice d. The *Marbury* ruling established judicial review, one of the most important principles of American constitutional law. Choice **a** is incorrect because there is no evidence in the passage to support this statement. The Court could rule on the constitutionality of legislation but not write it. Choice **b** is incorrect because the Constitution remained intact and was not voided by the *Marbury* decision. Choice **c** is incorrect because there is not enough information to make this inference.

27. The correct answer is choice b. This is the best summary of the judiciary's main duty according to Justice Marshall. Choice **a** is incorrect because Marshall does not state that the judiciary should have law-writing powers. Marshall writes that it is the duty of judicial department to say, or interpret, what the law is. Choice **c** is incorrect because Marshall's words do not support this statement. Choice **d** is incorrect because Marshall states that the judiciary should interpret the law, not rewrite the Constitution.

28. The correct answer is choice c. Jefferson's quote suggests that he is concerned that one branch of government—the judicial—might have authority over the others because of judicial review. This would go against the principles of separation of powers. Choice **a** is incorrect because there is no evidence in the quote to support this assumption. Choice **b** is incorrect because Jefferson is not implying that constitutional meaning is not necessary, only that each branch can arrive at individual meanings. Choice **d** is incorrect because Jefferson does not discuss amending the Constitution but rather finding the most appropriate meanings within it.

29. The correct answer is choice a. Article III of the Constitution describes the makeup and powers of the judicial branch, including the Supreme Court. The power of judicial review is not granted to the Supreme Court, which has led to disagreements over whether the Court should have that power. Choice **b** is incorrect because there is not enough evidence to support this statement. Choice **c** is incorrect because there is no evidence that judicial review has been proven ineffective as a rule. Choice **d** is incorrect because there is nothing in the Constitution describing judicial review or prohibiting the other branches from recognizing the principle.

30. The correct answer is choice c. Since its founding, the Soviet Union was tightly controlled by the government, limiting free expression and the press. Its economy was also controlled by the state. As the passage states, Gorbachev was a life-long communist bureaucrat who had followed Marxist ideologies, so to introduce *glasnost* and *perestroika* would seem out of place. Choice **a** is incorrect because Soviet secretary generals could have a great deal of power. Choice **b** is incorrect because it is implied in the passage that *glasnost* and *perestroika* were new policies. Choice **d** is incorrect because Gorbachev's actions refute this claim.

31. The correct answer is choice a. The passage describes the struggling Soviet economy, suggesting that changes had to be made or else it would collapse. The reference to the arms race also suggests that the Soviet Union was struggling to keep pace with the U.S. Choice **b** is incorrect because the passage describes significant actions Gorbachev took in the Soviet Union, illustrating his considerable influence. Choice **c** is incorrect because there is not enough information in the passage to support this statement. Choice **d** is incorrect because even though Gorbachev initiated policies that were uncommon in a communist government, there is not enough information to suggest that he abandoned his Marxist ideology.

32. The correct answer is choice c. The final sentence implies that the citizens' new freedoms were popular and caused civil unrest, which suggests protests against governments demanded greater freedoms. Choice **a** is incorrect because freedom of speech does not always lead to unrest. Choice **b** is incorrect because there is not enough information in the passage to make this inference. Choice **d** is incorrect because there is not enough information in the passage to make this inference.

33. The correct answer is choice b. A hardline critic of the Soviet Union and knowing its history, Reagan would have been unconvinced that the Soviet government and its people would support Gorbachev's initiatives. Choice **a** is incorrect because Reagan supported the democratic ideals of *glasnost*. Choice **c** is incorrect because Reagan supported free-market capitalism. Choice **d** is incorrect because Reagan was open to more interaction with the Soviet Union, but only if it softened or abandoned its communist principles.

34. The correct answer is choice b. A focus of *perestroika* was to introduce some free-market mechanisms to the Soviet economy. A government takeover of industries is not in line with free-market principles. Choice **a** is incorrect because one of the goals of *perestroika* was to democratize the Soviet political system. Choice **c** is incorrect because private ownership of businesses is indeed an aspect of free-market economies. Choice **d** is incorrect because the secret ballot is an aspect of democratic elections.

35. The correct answer is choice d. In a weak-mayor system, the city council makes policy decisions and appoints department heads, removing the mayor from decision-making in important city affairs. Choice **a** is incorrect because in a weak-mayor system, mayors usually lead council meetings. Choice **b** is incorrect because in this system, mayors do not get to appoint department heads. Choice **c** is incorrect because mayors often must vote to break ties.

36. The correct answer is choice d. One of the key features of a weak-mayor system is the council's authority to make policy decisions. Choice **a** is incorrect because mayors do not have the authority to veto council decisions in a weak-mayor system. Choice **b** is incorrect because mayors do not have hiring authority in a weak-mayor system. Choice **c** is incorrect because mayors do not have this authority in a weak-mayor system.

37. The correct answer is choice a. One of the key features of a strong-mayor system is the mayor's authority to hire and manage city department heads. Choice **b** is incorrect because mayors do not have the authority to prepare city budgets in a weak-mayor system. Choice **c** is incorrect because in a strong-mayor system, mayors do have the authority to veto council decisions. Choice **d** is incorrect because in a strong-mayor system, mayors have a great deal of power and can use this to set agendas and lead.

38. The correct answer is choice c. It best explains the importance of who controls the leaders of city departments. Clear goals and procedures lead to more efficient government. Choice **a** is incorrect because mayors must still operate within the law and within budgets. Even strong mayors must be held accountable. Choice **b** is incorrect because many people are involved in the planning and implementation of city projects. Choice **d** is incorrect because department heads still must operate within a budget and would not be allowed to spend money indiscriminately.

39. The correct answer is choice b. Europe is the region that has experienced the greatest decrease in immigration to the United States, from 75% in 1960 to 12% in 2010. Choice **a** is incorrect because immigration numbers from Latin America have increased since 1960. Choice **c** is incorrect because immigration numbers from Asia have increased. Choice **d** is incorrect because Northern American immigration has dropped 8 percentage points, considerably less than European.

40. The correct answer is choice d. As of 2010, Latin America accounts for more than half of all immigrants; the rest of the regions account for 47%. Choice **a** is incorrect because Asia accounts for 28% of all immigrants. Choice **b** is incorrect because Europe and Asia account for 40% of all immigrants, less than half. Choice **c** is incorrect because Europe's share of immigrants has declined significantly since 1960.

41. The correct answer is choice a. Because more than half of all immigrants as of 2010 have come from Latin America, and since 67% of all immigrants live in states in the West and South, it is a valid assumption to say that Texas, California, and Florida have large numbers of immigrants from Latin America. Choice **b** is incorrect because there is not enough information to make that assumption. Choice **c** is incorrect because few immigrants originate from Northern America. Choice **d** is incorrect because immigration data and information for the other states is not provided, making this an unfounded assumption.

42. The correct answer is choice d. The Constitution is the supreme law of the United States, and even the president must follow it. Choice **a** is incorrect because limited government reflects the idea that the government can only exercise the powers granted to it by the people. Choice **b** is incorrect because the Twenty-Second Amendment does not concern individual rights. Choice **c** is incorrect because representative government concerns electing people to represent others in a government.

43. The correct answer is choice c. Casting a ballot in an election is a very good example of the principle of representative government in action. Choice **a** is incorrect because public polling companies research public opinion on a variety of subjects, not necessarily politics. Choice **b** is incorrect because writing a letter to the local newspaper illustrates civic participation, not representative government. Choice **d** is incorrect because serving on a jury is a legal duty American citizens must perform.

44. The correct answer is choice b. American citizens, through the process of voting, are the source of power in our democracy. Choice **a** is incorrect because the Constitution is the framework that outlines the rights of Americans and the powers of government. Choice **c** is incorrect because American citizens elect representatives to serve in government. Representatives are bound to the laws of the Constitution. Choice **d** is incorrect because American citizens elect the president, who, like other representatives, is bound to the laws of the Constitution when fulfilling the duties of the office.

45. The correct answer is choice c. Supplies increase because of lack of demand, leading to a surplus. Choice **a** is incorrect because consumer demand decreases above $30. Choice **b** is incorrect because the graph shows that consumer demand decreases. Choice **d** is incorrect because supplies increase at a price of more than $30.

46. The correct answer is choice d. At the equilibrium price, producers will supply about 200 units. Choice **a** is incorrect because the graph shows that there will be a surplus of units. Choice **b** is incorrect because at the equilibrium price, consumers will demand much less than 400 units. Choice **c** is incorrect because demand will hold steady at that price.

47. The correct answer is choice a. When consumer demand drops, producers also decrease supplies. Choice **b** is incorrect because a producer will most likely lower the price. Choice **c** is incorrect because the producer will have to make adjustments or risk losing money. The producer will decrease the supply. Choice **d** is incorrect because as the graph shows, the producer will decrease supplies and most likely lower prices.

48. The correct answer is choice b. The cartoonist is clearly portraying Gould as a ruthless and dishonest businessman. Labels on the bowling balls reveal how Gould had been knocking down other business people. Choice **a** is incorrect because Jay Gould was a railroad tycoon, and he was taking out the Wall Street people, suggesting he was not inexperienced. Choice **c** is incorrect because in the cartoon, the Wall Street banks and others associated with the financial world in New York have been knocked down. Choice **d** is incorrect because bowling is used as a metaphor.

49. **The correct answer is choice b.** The cartoonist depicts Gould bowling on Wall Street, using "dishonest" bowling balls to take out less powerful or experienced individuals. The cartoonist is portraying Gould as a ruthless and dishonest businessman. Choice **a** is incorrect because the cartoonist provides details that suggest that Gould is corrupt and not simply lucky. Choice **c** is incorrect because the cartoonist depicts Gould knocking over or taking out other investors or bankers. Choice **d** is incorrect because the cartoonist provides details that suggest Gould earned his wealth through dishonest methods.

50. **The correct answer is choice c.** Gould's businesses, from the outside, looked prosperous and legitimate. However, Gould's "gilded" exterior was covering up his true nature, one made of corruption and dishonesty. Choice **a** is incorrect because Gould's decisions were often corrupt and illegal. Choice **b** is incorrect because most Americans do not respect or want to emulate those who achieve prosperity through dishonest methods. Choice **d** is incorrect because the idea of the Gilded Age is one of outside beauty covering up something less appealing.

ADDITIONAL ONLINE PRACTICE

Using the codes below, you'll be able to log in and access additional online practice materials!

Your free online practice access codes are:

FVE5G5J7Q85Q5ERTRD7D

FVE6BFNDUF75KFJSN552

FVEV5J16XIU6UPFG1N27

FVEBT56DH2D27050A4M4

FVEMXG7TRFE3B6V3I3UC

Follow these simple steps to redeem your codes:
- Go to **www.learningexpresshub.com/affiliate** and have your access codes handy.

If you're a new user:
- Click the **New user? Register here** button and complete the registration form to create your account and access your products.
- Be sure to enter your unique access code only once. If you have multiple access codes, you can enter them all—just use a comma to separate each code.
- The next time you visit, simply click the **Returning user? Sign in** button and enter your username and password.
- Do not re-enter previously redeemed access codes. Any products you previously accessed are saved in the **My Account** section on the site. Entering a previously redeemed access code will result in an error message.

If you're a returning user:
- Click the **Returning user? Sign in** button, enter your username and password, and click **Sign In**.
- You will automatically be brought to the **My Account** page to access your products.
- Do not re-enter previously redeemed access codes. Any products you previously accessed are saved in the **My Account** section on the site. Entering a previously redeemed access code will result in an error message.

If you're a returning user with a new access code:
- Click the **Returning user? Sign in** button, enter your username, password, and new access code, and click **Sign In**.
- If you have multiple access codes, you can enter them all—just use a comma to separate each code.
- Do not re-enter previously redeemed access codes. Any products you previously accessed are saved in the **My Account** section on the site. Entering a previously redeemed access code will result in an error message.

If you have any questions, please contact Customer Support at Support@ebsco.com. All inquiries will be responded to within a 24-hour period during our normal business hours: 9:00 A.M.–5:00 P.M. Eastern Time. Thank you!